Seeking God

Seeking God

The Recovery of

Religious Identity in

Orthodox Russia,

Ukraine, and

Georgia

Edited by

STEPHEN K. BATALDEN

NORTHERN ILLINOIS UNIVERSITY PRESS

DeKalb   1993

© 1993 by Northern Illinois University Press
Published by the Northern Illinois University Press, DeKalb, Illinois, 60115
Manufactured in the United States using acid-free paper   ∞
Design by Julia Fauci

Library of Congress Cataloging-in-Publication Data
Seeking God : the recovery of religious identity in Orthodox Russia,
    Ukraine, and Georgia / edited by Stephen K. Batalden.
        p.   cm.
    Includes bibliographical references and index.
    ISBN 0-87580-178-1
    1. Orthodox Eastern Church—History. 2. Russia (Federation)—
Religious life and customs. 3. Ukraine—Religious life and
customs. 4. Georgian S. S. R.—Religious life and customs.
    I. Batalden, Stephen K.
    BX310.S29 1993
    281.9'47—dc20   93-16553
                        CIP

Photo of Men', from *Kirchen im Kontext Unterschiedlicher Kulturen*, edited by Karl Christian Felmy et al., courtesy of Vandenhoeck & Ruprecht, used with permission.

Figure 4 from *Staroobriadcheskii tserkovnyi kalendar' 1990* (Moscow: Izdanie Staroobriadcheskoi Mitropolii Moskovskoi i Vseia Rusi, 1990).

Figure 5 from George Heard Hamilton, *The Art and Architecture of Russia* (New York: Penguin Books, 1957), used with permission.

Figure 7 from Alexander Opolonikov and Yelena Opolonikova, *The Wooden Architecture of Russia: Houses, Fortifications, Churches* (New York: Harry N. Abrams, 1989), used with permission.

To the memory of

FATHER ALEKSANDR MEN'

Contents

PART ONE

Popular Religious Culture and Orthodox Identity

Acknowledgments

With the exception of the essay by Roy Robson, the contributions to this volume were read in earlier versions at the symposium on "The Recovery of Religious Identity in the Soviet Union," held at Arizona State University in March 1991. It is a pleasure to acknowledge the generous support for that symposium provided by the Arizona State University Russian and East European Studies Consortium, the Arizona State University College of Liberal Arts and Sciences, the College's Alumni Association, the Arizona State University Libraries, the Arizona Council of Eastern Orthodox Churches, and the Friends of the Phoenix Public Library.

I am grateful for the assistance of Patricia Nay both during the original symposium and in the subsequent preparation of the manuscript for submission. Several people have read parts or all of the manuscript, and I wish to thank them all for their suggestions. In particular, I am grateful for the timely suggestions of Mary Lincoln at Northern Illinois University Press. Most important at each stage of this project has been the support and encouragement of Sandra Batalden, who has read and commented on the entire manuscript.

Seeking God

Introduction

Those who herald the heightened sense of religious identity in former Soviet lands invariably discover that such religious consciousness has long been part of the Orthodox world, even in the twentieth century. Writing of his memory of early twentieth-century Russia, the émigré philosopher Nikolai Berdiaev noted that "it was a time marked by profound spiritual disquiet and religious searching. . . . The end of an old age seemed to coincide with a new era which would bring about a complete transfiguration of life."[1] For many of Berdyaev's generation, *bogoiskatel'stvo* (God-seeking) became the identifying mark of an intelligentsia driven by intensified religious consciousness. These *bogoiskateli*, or God-seekers, combined a critique of Marxism and a challenge to positivism with new and experimental forms of spirituality. From a marginal group such as the Universal Order of Infant Prodigies to the circle of philosophical idealists associated with the anthology *Vekhi* (Landmarks, 1909), the God-seeking movement fundamentally rejected the materialism and atheism of radical nineteenth-century polemicists. Its call was, rather, for the recovery of religious identity, an identity that came to be associated with the values of individualism and the creative human personality. While not all these *bogoiskateli* found their way back to the Orthodox church, many did, and their impact was profoundly felt by subsequent generations both in the Soviet Union and in the Russian emigration.[2]

Today, at the other end of the twentieth century, following more than seventy years of official state atheism, the recovery, or rediscovery, of religious identity is once again clearly observable—and not just among a narrow religious intelligentsia. The signs of this "complete transfiguration," to use Berdyaev's phrase, are everywhere. They can be seen in the opening of thousands of Orthodox, Catholic, and Protestant churches (as well as numerous monasteries and seminaries), in the renewal of Jewish identity exemplified by revitalized Hebrew language instruction, and in the widening claims of Islamic institutions and leaders upon the loyalties of Turkic peoples of Tatarstan, Central Asia, and Transcaucasia. The public face of this new religious consciousness is even apparent on local television programs that find it fashionable to include ecclesiastical representation on panel discussions, and in the publishing offices of *Pravda*, where they seek to print mass editions of Holy Scripture for profit.

Seeking God examines the roots of the recovery of religious identification in the Orthodox world of Russia, Ukraine, and Georgia. The underlying assumption of the volume is that the new religious consciousness, although partially occasioned by the death of communism, is firmly rooted in living traditions that antedate by centuries the relatively brief period of Soviet rule in Eurasia. Thus, the essays in the collection focus upon the historical sources of religious identity in Orthodox culture.

In examining such sources of modern Orthodox religious identity, contemporary scholarship has increasingly been drawn into consideration of two complementary subjects. The first is the multifaceted phenomenon of popular religious culture and its importance for Orthodox spiritual identity. In 1982, Natalie Zemon Davis, in her historiographical overview, "From 'Popular Religion' to Religious Cultures," noted that Western historians of religion have increasingly devoted their attention to religion "as practised and experienced and not merely as defined and prescribed."[3] Recognizing the concern that historians such as Carlo Ginzburg expressed over possible misunderstanding of the term "popular religion," Professor Davis suggested that the new focus on religion in early modern Europe ought to be directed toward the portrayal of "religious cultures," which she defined as frameworks for identifying interconnected beliefs and practices. What is important, she argued, is not whether a case in question is "popular" but rather what that case represents. For the study of religious cultures is by its very nature contextual, comparative, and relational.[4] It is in such a contextual and relational sense that this volume addresses the beliefs and practices of Orthodox religious culture.

Today, the outward signs of the recovery of Orthodox religious culture are dramatic and far-reaching. For some, the recovery has taken the form of a renewed appreciation for the art of bell-casting and the sound of Russian church bells. For the circle of artists at Pskov, it has taken the form of the revival of an early Russian school of icon painting. For thousands of pious believers who stood at a Moscow rail station in February 1991, waiting for the arrival of the relics of Saint Serafim of Sarov (b. 1759), the recovery of Orthodox identity has been symbolized by the discovery of the relics that were confiscated during the Russian Revolution and stored in the cellar of the Kazan Cathedral in Leningrad. For others, the recovery of Orthodox identity is to be seen in expressions of religious charity (*miloserdie*) now recognized as lawful in official charters affecting church-state relations. For still others, the recovery of Orthodox identity is sought in the reestablishment of Sunday schools and Bible study. At one of the dozen or more such institutions in Moscow, over two-hundred children attend a Sunday school run by the Church of the Resurrection of Slovushchii. And for some, such as Academician Dmitrii S. Likhachev, the revival of monasticism, given new energy by the movement for historic preservation and the reopening of early "cultural monuments," is critical to the recovery of a religious culture that fostered the book, at the same time that it contributed to agricultural and economic development.[5]

Within the popular religious culture, there also remain elements of what some consider a sign of renewed paganism. The ancient symbol of the ax, for example, resurfaced in the 1980s as a powerful sign of the right-wing, anti- Semitic organization Pamiat' (Memory). In the youth culture, signs of a revived paganism reside next to religious symbols in the graffiti of Moscow, where the *fanaty, metallisty, rokery,* hippies, fascists, and punks vie for the loyalties of local gang members.[6] There are also unions for the renewal of Old Slavic paganism.

It is in the context of this current refashioning of religious identity that the essays in the first part of the volume reexamine the rich diversity of traditional Eastern Orthodox religious culture—the religious practices of peasants, of clergy, of nuns, and of Old Believers interacting within the traditions and authority of Eastern Orthodox confessional practice. Eve Levin's essay opens the consideration of religious culture by addressing the question of *dvoeverie,* a Russian term referring to the popular religious system in which pagan beliefs and practices were preserved alongside or under the veneer of Christianity. Using the examples of the Orthodox cult of Saints Ioann and Iakov Meniuzhskie in the north, and the cult of Saint Paraskeva from the Balkans, Professor Levin suggests that the prevailing pagan/Christian dualist or conflict model of *dvoeverie* needs to be more nuanced, in order to reflect the manner in which "religious beliefs and observances grew out of people's own understanding of the supernatural and the natural and social world around them."

Gregory Freeze extends this investigation of popular religious practice into the modern period by evaluating the Russian church's use of *epitimiia* (public penance in the form of monastic seclusion) as a weapon against religious deviance, crime, and immorality. Offering an interesting profile of the 844 penitents of 1850, Professor Freeze provides insight into why the institution of *epitimiia* continued to decline in importance, until by 1868 it "ceased to serve as an instrument either of intimidation or of correction." In a sense, Freeze's essay, by demonstrating the marginal effectiveness of coercive efforts to shape popular religion from above, indirectly reinforces the point of Professor Levin's article regarding the popular sources behind Orthodox spirituality. Freeze's essay complements his earlier article, "The Rechristianization of Russia," in which he documented how the Russian church ultimately was obliged to appeal beyond the liturgy, to public education and the religious press, in order to reshape popular religion more effectively.[7]

With Brenda Meehan's essay the focus of Part I shifts to the religious culture of women's monastic communities in modern Russia. Like Levin in her approach to Orthodox spirituality, Professor Meehan views the remarkable growth of the women's communities as testimony to the importance of popular developments—in this case, to a popular piety that arose out of the lives of the women themselves, a piety that was "spontaneous, genuine, and local." There is, one senses, a significant point of linkage between the popular piety of these pre-1917 women's communities and the recovery of interest in monasticism in the contemporary popular culture.

Three of the essays in Part I address the religious culture of Old Belief from the seventeenth century to the present. In defining the origins of this religious culture, Boris Uspensky, philology professor at Moscow University, sees the schism arising out of deeper philological, theological, and linguistic or semiotic divisions in seventeenth-century Russian culture. In this context, the Old Believers are seen as preserving not only the old symbols but also, through these symbols, powerful traditions of old Russian culture. While Uspensky's arguments bring fresh semiotic insight to the Old Believer issue, his identification of Old Believer culture with Russian culture calls to mind the argument of N. S. Trubetskoi and others that, in the face of the Ukrainianization of the intellectual and spiritual culture of Great Russia in the seventeenth and early eighteenth centuries, the Old Believers alone retained a sense of continuity with old Russian culture.[8]

In his essay interpreting the subsequent fate of Old Believer communities, Robert Crummey notes the ongoing division between church historians and populists regarding the substance and significance of the Old Believer movement. Noting the resilience of their interpersonal connections, the attractiveness of their relative economic prosperity, and the independence exhibited in their monastic and lay lifestyles, as well as in their attitudes toward authority, Professor Crummey sees the Old Believer communities as part of a "sophisticated cultural system"—an interconnected religious culture.

The twentieth-century renewal of these Old Believer communities following Nicholas II's edict of religious toleration is the subject of Roy Robson's essay on Old Believers. Robson takes as his point of departure Old Believer architecture, noting that architectural innovation was possible within prescribed norms. Indeed, as William Brumfield has noted elsewhere, the application of new construction techniques had the effect of making these early twentieth-century Old Believer churches compatible with the "new style" in modern Russian architecture—despite the fact that the structures were ostensibly modeled after seventeenth-century churches of the Russian north.[9] Robson's essay clarifies how, alongside the external elements of innovation, Old Believer architecture conformed to the specific worship needs and practices of the believing community.

Part II of this volume addresses the interface between Orthodox confessional identity and modern nationalism. The importance of confessional identity for the rise of the nation has often been the subject of analysis. Historians of modern Europe are accustomed to noting the post-Reformation division of the Latin West along confessional lines that invariably mirrored underlying regional and state interests. From at least the time of Peter the Great, the Russian Empire retained a comparable interest in the conformity of confessional identity to state interest. Within the empires of eastern Europe, however, the rise of authentic national movements often was buttressed by religious or confessional loyalties at variance with that of the official state. The importance of Greek Catholic or Uniate confessional identity for the Rusyn and western Ukrainian population served to differentiate the region from the Great Russian heartland of the empire. Russian imperial efforts to undermine the legal and confessional status of Uniates in the nineteenth century recognized the threat that confessional heterodoxy posed as a potential support for national resistance. Even in the case of the Russian Slavophile nationalists of the 1830s and 1840s, who based their ideology upon what they perceived to be the unique historical role and mission of the Orthodox church, their romantic nationalism invariably set them at odds with the more confining "official nationality" of Nicholas I's ancien régime. In Georgia, as Fairy von Lilienfeld notes in her article, it is virtually impossible to separate the drive for Georgian church autocephaly from the wider aspirations of Georgian national autonomy and independence—aspirations that were by their very nature contrary to imperial policy.

What is remarkable, however, is the speed with which this linkage between confessional and national identity has reasserted itself in the wake of the collapse of the Soviet empire. In describing the resurgent national movements within post-Soviet society, one historian in 1991 suggested the analogy of the old linoleum floor, which, having worn away, reveals the original wooden floorboards.[10] The sudden demise of Soviet institutions has been paralleled by the rapid resurfacing of underlying confessional and national identities. In this process, the recovery of national identity remains powerfully grounded in religious and confessional symbols.

Focusing upon Ukrainian, Georgian, and Russian cases, the essays in Part II of the volume consider some of the less well understood elements of the interface between confessional and national identity. While the dramatic events of the failed coup d'état in August 1991 became the occasion for climactic declarations of national independence in the constituent Soviet republics, the recovery of confessional identity developed more quietly behind the scenes, often in more complicated circumstances. The interplay between confessional and national identity has also led to conflict and division within national movements in cases where there is not strict confessional uniformity. As Frank Sysyn's work documents, the three-way struggle among Greek Catholics, autocephalous Orthodox, and more Moscow-oriented Orthodox followers in Ukraine represents, in part, a confessional struggle over national identity in which the historical and regional complexities of modern Ukraine have once again been reopened.

Sysyn's account of the situation in Ukraine is paralleled by developments in the newly independent Republic of Belarus. There the much smaller Greek Catholic or Uniate church, reopened in 1990, has been launched with a primarily Polish Catholic clergy. Its journal, *Uniya*, rushed into press in Riga to meet the church's opening August 1990 assembly, hailed the reemergence of the long-suppressed Eastern rite Catholic church of Belarus. In a passage no doubt intended to claim authority as the national voice of Belarus, *Uniya* intuitively hit upon the linkage of confessional and national identity in eastern Europe: "Every person and every nation must seek its own path to God. . . . For every nation in the world it is of great significance to have its own faith, which is the essence of its national world view. But what is our faith, Belorussians?"[11] While the answer to the question was intended to be self-evident, the search for God in Belarus, as in Ukraine, remains complicated by historic confessional divisions that date to the sixteenth and seventeenth centuries, and have their origins in the Eastern Slav borderlands of the Polish-Lithuanian Commonwealth.

For modern Georgian Orthodoxy the problems are not those of confessional conflict but the threat of being marginalized by secular, political struggles that disregard the moral authority of religious leadership. In her "Reflections on the Current State of the Georgian Church and Georgian Nation," Fairy von Lilienfeld, professor emeritus of Byzantine and East Slavic history and theology, assesses the relationship between confessionality and nationality in modern Georgia. Frequently underrepresented in the literature on Georgian nationalism, the role of religious leadership, according to Lilienfeld, continues to be of central importance in current internal Georgian conflicts. Evidence of this is found in the way Georgian religious leaders have, on occasion, become figures of national stature. Professor von Lilienfeld suggests that this may also be true today in the case of the revered Catholicos, Patriarch Ilia II, an advocate of nonviolence who has remained a national and moral leader relatively untarnished by recent fratricidal, intra-ethnic turmoil.

Shortly after his forced exile from the Soviet Union in 1974, Aleksandr Solzhenitsyn and several of his associates sought to reframe the early twentieth-century debate over Russian religious consciousness by publishing a series of essays that linked Russian national identity with the moral authority of confessional, religious identity. Those essays, entitled *Iz pod glyb* (From Under the Rubble), took as their point of departure the early twentieth-century rejection of Marxian materialism found in the *Vekhi* (Landmarks) anthology. Solzhenitsyn and his circle used the *vekhovtsy* appeal to the organic human personality as a model for what they perceived to be the larger organism of the Russian nation, and they called for the recovery of the moral and religious conscience of the Russian nation.[12]

Today, in the aftermath of the collapse of the Soviet Union, the Solzhenitsyn appeal for the recovery of religious identity, while not without its articulate supporters in Russia, is complicated by the intense political and factional divisions within the Orthodox confession. Despite the more dynamic leadership provided by Moscow Patriarch Aleksii (elected in 1990), some of the Russian faithful have lost confidence in an official church hierarchy that they associate with earlier church-state compromises. Others, reflecting (and occasionally manipulating) the conservative instincts of many Russian believers, seek to cleanse the church of its ecumenical, interconfessional alliances built since the 1960s under considerable state pressure. For such groups, the preoccupation today is confessional exclusivity and purity, a purity some find in the parishes of the Free Russian Orthodox church, a name now used in Russia for the Russian Orthodox Church Abroad, the former Karlovatskii Synod that definitively broke with the Moscow church in 1927. As of the end of 1991, the Free Russian Orthodox church had three bishops and a growing number of parishes stretching from Moscow and St. Petersburg to the far reaches of Siberia.

Faced with a potential schism within its ranks, the official Russian Orthodox confessional leadership has turned inward, fearful of launching bold innovations that might be used against them by the splinter Free Russian Orthodox church. Moreover, the controversial issues relating to new, legal relationships with the former Soviet and post-Soviet Russian governments have been closely tied to the problems of a looming schism. To protect itself and its constituent parishes from defection, Moscow Patriarch Aleksii sought to secure for the Russian Orthodox church recognition as a legal person. Instead, the 1990 Soviet law titled "Freedom of Conscience and Religious Organizations" granted the status of legal person to individual religious organizations, including parishes, but not to the Russian Orthodox church as a collective institution.[13]

It is in the context of such confessional politics—politics that tend to fragment the impact of confessional identity upon the Russian nation—that the hotly debated nineteenth-century issue of the modern Russian Bible has been reopened. Part II of this volume closes with a look at the politics of Russian biblical publication, noting that despite the increasing circulation of the Russian Bible, the liturgical text of the Orthodox confession continues to be the Church Slavonic translation, the eighteenth-century Elizabethan Bible.

Part III of this volume is titled "Sources for Study of Religious Identity in the Orthodox East." Typically regarded as an auxiliary or helping discipline for historians, the critical study of sources (*istochnikovedenie*) was one of the areas in which Soviet scholarship was most productive. Exemplary in that regard has been the unbroken tradition of Greek paleography in St. Petersburg and Moscow. Building upon the work of his predecessors, V. N. Beneshevich and E. E. Granstrem, the Moscow paleographer and historian Boris Fonkich has brought to scholarly attention the extraordinary degree to which Russian and Ukrainian library and archival repositories remain the finest resources for study of Orthodox religious cultures in the Slavic world, as well as in the Greek, Levantine Near East.[14] Currently preparing a multivolume guide to the massive archival collection on Russian relations with Greece in the Moscow Central State Archive of Ancient Acts (*Fond 52, Otnosheniia Rossii s Gretsiei*), Fonkich has documented the important religious and cultural ties that continued to link the wider Greek and Slavic Orthodox world after the fall of Constantinople.

Western scholars whose access to Russian and Ukrainian holdings is necessarily limited by time constraints and distance, have nevertheless supplemented the work of paleographers such as Fonkich by opening up those Western collections that complement archival and library holdings in Eastern Slav lands. The two essays in Part III reflect the importance of Western sources for work on Greco-Slavic Orthodox culture. The first of these, an essay on the fate of Russian landholding in Jerusalem in the twentieth century, uses previously unexamined British records of the Palestine Mandate to document the insistent efforts of the Soviet state in the interwar period to claim ownership of the vast holdings in Jerusalem of the prewar Russian Ecclesiastical Mission and the Palestine Orthodox Society. The contested claims upon the Jerusalem properties, as in the case of other issues raised in this volume, exhibit a peculiar timeliness. For not only did the issue of the properties resurface in the recent Israeli-Soviet rapprochement, but the underlying Orthodox cultural dynamic that contributed to Russian investment in Jerusalem in the first place—the popular religious practice of *palomnichestvo* (pilgrimage)—has resurfaced as an identifiable element of Orthodox popular piety and free expression in the 1990s, a modern-day form of *bogoiskatel'stvo*.[15] Twentieth-century Soviet efforts to reclaim Jerusalem properties must also be seen in the light of earlier nineteenth-century efforts to compete with other imperial powers for precedence in the Holy Land.

In the other essay of Part III, Charles Frazee, a scholar of Levantine church history, explores the importance and accessibility of Vatican archives for study of the Orthodox East. His essay, a contribution to Western *istochnikovedenie,* provides an up-to-date guide to published descriptions of Vatican collections.

The title of this volume takes its inspiration from the life and works of the late Father Aleksandr Men' and his religious followers. A former student of Father Men', Michael Meerson, presents in the lead essay a biographical tribute to this remarkable Moscow Orthodox priest. The parish of Aleksandr Men', on the outskirts of Moscow, became in the 1970s and 1980s the spiritual center for a Moscow religious intelligentsia committed to *bogoiskatel'stvo*. The life and tragic death of Aleksandr Men' serve to demonstrate the potential peril to confessional leaders when the passions of modern nationalism are inappropriately linked with confessional identity in the popular imagination. Of Christian and Jewish parentage, Aleksandr Men' was a scholar and churchman whose remarkable contributions testified to a world beyond ethnic passion and confessional rigidity. Yet his murder by ax, likely at the hands of those who sought greater national or confessional exclusivity, has demonstrated how potentially vulnerable is confessional integrity in an environment that seeks to bind religious identity to narrowly national agendas. It is to the memory of Aleksandr Men' that this volume is dedicated.

NOTES

1. Nicholas Berdyaev, *Dream and Reality*, trans. Katherine Lampert (London: Geoffrey Bles, 1950), p. 141. The quotation is from Lampert's translation. For the original Russian edition, see *Samopoznanie: Opyt filosofskoi avtobiografii* (Paris: YMCA, 1949). Berdyaev wrote the work in 1940.

2. On God-seeking, see V. F. Botsianovskii, *Bogoiskateli* (St. Petersburg/Moscow, 1911). In English, see the discussions of Nicholas Zernov, *The Russian Religious Renaissance of the Twentieth Century* (New York: Harper & Row, 1963); and Christopher Read, *Religion, Revolution and the Russian Intelligentsia, 1900–1912* (London: Macmillan, 1979).

3. Natalie Zemon Davis, "From 'Popular Religion' to Religious Cultures," in *Reformation Europe: A Guide to Research*, ed. Steven Ozment (St. Louis: Center for Reformation Research, 1982), p. 322.

4. Ibid., p. 323. This approach to the study of religious cultures is also reflected in a broad range of current scholarship on early modern and modern Europe. See, for example, the collection of essays in *The German People and the Reformationion,* ed. R. Po-Chia Hsia (Ithaca, N.Y.: Cornell University Press, 1988); see also Eve Levin's "*Dvoeverie* and Popular Religion" in this volume, note 33.

5. Likhachev's strong feelings on Russian monastic traditions have been published in a number of different forums in recent years. See, for example, his articles "Predvaritel'nye itogi tysiacheletnego opyta," *Ogonek*, no. 10 (1988); and "Ot pokaianiia k deistviiu," *Literaturnaia gazeta,* 9 September 1987. On the recovery of Sunday schools, see Oxana Antic, "Sunday Schools in the Soviet Union," *Report on the USSR,* 30

March 1990 (RL149/90), pp. 11–13. For most of the Soviet period, even the word *miloserdie* (charity) was either eliminated from official dictionaries or marked as obsolete or bourgeois. After sixty years the expression has been reborn with the practice itself.

6. On graffiti, see John Bushnell, *Moscow Graffiti: Language and Subculture* (Boston: Unwin Hyman, 1990).

7. Gregory L. Freeze, "The Rechristianization of Russia: The Church and Popular Religion, 1750–1850," *Studia Slavica Finlandensia* (Helsinki), 7 (1990), pp. 101–136.

8. Nikolai Sergeevich Trubetzkoy, "The Ukrainian Problem," in his *The Legacy of Genghis Khan and Other Essays on Russia's Identity,* ed. Anatoly Liberman (Ann Arbor: Michigan Slavic Publications, 1991), pp. 245–267.

9. William C. Brumfield, "The 'New Style' and the Revival of Orthodox Church Architecture, 1900–1914," in *Christianity and the Arts in Russia,* ed. William C. Brumfield and Milos M. Velimirovic (Cambridge: Cambridge University Press, 1991), pp. 109–112.

10. Edward L. Keenan, "Rethinking the U.S.S.R., Now That It's Over: A Historian's Perspective," *New York Times* (The Week in Review), 8 September 1991, p. 3.

11. The *Uniya* passage is quoted in Elizabeth Ambrose, "The Reemergence of Eastern-Rite Catholicism in Belorussia," *Report on the USSR,* 19 October 1990, pp. 21–23.

12. Aleksandr Solzhenitsyn, *From Under the Rubble* (New York: Little, Brown, 1975). The original Russian edition was published in Paris by YMCA Press, 1974.

13. Oxana Antic, "The New Law on Religion," *Report on the USSR,* 23 November 1990, pp. 9–10.

14. Along with his numerous articles in *Vizantiiskii vremennik,* other journals, and *sborniki* (collections), see the book-length study by Boris L. Fonkich, *Grechesko-russkie kul'turnye sviazi v XV–XVI vv.: Grecheskie rukopisi v Rossii* (Moscow: Nauka, 1977).

15. On the renewed interest in pilgrimage, see Oleg Peresypkin, "Palestina, blizkaia nam," in a special issue of *Ekho planety,* no. 1(92), 1–5 January 1990, pp. 26–33. The cover of the issue features a picture of Jerusalem, and has the caption "Sviataia zemlia: Budet-li ona vnov' dostupna dlia nashikh palomnikov?" [The Holy Land: Will it again be accessible for our pilgrims?]. It should be noted that some of the renewed interest in pilgrimage has been tied to negotiations over Soviet-Israeli rapprochement. The author of this article, Oleg Peresypkin, is a former Soviet ambassador to Arab lands, and has been serving as president of the renamed Russian Palestine Society [Rossiiskoe Palestinskoe Obshchestvo], formerly the Orthodox Palestine Society [Pravoslavnoe Palestinskoe Obshchestvo], now affiliated with the Academy of Sciences.

The Life and Work of
Father Aleksandr Men'

In the morning twilight, the village priest opened the door and headed for the train platform less than a half-mile away. It was Sunday, and Father Aleksandr Men' always caught the 6:50 A.M. *elektrichka* from his village near Zagorsk to his parish church in Novaia Derevnia, a small town outside Moscow. The priest kept walking along the asphalt path through the Semkhos Woods. Suddenly, from behind an oak, someone leapt out and swung an ax at Aleksandr Men'. An ax—the traditional Russian symbol of revolt, one of the symbols of the neo-fascist group Pamiat'. The blow hit Men' on the back of the skull. The wound was not very deep, but it severed major arteries. The killer, police sources said, grabbed the priest's briefcase and disappeared into the woods. Father Aleksandr, bleeding, stumbled toward his home, walking a full three-hundred yards to his front gate at 3-A Parkovaia Street. Along the way, two women asked if he needed help. He said no, and they left. From her window, Natasha Men'[1] saw a figure slumped near the gate and pressing the buzzer. She could not quite make out who it was in the half-light. She called an ambulance. In minutes, her husband was dead.[2]

*A*leksandr Men's funeral in the small church of the Meeting of the Lord, where he served for more than twenty years, gathered several thousand believers, who crowded in the yard and street outside the church to bid a last farewell to their spiritual leader, father-confessor, teacher. In the aftermath of this assassination, articles in the Soviet press compared Fr. Men' with Andrei Sakharov. *Ogonek* compared his murder with the Polish security police's assassination of Fr. Jerzy Popieluszko, a pro-Solidarity priest, in 1984.

Fr. Men' did not associate himself with any political movement, but his impact on society was immense. He was an apostle, a preacher of the Gospel in a militantly atheistic society, in a post-Christian era. Aleksandr Men' grew up amid Stalin's totalitarian materialism and as a teenager defined his life's goal as fighting this ideological fortress. He fought it for thirty years, and he won. Today atheism is dead in the former Soviet Union. *Nauka i religiia,* the leading organ of atheist propaganda for decades, is ashamed today to call atheism "scientific" and is publishing interviews with clergymen.

The ruling party elite changed its attitude to religion because it came to realize that atheistic materialism was dead in the Soviet Union. The ideocratic regime, whose very essence depends on ideology, could not afford dead ideology. With this awareness of new trends in the nation's culture and of the need for ideological readjustment, the new policy of glasnost and perestroika began.

In recent articles on Fr. Men' it is said that he was a personal friend, if not father-confessor, to leading figures in contemporary Soviet culture. He baptized Aleksandr Galich and Nadezhda Mandelshtam in the 1960s. He had long conversations on religion, Christianity, and Eastern Orthodoxy with Aleksandr Solzhenitsyn that eventually brought him back to the church. Thousands of leading Soviet intellectuals knew Fr. Men', saw him, and talked with him. He impressed them all with one thing: the thousand-year-old Russian Orthodox tradition spoke to them through him in a clear, joyful, comprehensible, and thoroughly meaningful language. One could agree or disagree with him, but after meeting him, one abandoned the Soviet myth that religion is a "vestige of the past." In him religion was alert, contemporary, modern, dynamic. He made it speak even more powerfully and universally through his writings.

One can apprehend his writings fully only by taking into account their ideological background. Fr. Men' was often criticized by Orthodox zealots for not defending Orthodoxy enough. When he began writing, it was not Orthodoxy, Protestantism, or Catholicism but religion itself— religion as such—that was questioned. The materialistic world view made no distinction among various creeds. The Orthodox church presented an even greater problem for the average Soviet person. How could one comprehend and intelligently practice a religion that was formed in an extinct civilization (Byzantium) and did not change or develop for a thousand years?

To make the language of the Orthodox faith meaningful to a Soviet person became the life task of Fr. Aleksandr Men'. He met the challenge of his time so successfully that in the last few years of relative freedom he became the main spokesman for the church. He became a Soviet Billy Graham, addressing thousands directly or through the media. In his own words, as he said to his brother Pavel, he felt, after all the years of imposed public silence, like "an arrow finally sprung from the bow."[3] His biography, which Men' recalls in several interviews published in the Soviet press, brings some light to this phenomenon of the unity of loving pastoral care, of fearless Gospel preaching, of wise spiritual leadership, and of keen intellectual insight.

Aleksandr Men' was born in 1935, on January 22, the birthday of Fr. Pavel Florenskii, another great apologist for the Christian faith in Russia.[4] Fr. Men' humorously recalled this coincidence to underline the continuity of the intellectual ministry in the church. His parents were

Jews. In the 1930s his aunt and mother, during the time of bloody antireligious persecution, met Fr. Serafim Batukov, a catacomb priest, were impressed by him, were baptized, and joined his community.[5] From his early childhood, Aleksandr Men' was reared by this man of outstanding holiness and spiritual gifts. After Fr. Batukov's death, Men' was educated by a nun, Mother Mariia, who ran an unofficial women's monastic community in Zagorsk, near the monastery of St. Sergius of Radonezh, which Fr. Men' considered his spiritual cradle. Mother Mariia, with her joyful, bright spirituality, so vividly described by Dostoevsky in the elder Zosima of *The Brothers Karamazov,* impressed young Aleksandr throughout his life. The message of his works and his pastoral ministry, as well as of his personal behavior, was of joy in the Holy Spirit. Christ is the Liberator; therefore men should rejoice in giving Him thanks.

In the 1940s Men' was educated in the catacomb Sunday school of Boris Vasil'ev, a scientist, ethnographer, anthropologist, and theologian, who was a friend of the family and a member of the catacomb community of Fr. Batukov during the 1930s. Fr. Men' said that, if he never experienced any contradiction between faith and scientific knowledge, it was due to these formative years under the tutorship of Vasil'ev.[6] Under his influence, Men' in his teenage years started to work on the Bible's sacred history, and this brought him to the study of ancient oriental history.[7] Fr. Men' recalled that he then began to feel that the existing accounts of sacred history in Russian were hopelessly outdated and had to be written afresh. He had already decided to become a priest. As he remembered, the occasion for this decision was the emergence of the independent state of Israel in 1948.

Aleksandr's family had an acute Jewish awareness. His mother as a young girl was active in the Russian Zionist movement. His father, although not a practicing Jew or a religious person, felt deep solidarity with the Jewish community. His brother Pavel, a member of the Orthodox church, at one time was one of the best teachers of Hebrew in Moscow. The creation of the state of Israel in 1948, at the outset of Stalin's growing anti-Semitic campaign, was greeted by the Soviet Jews with great joy. Aleksandr's family was no exception. Young Men' also wanted to serve the Zionist cause and decided to become a priest. At the age of thirteen he knocked at the door of the Moscow Theological Seminary (in Zagorsk) and asked to be admitted. He was politely turned down because of his age, but made the acquaintance of the dean of students at the seminary, Anatolii Vedernikov, who came to be his lifelong friend and supporter. Later, as the editor of the *Zhurnal Moskovskoi patriarkhii* (Journal of the Moscow Patriarchate), Vedernikov published articles by Men' under various pen names.

The paradoxical decision of the young Zionist to greet the state of Israel by becoming an Orthodox priest had a logic of its own. Men' thought that if Jesus is the Messiah of Israel, the time for the people of Israel to acknowledge Him as such will eventually come. The emergence of the Jewish state was a sign. Living in diaspora, the Jews had to preserve their identity. The walls of uncompromising rabbinical Judaism were absolutely necessary for the preservation of the people's existence. With the restoration of the Jewish state, the danger of assimilation would eventually disappear. The people, liberated internally from the fear of losing their national identity, would become ready to look at what Men' considered the earliest Jewish legacy—the New Testament. At this point the need for Jewish priests and preachers of the Gospel would be felt.

Having failed to enter theological seminary at the age of thirteen, Men' started, at the age of fourteen, to write a new account of the life of Christ. In 1949 the first draft of his book *Syn chelovecheskii* (The Son of Man), the initial volume of his series on the religious history of mankind, was written.

His life's other interest was biology. He began to study it as a schoolboy at the Children's Society of the Moscow Zoo.[8] After graduating from high school, Men', in order to acquire a broader background in science, entered the Moscow Institute of Fur Animals to continue his study of biology. For Men', the book of living nature was another Bible. He had a deep respect for every expression of life, and he felt himself to be a part of the immense ocean of life that glorifies its Creator by the sheer fact of being. He began his studies in 1953, spending the last years (1955–1958) in Irkutsk, Siberia, where the institute was relocated. In Irkutsk, Men' shared a room with Gleb Yakunin, another student of biology, who at that time was an atheist. The friendship with Men', however, had its impact on Yakunin. He rejoined the church in which he had been baptized in his childhood, and later became a famous priest, dissident, and human rights activist.

Men' did not have a chance to graduate. Khrushchev's antireligious campaign caught him in the middle of the comprehensive examinations, and he was expelled as a practicing church member. Aleksandr accepted it as a sign to enter the church ministry, married his wife, Nataliia, and in the summer of 1958, on the feast of Pentecost (June 1) was ordained a deacon in Moscow. Two years later he was ordained a priest in the Donskoi Monastery by Bishop Stefan Nikitin, a follower of Fr. Aleksei Mechev and a member of a catacomb church in the 1930s. The circumstances of his ordination demonstrated that Fr. Men' belonged to the best tradition in the Russian Orthodox church. He personally knew many confessors of faith and outstanding ministers.

Two priests played important roles in his spiritual life during these years. One was Fr. Peter Shipko, a priest who spent thirty years in prison camps and in exile. From him Men' learned uncompromising faithfulness to the church and the value of perseverance in suffering for Christ.

When Fr. Men' was asked in an interview how he felt when he was persecuted by the KGB, especially in the worst years, 1980–1985, he answered that he always measured his personal troubles against the sufferings of people like Shipko. This measuring prompted him to thank God for allowing him to serve the church for almost four decades without interruption.[9]

The other priest was Fr. Nikolai Golubtsov, also a former biologist. Fr. Golubtsov baptized Stalin's daughter Svetlana and future dissident writer Andrei Siniavskii, among others. As Fr. Men' recalled regarding Golubtsov, "He told me that I would suffer most with the intelligentsia. He himself, however, was a pastor of this abandoned flock and bequeathed the same to me. His rule was the principle of personal spiritual freedom."[10] This principle of liberty was always a striking feature of his own spiritual leadership, and Men' himself was the best example of this spiritual freedom, feeling and behaving as a son in his Heavenly Father's house.

After his ordination, Fr. Men' served in parishes of the Moscow region. He graduated by correspondence from the Leningrad Seminary and then from the Moscow Theological Academy with a master's degree in theology. Beginning in 1959 he published articles under a pen name in the *Zhurnal Moskovskoi patriarkhii* and in various church publications in East Germany and Bulgaria, but his main theological work was done in samizdat. What inspired this work? When Fr. Men' was asked in an interview about his relationship with Solzhenitsyn, he answered that he respected Solzhenitsyn's talent, his wit, his prophetic zeal; but that they respected each other while differing in opinions. When asked about the difference, Fr. Men' answered that Solzhenitsyn emphasized the external difficulties of the church, while he pointed to its inner crisis.[11]

What was the crisis he was talking about? Western churches have long been speaking about the crisis in Christianity. The Russian Orthodox church started to become aware of this crisis only at the turn of the century. The movement in the church and among intellectuals that reflected the crisis and worked to heal it is called the Russian religious renaissance. The work was aborted by the Revolution and then was resumed in a caricatured and violent form by the Renovationists (the so-called Living Church) in the 1920s. The Renovationists, who wished to update church life, in fact helped the Soviet regime to destroy it. When church life was restored under the aegis of the Moscow Patriarchate after the war, it reemerged in the most conservative, stagnant form.

The regime that permitted the existence of the church wanted it in precisely this form, to make it "the vestige of the past." Fr. Men', ordained into this church and into this sluggish form of it, set out alone to tackle the task of presenting the faith hidden under this form as a universal and timeless message. His heroic ministry was met with suspicion on every side. The church establishment suspected and hated him because he was always surrounded by crowds of people and of youth, and only created trouble with the atheist authorities. The best clergy, survivors of Stalin's labor camps and of persecution by the Living Church, were afraid of church reforms and of "innovation" because they associated it with the Renovationist schism. They looked askance at Aleksandr's bold work, suspecting that his spirit of freedom contained a lack of respect for the Orthodox tradition. In a general church atmosphere of cultural and religious obscurantism, Fr. Men', with his extremely broad cultural and religious horizon, could arouse only suspicion.

Thus Men' had to move from a big church in Tarasovka in the Moscow region to a small wooden church in Novaia Derevnia, because his rector kept denouncing him to church and civil authorities. In his new church, where he served more than twenty years, he was always a second priest, and his superiors continually humiliated him. Only recently, with perestroika well under way, was Men', by this time an internationally known theologian and pastor, made a rector.

The same thing happened with the theological academic establishment. The brightest living theologian of the Russian church, Fr. Men' was not invited to teach either at the Moscow Theological Academy or at its seminary, although he lived within walking distance. The author of many books published in the West, he managed to publish only one article under his own name in a Soviet theological journal. In 1987, *Bogoslovskie trudy* published his article on Russian biblical theology. It is the best concise survey of the history of Russian scriptural studies in print.[12] Biblical studies were, in fact, his chief field of research. Men' was the only biblical scholar in the Soviet Union who met the standards of modern scriptural studies. He was familiar with the current theories and findings of biblical criticism and took them into account. His last works were an eight-volume biblical dictionary[13] and an introduction to the Old Testament, a textbook for seminary students.[14] Both were written for the church's use, but the hierarchy declined to use them.

Though Men' carefully avoided involvement in political or church dissent, and declined to speak out on human or religious rights issues, he was feared for the boldness of his apostolate. In a society in which freedom, political as well as spiritual, was a rare commodity, he was a pillar of freedom. He educated his numerous flock in this spirit. In his last years someone asked Men' how he would define his creed. Fr. Aleksandr responded with a short statement, about five pages long. His creed did not run against the Orthodox creed. It was the church faith, however personalized, internalized, expressed in the expectations of today. But it was not a denominational faith either. It was the faith of universal victory in Jesus Christ. Men' always lived and acted according to this creed, though he had expressed it only recently.

For me, the Christianity I profess is the dynamic force that encompasses all aspects of life, open to everything that God created in nature and man. I regard it not so much as a religion that is twenty centuries old . . . as the way to the future. This Christianity is a religion of freedom, it professes freedom as a basic law of the Spirit and regards sin as a form of slavery. It rejects authoritarianism and paternalism, which are grounded not in the spirit of faith but, rather, in fallen human nature. This Christianity weeps over divisions among Christians as our common sin and transgression against the will of Christ [John 10:16], but it believes that in the future this sin will be overcome in the spirit of brotherly love, rather than by the way of pride, self-righteousness and self-exaltation. Therefore, the Christianity that I profess is open to everything valuable in other Christian denominations. It does not reject the good which comes from unbelievers, but it rejects violence, dictatorship, hatred even if they use Christ's name as a cover. It takes public life as a domain for the Gospel's principles to be applied, it measures a political system by its humaneness, by what it gives to a human being. It considers separation of church and state the most favorable condition for the church and sees a danger in the very idea of "state religion."[15]

In the sacrament of confession, in his prayers, and in his formulation of sins, Fr. Men' emphasized personal freedom and dignity. In the questionnaire to help confessors that he compiled, he asked, among other things: "How would you react if a circumstance, or a person, or a group of people, or an organization, intervened in your life, humiliated you, challenged you, threatened you? Would you fall into despair and hatred, or attempt to avoid it and shy away? Or would you encounter the danger with faith, and manliness, would you struggle in the spirit of hope?"[16]

In a society poisoned by slavishness and fear as if by leprosy, he was educating people to be free and fearless. No wonder he was feared and envied by his less courageous or creative colleagues and persecuted by the authorities. In the past he was constantly under surveillance by the KGB and slandered in the Soviet press, betrayed by former disciples who denounced him openly. He was several times on the brink of being arrested.[17] In 1985 he was summoned to meet with the KGB many times a week for several months. The KGB tried to drive him out of the country or to force him to sign a public denunciation of his own ministry, as it had forced Fr. Dudko to do. Fr. Men' finally produced a public statement. One can see how hard he negotiated with the dreaded secret police. He stated that he had sometimes behaved without proper caution in the past and that he had made several mistakes. The statement did not specify what the mistakes were. Fr. Men' was a tough negotiator and managed to pay the least possible price to the KGB for being able to continue his ministry. When he was asked how he felt having to visit KGB headquarters so often and being forced to talk to the KGB officers, Fr. Men' replied: "I am a priest, I can talk to everybody. And to me it is never difficult."[18]

Obviously, priesthood alone would not suffice. Fr. Men' had a special spiritual gift for accepting other human beings into his heart, a gift that has also been described to the Optina elders, to Fr. Serafim Batukov, who baptized him, and to Fr. Nikolai Golubtsov, who was his spiritual teacher. His ability to talk to everybody, from Solzhenitsyn to a peasant woman or from Cardinal Lustige of Paris to a KGB lieutenant, was grounded in his deep faith that the image of God sparkled in every person. But it was also grounded in his ability to speak several cultural languages. Men' was perfectly at home discussing Greek gnosticism with Academician Sergei Averintsev (his old friend), the Dead Sea Scrolls and Aramaic layers of the Bible with Soviet scholar I. D. Amusin, or genetics with Antoine Elens, the Belgian Jesuit and professor of biology at Notre-Dame University in Namur, as well as talking in simple words about Russian saints or Gospel stories with his village *babushki,* the peasant and worker women of his parish, who adored him for his simplicity and accessibility.

All these cultural languages grew as branches out of one solid root—a universal human culture. For Fr. Men', culture—first of all European and Russian culture, the culture of the world of the Bible and of the East—was not a matter of professional knowledge; it was the intellectual atmosphere in which he lived and which allowed him to survive intellectually in the narrow, obscurantist world of his colleagues, superiors, and the bulk of his flock. I recall once when I visited him at home, I found him working in his garden, watering plants. He was reading a book held in his left hand, reciting something to himself, while watering with his right hand. "What are you reciting, Father?" I asked him. "Dante's *Divine Comedy,*" he replied. "I cannot live without it, I know it almost by heart, and reread it several times a year to keep it in my memory." The *Divine Comedy* was not the only piece of literature he knew by heart. Conversation with him was an intellectual feast: his language was picturesque, full of puns, literary allusions, and quotations from memory of poetry, of the mystical literature of East and West, and of the Scriptures, which he knew brilliantly.

What was the philosophy that inspired this life totally dedicated to ministry, a philosophy also espoused in his writings? Fr. Men' was influenced by, and considered himself a successor to, the Russian religious renaissance, to Nikolai Berdiaev, Nikolai Losskii, Pavel Florenskii, Sergei Bulgakov, Semen Frank, and Sergei Trubetskoi.[19] His main contribution lies, however, in the history and philosophy of culture and religion. A man of encyclopedic knowledge, he wrote several volumes covering the history of the religious life and philosophical thinking of humanity before Jesus Christ. These seven volumes, more than four thousand pages in all, have been published in the West in Russian, under his two pen names (Bogoliubov and Svetlov).[20]

His first published book, *The Son of Man*, a historical portrait of Jesus Christ, His life, and His teaching, serves as an introduction to the series.[21] It is connected with the last volume of the series, which after a long journey through the history of mankind's religious search brings the reader to the threshold of the New Testament. Following the introduction, the first volume of the series, *The Origins of Religion*, discusses religion in general. It treats topics dealing with the nature of faith and with the philosophical orientation of humanity in the light of modern science.[22] The second volume, *Magism and Monotheism*, describes the religious life of primitive society; of the first politically organized civilizations of Egypt, Sumer, India, and Greece; and, against this background, the emergence of Hebrew monotheism among the patriarchs. The history of Israel is traced through the first united monarchy under Solomon and its division under his successors. In this work Fr. Men' eloquently advocates the theory of original monotheism.[23]

The third volume, *At the Gate of Silence*, deals with the religious life of ancient India and China.[24] In the fourth volume, Fr. Men' presents the history of religious life, mysticism, and philosophical thought in ancient Greece up to the time of Alexander the Great.[25] In the fifth volume, he returns to the world of the Old Testament. The message of the prophets is discussed against the background of the political and cultural history of Israel.[26] Following Abraham Heschel,[27] Fr. Men' emphasizes the social and political dimension of the prophetic message, and following Martin Buber,[28] he points out the prophets' faith in Yahweh's reign in the midst of Israel, their political philosophy of God's kingship. He sets the prophets' ministry, however, into messianic perspective because the whole series is emphatically Christocentric.

The last volume gives an overview of the religious and cultural life of Hellenistic, Roman, Indian, and Judaic civilizations prior to and during the time of Jesus Christ, and thus provides the historical background for Jesus' preaching.[29] In this volume one can feel particularly that Fr. Men' is swimming in his native waters. He discusses at length the Judaism of the first century, introduces the reader to the drama of the fatal struggle between Israel's various religious-political parties, and paints a broad eschatological canvas of this momentous century of Jewish history that prepared the way for the preaching of the Messiah and for the ultimate destruction of Israel's statehood by the Romans.

The primary target of Fr. Men' was, obviously, the Soviet reader, who was usually totally ignorant in religious matters. The amount of information given in his series is enormous. Numerous appendixes deal with the various challenges that modern science and ideologies present to religious beliefs. Darwinism, Freudianism, Marxism, various problems in biblical criticism, the newest theories in physics, biology, astronomy, and psychology—all these issues are discussed from the

Christian perspective in these appendixes.

What makes the writing of Fr. Men' the most readable for an average Russian intellectual is not only its scientific quality, its fine style, and easy language, but also numerous and transparent allusions to the contemporary world and Soviet history. History is presented as a perpetual drama in which humanity is caught by the necessity to choose between good and evil, between right and wrong. History repeats itself, particularly when people forget about the lessons that the wisdom of faith provides. Thus, in describing the tyrannies of ancient Assyria and Babylonia, Fr. Men' makes the reader think about Hitler's and Stalin's atrocities in the twentieth century.[30] One reads this religious history of mankind and finds in it one's own spiritual biography.[31]

The entire series is dedicated to the memory of Vladimir Solov'ev, a dedication that is not accidental. Behind the vast canvas of the universal history of culture and religion stands the idea of the fundamental unity of mankind's spiritual quest for the ultimate truth. Men' considered Solov'ev to be his primary teacher. His books present historical, anthropological, and cultural material as an unfolding of Solov'ev's philosophy of religion and his vision of history as a process of developing "Godmanhood."

Vladimir Solov'ev, with whom genuine Russian philosophy began, was inspired by the philosophical task set by Hegel. In his *Lectures on the Philosophy of Religion,* Hegel defined Christianity as a superior, absolute religion.[32] For Hegel the superiority of Christianity is expressed in its all-encompassing character. As a religion Christianity is one among many. In its philosophy, however, Christianity is universal and represents a philosophical synthesis that embraces, or even contains in itself, principles of other religions. Hegel, however, failed to demonstrate the philosophical universality of Christianity. In his presentation, Christianity loses its own essence, becoming an abstract philosophical religion in which the unraveling absolute idea replaces the Christian doctrine of the Trinity and the Incarnation.

Solov'ev inherited Hegel's task and succeeded in achieving it philosophically through his concept of developing "Godmanhood." Solov'ev interprets world evolution as a process that is teleologically oriented toward humanity, which is the goal and the end of the evolutionary process. The history of humanity, in turn, is a religious-cultural process of seeking to encounter God. This encounter takes place in its fullness in the Incarnation of the second person of the Trinity, Jesus Christ, perfect God and perfect man, in whom deity and humanity are united in the "Godman." Solov'ev demonstrated philosophically that the substance of every religion that he considered as a part of the whole truth finds its fulfillment in Christianity, which, for Solov'ev, as for Hegel, encompasses the fullness of truth.[33]

What Solov'ev did as a philosopher, Fr. Men' attempted to demonstrate as a cultural historian of religion. For Men', as well as for Solov'ev, all history is the movement of the human spirit toward an encounter with God; the heart of human history is the history of beliefs and ideas, or religions. It is the great quest of humanity, searching for God in different ways. God became man at the fullness of time, which means for Fr. Men', as it meant for Solov'ev, the ripeness of mankind's spiritual effort to discover God. God responds to this ripeness with His ultimate revelation, the incarnation of His Son. This vision permeates the whole series of volumes, making them a fascinating historical survey of the religious adventure of the human spirit.

Before the books were published in the West, they were widely circulating in samizdat, and Fr. Men' took a lion's share in their printing. He richly illustrated all volumes by collecting pictures, photos, and charts from old magazines, books, albums, and encyclopedias. The impact of this series was enormous. The 1960s and 1970s were years of mass conversion of intelligentsia youth to the church. They needed to be educated in the basics of church practice. Fr. Men' wrote two concise introductions: one to Eastern Orthodox worship,[34] the other to the Bible.[35] His own community kept growing, and it was this growth that made Fr. Men' a direct target of the KGB in 1982–1986.

With glasnost things began to change. When the church was finally allowed to speak freely to the public, Fr. Men' was one of the few clerics able to address the average Soviet citizen with the Gospel message in straightforward, understandable, and eloquent language. Well versed in fiction, poetry, and philosophy, open to secular culture, interested in theater and cinema,[36] Fr. Men' was always at ease with people of a secular mentality molded at an atheist hearth. When Soviet society turned to the church for Christian testimony, Fr. Men' began to gain recognition as one of the most outspoken church theologians and preachers, and was invited to give talks on Soviet television, as well as in high schools and colleges. He became so popular a preacher that sometimes he gave several talks a day.

His activity and growing visibility ignited jealousy among some clerics. The conservative Orthodox accused him of destroying the Russian church by being too ecumenical and tolerant toward other Christian confessions and other religions. Being an ethnic Jew, he also provoked open hatred among extreme Russian nationalist and fascist groups.[37] Some zealots within Russian Orthodox quarters slandered him as a crypto-Catholic or a crypto-Jew. Whatever pretexts were used, the deep-seated fear of freedom that his Gospel conveyed was at the bottom of these accusations. He had old enemies in the KGB as well.

During his last year, Fr. Men' began to receive anonymous threatening letters that urged him either to leave the country or to reduce his public appearances. In September 1990 he was invited to host a Moscow television show on religion and culture, and to take a position as rector of the Moscow Sunday Christian University. He received threats that if he took these positions, he would be assassinated. Fr. Men' disregarded the letters and continued his work. Usually he was surrounded by people, parishioners and friends who accompanied him on his way home from the church to have a moment to talk to him. A killer, or killers, watched closely to find a time when he was alone: very early on Sunday morning, while everybody was asleep, when he left home to go to the church to celebrate early liturgy. Sunday, September 9, 1990, instead of the bloodless sacrifice of the Eucharist, he had to offer his own blood.

He was buried on September 11, when the Russian Orthodox church celebrates a great feast day, the beheading of John the Baptist. This symbolic coincidence was unearthed, not without some spirit of awesomeness, by the Soviet press.[38] The people at the funeral, as well as authors of the liberated Russian press, compared this loss for the nation with another loss—that of Andrei Sakharov.[39] There was something else common to both of them, as Alexis Zvelik, a Russian physicist who knew both well, said to me: "It seemed that they were the only two people who did not have fear in their eyes. Now in Russia everyone is fearful, from top to bottom. But these two looked straight into the future with calm and courageous hope. They looked ahead without fear."

NOTES

1. Fr. Men' was survived by his wife and two children: Michael, a jazz musician, and Helen, an icon painter who now lives with her husband in Italy.

2. "Lament for a Murdered Russian Priest," *The Washington Post,* October 18, 1990, p. B1.

3. Ibid.

4. Sergei Bychkov, "Syn chelovecheskii," interview with Fr. Aleksandr Men', *Moskovskii komsomolets,* September 16, 1990.

5. His aunt, Vera Vasilevskaia, wrote a book, *Katakomby dvadtsatogo veka* (The Catacombs of the Twentieth Century), in which she gives a portrait of Fr. Batukov and describes the life of the catacomb church community in the 1930s. A part of it has been published in "Dva portreta" (Two Portraits), *Vestnik RKhD* (Paris), no. 124 (1978), pp. 269–298; the rest remains in manuscript.

6. "Autobiographie du Père Alexander Men sous forme d'interview," *(Plamia)*, Centre d'Études Russes Saint-George (Medon, France), no. 80 (Jan. 1991), p. 7.

7. Bychkov, op. cit.

8. The society's hymn written in the 1940s had a verse about

young Men' in it. He left the imprint of his personality even there.

9. Bychkov, op. cit.

10. Ibid.

11. Ibid.

12. Protoierei Aleksandr Men', "K istorii russkoi pravoslavnoi bibleistiki," *Bogoslovskie trudy* (Moscow), no. 28 (1987), pp. 272–289.

13. Fr. Aleksandr Men', "Bibliologiia (Opyt pravoslavnoi bibleistiki)" (manuscript).

14. Fr. Aleksandr Men', "Opyt kursa po izucheniiu sviashchennogo pisaniia" (manuscript).

15. "Kredo," in Aleksandr Men', *Smertiiu smert' poprav* (Minsk: Eridan, 1990), pp. 9–11.

16. "Prigotovlenie k ispovedi," ibid., pp. 47–48.

17. Mark Popovskii, "Za chto traviat o. Aleksandra Menia" (Why Is Fr. Men' Persecuted?), *Put'* [The Path], no. 2 (New York: Christ the Savior Orthodox Church, 1984).

18. Vladimir Zelinskii, "Slova proshchaniia," *Russkaia mysl'* (Paris), no. 3845, September 14, 1990, p. 8.

19. Bychkov, op. cit.

20. His works are now published in Russia.

21. Andrei Bogoliubov, *Syn chelovecheskii* (Brussels: Izd. Zhizn' s Bogom, Foyer Oriental Chrétien, 1969), p. 336.

22. *Istoki religii.* The first edition was published under his pen name Emmanuil Svetlov (Brussels: Foyer Oriental Chrétien, 1970); the second, revised edition, under the name Aleksandr Men' (Brussels: Foyer Oriental Chrétien, 1981).

23. Emmanuil Svetlov, *Magism i edinobozhie. Religioznyi put' chelovechestva do epokhi velikikh uchitelei* [Magism and Monotheism: The Religious Path of Humanity Until the Epoch of the Great Teachers] (Brussels: Izd. Zhizn' s Bogom, Foyer Oriental Chrétien, 1971).

24. Emmanuil Svetlov, *U vrat molchanie. O dukhovnoi zhizni Kitaia i Indii* [At the Gate of Silence: On the Religious Life of China and India] (Brussels: Izd. Zhizn' s Bogom, Foyer Oriental Chrétien, 1971).

25. Emmanuil Svetlov, *Dionis, Logos, Sud'ba (Grecheskaia religiia i filosofiia)* [Dionysus, Logos, Fate: Greek Religion and Philosophy] (Brussels: Izd. Zhizn' s Bogom, Foyer Oriental Chrétien, 1972).

26. Emmanuil Svetlov, *Vestniki tsarstva Bozhiia. Bibleiskie proroki ot Amosa do restavratsii (VIII–IV vv. do nashei ery)* [The Messengers of the Kingdom of God: Biblical Prophets from Amos to the Restoration, VIII–IV B.C.] (Brussels: Izd. Zhizn' s Bogom, Foyer Oriental Chrétien, 1972).

27. Cf. Abraham J. Heschel, *The Prophets* (New York: Harper & Row, 1962).

28. Cf. Martin Buber, *The Prophetic Faith* (New York: Harper &

Row, 1960) and *Kingship of God* (New York: Harper & Row, 1973).

29. Emmanuil Svetlov, *Na poroge Novogo Zaveta. Ot epokhi Aleksandra Makedonskogo do propovedi Ioanna Krestitelia* [On the Threshold of the New Testament: From the Time of Alexander of Macedonia to the Preachings of John the Baptist] (Brussels: Izd. Zhizn' s Bogom, Foyer Oriental Chrétien, 1983).

30. *Vestniki tsarstva Bozhiia*, pp. 118–119.

31. The series is pedagogical in the old romantic sense of the word. It was Hegel's primary task to reveal the immanence of human history in individual consciousness. Hegel gives his philosophy of world history as the way of educating an individual who must acquire knowledge by becoming aware of the world history that is his or her own substance. An analogous pedagogical task inspired Rousseau's *Emile*, in which the child's education must largely reproduce the general movement of humanity. See Jean Hyppolite, *Genesis and Structure of Hegel's Phenomenology of Spirit* (Evanston, Ill.: Northwestern University Press, 1974), p. 39.

32. Georg W. F. Hegel, *Lectures on the Philosophy of Religion: The Lectures of 1827,* ed. Peter C. Hodgson (Berkeley: University of California Press, 1988), p. 109.

33. The development of human religion according to Vladimir Solov'ev is demonstrated in the work of Msgr. Jean Rupp, *Message ecclésial de Solowiew: Présage et illustration de Vatican II* (Paris: Lethielleux, 1975). Rupp, however, played down Hegel's influence on Solov'ev (see p. 119).

34. Aleksandr Men', *Tainstvo, slovo i obraz* [Sacrament, Word and Image] (Brussels: Izd. Zhizn' s Bogom, Foyer Oriental Chrétien, 1980). This introduction to Orthodox worship was published twice under the title *Nebo na zemle* [Heaven on Earth], after which it appeared under its present title.

35. Aleksandr Men', *Kak chitat' Bibliiu* [How to Read the Bible] (Brussels: Izd. Zhizn' s Bogom, Foyer Oriental Chrétien, 1981).

36. Nataliia Bolshakova's interview with Fr. Men', "O dukhovnosti" [On Spirituality], *Kino* (Riga), no. 7 (1989), pp. 14–16.

37. On accusations against him as a Jew who destroys the Russian Orthodox church from inside, see Guy Sitbon, "Qui a tué Alexandre Men, pope et juif?" *Le nouvel observateur* (Paris), no. 1350 (1990), pp. 50–51.

38. A. Vasinskii, "Po doroge k khramu," *Izvestiia,* September 12, 1990, p. 6.

39. "On Tuesday, by the grave of Fr. Alexander, I tried to remember where I had seen this crowd before, who came to bid him farewell.... Then I recalled. It was the same crowd that came to Sakharov's funeral. The same brightened faces, the same expression in their eyes. It was our

people's remnant untouched by cynicism, degradation, despair. They always come when misfortune befalls not only relatives, but the very society, the very age. As if the same bright crowd wanders from grave to grave, from one righteous man to another." Ibid., p. 6.

Part One

Popular Religious Culture
and Orthodox Identity

Dvoeverie
and Popular Religion

Adiscussion of the recovery of religious identity in the Soviet Union assumes the existence of a strong religious identity in pre-Revolution Russia. While no one would dispute the official status of the Russian Orthodox church, or the profound Christian inspiration in the oeuvres of many Russian *intelligenty*, the depth and content of the religious belief of the lower classes remain an area of scholarly dispute. Premodern Russian peasants have been characterized as deeply pious, or ignorant and superstitious, or scoffing and amoral, as has suited the intellectual or political agenda of the observer. Certainly the quality of popular Christianity before the Revolution has implications for the process of the recovery of religious identity in post-Communist Russia.

Scholars have long used the term *dvoeverie* to describe popular religion in Russia. In the common parlance of the profession, it means a religious system in which pagan beliefs and practices are preserved under a veneer of Christianity. The common people of Russia kept their traditional pagan practices, a situation that brought them into conflict with the church hierarchy, which was backed up by the state. The frequent repetitions of ecclesiastical prohibitions on consulting "sorcerers" and participating in "satanic rituals" demonstrated that the struggle was both protracted and generally unsuccessful. When the church accommodated popular beliefs, it did so under duress, in order to gain wider acceptance. Because the religious milieu of the nineteenth-century peasantry seemed so little Christian, the concept of *dvoeverie* was extended to it as well.[1] In this way, *dvoeverie* and popular religion became virtually synonymous.

Few scholars have challenged this view. In 1962, Nikolay Andreyev stated that this perception of popular religion "is confirmed by historians of all schools."[2] But as Gregory Freeze observed:

> most observers in late imperial Russia—and historians ever since—have tended to concur that the Russian people were only semi- (or even pseudo-) Christianized, that their religious world changed but little over the centuries, and that the Orthodox Church bore much of the responsibility for failing to implant a proper understanding of the faith among its flock.

Such assumptions are manifestly in acute need of reconsideration. For the most part, they derive not from serious empirical research, but from the a priori assumptions and the obiter dicta of Russia's urban intelligentsia. The fact is that we know precious little about popular piety, its wellsprings, forms, and influence. . . .[3]

A thorough reconsideration of popular religion would require much more elaboration than can be accomplished here. My goal in this essay will be more modest: to lay out problems of past scholarship on Russian *dvoeverie*, to examine recent innovations in the historiography of popular Christianity in the medieval West as a possible guide for Russianists, to discuss two examples that do not fit well into the two-sided conflict paradigm of popular religion, and finally to suggest better ways of conceptualizing medieval Russian popular religion.

THE HISTORIOGRAPHICAL TRADITION OF *DVOEVERIE*

The word *dvoeverie* originated in the medieval period. It is recorded in sermons directed against Christians who continued to worship pagan deities: "The Lord Almighty thus cannot abide Christians who live in *dvoeverie*...when those in the faith and baptism do this, not only the ignorant but also the knowing, priests and bookmen."[4] Some purists among modern scholars still prefer to restrict usage to the Kievan period, when some East Slavs still remained unbaptized.[5] Pre-Petrine authors also used it to describe other diabolical schisms in Christian unity, such as the Oprichnina.[6]

Even at that time, it had a negative connotation. *Dvoeverie* implied that Russian Orthodoxy as it was commonly practiced was imperfect. From its medieval roots, *dvoeverie* came to signify conflict between two different religious systems, whether conscious or unconscious. The term itself implies a dualism: paganism and Christianity still distinct and separable. This connotation is not present in the term "syncretism," which instead emphasizes fusion.

N. M. Gal'kovskii wrote the seminal work on *dvoeverie*, the two-volume *Bor'ba Khristianstva s ostatkami iazychestva v drevnei Rusi.*[7] He argued that the populace of medieval Russia rapidly accepted a new, Christian identity, but their ways remained pagan, especially in borderlands, rural communities, and among women:

not as a result of stubborn refusal to live as Christians, but as a result of a poor knowledge of Christian tenets of the faith. . . . The hierarchy condemned popular *dvoeverie*, but the people themselves lived in *dvoeverie* considering themselves to be true believers, not noticing and not knowing that there was much paganism in their lives. . . . The strength of paganism is found in the ignorance of the popular masses.[8]

In this schematization, the church originated the struggle, trying to stamp out the relics of paganism in popular observances. The people did not openly resist Christianity, but until the time of Alexei or even Peter the Great, simply did not know any better.[9] In this way, Gal'kovskii endorsed the conflict model of *dvoeverie,* and confirmed the pagan content of popular religion, even while denying that peasants were consciously pagan. The inculcation of a truly Christian faith among the masses was part of the process of educating and civilizing them. Working independently at the same time, E. V. Anichkov arrived at similar conclusions. He dated the period of conflict between Christianity and the paganism of the peasant masses later than Gal'kovskii. Until the fifteenth or sixteenth century, *dvoeverie* was exclusively an urban phenomenon; the peasants knew nothing of Christianity, and retained their agricultural cults. The struggle to Christianize the peasantry occurred in the fifteenth through seventeenth centuries. Many pagan rituals survived, with the late addition of Christian meanings.[10]

George P. Fedotov largely agreed with Gal'kovskii's and Anichkov's characterization of *dvoeverie.* He argued that the church was uncompromising in its attacks on pagan traditions in the Kievan period, when Christianity was "mainly the civilized, urban religion, the faith of the aristocratic society."[11] While Fedotov saw more active resistance from pagans than Gal'kovskii did, he attributed most of the later outbreaks to non-Russian Finno-Ugric or steppe nomadic peoples. He further argued that Orthodox Christianity finally permeated the masses only when it became receptive to traditional Russian veneration of the forces of nature and divine womanhood.[12] While Fedotov did not emphasize the "conflict" aspects of *dvoeverie,* he did accept the two-sided model, and agreed with his predecessors that the substance of popular religion long remained pagan.

One Western scholar cautiously moved away from the the two-sided model and the definition of popular religion solely as *dvoeverie.* In a short article intended as an initial foray into terra incognita, Dmitri Obolensky suggested four levels of interaction between official Orthodoxy and popular religion. At the first level, the church's teachings became popular; Obolensky's example is the cult of Boris and Gleb. At the second level, the people embraced Christian ideas, and expressed them in the terms of folk tradition, in particular in popular spiritual poems (*kaliki*). The church supported both of these manifestations of popular religion. The third level consists of pagan survivals. The church generally opposed customs of pagan origin but could occasionally tolerate Christianized forms. The fourth level is the dualistic heresy of Bogomilism, which church and state united to annihilate.[13] Obolensky thus revised certain aspects of the two-sided model. First, he noted that popular religion was not synonymous with paganism. Second, he pointed out that the church's relationship with the people was not marked primarily by hostility. At the same time, he, like Gal'kovskii, Anichkov, and Fedotov, continued to measure popular religion by the standard of the most educated and philosophical version of Christianity.

To these scholars, the source of conflict was primarily the church's ideological hostility to pagan customs, although in practice it could tolerate a certain amount of syncretism. The people continued their pagan customs largely because of insufficient assimilation of the new faith rather than of deliberate opposition to Christianity. Two groups of scholars, Soviet Marxists and Western feminists, have challenged the interpretation of popular ignorance, arguing that the majority deliberately and consciously espoused paganism in defiance of church and state. In this way, Marxists and feminists also endorsed the concept of a two-sided conflict between religious traditions.

To Soviet scholars such as N. Matorin and B. A. Rybakov, the relationship between the church and the people was necessarily hostile.[14] The state adopted Christianity in order to use the church as a tool of social control over the peasantry and urban lower classes. Soviet Marxists emphasized the importance of pagan and heretical movements as the vehicles for popular rebellions as part of the class struggle. Even in the absence of overt protests, the lower classes actively chose to observe pagan customs as a method of expressing opposition to the alien ideology of the ruling class. Unlike most pre-Revolution and Western scholars, Soviet Marxists did not regard Christianity as fundamentally different from paganism in its system of beliefs. Instead, Christianity reflected the same universal myths of feminine deity and the forces of nature found in pagan religious systems, enshrined in a more oppressive institutional structure. Paganism, by contrast, was a manifestation of folk culture of great antiquity and rich heritage. In this way, Soviet Marxists downgraded Christianity as superstitious and exploitative—a view that fit nicely with the Soviet state's antireligious policies—while extolling paganism as part of Russian national identity.

Under glasnost, some adventurous Soviet scholars dared to break with the class antagonism model of their seniors. Iu. V. Krianev and T. P. Pavlova downplayed overt conflict but retained the favorable and unfavorable views of paganism and Christianity, respectively, of the Soviet Marxist tradition. They stressed that Christianity's pessimistic and ascetic outlook was alien to the optimistic, realistic, and democratic spirit of traditional Russian pagan culture. The authors extolled medieval Russia's "secular" culture, derived from paganism, but said little about Russian Orthodoxy, except to argue that it ultimately was transformed to fit the predominant pagan base.[15]

V. G. Vlasov granted a greater influence to Christianity, asserting "the willing and spontaneous acceptance of Christianity by Russian agricul-

turalists" while granting that "popular Orthodoxy was far from orthodox, as the preservation of *dvoeverie* testifies."[16] In many ways he revived
Anichkov's position, seeing peasant religion as a recasting of the pagan
world view in Christian form: "Paganism simply and spontaneously
flowed into Christianity, pagan sorcery developed into Christian miracles, the magus-sorcerer became a Christian saint—that is the popular
philosophy of that time.[17] Vlasov also agreed that the Christianization of
rural Russia dated to the fifteenth century, when the first peasant saints
lived, and when the peasantry adopted the Church's calendar to mark the
agricultural cycle. Unlike his pre-Revolution predecessors, Vlasov devoted more space to influences, from the elite to the peasantry and from
the peasantry to the elite, than to conflict.

The semiotic school of Boris Uspensky and Iurii Lotman proposed
that duality—unrelated to social class—is the essential underlying characteristic of Russian culture. In their "binary" system, from "the subjective perspective of the 'native speaker'" the most basic opposition is
between old and new.[18] In the medieval period, the "old" was paganism;
the "new," Christianity. The "native speaker's" sense that the oppositions
must be dualistic was so strong that all non-Orthodox movements, including Russian heresies and Roman Catholicism, had to be understood
as a form of paganism. While the "native speaker" might condemn and
deny the "old," that opposition in itself kept the "old" alive.[19] Uspensky
applied this theory to the specific phenomenon of the cult of St. Nikola,
explaining the irregular features of the popular cult primarily by reference to the pre-Christian cult of the pagan god Volos. Although Uspensky prefers to speak of "stratification" (*naplastovanie*) of beliefs rather
than of *dvoeverie,* his conception is still essentially two-sided.[20]

While Soviet scholars have been abandoning the Marxist antagonistic
model of popular religion, Western feminists have taken inspiration from
it. Feminists, like Marxists, challenged the positive image of Christianity
in older studies of popular culture. To Mary Matossian and Joanna
Hubbs, Christianity is a "male" ideology dedicated to the suppression of
the "female" pagan system of belief. Pre-Christian Russian society was
woman-centered: its religion focused on the great mother goddess, and
its social structure was matrilocal and egalitarian. Both church and state
represented the forces of patriarchy, imposing their will on the resisting
Russian peasantry. The church's tradition of misogyny and its condemnations of evil women proved the continuing existence of a pagan resistance, led primarily by "witches." Even though Christianity ultimately
dominated, the church was not truly victorious, because the women succeeded in altering the content and rituals of the new faith to match those
of their pagan traditions.[21]

Thus the *dvoeverie* paradigm of popular religion in medieval Russia
has been perpetuated among historical schools as diverse as imperial

progressivists, émigré Orthodox, semioticians, Marxist and post-Marxist Soviets, and Western feminists. All view the religion of the people in the Middle Ages—if not later—as basically pagan. They understand the relationship between the elite of church and state and the masses to be primarily—if not exclusively—antagonistic. The scholars themselves have frequently taken sides, either with Christianity against ignorance and superstition, or with paganism against exploitation and intolerance. In short, the two-sided model has, since Gal'kovskii's time, become increasingly less subtle and more partisan.

Despite their limitations, the various versions of the two-sided model made their contribution to our understanding of medieval popular religion. The concept of *dvoeverie* led scholars to trace the distant roots of pagan beliefs, so that we know much more about them. The Soviet approach alerted us to the use of religion as political protest, and directed our attention to the economic and social context of religious issues. The feminist approach taught us that women and men often have different perspectives on religion, especially in a strongly patriarchal society. Much of the source material about popular religion in its conflict with the official church has been gathered and published.

The emphasis on conflict has distorted the evidence, however. The concept of *dvoeverie* demanded that scholars attempt to sort out what is pagan from what is Christian, leaving no room for overlap between the two systems, or for the development of beliefs that draw on both pagan and Christian concepts. The diversity within paganism and Christianity has been ignored. The emphasis on conflict led scholars to overestimate the hostility between the state and the church, on the one hand, and the peasants and the urban lower class, on the other, thus obscuring common elements in beliefs and practices. By visualizing the existence of two distinct parties, scholars too often assumed that attempts at accommodation between the two sides had to be deliberate: the church developed cults designed to supplant specific pagan observances; the people recast their traditional practices under the facade of Christian names.

In general, scholars have been too credulous of the labels medieval polemicists and modern ethnographers have used to describe religious phenomena. As Lotman and Uspensky pointed out, ecclesiastical authors and secular rulers used the term "pagan" indiscriminately to condemn "non-Christian" activities, whether actually pagan, heretical, foreign, or otherwise alien.[22] Scholars have compounded the problem of identifying actual paganism by interpreting any medieval complaint about "the devil's work" as pagan activity rather than as mere sin.[23] They frequently have conflated paganism with witchcraft, heresy, political protest, and folk medicine. As studies of witch scares in western Europe have demonstrated, witchcraft should be understood not as the survival of agrarian cults but, rather, as a complex phenomenon integrating paganism, magic, astrology, heresy, and Christianity in a setting of social and political tension.[24] Folk healers—especially women—might be accused of paganism or sorcery, but the labels are not interchangeable.[25] The church did not condemn all non-ecclesiastical medicine but instead accepted some manifestations of it—for example, midwives.[26] And while curing illness was a significant motivator to consult "sorcerers," some instances of witchcraft and paganism were totally unconnected with healing. Greater skepticism and caution are necessary in evaluating the labels in medieval sources.

Even when the designation "pagan" is accurate, more precision is necessary. Medieval Christianity had assimilated much from the pagan cultures of the late Roman world long before the conversion of Russia, thus complicating the separation of pagan and Christian elements. The Russian state always contained substantial populations of unassimilated Finno-Ugric, Baltic, Iranian, and Turkic peoples, who had not yet adopted Christianity. Many of the incidents of pagan resistance involved non-Russians, and much of the terminology in medieval sources for pagan people and practices is Finno-Ugric rather than Slavic.[27] Even as Finno-Ugric tribes living among the East Slavs became converted and assimilated, the expansion of the Russian state guaranteed that new, still pagan tribes would always inhabit the geographic and social fringes of Russian society. These peoples were a constant reservoir for pagan ideas within the Russian population. But despite centuries of close association, Slavs and Finns remain ethnically different. Slavs are Indo-European, and some plausible guesses can be made about Slavic religious beliefs from comparison with other Indo-European cultures, such as the Greeks. The Finno-Ugric language family spans an immense territory, from Europe to North America, and an equally wide range of cultural traditions. In addition, ancient astrological and fortune-telling traditions penetrated into medieval Russia.[28] Clearly, early Russia was influenced not by one pagan belief system but by many.

A further problem in extant scholarship is its reliance on folklore from the nineteenth and twentieth centuries to reconstruct medieval religious conceptions. Gal'kovskii and Anichkov centered their studies on medieval texts, but found them too fragmentary to interpret without reference to folk custom. Rybakov and Uspensky mixed ethnographical evidence, art, and medieval primary sources with abandon. Hubbs virtually abandoned medieval sources to concentrate solely on Neolithic archaeology and folklore. This approach assumes that peasant society within living memory accurately preserved the beliefs and practices of earlier periods.[29] If there was any change at all, it consisted of the erosion of paganism and the addition of a superficial Christianity. The former could be corrected by comparison with other Slavic peoples and better-known Indo-European pagan systems. The latter problem was corrected by deleting obvious Christian references.

However, peasant society, although conservative, is hardly unchanging. If folklore reflects the *mentalité* of nineteenth-century peasants, as Maureen Perrie argues so persuasively,[30] it cannot simultaneously reflect the values of peasants in the pre-Petrine period, when the legal, political, and economic milieu differed. Furthermore, peasant custom when it was recorded in the nineteenth century was highly localized: religious observances were often peculiar to one region or even one village. This diversity suggests the development of new rituals locally, rather than erosion of ancient traditions. The very conservatism of peasant culture complicates the process of dating religious beliefs. Folk rituals enshrine relics from the distant past—even from the Paleolithic period—but it is difficult to know when these relics lost their living religious significance. The ethnographers who recorded folk custom were entranced by the "pagan" elements, and preferred speculative pagan explanations for rituals to the peasants' own Christian meanings.[31] Scholars fell into the trap of circular reasoning as concerns folklore, paganism, and medieval popular culture. They reconstructed the pre-Christian belief system on the basis of nineteenth-century ethnography, then presented the consequent congruence as proof of continuity through the medieval period.

The biases of the sources complicate reconstruction of medieval popular religion. We learn about the lower classes only when they intersect with the elite, from the perspective of the elite. Sermons, laws, episcopal letters, penitential materials, and chronicles focus disproportionally on problems, rather like modern newspapers. But because these texts could reach only an audience that already accepted a Christian identity, the epithet "pagan" must be regarded with skepticism. The discovery of "pagan" activity depended largely upon the willingness of the individual to confess misconduct to a priest; the usual punishment consisted of penances of prayers and fasting. This method of dealing with violations suggests a measure of cooperation on the part of the offender—something hardly possible in a system of conflict and resistance. Furthermore, upon closer examination, it becomes clear that most of the "pagan" practices occurred on the occasion of Christian holidays, and alongside officially accepted ecclesiastical observances.

STUDIES OF POPULAR CHRISTIANITY IN MEDIEVAL WESTERN EUROPE

Scholars of medieval and early modern Western European popular religion have successfully extended their source base and analytical perspective, and can provide Russianists with instructive observations. In general, research on popular religion in medieval and early modern western Europe is more sophisticated than the works on Russia discussed above. Since the 1970s, Western medievalists have made great strides, abandoning the conceptualization of popular religion in terms of pagan survivals and deviation from canonical norms.[32] Since that time, studies of the economic and social structures of rural and urban communities have enriched understanding of everyday life, and generated a more sophisticated view of popular culture. Medievalists no longer regard it as a backward imitation of elite culture but, rather, as a creative blend of many religious and ethnic traditions, adapted to the societal realities and imperatives of lower-class life.

Keith Thomas wrote the seminal reinterpretation of popular religion, *Religion and the Decline of Magic*. Working primarily from the example of England, he dated the adoption of a "religious" mentality—approaching the divine for spiritual enlightenment and moral guidance—only to the seventeenth century, in the wake of the Protestant Reformation, Catholic Counter-Reformation, and Scientific Revolution. Before that time, most western Europeans, elite and common, clergy and laity, shared an essentially "magical" mentality, believing that individuals could tap into supernatural powers through rituals and words. Although well-educated theologians of the later Middle Ages emphasized the tenets of the faith and moral conduct to win God's blessing, in actuality the church condoned most aspects of popular piety, serving "as a limitless source of supernatural aid, applicable to most of the problems likely to arise in daily life. It offered blessings to accompany important secular activities, and exorcisms and protective rituals to secure them from molestation by evil spirits or adverse forces of nature."[33] As long as the church sanctioned a practice, it was not "superstitious," much less pagan. While the rural lower classes participated fervently in a multitude of religious ceremonies, they frequently lacked the most basic understanding of dogma, and attended services irregularly, even after the Reformation.[34]

The rituals and beliefs in the medieval West sound hauntingly familiar to students of medieval Russian popular religion: patron saints for every enterprise, wonder-working springs and images, protective amulets, invocations of agricultural and human fertility, lay and ecclesiastical faith healers.[35] But Thomas and his colleagues do not regard these phenomena as evidence of persisting pagan consciousness. As a Soviet historian of the medieval West, A. Ia. Gurevich, wrote, "This 'paganism' of which parish priests accused their flock, was highly conditional; as soon as people attended church services, came for confession and were able to comprehend the symbols of the faith . . . it is difficult not to consider them Christians."[36] In their explanations of popular religion, Western medievalists do not invoke descriptors such as "pagan survival" or the value-laden "superstition"; instead, they speak of "magic" as an attitude toward the supernatural independent of theological systems.

Unlike Russianists, Western specialists are aware that identifying Christian and pagan or "religious" and "magical" elements need not be the limit of scholarly analysis of popular religion. They do not make the mistake of assuming that "simple folk" are incapable of abstract theological thought, recognizing that peasants express their ideas in the metaphors of their daily experience.[37] Natalie Davis described the approach she shares with her colleagues:

> [We] examine the range of people's relation with the sacred and the supernatural, so as not to fragment those rites, practises, symbols, beliefs and institutions which to villagers or city dwellers constitute a whole. We consider how all of these may provide groups and individuals some sense of the ordering of their world, some explanation for baffling events or injustice, and some notion of who and where they are. We ask what feelings, moods and motives they encourage or try to repress. We look to see what means are offered to move people through the stages of their lives, to prepare for their future, and to cope with suffering or catastrophe. And further, we try to establish the ways in which religious life gives support to the social order . . . and in which it can also criticize, challenge or overturn that order.[38]

In short, Western medievalists have striven to understand religious life of the premodern believers through their eyes, tied well into the context of the realities of social, economic, and political life in general. They see that popular and elite religion overlap more than they conflict, that the two form part of a single community, an "inextricable unity."[39] They recognize that religious influences can move in both directions, from the ecclesiastical elite to popular culture, and from the peasant majority into the official church. They accept the idea that "conservative" popular culture does indeed change, and have documented some of those changes.[40] All these insights are important lessons for Russianists.

However useful the model of scholarship on western European popular religion in the premodern period, Russian specialists cannot adopt their conclusions incautiously. The Eastern Orthodox and Roman Catholic churches had differences in structure that directly impinged on popular piety. The Patriarch of Constantinople, unlike the Pope, claimed no universal dominion, and made no attempt to centralize ecclesiastical administration or to standardize procedures and laws. The married parish clergy in the Orthodox East were socially and culturally more similar to their parishioners than were their celibate Catholic counterparts. The use of Church Slavonic in the Russian liturgy meant that the words sounded familiar even to uneducated speakers of the Old Russian vernacular, although the meaning of whole passages might remain obscure.[41]

Theological differences matter, too. The concept of Purgatory that generated popular phenomena such as the sale of indulgences and masses for the dead in the West never developed in the Orthodox world. Icons bear a mystical significance that Western statuary, paintings, and stained glass do not. The adoption of Christianity came later in Russia than in the rest of Europe, Scandinavia excepted. When England, for example, had seven centuries of Christianity behind it, Russia had only two. Unlike most of western Europe, Russia included large numbers of various *inovertsy* (other-believers) within its borders throughout its history. Given these differences, Russia must be treated as a separate case.

POPULAR VERSIONS OF CHRISTIANITY: TWO EXAMPLES

Much of the information about religion in the medieval period, either in Russia or in the West, cannot be explained simply as a manifestation of either paganism or official Christianity. Evidence of peaceful, even cordial, interaction between the Church hierarchy and the common folk does not fit with a model of conflict and resistance. Most telling of all, peasants identified themselves primarily as "Christians" (*khrest'iane* in Old Russian), giving no indication that they retained a conscious pagan identity.[42]

Two examples will suffice to demonstrate that the two-sided paradigm of *dvoeverie* falls short in explaining the phenomena of popular religion in medieval Russia. The first example concerns the cult of Saints Ioann and Iakov Meniuzhskie, two young innocents venerated in the Novgorodian north. The second example is the cult of St. Paraskeva Piatnitsa, the patroness of women's housework, who was revered throughout the Orthodox countries of eastern Europe. In both cases, the cults enjoyed official sanction but were primarily laic. Neither cult can be explained simply as a pagan survival in Christian form.

Ioann and Iakov Meniuzhskie are among the many local saints of the sixteenth and seventeenth century who were eventually canonized by the Russian Orthodox church. Scholarly research on the cult of the brother-saints is entirely lacking. V. O. Kliuchevskii and L. A. Dmitriev do not mention them in their books on Russian vitae.[43] Modern ecclesiastical dictionaries record the pair as official saints, categorizing them as martyrs, but give little information beyond the day of veneration (June 24).[44] No vita has been published, but I was fortunate to find one, in a nineteenth-century copy, at the Novgorod State Museum.[45] This vita cites 1570 as the year of the children's martyrdom, but one source places it in the year 7000 (1492) by the Byzantine calendar.[46]

While the later official accounts assert that Ioann and Iakov died for their faith because of evil, the vita states otherwise. Ioann and Iakov, at ages five and three, were mimicking their parents' activities, butchering a sheep. Ioann struck his brother in play, and Iakov died as a result. Then, frightened, Ioann hid in the stove, and died when his mother lighted a fire. The boys' bodies were preserved uncorrupted, an early indication of their sainthood. In their first miracle, the graves of the boys, magically floating on a lake, guided lost hunters safely home. Later the saints appeared to the hunters again, asking them to bury their bodies at an abandoned monastery at Meniusha and to restore its buildings. In a third miracle, a monk received a cure of his illness from the relics of these saints. He then took up residence in the Meniusha monastery and began to receive pilgrims.

The evidence suggests that the cult of Ioann and Iakov began among the peasantry, and spread from there to the clergy. The peasants seem to have taken the lead in establishing the relics as a local pilgrimage site. Ecclesiastical interest, in the form of the healed monk, grew out of popular veneration. The monastery gained official recognition only in the late eighteenth century. The vita preserves details of peasant life—butchering a sheep, lighting a fire in the stove, hunters lost in the forest—so we may hypothesize that the religious sentiments expressed also reflect a peasant view, albeit filtered through an ecclesiastical writer. Neither boy died in defense of Orthodox Christianity. Iakov, the "sheep" in their game, imitates the Lamb of God's purity and sacrifice; he was "killed without guilt." Ioann earned sainthood because he had expiated his unknowing sin, "dying in martyrdom by fire for the murder."

The Russian church accepted with fervor the idea of canonizing young innocents. The cult of Boris and Gleb is the best-known example; these young men died not as martyrs for the faith but as imitators of Christ's passion, in complete innocence.[47] The Russian veneration of young innocents might find its roots in pagan ideas of the supernatural power of youth cut short (the *vila*) or a more general worship of deceased members of the *rod* (clan), but it also fits with Christian examples, such as Abel or Jesus Himself. But Abel and Jesus both accepted death in service to God, while Boris and Gleb died in a fratricidal civil war and Ioann and Iakov in a domestic accident. The author of the vita of Boris and Gleb attributed to them statements of faith at the moment of death, in a move to try to accommodate Christian notions of martyrdom as death for Christ. The author of the Meniusha vita, however, thought it sufficient to say that the boys had been baptized to demonstrate their Christian faith. While Boris and Gleb defended the interests of the Rurikovich princes and the Russian state, Ioann and Iakov protected the common people of Meniusha. The graves of both pairs of brother-saints were the sites of supernatural phenomena, amenable to both pagan and Christian explanation: fire in the case of Boris and Gleb, floating on water for Ioann and Iakov. Both pairs granted believers miraculous healing—a trait shared by many saintly persons, both living and dead.[48] In the cult of Ioann and Iakov Meniuzhskie, we see a religious phenomenon that cannot be explained solely by reference to Slavic paganism or to Orthodox Christian teaching, but only as a reinterpretation of Christian and pre-Christian motifs in the popular imagination.

All scholars, whether Orthodox, Marxist, feminist, or none of the above, agreed that the Russian cult of St. Paraskeva was a prime example of *dvoeverie:* the name of an obscure Christian saint covering veneration of a prehistoric goddess (perhaps the Neolithic great mother) in the guise of the Russian deity Mokosh.[49] Indeed, the characteristics of St. Paraskeva in the popular view seem to match those of Mokosh almost exactly: both are special to women; are venerated on Fridays; are responsible for spinning and housework; are a source of healing (especially of eye ailments); guarantee happy marriages; are connected with springs and tree branches. However, little is known about Mokosh from medieval or even ethnographical sources;[50] her traits were reconstructed from the peasant cult of St. Paraskeva! The close match, then, must be discounted as the outcome of circular reasoning.

Further investigation of the cult of St. Paraskeva reveals much evidence that does not fit with a pagan origin. She is venerated not only in Russia but also in Bulgaria, Serbia, Greece, and Romania, everywhere with the same characteristics. If Mokosh were the source, the cult of Paraskeva in its recognized form would be found only in Russia, for Mokosh was unknown farther south. Furthermore, the earliest evidence of veneration for Paraskeva arose among merchants, not among women.[51] Even in the fourteenth century, Metropolitan Kiprian described the holiday of St. Paraskeva as a merchants' festival.[52]

The first evidence of Paraskeva's association with women arose in fourteenth-century Bulgaria, where vitae were produced of the two saints of that name—a Roman martyr and a Bulgarian recluse—both highly favorable to women.[53] The traits attributed to Paraskeva in the popular tradition can be ascribed to incidents in one of three ecclesiastical sources: the vita of the martyr Paraskeva, the vita of the recluse Paraskeva, and chapter 31 of Proverbs, the Old Testament reading assigned for the Good Friday *paraskeve* (preparatory) service.[54] Her connection with spinning and housekeeping comes from the Proverbs reading, in which the admirable woman devotes herself to these tasks. The merchant veneration of Paraskeva might also be derived from this text: the good woman is "like a merchant ship; she brings food from afar." The martyr Paraskeva blinds her tormentor, then heals him to demonstrate the power of the Christian faith, thus explaining her patronage of eye ailments. The Bulgarian recluse Paraskeva was connected with healing springs both in Trnovo and in Belgrade while her relics were at those sites in the fourteenth and fifteenth centuries. The martyr Paraskeva received healing of her wounds from the Virgin Mary, who carried a branch of blackthorn (*túrnov,* a pun on the name Trnovo), explaining the appearance of branches in the popular cult. In short, the immediate inspiration for the popular cult of St. Paraskeva came from three distinct ecclesiastical traditions, not pagan ones.

The popular veneration of Paraskeva cannot be reduced to selective borrowing from the ecclesiastical tradition, however. On the contrary, the cult evolved further through popular imagination, particularly among women. Nothing in the ecclesiastical tradition hinted of Paraskeva's patronage of childbirth, but this development is understandable for the patroness of women's work and healing.[55] Paraskeva's patronage of marriage also reflects innovation from the ecclesiastical base, because according to official vitae neither saint married. But the martyr Paraskeva rejected a marriage proposal from her tormentor, averring that "I have a true bridegroom, Christ, and I need no other husband,"[56] thus becoming a model to young girls of exercising the right to choose or reject a spouse.

The records of the Stoglav Church Council of 1551 give further evidence of how the cult developed among the populace, and the official reaction to it:

> False prophets are wandering among the rural districts and villages. Men and [married] women and maidens and old grannies, naked and barefoot, with loose hair, and dissolute, shake and beat themselves. They say that Saints Piatnitsa and Anastasia appear to them and order them to teach Christians and observe the canons. They teach that manual labor should not be performed on Wednesdays and Fridays: women should not spin or wash clothes or heat stones. And others teach the doing of things offensive to God and against the divine scriptures.[57]

The council responded only to the problem of the disturbance of the peace, that is, wandering homeless and advising against working on Wednesdays and Fridays. These were properly days of fasting and sexual abstinence, the council ruled, but work was mandated. While the council worried about disorder and the suspicious teachings of these adherents of St. Paraskeva, it made no move to stamp out the cult. Indeed, Metropolitan Makarii gave the two Paraskevas a prominent place in the new official ecclesiastical calendar.

Little in the description of the popular Paraskeva cult suggests paganism rather than Christianity. Even the critics agreed that the heretics were teaching Christianity, even if their version of it was "offensive to God." The heretics demanded stricter observance of Wednesdays and Fridays as days of abstinence. They preached itinerantly, in imitation of Christ. By wandering naked and barefoot, they took on the role of the *iurodivye*, the "fools-in-Christ" whom the church accepted as legitimate even if they did point out the misdoings of ecclesiastical and governmental authorities.[58] The vitae of the two saints Paraskeva themselves illustrate official approval: the martyr Paraskeva traveled and preached;[59] the Bulgarian recluse left home to seek Christ in the wilderness, impervious to physical discomfort.[60] Self-mortification and ecstatic shaking were common elements of medieval Christian cults, in both the Eastern and the Western traditions, where self-torture was often accompanied by itinerant preaching and nudity for both sexes.[61] Flagellation survived as part of the folk rituals surrounding Paraskeva into the nineteenth and twentieth centuries.[62]

In short, the popular cult of St. Paraskeva can be understood much more fully as a manifestation of folk Christianity than as a pagan survival. The search for ancient pagan roots blinded scholars to the changes in the cult, and the multilayered interaction of ecclesiastical image and popular veneration.

TOWARD A RECONCEPTUALIZATION
OF POPULAR RELIGION

The inspiration for the popular cults such as those of Sts. Ioann and Iakov and St. Paraskeva may be Christian, but it is far from the "cognitive Orthodoxy"[63] of the modern world. The contemporary understanding of Christianity as a religion of individual faith and sophisticated theology rooted in Scripture is largely an outgrowth of the Protestant Reformation and Catholic Counter-Reformation. There were spokesmen for this intellectualized Christianity long before, of course: Augustine and Thomas Aquinas in the West; John Chrysostom and Gregory Palamas in the East. But medieval lay Christianity emphasized communal observance more than individual faith. A person became a Christian through participation in the rituals, most notably baptism, and observance of a "Christian life," however that was defined in the community. To judge from the penitentials, the content of the individual's faith—at least before the reforms of the seventeenth century—was of little import; confessors did not even inquire about it. Heresies became threats not because they included "wrong" ideas about God but because they disrupted the structures of society and challenged secular and ecclesiastical authorities.[64]

Medieval Christians, including the highest prelates, also accepted the validity of magic—that is, that humans could manipulate supernatural power mechanistically through proper words and procedures, apart from their moral virtue. The saints were revered not primarily as models of the Christian life who had attained eternal glory, but as heavenly persons who could be cajoled into acting at the behest of people on earth. The relics of the saints, holy water, incense, the bread of the Host really contained thaumaturgic power that was effective regardless of the spiritual state and motivations of the recipients. The proper performance of rituals and recitation of prayers were essential to gaining their beneficial effects. The timing of events to coincide with religious services and the Church calendar truly affected their outcome. Natural phenomena such as heavenly signs and earthquakes directly reflected God's will. Misfortune resulted from divine retribution against those guilty of some moral or ritual offense. Much of official Christianity from the Middle Ages looks like pagan superstition from the perspective of a modern spiritualized faith. Judging medieval religion by the standard of a contemporary intellectualized and rationalized philosophical system can result only in a distortion of premodern religious phenomena.

A better understanding of the nature of premodern official Orthodoxy is essential to replacing the old two-sided model of *dvoeverie* with a more nuanced conceptualization. The emphasis cannot be on tracing the distant origins of customs, but on uncovering their significance in the medieval milieu.[65] Many—but not all—elements in the religious system of pre-Petrine Russia were common to both the popular masses and the ruling classes, to the laity and the clergy, to rural and urban dwellers, to women and men. Religious beliefs and observances grew out of people's own understanding of the supernatural and the natural and social world around them.

Reinterpreting the popular religion of medieval Russia as a folk version of Christianity will have a final benefit: the term *dvoeverie* will no longer need to serve that function. Instead, it can be returned to its original meaning, cleansed of its pejorative connotation: the conscious and deliberate practice of Christianity and paganism by the same person. In this new/old guise, *dvoeverie* might again become a useful concept.

NOTES

ACKNOWLEDGMENTS: The author would like to express her appreciation to the International Research and Exchanges Board and the Fulbright-Hays Faculty Research Abroad program for funding visits to the Soviet Union in 1981–1982 and 1990; the Summer Research Laboratory of the University of Illinois; and the Hilandar Research Library at Ohio State University. Views expressed in this paper are those of the author, and may not be shared by facilitating agencies.

1. See, for example, S. A. Tokarev, *Religioznye verovaniia vostochno-slavianskikh narodov XIX-nachala XX v.* (Moscow-Leningrad, 1957), pp. 147–155; Stephen P. Dunn and Ethel Dunn, *The Peasants of Central Russia* (New York: Holt, Rinehart and Winston, 1967), pp. 104–109.

2. Nikolay Andreyev, "Pagan and Christian Elements in Old Russia," *Slavic Review*, 21, no. 1 (1962), p. 17.

3. Gregory L. Freeze, "The Rechristianization of Russia: The Church and Popular Religion, 1750–1850," *Studia Slavica Finlandensia*, 7 (1990), p. 101.

4. F. Buslaev, *Istoricheskaia khrestomatiia tserkovno-slavianskago i drevne-russkago iazykov* (Moscow, 1861), p. 99. See also I. I. Sreznevskii, *Materialy dlia slovaria drevnerusskago iazyka* (St. Petersburg, 1893), vol. I, p. 640.

5. B. A. Rybakov, for example, calls the eleventh through the thirteenth centuries the "period of *dvoeverie*," while for V. D. Otamanovskii it was the late eleventh to early twelfth century. See Rybakov, *Iazychestvo drevnei Rusi* (Moscow, 1987), pp. 456–459; and Otamanovskii, *Bor'ba meditsiny s religiei v drevnei Rusi* (Moscow, 1965), p. 59. Both scholars agree that popular religion remained largely pagan in content up to modern times.

6. From Ivan Timofeev's *Khronograf* of 1617, quoted in Daniel Rowland, "Did Muscovite Literary Ideology Place Limits on the Power of the Tsar (1540s–1660s)?" *Russian Review*, 49, no. 2 (April 1990), p. 132.

7. N. M. Gal'kovskii, *Bor'ba Khristianstva s ostatkami iazychestva v drevnei Rusi*, vol. I (Khar'kov, 1916); vol. II (Moscow, 1913), published in Zapiski Moskovskago arkheologicheskago instituta, no. 18.

8. Ibid., vol. I, p. 142.

9. Ibid., vol. I, p. 309.

10. E. V. Anichkov, *Iazychestvo i drevniaia Rus'*, Zapiski istoriko-filologicheskago fakul'teta imperatorskago S.-Peterburgskago Universiteta, 117 (St. Petersburg, 1914), esp. pp. 303–307.

11. George P. Fedotov, *The Russian Religious Mind* (Belmont, Mass.: Nordland, 1975), vol. I, p. 357. The original edition was published in 1946.

12. Ibid., vol. I, pp. 344–362.

13. Dimitri Obolensky, "Popular Religion in Medieval Russia," in *The Religious World of Russian Culture* [Russia and Orthodoxy, vol. II], ed. Andrew Blane (The Hague: Mouton, 1975), pp. 43–54.

14. N. Matorin, *Zhenskoe bozhestvo v pravoslavnom kul'te* (Moscow, 1931); B. A. Rybakov, *Iazychestvo drevnei Rusi* (Moscow, 1987) and *Iazychestvo drevnykh slavian* (Moscow, 1981).

15. Iu. V. Krianev, and T. P. Pavlova, "Dvoeverie na Rusi," in *Kak byla kreshchena Rus'* (Moscow: Izdatel'stvo Politicheskoi Literatury, 1989), pp. 304–314, esp. p. 313.

16. V. G. Vlasov, "Khristianizatsiia russkikh krest'ian," *Sovetskaia etnografiia* (1988), no. 3, p. 15.

17. Ibid., p. 12. His example of this phenomenon is the tale of Peter and Fevronia; he argues that the text actually describes Fevronia's conversion from paganism to Christianity.

18. Iurii M. Lotman and Boris A. Uspensky, "Binary Models in the Dynamics of Russian Culture (to the End of the Eighteenth Century)," in *The Semiotics of Russian Cultural History*, ed. Alexander D. Nakhimovsky

and Alice Stone Nakhimovsky (Ithaca, N.Y.: Cornell University Press, 1985), p. 33.

19. Ibid., pp. 39–42.

20. B. A. Uspenskii, *Filologicheskie razyskaniia v oblasti slavianskikh drevnostei (Relikty iazychestva v vostochnoslavianskom kul'te Nikolaia Mirlikiiskogo* (Moscow, 1982).

21. Mary Matossian, "In the Beginning, God Was a Woman," *Journal of Social History,* 6 (Spring 1973), pp. 337–338; Joanna Hubbs, *Mother Russia: The Feminine Myth in Russian Culture* (Bloomington: Indiana University Press, 1988). Although not a feminist, S. Smirnov accepted the notion that women preserved paganism; see "Baby bogomerzkiia," in *Sbornik statei posviashchennykh Vasiliiu Osipovichu Kliuchevskomu* (Moscow, 1909), pp. 217–243. None of these authors noted that condemnations of women in general as prone to witchcraft were not exclusive to Russia but were found in western Europe as well; see Robert Muchembled, "The Witches of the Cambresis: The Acculturation of the Rural World in the Sixteenth and Seventeenth Centuries," in *Religion and the People, 800–1700,* ed. James Obelkovich (Chapel Hill: University of North Carolina Press, 1979), p. 221. Similar statements about women and witchcraft may also be found in the Talmud.

22. Lotman and Uspensky, "Binary Models," pp. 40–43.

23. For example, see Anichkov, *Iazychestvo i drevniaia Rus',* p. 301.

24. The literature on witchcraft in the medieval and early modern West is immense. For an overview of approaches to witchcraft, see Jeffrey Burton Russell, *Witchcraft in the Middle Ages* (Ithaca, N.Y.: Cornell University Press, 1972), esp. ch. 1, pp. 1–26. There has been minimal study of witchcraft in Russia, but preliminary work suggests both similarities and differences, especially in the significant participation of men. See Valerie A. Kivelson, "Through the Prism of Witchcraft: Townswomen in Seventeenth-Century Muscovy," in *Russia's Women: Accommodation, Resistance, Transformation,* ed. Barbara Evans Clements, Barbara Alpern Engel, and Christine D. Worobec (Berkeley: University of California Press, 1991), pp. 74–94.

25. Despite his valuable compilation of sources and information, V. D. Otamanovskii confuses folk healers with sorcerers and witches; see *Bor'ba meditsiny.* On folk healing in the religious context in the medieval West, see Keith Thomas, *Religion and the Decline of Magic* (New York: Scribner's, 1971), pp. 177–211.

26. See Eve Levin, "Childbirth in Medieval Russia: Canon Law and Popular Traditions," in *Russia's Women,* pp. 44–59.

27. James H. Billington makes this point briefly in his classic study of Russian culture, *The Icon and the Axe* (New York: Vintage Books, 1970), p. 18; as does Fedotov, *The Russian Religious Mind,* vol. I, p. 356, and Ewa M. Thompson, *Understanding Russia: The Holy Fool in Russian*

Culture (New York: University Press of America, 1987), pp. 97–123.

28. For example, see the texts "Gadal'nye knigi" included in the Soviet publication of *Domostroi* (Moscow, 1990), pp. 260–270. Anichkov referred briefly to "Chaldean astronomy and alchemy" as a source of an urban version of *dvoeverie* in medieval Russia, but did not elaborate; see *Iazychestvo*, p. 304.

29. See Tokarev, *Religioznye verovaniia*, pp. 4–19, for a discussion of the scholarly tradition of using folklore to reconstruct pagan beliefs. Raoul Manselli, *La religion populaire au moyen âge: Problèmes de méthode et d'histoire* (Montreal: Instituat d'Etudes Médiévales, 1975), pp. 36–41, has some valuable observations concerning the value and difficulty of using folklore as a source for popular religion.

30. Maureen Perrie, "Folklore as Evidence of Peasant *Mentalité*: Social Attitudes and Values in Russian Popular Culture," *Russian Review*, 48, no. 2 (1989), pp. 119–143.

31. Christine Worobec brought this fact to my attention in a private communication. For an example of this approach at its most sophisticated, see S. V. Maksimov, *Nechistaia, nevedomaia i krestnaia sila* (St. Petersburg, 1903).

32. See Natalie Zemon Davis, "Some Tasks and Themes in the Study of Popular Religion," in *The Pursuit of Holiness in Late Medieval and Renaissance Religion,* ed. Charles Trinkaus and Heiko A. Oberman (Leiden: E. J. Brill, 1974), pp. 307–310, for a brief summation of this older view and a thoughtful critique of it. It is beyond the scope of this essay to provide a complete bibliography of the immense literature on popular religion in the medieval and early modern West. A few milestones are Natalie Zemon Davis, *Society and Culture in Early Modern France* (Stanford, Calif.: Stanford University Press, 1965); Thomas, *Religion and the Decline of Magic;* Manselli, *La religion populaire,* pp. 307–336; Carlo Ginzburg, "Cheese and Worms: The Cosmos of a Sixteenth-Century Miller," in *Religion and the People, 800–1700,* ed. James Obelkovich (Chapel Hill: University of North Carolina Press, 1979), pp. 87–167; *Popular Belief and Practice,* ed. G. J. Cuming and Derek Baker (Cambridge: Cambridge University Press, 1972); Rosalind Brooke and Christopher Brooke, *Popular Religion in the Middle Ages: Western Europe 1000–1300* (London: Thames and Hudson, 1984); A. Ia. Gurevich, *Problemy srednevekovoi narodnoi kul'tury* (Moscow: Iskusstvo, 1981), translated by János M. Bak and Paul A. Hollingsworth as *Medieval Popular Culture* (Cambridge: Cambridge University Press, 1988); A. Ia. Gurevich, *Srednevekovyi mir: Kul'tura bezmolvstvuiushchego bol'shinstva* (Moscow: Iskusstvo, 1990).

33. Thomas, *Religion and the Decline of Magic,* p. 77, cf. pp. 3–50 and *passim.* See also Gurevich, *Srednevekovyi mir,* pp. 279–306; Manselli, *La religion populaire,* pp. 32–35, where he invokes the conversion of

Russia as an example of popular faith not in Christianity but in the prince's power to choose the best supernatural protector.

34. Thomas, *Religion and the Decline of Magic,* pp. 159–166.

35. The similarities become particularly striking when reading about the medieval West in Russian, as in the Soviet publications of A. Ia. Gurevich.

36. Gurevich, *Srednevekovyi mir,* p. 49.

37. Ginzburg, "Cheese and Worms," pp. 87–88, 162–163, and *passim.*

38. Davis, "Some Tasks and Themes," p. 312.

39. Brooke and Brooke, *Popular Religion,* pp. 12, 61–62; see also Gurevich, *Srednevekovyi mir,* pp. 306–307.

40. James Obelkovich, "Introduction" to *Religion and the People, 800–1700,* pp. 5–6; Colin Morris, "A Critique of Popular Religion: Guibert of Nogent on *The Relics of the Saints,*" in *Popular Belief and Practice,* p. 55; Manselli, *La religion populaire,* pp. 17–32.

41. A few scholars—most notably B. A. Uspensky and Edward L. Keenan—have emphasized the divergence between Church Slavonic and the vernacular Russian of the sixteenth and seventeenth centuries; see Edward L. Keenan, *The Kurbskii-Groznyi Apocrypha* (Cambridge, Mass.: Harvard University Press, 1971), pp. 53–56. However, there was considerable crossover between the two, and in any case the difference was no greater than between Shakespearean and modern English.

42. Peasants often referred to themselves as "Christians" in birch-bark letters; see the word index in *Novgorodskie gramoty na bereste,* vol. VIII, ed. V. L. Ianin and A. A. Zalizniak (Moscow, 1986), p. 303.

43. V. O. Kliuchevskii, *Drevnerusskaia zhitiia sviatykh kak istoricheskii istochnik* (Moscow, 1871); L. A. Dmitriev, *Zhitiinye povesti russkogo severa kak pamiatniki literatury, XIII–XVII vv.* (Leningrad, 1973).

44. *Zhitiia sviatykh: 1000 let russkoi sviatosti,* ed. Nun Taisiia, 2d ed., vol. I (Jordanville, N.Y.: Holy Trinity Monastery, 1983), p. 282; E. Golubinskii, *Istoriia kanonizatsii sviatykh v russkoi tserkvi* (Moscow, 1903), p. 151; N. Barsukov, *Istochniki russkoi agiografii* (St. Petersburg, 1882), p. 238; *Slovar' istoricheskii o sviatykh proslavlennykh v rossiiskoi tserkvi i o nekotorykh podvizhnikakh blagochestiia mestno chtimykh* (St. Petersburg, 1836), p. 1090.

45. Novgorod State Museum, no. 11179, fols. 221v–224, 19th c. The dating information is based on A. I. Semenov, *Opisanie rukopisnykh knig Novgorodskogo muzeia po XVII-yi vek vkliuchitel'no i naibolee interesnykh XVIII–XIX vekov* (Novgorod, 1968). The content of the text itself may be used to estimate its date of composition. The last paragraph refers to the co-tsars Ivan V and Peter I, and is obviously a later addition to the original text. Thus the original was written between the putative date of the saints' death, 1570, and 1696.

46. Barsukov, *Istochniki russkoi agiografii,* p. 238.

47. On the cult of Boris and Gleb, see Gail Lenhoff, *The Martyred Princes Boris and Gleb: A Socio-Cultural Study of the Cult and the Texts* (Columbus, Ohio: Slavica, 1989); S. Maczko, "Boris and Gleb: Saintly Princes or Princely Saints?" *Russian History* 2, no. 1 (1975), pp. 68–80; Michael Cherniavsky, *Tsar and People* (New Haven: Yale University Press, 1961), pp. 7–13; Obolensky, "Popular Religion in Medieval Russia," pp. 45–47.

48. For the miracles of Boris and Gleb, see Lenhoff, *The Martyred Princes,* pp. 37–45. Even in the seventeenth century, when Western medicine had appeared in Muscovy, the church promoted belief in faith healing. Patriarch Nikon was a noted faith healer: see Sergei Belokurov, ed., "Dela sviat. Nikona patriarkha pache zhe reshchi chudesa vrachebnaia," *Chteniia v Imperatorskom obshchestve istorii i drevnostei rossiiskikh pri moskovskom universitete* (1887), bk. 1, pp. 83–114.

49. The main scholars who have discussed the Russian cult of St. Paraskeva are S. V. Bulgakov, *Nastol'naia kniga dlia sviashchenno-tserkovnosluzitelei* (Kharkov, 1900), pp. 392–394; Konrad Onasch, "Paraskeva-Studien," *Ostkirchliche Studien,* 6 (1978), pp. 121–141; Matorin, *Zhenskoe bozhestvo;* Joan Delany Grossman, "Feminine Images in Old Russian Literature and Art," *California Slavic Studies,* 11 (1980), pp. 38–42; Rybakov, *Iazychestvo drevnykh slavian,* pp. 379–392, esp. p. 387; and *Iazychestvo drevnei Rusi,* pp. 658–659; Matossian, "In the Beginning, God Was a Woman"; Hubbs, *Mother Russia,* pp. 116–123; Uspenskii, *Filologicheskie razyskaniia,* pp. 33–34, 75, 95n, 113, 134–138.

50. See Gal'kovskii, *Bor'ba khristianstva,* vol. I, pp. 33–35, for a compilation of all solid medieval evidence on Mokosh.

51. Paul Bushkovitch, "Urban Ideology in Medieval Novgorod: An Iconographic Approach," *Cahiers du monde russe et soviétique,* 16, no. 1 (1975), pp. 19–26.

52. "Otvety mitropolita Kipriana igumenu Afanasiiu," in *Pamiatniki drevne-russkago kanonicheskago prava,* Russkaia istoricheskaia biblioteka, 6 (St. Petersburg, 1908), p. 253.

53. *Bdinski Zbornik: Ghent Slavonic Ms 408 A.D. 1360 Facsimile Edition* (London: Variorum Reprints, 1972), ii, vi–vii, fols. 58–72; St. Novaković, "Apokrifsko itije svete Petke," *Spomenik Srpske kraljevske akademije,* 29 (1895), pp. 23–32; Emil Kaluzniacki, "Zur älteren Paraskevalitteratur der Griechen, Slaven, und Rumanen," *Sitzungsberichte der Philosophisch-historischen Klasse der Kaiserlichen Akademie der Wissenschaften* (Vienna), 141, no. 8 (1899), pp. 1–93; and *Werke des patriarchen von Bulgarien Euthymius (1375–1393)* (London: Variorum Reprints, 1971), pp. 59–77; François Halkin, "Sainte Parasceve la Jeune et sa vie inédite BHG 1420z," *Studia Slavico-Byzantina et Mediaevalia Europensia,* vol. I (Sofia, 1989), pp. 281–292. The *Velikii chetii minei* of Metropolitan

Makarii of Russia, compiled in the mid-sixteenth century, contains versions of both vitae: *Velikiia minei chetii sobrannyia vserossiiskom mitropolitom Makariem. Oktiabr' dni 4–18* (St. Petersburg, 1874), pp. 1021–1042; *Velikiia minei chetii sobrannyia vserossiiskom mitropolitom Makariem. Oktiabr' dni 19–31* (St. Petersburg, 1880), pp. 1968–1969. For the appeal of Evtimii's version of the vita to women, see Donka Petkanova, *Starobulgarska literatura*, vol. II (Sofia, 1987), pp. 69–71. Although modern ecclesiastical calendars occasionally list additional early saints named Paraskeva, these citations are apparently the result of recent confusion, and do not reflect medieval traditions.

54. Nicolaus Nilles, *Kalendarium manuale utriusque ecclesiae orientalis et occidentalis* (Westmead, U.K.: Gregg International Publishers, 1971), vol. II, pp. 253–256. I am grateful to Predrag Matejic for drawing my attention to the Proverbs reading and its place in the Orthodox liturgy of the Middle Ages. This choice of reading was apparently a carryover from the home service for the beginning of the Jewish Sabbath, on Friday evening.

55. On Paraskeva's role in popular legends about childbirth, see Maksimoimov, *Nechistaia*, pp. 516–518.

56. Hilandar Research Library, Uppsala Collection 53 (*Sbornik*, Russian, 17th c.), fol. 121v.

57. *Stoglav*, ed. D. E. Kozhanchikov (St. Petersburg, 1863), pp. 138–139.

58. The most accessible study of *iurodivye* is Ewa M. Thompson, *Understanding Russia*, but it is marred by the author's antipathy for a tradition she deems to be pagan rather than Christian in origin.

59. *Bdinski Zbornik*, fols. 59–60.

60. *Velikiia minei chetii . . . Oktiabr' dni 4–18*, p. 1025; Kaluzniacki, *Werke*, pp. 62–63.

61. Norman Cohn, *The Pursuit of the Millennium* (New York: Harper Torchbooks, 1961), pp. 124–148.

62. Matorin, *Zhenskoe bozhestvo*, pp. 5–6; Matossian, "In the Beginning, God Was a Woman," p. 330; Uspenskii, *Filologicheskie razyskaniia*, p. 135.

63. I take this useful term from Freeze, "The Rechristianization of Russia," p. 111.

64. On medieval Russian heresies in the social context, see N. A. Kazakova and Ia. S. Lur'e, *Antifeodal'nye ereticheskie dvizheniia na Rusi XIV-nachala XVI veka* (Moscow-Leningrad, 1955); and Robert O. Crummey, *The Old Believers and the World of Antichrist* (Madison: University of Wisconsin Press, 1970).

65. Chs. 4 and 5 of Paul Bushkovitch's *Religion and Society in Russia: The Sixteenth and Seventeenth Centuries* (New York: Oxford University Press, 1992), may serve as a model in this direction.

The Wages of Sin

The Decline of Public Penance in Imperial Russia

S erious scholarship on institutional and, especially, popular religion in Imperial Russia has only just begun. Although the published literature (chiefly prerevolutionary) is immense, it is too old-fashioned to pose the significant questions, to employ modern methodologies and conceptual tools, or to contextualize findings in a larger comparative framework.[1] Hence Russianists *volens-nolens* must rely upon the crude stereotypes and simpleminded assumptions bequeathed by the urban intelligentsia, which, with rare exceptions, had little understanding and still less empathy for the traditional religious culture. As a result, the historiography is befuddled with contradictory images—of the people as pious and pagan, of the Church as a moribund relic of the past and a powerful tool of repression. It is indeed difficult to identify any other sphere of modern Russian history that has been more neglected and distorted than institutional and popular religion.

The present essay examines one important sphere of institutional and popular interaction—public penance. In contrast to private penance rendered in the home parish,[2] public penance (*epitimiia*) entailed monastic seclusion from several weeks to several years. Incarceration of public penitents (*epitiimtsy*) represented the Church's most aggressive attempt to combat religious deviance, crime, and immorality; in theory, at least, it was a powerful instrument for social disciplining that could augment community control and state law. In that sense, public penance was a yardstick of ecclesiastical power and authority, directly reflecting the Church's capacity to influence social behavior. Public penance reveals much about the Church's prescriptive norms, how it assessed and ranked the various transgressions, civil and spiritual, by its flock. Above all, it is essential to study the penitents, not the penitentials—that is, the real practice, not the prescriptions in dogma and decree. Only then can one determine what meaning, if any, the formal prescriptions had in religious life and social behavior.

Given the primitive state of scholarship on institutional and popular religion in Imperial Russia, it is hardly surprising that public penance has been largely neglected. To be sure, penance has been the subject of studies on canon law and penitentials,[3] surveys of state law,[4] and abstruse discourses on theological dogma.[5] Most of this literature treats only the theological or juridical dimension, with no serious attempt to consider the meaning of public penance in everyday life.

That quotidian public penance is the subject of this essay. I shall first examine the evolution of Church teaching on penance and then turn to the far-reaching reforms of the eighteenth century.[6] To determine how the new order subsequently functioned, the following section will present a close analysis of the penitents in 1850; the archival records on these 844 *epitiimtsy* reveal much about their status and the kinds of transgressions that brought them to the monastery. The final section examines the ensuing penance reforms that led to a gradual dismantling of public penance for most transgressions.

FROM PUNISHMENT TO PENANCE

In its earliest phases the Eastern Church ascribed a therapeutic, not a punitive, meaning to penance. Its purpose, the Church taught, was primarily to make the sinner conscious of his or her transgressions and thereby to evoke the appropriate sense of contrition. Hence it bore chiefly a pedagogical rather than a punitive function. It also held some broader social significance when it entailed the visible exclusion from Communion and gradual readmission to fellowship (symbolized by permission to reenter sacred space—the church itself). Such ritualized ostracism served to make both the sinner and the other parishioners cognizant of the gravity of a particular transgression. The dual exclusion, from community and Communion, emphasized at once the significance of the sacred and the fellowship of believers. Most important, the early Church sought to convert, not to govern; its purpose was to evoke the proper sense of contrition, not to punish or to deter crime.

Hence this conception of penance did not imply the notion of compensatory atonement ("satisfaction") that became so important in the Catholic church. That is why the early Church did not generate complex systems of penance (with an intricate algebra of sin and atonement) and fines, much less indulgences. Instead, it limited penance to exclusion from the Eucharist and church; it knew neither fasts nor vigils, neither prostrations nor monastic incarceration, neither fines nor indulgences.[7] That doctrinal difference corresponded to the relative authority each church accorded its clergy: whereas the Catholic church inclined toward sacerdotalism (empowering the priest to grant absolution on behalf of the Lord), the Eastern church taught that the priest could merely intercede before God and seek divine mercy. Accordingly, the rite of "absolution" in the Eastern church bore a purely deprecative character: it did not proclaim forgiveness of sins (in contrast with the Catholic church) but beseeched the Lord to forgive the sinner.

That differed fundamentally, of course, from the Western church, where annual confession became obligatory in 1215 and penance constituted an important ancillary of secular justice. Given the weakness of medieval states, penance came to function as an important instrument not only for moral education but also for social control. Ecclesiastical courts correspondingly gained in secular significance; the introduction of the confessional booth and the proliferation of literature on confession in the late Middle Ages bear witness to this. Indeed, the intensification of ecclesiastical power through these sacraments may have played a significant role in provoking the Protestant Reformation, not only because of the scandalous sale of indulgences but also because of the clergy's increasing intrusion into the laity's private daily lives.[8]

Subsequently, however, the Eastern church (including its Russian subsidiary) began to assign a punitive function to public penance and thereby to substitute for an underdeveloped system of state law and judiciary. That ecclesiastical power was especially pronounced in the Russian case, where neither the Kievan state nor its immediate sequels could exercise more than nominal control of civil, let alone criminal, affairs. All this had a profound impact upon the confessional and penance system in pre-Petrine Russia. As the Russian penitential books from the fourteenth to the sixteenth centuries (especially the instructions in the *Trebnik*) show, the Church acquired a broad judicial competence that empowered it to impose penance for adultery and vice, for theft and crime, for drunkenness and murder, for the sale or abuse of children, and for sexual intercourse on Sundays or the numerous church holidays. No less striking was the severity of penance, even for minor transgressions; hence those who laughed to the point of tears risked—at least theoretically— the sobering prospect of fasting for forty days on bread and water. Serious offenses, predictably, were treated with commensurate severity. For example, as penance for extramarital sexual relations, the *Trebnik* prescribed a penance of fifteen years, with numerous (even hundreds) of daily genuflections and prolonged fasting on bread and water. Given the institutional backwardness of early modern Russia, one should not exaggerate the Church's real capacity for control; indeed, the very weakness of ecclesiastical or state institutions was one reason for the prophylaxis of draconian law. Nevertheless, the Church's temporal power included its own armed forces, thus conferring some capability of enforcement.

This temporal power of the Church inexorably came into conflict with the absolutist aspirations of the secular state seeking to arrogate prerogatives and power.[9] The struggle for predominance had been inconclusive in the seventeenth century, but the Petrine reforms firmly established the state's predominance in civil and criminal affairs. Peter did not, however, altogether terminate the Church's authority in these spheres: once the proper civil punishment had been administered, the Church retained the right to affix ancillary penance (reduced by half to account for any prior penalties by civil authorities).[10] Like other practitioners of contemporary absolutism, Peter sought to enlist the Church's assistance as a separate auxiliary instrument for social control and discipline, thereby forming a complement to the nascent bureaucracy.[11] That status matched perfectly the Petrine conception of Church-state relations, envisioning an "ecclesiastical government" that was parallel, not subordinate, to the "civil government."[12]

Perhaps even more important, Peter also challenged the imposition of severe penance and specifically any prolonged exclusion from Communion. In the words of the Supplement to the Ecclesiastical Regulation: "Many clergy, who are poorly educated, adhere blindly to the *Trebnik* in that they exclude penitents for many years from the Eucharist."[13] That practice, of course, directly subverted Peter's demand that members of the Orthodox church confess and take Communion at least once each year. Although the Petrine reform did not explicitly challenge the principle of penance or the use of monastic incarceration, the castigating critique of the *Trebnik* implicitly challenged the propriety of penance that was unduly severe and onerous.

The demand to moderate and limit penance derived from a variety of motives. One was ostensibly religious: as the Supplement warned, excessive penance could evoke "the poison of despair instead of cure," thus failing altogether to achieve its main objective. In that sense, the Petrine reform sought to restore the therapeutic, nonpunitive conception of penance adumbrated in the teaching of the early Church.[14] The Supplement referred directly to a second impulse—suspicion that excommunication served to conceal the schismatic Old Believers:

> Although [penance] was previously designed for the care of souls (by demonstrating the abomination of sins and restraining the evil desires of the flesh), it has now, however, not only ceased to be frightful to many, but has become desirable to indolents. It is even highly favored by secret schismatics, and it is purposely sought after through the confession of false sins.[15]

Finally, it bears noting that the secularization of justice was a broader phenomenon of early eighteenth-century states; Friedrich Wilhelm I of Prussia, for example, adopted remarkably similar measures in his effort to restrict the role of ecclesiastical courts.[16]

As in so many other spheres, this Petrine reform was slow to take effect, in good measure because it sought to moderate, not to abrogate, penance. Excommunication, for example, remained a clerical prerogative, as an oft-printed guide on clerical duties made clear: "Do not give the divine sacrifice to the unfaithful, heretics, immoral, adulterers, thieves, bandits, merciless authorities, drunkards, usurers, members of robber bands, slanderers, those who make false denunciations, sorcerers, magicians, clowns, or those who torture their slaves with hunger and wounds." The guilty and unrepentant, it declared, were not to be given Communion.[17] Confession and Communion reports from the late eighteenth century, moreover, show that nearly 6 percent of the laity had gone to confession but not received Communion; proportions were especially high in certain provinces of the north and east, reaching 28.1 percent in Irkutsk.[18] Although the reasons for the semicompliance were varied, nominal lists from St. Petersburg and Vladimir show that many failed to take Communion "on the advice of the spiritual father" (po sovetu dukhovnogo ottsa).[19]

Nor did the penchant for harsh public penance quickly subside. Some bishops, like the prelate in Viatka, did not abjure even corporal punishment, ordering that adulterers not only undergo excommunication and pay fines but also be birched and flogged for their transgressions.[20] Two decades later the metropolitan of Moscow similarly prescribed "merciless corporal punishment" for a woman who had committed adultery and deserted her husband. Nor did he mollycoddle blasphemers: "Give [the penitent] only bread and water to eat for sustenance, but only in sufficient quantity so that he does not die of hunger."[21] A report from 1742 confirmed that offenders, even minors, were dispatched to monasteries for terms as long as fifteen years.[22] In 1756 the Synod complained that "in some places a large number [of penitents] are held" in monasteries.[23] The issue became even more acute after 1764, when the secularization of church peasants and property produced an acute crisis in providing adequately for the monastic clergy, let alone penitents. A few years later, in 1767, the Synod again issued a sharp reproof to diocesan authorities for remanding many to monasteries.[24] Ecclesiastical authorities in St. Petersburg also received complaints from Tobol'sk diocese, reporting that fifty-one penitents had been incarcerated in monasteries for more than fifteen years, with ruinous consequences for their families.[25]

From midcentury, however, the Church took steps to avert unduly harsh punishments. Official Church publications, such as the standard pastoral guidebook, admonished the priest to exclude only the unrepentant from Communion.[26] Similarly, the prelate of Voronezh (Tikhon [Sokolov], later canonized) empowered the priest to impose penance but directed that it not be set according to the Trebnik; rather, it was to take into account the penitent's age, rank, and similar circumstances.[27] Over the subsequent decades this demand for moderate penance became ubiquitous in ecclesiastical publications, which emphasized that penance should seek to be therapeutic, not punitive.[28]

The Church also took administrative steps to deter excessive public penance. In 1758, for example, it reprimanded the imperious metropolitan of Rostov, Arsenii Matseevich, for immoderate use of penance.[29] In the 1760s it expressly directed bishops to avoid unduly harsh public penance, and in 1780 sent a circular to local authorities with the admonition "that the penitent neither be overburdened nor driven to despair."[30] After 1774 the Synod began to exercise direct supervision over public penance, requiring diocesan authorities to submit annual reports on penitents (including details on age, rank, and gender) as well as information about their transgressions and prescribed penances.[31]

The Church, moreover, sought not only to shorten the term of public penance but also to emphasize its strictly spiritual ends. Although commoners typically had to perform manual labor during their confinement (both as compensation for support and as spiritually beneficial), the primary purpose of monastic incarceration was to ensure closer supervision of the penitents. The monastery not only could isolate the penitent from temptation and repetition of the offense, but also could provide close supervision over the fulfillment of specific duties, such as genuflections and fasting. In a typical resolution, for example, the abbot of one monastery was instructed

> to accompany [the penitent] to all church services, to force him to pray zealously to the Lord, to perform 100 genuflections every day (except on Sundays and religious holidays), to purify his conscience every day, to perform the genuflections after individual church services, to admit the harm of the sins he had committed, and to guide him to sincere contrition before God. During Lent he may not (except in the event he falls mortally ill) take Communion; he is to eat with moderation and, on Wednesdays and Fridays, to take only bread and water for nourishment.[32]

Sincere repentance could serve to reduce the term of penance: monastery authorities filed regular reports on penitents' conduct and, if the contrition seemed genuine and a penitent unlikely to repeat his or her offense, diocesan authorities could reduce the term of incarceration and permit the remainder of the penance to be performed in the home parish.[33] These reports were especially important in the case of penitents with no fixed term: evidence of reform and contrition were essential if they were to obtain their release.[34]

This system of public penance, subject to the Synod's supervision, remained essentially unchanged until the second half of the nineteenth century.

THE PENITENTS OF 1850

Although one can only speculate about the number of penitents before the late eighteenth century,[35] data for the 1840s show a maximum of 1,000 to 2,000 penitents.[36] The list of 844 penitents examined here is

slightly smaller, because several dioceses failed to submit their annual report for 1850.[37] Although the exact profile varied from year to year,[38] an
analysis of the penitent list for 1850 can reveal much about the operating
principles, routine practices, and social impact of public penance.

Certainly the most striking datum is the small number of penitents.
Given the broad range of offenses that potentially could justify monastic
incarceration, and the frequency of such crimes and moral offenses, it is
clear that few transgressors had to undergo public penance. Data on
crime, to be sure, are notoriously unreliable, and exact comparisons are
hardly feasible. But compared with the population of penitents in the
whole empire, the number of offenders in a single province (Orenburg)
was many times higher—nine times higher for bestiality, twelve times for
premeditated murder and theft.[39] The discrepancy was even greater for
moral offenses like illicit sex and having an illegitimate child. Thus in
each of the populous dioceses several thousand women gave birth to illegitimate children each year, but only a handful underwent penance in a
monastery.[40] In the Moscow diocese, for example, authorities incarcerated eleven laity in 1850 for fornication and adultery (usually demonstrated through illegitimate births), but that very year the diocese
formally registered 3,137 illegitimate births.[41] Characteristically, the offenders often had given birth to multiple illegitimate children before finally undergoing public penance.[42] In short, monastic confinement may
have been important as a threat, but it hardly constituted a system of regular detection and correction.

The frequency of penance did not correspond to the incidence of
crime and immorality, but it did reflect the religious geography of the
prereform Church. As Table 1 shows, the number of penitents varied
considerably, from a single penitent in Viatka diocese to ninety-eight in
Simbirsk. To some extent, the number of penitents reflected the zeal of
an individual bishop in meting out public penance. It was, after all, a
highly arbitrary decision, given the ambiguity in law and the Synod's
attempt to discourage monastic incarceration. At the same time, the
bishop's zeal was inevitably tempered by the strength of monastic institutions. As a result, incarceration tended to be highest in central and
south-central dioceses, which had substantial numbers of monasteries
and a well-established ecclesiastical apparatus. Disproportionately high
numbers also came from sparsely populated dioceses like Perm, probably
reflecting the bishop's determination to combat the Old Belief as well as
the governor's willingness to collaborate. By contrast, incarceration rates
tended to be low in the northern dioceses, either because of the weakness
of administration astride huge territories, or because of the remoteness of
monasteries. The western dioceses also reported relatively few penitents,
partly because religious observance tended to be generally high but also,
perhaps, because local prelates avoided antagonizing the laity in an area

Table 1. Distribution of Penitents Among Dioceses

Diocese	Penitents	Percent
Viatka	1	0.12%
Ekaterinoslav	2	0.24%
Smolensk	2	0.24%
Kishinev	3	0.36%
Kherson	3	0.36%
Astrakhan	5	0.59%
Mogilev	5	0.59%
Don	5	0.59%
Warsaw	6	0.71%
Vologda	6	0.71%
Lithuania	10	1.18%
Nizhnii Novgorod	11	1.30%
Tambov	12	1.42%
Voronezh	12	1.42%
Kursk	14	1.66%
Podolia	15	1.78%
Moscow	15	1.78%
Orel	19	2.25%
Volhynia	19	2.25%
Tver	20	2.37%
Kaluga	21	2.49%
Kostroma	21	2.49%
Kiev	22	2.61%
Novgorod	24	2.84%
Riga	25	2.96%
Arkhangel'sk	26	3.08%
Kharkov	28	3.32%
Polotsk	30	3.55%
Iaroslavl	31	3.67%
St. Petersburg	32	3.79%
Perm	48	5.69%
Riazan	52	6.16%
Poltava	61	7.23%
Tula	69	8.18%
Vladimir	71	8.41%
Simbirsk	98	11.61%
Empire	844	100.00%

Source: RGIA, *f.* 796, *op.* 132, *g.* 1851, *d.* 124.

already seething with confessional discontent and competition.

The grounds for incarceration were extremely diverse but very broadly can be grouped into four main categories (see Table 2). The smallest contingent of penitents (4.7 percent) had committed a strictly religious offense, either flagrant religious deviance or religious nonfeasance (mainly the failure to perform the annual confession and Communion duty). The second broad category consisted of sexual misconduct, chiefly fornica-

Table 2.   Categories of Transgression

Category	Offense	Penitents	Percent
RELIGIOUS	Apostasy	4	0.47%
	No Confession/Communion	23	2.73%
	Schismatic	6	0.71%
	Illegal Burial	1	0.12%
	Sectarian Meetings	3	0.36%
	Blasphemy	1	0.12%
	Self-Castration	2	0.24%
SEXUAL	Fornication	346	41.00%
	Adultery	122	14.45%
	Incest	13	1.54%
	Bestiality	1	0.12%
CRIME	Theft	23	2.73%
	Arson	12	1.42%
	Suicide Attempt	34	4.03%
	Manslaughter	62	7.35%
	Homicide	5	0.59%
	Battery	13	1.54%
	Perjury	2	0.24%
	Child Neglect	5	0.59%
	Political	2	0.24%
	False Denunciation	2	0.24%
	Child Abuse	2	0.24%
	Fourth Marriage	1	0.12%
	Third Marriage	2	0.24%
	Bigamy	1	0.12%
	Pogrom of Jewish woman	1	0.12%
	Infanticide	2	0.24%
	Homicide Attempt	1	0.12%
	Rape	1	0.12%
CLERGY	Drunkenness	65	7.70%
	Illegal Marriage	26	3.08%
	Nonfeasance	17	2.01%
	General Misconduct	34	4.03%
	Insubordination	5	0.59%
UNKNOWN		4	0.47%
TOTAL		**844**	**100.00%**

Source: RGIA, f. 796, op. 132, g. 1851, d. 124.

tion and adultery; altogether, these penitents represented 57.0 percent of the list. Another large congeries included various civil and criminal offenses, from homicide to perjury; although no single category was preponderant, altogether they accounted for 20.4 percent of the penitents. The final, distinct set consisted of professional malfeasance and personal misconduct by clergy, who comprised 17.4 percent of the list. For four individuals (0.5 percent), the offense was not identified.

The number of penitents who had committed religious offenses is surprisingly small: a mere forty laymen for the whole empire. Over half of these consisted of short-term penitents who had neglected confession and Communion for three or more years consecutively. Left out of account, to be sure, are the prisoners in special monastic detention (*kolodniki*), who were deemed incorrigible and dangerous sectarian leaders, and consigned to virtual life imprisonment.[43] The paucity of religious offenders, it should be emphasized, was not an index of piety and conformity. Rather, it reflected far more the weakness of ecclesiastical control: the Church simply lacked the instrumentalities (if not the will) to ferret out and prosecute the *poluraskol'niki* who were nominally Orthodox but actually clandestine schismatics or sectarians. The small number of penitents, however, was also a result of deliberate policy: the Church sought to excoriate only the "instigators" and leaders, not rank-and-file adherents. Implicitly accepting the premise that the ordinary dissenter was still at least half Orthodox, the Church feared that excessive repression might only alienate them conclusively. The Church was still more tolerant toward recent converts: apart from two Jewish apostates, the list contained no penitents from the substantial list of converted minorities who were often remiss in adhering to the faith.[44] In short, the stereotypes of ruthless clerical oppression—especially those from Soviet antireligious literature—bear little resemblance to reality.

Sexual offenders, the largest category of penitents, consisted mostly of those who had committed fornication or adultery. It bears noting that the Church drew a distinction between extramarital fornication (*blud* or *liubodeianie*) and adultery (*preliubodeianie*), with most penitents coming from the former category. The reason, no doubt, is that most penitents were women who had given birth to illegitimate children—ipso facto demonstrably guilty, especially if unmarried. It should be noted that the number of incest cases (thirteen) was relatively low, especially if any credence is to be given to the infamous *snokhachestvo* (the claim for sexual favors from daughters-in-law by peasant patriarchs). The 1850 records, finally, did not list any cases of homosexuality; such cases, rarely reported, usually came to light in the army and fell to the personal disposition of the emperor.

The penitents also committed a variety of civil and criminal offenses. Above all, the aggregate number of ordinary criminals among penitents was low: most criminals convicted by state courts were sentenced to more severe punishment (imprisonment, banishment to Siberia, and hard labor) and could hardly be remanded to the custody of ill-equipped monasteries. Moreover, it should be noted that the offenses were of considerable gravity; mere drunkenness, for example, was not grounds for incarceration for the laity (in contradistinction to the clergy). Rather, the penitents had committed a host of serious crimes against property (theft and arson) or of violence (homicide, attempted suicide, infanticide, child abuse, battery, and the like). The offense of manslaughter in most instances actually represented cases of probable but unproven homicide.

The final and rather substantial category of penitents was the Orthodox clergy. Their numbers do not, of course, testify to extraordinary immorality, but only to the Church's stronger administrative control, the clergy's unmediated vulnerability to detection and prosecution, and the bishops' sensitivity to clerical misconduct. Fully subordinated to the ecclesiastical domain and subjected to biannual visitations by superintendents, the clergy were easily apprehended and prosecuted. Moreover, the Church held them to higher levels of conduct, not only in the performance of their spiritual duties but also in their personal lives. Hence 39.2 percent of the clergy were performing penance for drunkenness, and many of the others (23.9 percent) for sundry acts of insubordination and "general misconduct." Relatively few had committed offenses against their professional duties; most of these pertained to the administration of that most difficult sacrament marriage, which invited strong pressure from laity to disregard laws regulating minimum age, kinship, and the like. Distinctly different was the case of one priest from Kiev diocese, who had been incarcerated "for interfering in the affairs of estate management"—a euphemism for involvement in peasant disorders.[45] As Table 3 shows, the length of penance varied considerably and bore little resemblance to the long terms of a century earlier. Nominally, penance terms conformed to the terms prescribed by the *Trebnik*, reduced by half if some form of civil punishment (birching or imprisonment) had already been meted out. Significantly, however, the term of monastic incarceration was further reduced: the Church generally limited it and allowed the penitent to serve the balance in the home parish. In the case of fornication and adultery, for example, the *Trebnik* prescribed seven years, which was reduced by half to take into account the civil punishment (corporal punishment and imprisonment, already administered by the state or community). Of that term, however, only a portion—usually six months to one year—was to be spent in monastic incarceration. Indeed, in many cases the prelate opted to suspend the public penance altogether; for example, Metropolitan Filaret (Drozdov) of Moscow generally suspended the monastic confinement if the woman married immediately. And the clerical penitents generally had very brief terms, intended chiefly as a chastisement but also to give authorities the opportunity to exercise close moral supervision.

The term of penance was highly variable, and the above averages conceal both arbitrariness and instances of severity. Thus those serving penance for adultery had received sentences from 6 months to 10 years; 1 perpetrator of infanticide faced 1 year of incarceration but another, 10 years; arsonists had to spend from 6 months to 15 years in monastic incarceration. Harsh penance, though rare, nevertheless persisted: 1

Table 3. Length of Public Penance

Category	Offense	Average Term	No Fixed Term
RELIGIOUS	Apostasy	0.25	2
	No Confession/Communion	0.47	5
	Schismatic	None Set	6
	Illegal Burial	0.50	0
	Sectarian Meetings	None Set	3
	Blasphemy	None Set	1
	Self-Castration	0.50	1
SEXUAL	Fornication	0.91	0
	Adultery	0.90	2
	Incest	3.26	1
	Bestiality	5.00	0
CRIME	Theft	1.47	1
	Arson	2.58	0
	Suicide Attempt	1.12	0
	Manslaughter	1.01	0
	Homicide	1.89	2
	Battery	0.88	0
	Perjury	0.33	0
	Child Neglect	0.40	0
	Political	0.00	1
	False Denunciation	0.00	1
	Child Abuse	0.50	1
	Fourth Marriage	0.00	0
	Third Marriage	2.50	0
	Bigamy	3.00	0
	Pogrom of Jewish woman	1.00	0
	Infanticide	5.50	0
	Homicide Attempt	1.00	0
	Rape	1.00	0
CLERGY	Drunkenness	0.20	27
	Illegal Marriage	0.18	0
	Nonfeasance	0.19	5
	Misconduct	0.23	0
	Insubordination	1.46	1
UNKNOWN		0.09	3
TOTAL		0.93	63

Source: RGIA, f. 796, op. 132, g. 1851, d. 124.

penitent faced 15 years' incarceration, 26 (3.1 percent) had to serve a penance of 5 or more years, 15 (1.8 percent) had to serve 2 to 4 years, 330 (39.1 percent) had a sentence of 1 to 2 years, 402 (47.6 percent) had less than 1 year, and 70 (8.3 percent) had no specified term (*bessrochno*). As might be expected, the most severe sentences were for sexual deviance (incest and bestiality) as well as crimes against the sacrament of marriage (bigamy). The two instances of proven infanticide elicited a long average

Table 4. Transgressions of Lay Penitents by Gender

Category	Offense	Females	Percent	Males	Percent
RELIGIOUS	Apostasy	1	0.24%	3	1.05%
	No Confession/Communion	3	0.73%	20	7.02%
	Schismatic	1	0.24%	5	1.75%
	Illegal Burial	0	0.00%	1	0.35%
	Sectarian Meetings	1	0.24%	2	0.70%
	Blasphemy	0	0.00%	1	0.35%
	Self-Castration	0	0.00%	2	0.70%
SEXUAL	Fornication	281	68.20%	65	22.81%
	Adultery	95	23.06%	27	9.47%
	Incest	5	1.21%	8	2.81%
	Bestiality	0	0.00%	1	0.35%
CRIME	Theft	3	0.73%	20	7.02%
	Arson	6	1.46%	6	2.11%
	Suicide Attempt	6	1.46%	28	9.82%
	Manslaughter	3	0.73%	59	20.70%
	Homicide	0	0.00%	5	1.75%
	Battery	0	0.00%	13	4.56%
	Perjury	0	0.00%	2	0.70%
	Child Neglect	4	0.97%	1	0.35%
	Political	0	0.00%	2	0.70%
	False Denunciation	0	0.00%	2	0.70%
	Child Abuse	0	0.00%	2	0.70%
	Fourth Marriage	1	0.24%	0	0.00%
	Third Marriage	0	0.00%	2	0.70%
	Bigamy	0	0.00%	1	0.35%
	Pogrom of Jewish woman	0	0.00%	1	0.35%
	Infanticide	2	0.49%	0	0.00%
	Attempted Homicide	0	0.00%	1	0.35%
	Rape	0	0.00%	1	0.35%
UNKNOWN		0	0.00%	4	1.40%
EMPIRE		412	100.00%	285	100.00%

Source: RGIA, f. 796, op. 132, g. 1851, d. 124.

incarceration (5.5 years), and relatively lengthy penance was also set for theft (1.47 years), homicide (1.89 years) and especially arson (2.58 years). The most common offenses—fornication and adultery—elicited an average penance of 0.9 year. The seventy penitents with unspecified terms consisted of two very different groups: clergy (normally sentenced for short periods to attest their behavior) and religious deviants (who were likely to remain until they recanted).

Although the data on gender might suggest a superficial equality (416 females and 428 males), the correlation with specific offenses shows significant variations (see Table 4). If the clergy (whose penance constituted a special case) are omitted and only the laity is considered, males comprised only 38.6 percent of all penitents. The preponderance of females directly reflects the prominence of fornication and adultery as grounds for public penance, for females comprised 80.3 percent of all such prosecuted offenders. It was neither female promiscuity nor episcopal misogyny that explains the disproportion; rather, the female who gave illegitimate birth was immediately culpable, whereas paternity was far less easily demonstrated. Significantly, when sexual misconduct or paternity could be established, the Church meted out terms of penance with no discrimination as to gender. The fact of demonstrated illegitimacy probably accounts for the preponderance of premarital fornication over adultery; the latter, of course, even if it did result in birth, did not necessarily come to light. As a result, 91.2 percent of female penitents were for sexual misconduct, with only a smattering of other offenses. The 1850 list also included a few cases of infanticide, which often took the form of passive neglect of the newborn and therefore remained highly probable but not conclusively proven.[46]

Premarital fornication also constituted the single largest offense for males, but represented only a relatively small proportion (22.8 percent) of the reason for their public penance. Instead, the male offenders were scattered among the other main categories, including grave felonies, especially those involving interpersonal violence (22.6 percent). It is that category of transgression, no doubt, which explains the fact that the median penance for men was longer (1.19 years) than for women (0.96 year). Nevertheless, given the chilling brutality of many such crimes, the penance was quite moderate. Although reduced terms were dictated primarily by a reluctance to wreak harm on the innocent dependents of the offender, they also conformed to the new emphasis on the therapeutic, not punitive, function of penance. The latter was already administered by state authorities, and public penance had the sole purpose of making the perpetrator cognizant and contrite.

The penitents' age ranged widely, from a minimum of 12 to a maximum of 89, with 34.8 as the median.[47] Male penitents, as a rule, tended to be considerably older: the male median age was 38.6, compared with 31.0 for women. The structure of misdeeds doubtless accounts for the difference: the preponderance of illegitimacy as grounds for penance weighted the female population toward younger, more fertile years. Nevertheless, the age distribution (see Table 5) shows a large number in the middle and upper age brackets—disproportionate to their share of the general population. Youths under age 20 comprised only 6.2 percent of the penitents; by contrast, those over 40 comprised 30.1 percent. Public penance was evidently reserved for recidivists, who had exhausted the patience of the community and appeared impervious to private penance. The rather large population of "senior sinners" (15.2 percent were over 50 years of age) may also be attributable to their expendability, since they were too old to be of much value as labor for the family or community economy.

Table 5.	Age of Penitents
Age Group	**Number of Penitents**
12–19	48
20–29	211
30–39	196
40–49	99
50–59	63
60–69	20
70–79	10
80–89	4

Source: RGIA, *f.* 796, *op.* 132, *g.* 1851, *d.* 124.

The social composition registered in Table 6 likewise bears little resemblance to the population at large. Certainly the most striking overrepresentation was the clergy, not because of their foibles but a result of the tighter control and accountability imposed on the Church's servitors. Despite lamentations by priests about their own high moral condition and the abysmal state of deacons and sacristans,[48] the proportion of priests roughly approximated their share of those in service.[49] The monastic clergy were noticeably underrepresented; however, it is likely that most misbehaving monks simply underwent penance at their superiors' command, without recourse to formal action by ecclesiastical courts.

The second disproportionately large group was the military estate, which, together with Cossacks, comprised 12.7 percent of all penitents. Significantly, that proportion virtually omits the ordinary soldier (see Table 7). The reason was not uncommon virtue among Russian soldiery

Table 6.	Social Composition of Penitents		
Social Comp	**Penitents**	**Percent of Penitents**	**Percent of Laity Only**
Civil official	4	0.47%	0.59%
Clergy	166	19.67%	
Converted Jews	2	0.24%	0.29%
Cossacks	24	2.84%	3.54%
Dvorovoi	56	6.64%	8.26%
Factory Serf	9	1.07%	1.33%
Military	83	9.83%	12.24%
Noble	4	0.47%	0.59%
Peasant	445	52.73%	65.63%
Townspeople	51	6.04%	7.52%
Totals	844	100.00%	100.00%

Source: RGIA, *f.* 796, *op.* 132, *g.* 1851, *d.* 124.

Table 7. Social Composition of Penitents from Military Estate

Category	Number	Percent
Unspecified	3	2.8%
Officer	6	5.6%
Soldatka	64	59.8%
Soldier	10	9.4%
Cossacks	24	22.4%
Total	**107**	**100.00%**

Source: RGIA, *f.* 796, *op.* 132, *g.* 1851, *d.* 124.

but state fiat: a decree of 1799 ordered that they be exempted from monastic detention and be permitted to serve their penance at their place of service.[50] The Cossacks, however, constituted a self-perpetuating subsociety and therefore had nonserving members liable to penance; that is presumably why they were so saliently represented in the penitent list of 1850. However, the main contingent of people from the "military estate" was not men but women—recruits' wives (*soldatki*) who remained behind and occupied an indeterminate station in lay society. Although illegitimacy rates for these women may have been higher, it is also likely that they lacked special protection by either private or military authorities, and therefore proved especially vulnerable to prosecution for illegitimacy.

The fifty-one penitents from the urban estates (townspeople and merchants) were also relatively well represented: this 6 percent of the penitents roughly corresponded to their proportion in the general population.[51] That rate at least partly reflected their greater vulnerability to ecclesiastical control, given the clergy's higher density and tighter administration in urban areas. But another reason, curiously, was the omnipresent peril of conflagration in Russia's wooden towns: nearly half (twenty-five) of the urban penitents had allegedly committed arson or been blamed for causing a fire. The remainder had committed extramarital fornication, which in some instances may have been due to Old Believer sympathies and consequent refusal to accept rites in the official church.

The rural population, whether noble or peasant, was underrepresented. Only four of the penitents were listed as nobles, a fact that cannot be too surprising in view of the authority structures of Russia. Significantly, none of these were performing penance for mistreating their serfs; to judge from belles-lettres and memoir literature, such abuse constituted a serious problem in the village and often provided an explosive force behind squire-serf tensions. Penance was imposed on squires for such abuse, but rarely; it usually involved a squire who had committed such flagrant atrocities that the government was forced to intercede, sometimes remanding the culprit to the Church for an extended penance. It should be emphasized, however, that the culpability here rested not with the Church but with state authorities, who claimed the exclusive prerogative to investigate and prosecute but were all too remiss in performing their responsibilities. Once the Church did receive such cases, however, it was consistent and rigorous, within limits, in treating such offenders.[52]

The peasantry was similarly underrepresented: the combination of peasants, house serfs, and factory serfs—only 60.4 percent of the penitents—comprised only two-thirds of their proportion of the general population. Doubtless the shielding of community and squire, as well as the weakness of ecclesiastical control over far-flung and sparsely populated parishes, made it far less likely that they would have to undergo monastic incarceration. It is also likely that community or seigniorial control was greater, meting out swift corporal punishment and eschewing the luxury of extended penance in a remote monastery. The special subcategory of house serfs (*dvorovye*) was relatively large (6.6 percent of the population), probably because these offenders were more vulnerable to clerical control and unprotected by a rural community. The number of factory serfs, though small (nine), is nonetheless interesting, for it hints at the religious deviance (if not indifference, then schism) that characterized this new and growing segment of the population.

In short, the 844 penitents of 1850 hardly constituted a microcosm of Russian society or Russian sinners. They showed a high disproportion of lay females, clergy, older persons, and sexual or criminal offenders, and most spent less than a year in monastic incarceration. The most important fact about the group is its minuscule size: public penance in monastic confinement had become exceedingly unlikely and affected only a tiny proportion even of those who had been apprehended and convicted for perpetrating some breach of religious, civil, or criminal law. As a result, the Church plainly wielded neither the prophylactic terror of dire punishment nor the capacity for regular incarceration of offenders. Except for the clerical and military estates (where control and vulnerability were greater), most of the population had little reason to fear the *Trebnik*.

DISESTABLISHMENT OF PUBLIC PENANCE

Even in this attenuated form, public penance aroused growing resistance from the laity. In fact many laity, evidently in increasing numbers, refused to comply with the order for monastic penance. The most dramatic, if untypical, evidence comes from the diocese of Perm: for one twenty-year period (1831–1850) the bishop reported that 257 of those sentenced to penance in a monastery had failed to appear.[53] One clerical writer attributed the resistance to a decline in respect for the sacrament of penance itself. Ever more frequently, he argued, the faithful were challenging the need for penance and even were inclined to assert that penance was "an invention" of the clergy and devoid of scriptural foundations.[54] Such sentiments, if not widespread, were fueled by the fact that so few now had to bear public penance and that the grounds and terms of penance seemed utterly arbitrary. As one peasant woman (protesting monastic incarceration as penance for giving birth out of wedlock) complained in 1854, such penance was unjust when so many others committed the same transgression but had not had to undergo penance.[55]

Opposition sprang as well from the fact that public penance, even if substantially moderated, nevertheless remained exceedingly onerous. It still connoted hard labor, at least for commoners. Thus the consistory of Tver, for example, ordered one penitent "to attend church every day, but in the time free from prayer, to be used for labor in the monastery."[56] The justification partly rested in the demand that the penitent earn his or her own keep, but also in the notion that work was a good means for disciplining and educating. Furthermore, monastic detention entailed strict observance of the bishop's order on daily attendance at mass, numerous daily genuflections, and strict observance of fasts. Some monastic authorities also sought to instill heightened spirituality by imposing a generous dose of asceticism. As the archimandrite of Solovetskii Monastery admitted, he had reduced the nourishment of penitents to promote the "spiritual repentance" and zeal of those incarcerated.[57] Such methods were even applied to the wellborn, eliciting formal complaints by the penitents or by secular authorities.[58]

But by far the most onerous effect of public penance was economic. Apart from the fact that the penitents sometimes had to provide their own material support, the incarceration forced them to abandon their occupations and thus to forfeit their livelihoods. It was only natural, therefore, that laymen petitioned state and Church authorities to reduce or even excuse them from public penance, usually with the argument that monastic confinement would cause material hardship for themselves and especially for their families. As an unmarried female peasant from Tambov (the mother of an illegitimate child) explained: "I support myself by my own labor, and therefore to live an entire year without any means of support is a terrible situation for me. What should I do in this case? I do not know myself."[59]

State officials tended to support such appeals. Like squires and communities, they resisted the loss of able-bodied and taxpaying members, an inevitable consequence of prolonged penance in a monastery. Complaints about noncooperation, even overt resistance, by state officials appeared periodically in the eighteenth and early nineteenth centuries.[60] To some degree, government officials looked askance at the uncontrolled movement of penitents; in 1843 the minister of interior complained sharply to the Church about the influx of vagrants to St. Petersburg, nominally to perform their penance but (he claimed) actually to engage in various criminal activities.[61] But state officials were also concerned that penance would impair the laity's capacity to perform state obligations and pay taxes. Such concerns were paramount, for example, in a complaint from the governor of Arkhangel'sk in 1851. Protesting the case of a peasant woman (who had been given one year's monastic confinement for illicit sex), the governor stressed the ruinous consequences: "She runs the household for her family, which consists of an elderly father and three young sisters; she also lacks the proper clothing for the journey to the monastery. Hence to dispatch her there to perform penance will bring complete ruin to the family economy and deprive her father and sisters of the means of subsistence."[62]

The Church admitted that the economic consequences could be onerous, especially for married penitents, and therefore tended to reduce penance in such cases. Even so stalwart a conservative as Metropolitan Filaret of Moscow explicitly acknowledged these problems and, so far as possible, tried to accommodate the laity's worldly needs. In 1851, for example, he explained that "men should be sent to monasteries for penance only when necessary and for short terms, and peasants should not be sent during peak periods of field work."[63] In one case involving thirty-six peasants who had committed perjury, Filaret ordered that they perform the penance in stages (one small group after the other) to avoid emptying the small village, and further specified that this penance not be performed during the main agricultural working season.[64] Likewise, Filaret agreed to release adulteresses from monastic incarceration if their husbands were still residing at home and wished the women to return.[65] The prelate also agreed to release women guilty of premarital fornication if a man (presumably the former partner) consented to marry her.[66] The Synod likewise took marital status into account, reducing the penance by half in the case of married offenders.[67]

Quite apart from the impact on the laity, many clergy expressed concern about the impact of public penance on the Church and, especially, on monasticism. The issue gained in sensitivity in the late 1840s amid criticism, some from imperial quarters, about the religious and moral conditions prevailing in Russian monasteries. In response to such sentiments, some bishops warned that the presence of so many corrupt penitents had a demoralizing impact on the monks and nuns residing in those institutions. The problem was especially acute in dioceses that had only a few monastic institutions and therefore were more sensitive to the impact of penitents. Thus the bishop of Olonets wrote to the Synod that "so great a number of female penitents with bad and corrupt morals have been a burden for the monastery and caused it harm."[68] Likewise, the bishop of Irkutsk complained that the confinement of seriously corrupted laymen either compromised the reputation of monasteries or exerted a pernicious influence on the monks.[69] As participants at a conference of spiritual elders (*startsy*) later observed, it was manifestly contradictory to the goal of the monastery to admit the most depraved elements of this world into institutions that were specifically intended as a refuge from a corrupt world.[70]

The result was the Synod's resolution of 11 July 1851 to mandate a sharp reduction in the use of public penance. According to data collected by the Synod, the monasteries currently held some 648 lay penitents (an incomplete tally, since nine dioceses had failed to submit data). So large a number, complained the Synod, was unacceptable. First, monastic incarceration "diverted the laity from their usual employment and thereby subjected them to the most extreme hardship." The problem was most acute in the larger, sparsely populated dioceses, where the costs of transportation and support proved especially onerous for the laity. Furthermore, noted the Synod, monastic confinement often failed to achieve real repentance and served only to harden and alienate. It was far more desirable to rely upon public penance in the home parish: "The fulfillment of penance under the supervision of the spiritual father, as experience has shown, is the most effective measure, if it is performed privately and with zeal from the side of the confessor, who through his edification and in a spirit of gentleness and Christian love, is able to arouse consciousness of the sin and genuine contrition." The Synod therefore ordered that henceforth penance should be performed at the home parish and that monastic incarceration be applied only when the gravity of the crime and lack of contrition warranted.[71]

Because the decree left much to episcopal discretion and many prelates upheld the need for some public penance,[72] the number of penitents declined gradually but remained fairly substantial. In 1854, for example, diocesan reports indicated that the number of lay penitents had declined by less than half (to 376).[73] In a new resolution of 18 March 1868, the Synod observed that while the number of public penitents in monastic confinement had declined by the mid-1860s,[74] it was still unacceptably high, comprising some 200 laypersons and more than 300 parish clergy. It complained that monasteries had neither the fiscal means nor the proper quarters to confine so many penitents. It also found that most cases of public penance were not even prescribed by the existing Digest of Laws (*Svod zakonov*): according to the Synod's records, only 29.7 percent of the 212 lay penitents in 1865 had committed offenses entailing monastic detention. Some of the balance (7.1 percent) had been confined by special order of the emperor, but the majority (62.2 percent) had been interned in monasteries without proper legal grounds. The Synod thereupon ordered their immediate release and strictly admonished the diocesan prelates to order public penance only for offenses explicitly listed in the Digest of Laws.[75]

Although that decree did not eliminate public penances altogether, it did sharply reduce their number. By 1904 the number of lay penitents in monasteries was just 119—roughly a tenth of the number held before the 1851 reform. Moreover, most of the penitents were juveniles who had committed a felony (such as arson), along with a handful of incorrigible sectarian or schismatic leaders. For all practical purposes, after 1868 public penance ceased to serve as an instrument either of intimidation or of correction.

CONCLUSION

The devolution of public penance was not only gradual but also voluntary: the Church itself supported the amelioration and virtual abolition of monastic incarceration. Even if the Petrine reform provided the first initiative, from the mid-eighteenth century the Church acted to diminish the length and frequency of public penance. To be sure, some prelates resisted; Metropolitan Arsenii (Matseevich) defended massive application, and Metropolitan Filaret (Drozdov) opposed its complete abolition. But from the 1760s to the 1860s, most prelates gradually acceded to an ever more limited use of monastic incarceration.

That voluntary dismantling, it should be stressed, corresponded to the clerical elite's effort to "re-Christianize" the common people. Above all, that shift meant a systematic effort to excoriate the false and superstitious, still more to instill a new comprehension of Orthodoxy, to augment popular piety with greater comprehension of the essentials of the faith.[76] The notion of cognitive Orthodoxy extended as well to penance, which should be governed neither by custom nor by coercion. Instead, penance should represent an act of private volition, sustained not by external coercion but by inner conviction of the individual. Privatization of penance, at least potentially, promised to create a more conscious laity and hence one less susceptible to the blandishments of schism and sect. It was not without its dangers; in an age of rising crime and religious dissent, the Church lost the threat, much less the systematic use, of coercive powers. But the change—in penance as in other matters—was all the more essential if the Church was to maintain its place in an ever more secular state and multiconfessional empire.

If individuation was one motive, institutionalization provided the other: dismantling public penance was a necessary accommodation to the development of the modern state. It was not simply a matter of state absolutism or intrusion; rather, even when the state reserved powers for the Church to exercise, it proved manifestly impossible to institutionalize public penance and to absorb vast hordes of sinners and criminals. That problem had not existed in pre-Petrine Russia, where the minuscule system of justice, secular or ecclesiastical, exerted little prescriptive influence over popular life, especially in rural areas. In that sense, the Petrine state, with its expanding bureaucracy and judiciary, apprehended and convicted offenders—all of whom were potentially liable to public penance. Thus the new recordkeeping (parish registers, census revisions) detected illegitimate births; expanded courts prosecuted and convicted those who violated civil and criminal law.

At the same time the Church's capacity to control such penitents declined, especially after the secularization of church properties in 1764; even the renewed expansion of monasticism from the mid-nineteenth century could hardly compensate for the exponential growth of the state and its judicial apparatus. The growing contradiction between the pool of potential candidates and the Church's capacity to absorb them steadily widened. Hence the abolition of public penance was, ultimately, an inevitable consequence of the expansion of the state bureaucracy and formal justice. In a larger sense, the prophylactic function of medieval penitentials (employing the threat of unbearable penance as deterrent) was not only discordant with modern sensibilities but also incompatible with the institutionalization of regular justice.

NOTES

ACKNOWLEDGMENTS: The present essay, which is part of a larger study titled "Church, Society and Religion in Modern Russia, 1750–1930," has been supported by grants from the International Research and Exchanges Board, the Alexander von Humboldt-Stiftung, the Fulbright Faculty Research Program, and the American Council of Learned Societies. Special thanks are due to the staffs of various Russian archives (in particular, the Rossiiskii Gosudarstvennyi Istoricheskii Arkhiv, formerly the Tsentral'nyi Gosudarstvennyi Istoricheskii Arkhiv SSSR) and the Slavic Library of Helsinki University.

1. The sheer volume of scholarship on institutional history is astounding; see, for example, the synthesis and bibliographical apparatus in Igor Smolitsch, *Geschichte der russischen Kirche*, 2 vols. (Leiden and Wiesbaden: Brill, 1964–1991). The research on popular religion, conducted between 1870 and 1930, chiefly by anthropologists and ethnographers, suffers from the desire to record nonnormative religious practice. For the concept of popular religion, see C. Dipper, "Volksreligiosität und Obrigkeit im 18. Jahrhundert," in *Volksreligiosität in der modernen Sozialgeschichte*, ed. Wolfgang Schieder (Göttingen: Vandenhoeck & Ruprecht, 1986), pp. 73–96.

2. The private (*chastnaia*) penance was not necessarily secret, since it could entail genuflections, fasting, or even physical exclusion from the parish church. The latter practice, however, gradually abated, heighten-

ing the distinction between voluntary private and coercive public penance.

3. The classic studies of Eastern church penitential guides are the monograph and source publication by S. Smirnov: *Dukhovnyi otets v drevnei vostochnoi tserkvi* (Sergiev Posad, 1906) and *Materialy dlia istorii drevnerusskoi pakaiannoi distsipliny* (Moscow, 1912). Medieval penitentials are examined in Eve Levin, *Sex and Society in the World of the Orthodox Slavs, 900–1700* (Ithaca, N.Y.: Cornell University Press, 1989). See also "O publichnom pokaianii," *Pravoslavnyi sobesednik* (1868), no. 2, pp. 97–130, no. 4, pp. 282–320; I. Berdikov, *K voprosu o tserkovnoi distsipline* (St. Petersburg, 1902); V. Kiparisov, *O tserkovnoi distsipline* (Sergiev Posad, 1897); "Ob epitimiiakh i tak nazyvaemykh indul'gentsiiakh," *Khristianskoe chtenie* (1852), no. 2, pp. 406–441; N. Suvorin, *O tserkovnykh nakazaniiakh. Opyt issledovaniia po tserkovnomu pravu* (St. Petersburg, 1876); A. I. Aivazov, *Tainaia ispoved' pravoslavnoi vostochnoi tserkvi*, 3 vols. (Odessa, 1894); H. Koch, "Zur Geschichte der Bußdisziplin in der orientalischen Kirche," *Historisches Jahrbuch* 21 (1906), pp. 58–75; N. Milasch, *Das Kirchenrecht der morgenländischen Kirche* (Moscow, 1905); M. I. Gorchakov, *K istorii epitimnykh nomokanonov petentsialov pravoslavnoi tserkvi* (St. Petersburg, 1884). In *Ob"em distsiplinarnogo suda i iurisdiktsiia tserkvi v period Vselenskikh soborov* (Iaroslavl', 1884), N. Suvorin stressed that punitive penance was a belated and gradual development, thereby provoking a sharp debate among specialists in Russian canon law. See also N. Suvorov, *K voprosu o tainoi ispovedi i o dukhovnikakh v vostochnoi tserkvi* (Iaroslavl', 1886).

4. V. N. Shiriaev, *Religioznye prestupleniia. Istoriko-dogmaticheskii ocherk* (Iaroslavl', 1909); N. D. Sergeevskii, "K izucheniiu o prestupleniiakh religioznykh," *Zhurnal Ministerstva iustitsii* (1906), no. 4, pp. 13–49; A. F. Kostiakovskii, "O prestupleniiakh protiv very," *Nabliudatel'* (1882), no. 10, pp. 102–122. For polemical treatments of ecclesiastical repression, see critical treatments by prerevolutionary exponents of religious freedom—e.g., S. V. Pozdnyshev, *Religioznye prestupleniia s tochki zreniia religioznoi svobody* (Moscow, 1906)—as well as the antireligious tracts of the 1920s and 1930s, such as E. F. Grekulov, *K istorii inkvizitsii v Rossii*, 3d ed. (Moscow, 1930).

5. In particular, see Alois Bukowski, S. J., *Die Genugtuung für die Sünde nach der Auffassung der russischen Orthodoxie* (Paderborn, 1911); Gisela Schröder, "Die Lehre vom Sakrament der Buße in der Russisch-Orthodoxen Kirche" (Ph.D. diss., Ernst-Mortz-Arndt-Universität zu Greifswald [DDR], 1978); Georg Wagner, "Bußdisziplin in der Tradition des Ostens," in *Liturgie et rémissions des Péchés* (Rome, 1975), pp. 251–264.

6. Apart from the various published sources (laws, pastoral guides, sermons, and learned tracts on confession and penance), this essay draws

chiefly upon the ecclesiastical archives of the Holy Synod (Rossiiskii Gosudarstvennyi Istoricheskii Arkhiv [hereafter RGIA], *fond* 796). The most important sources are the regular reports, after 1774, on cases of public penance; the list from 1850, on the eve of the dismantling of private penance, is fairly typical of those from the first half of the nineteenth century and offers an extraordinary, comprehensive picture of the evolution of public penance in the imperial period.

7. For an overview, see the discussion in Schröder and the literature cited therein.

8. See Steven E. Ozment, *The Reformation in the Cities* (New Haven: Yale University Press, 1975).

9. The fullest exposition of the secularization of justice in areas of religion and morality is in Ardalion Popov, *Sud i nakazaniia za prestupleniia protiv very i nravstvennosti po russkomu pravu* (Kazan, 1904).

10. Hence the typical resolution from the Novgorod ecclesiastical consistory in 1853: "The time of penance prescribed by ecclesiastical laws (per the customs in ecclesiastical administration) can be reduced by half if the accused has been sentenced to other punishments by the secular government." RGIA, *fond* 796, *opis'* 135, *god* 1854, *delo* 2053, *list* 202 ob. (heareafter archival terms are abbreviated *f., op., g., d.,* and *l.,* respectively).

11. For an insightful comparative framework, see Walter Wendland, "Zur Geschichte der öffentlichen Kirchenbuße in Brandenburg im 18. Jahrhundert," *Jahrbuch für Brandenburgische Kirchengeschichte,* 15 (1917), pp. 45–65; and S. D. Kluge, "Die 'Kirchenbuße' als staatliche Zuchtmittel im 15.–18. Jahrhundert," *Jahrbuch für Westfälische Kirchengeschichte,* 70 (1977), pp. 51–62. The difference, and an important one, between Russia and central Europe was chronology: Peter was rebuilding this system as it was on the verge of disappearing in the West.

12. For a more extended argument, see Gregory L. Freeze, "Handmaiden of the State? The Church in Imperial Russia Reconsidered," *Journal of Ecclesiastical History,* 36 (1985), pp. 82–102.

13. *Polnoe sobranie zakonov Rossiiskoi imperii,* pervoe sobranie, 55 vols. (St. Petersburg, 1830), VI, 4022.

14. For the argument that Peter's chief ideologist, Feofan (Prokopovich), was more Byzantine than Western in his theological views, see Hans-Joachim Härtl, *Byzantinische Erbe und Orthodoxie bei Feofan Prokopovich* (Würzburg, 1971).

15. Alexander Muller, ed. and trans., *The Spiritual Regulation of Peter the Great* (Seattle: University of Washington Press, 1972), pp. 66–67 (modified).

16. See, for example, the decree of 1716 that demanded reductions in public penance, which was supposed to be not "eine Art von Strafe und Beschimpfung des Gefallenen, sondern ein Mittel, die Sünde und

nur Buße zu bringen." See Wendland, pp. 37ff.

17. *Pouchenie sviatitel'skoe k novopostavlennomu iereiu* (St. Petersburg, 1721; often reprinted), fols. 5 v.–6.

18. RGIA, f. 796, *op.* 63, *g.* 1782, *d.* 123, *ll.* 2–3.

19. The confessional books for 25,000 residents in Suzdal district showed that 30 percent (103 of 346) had confessed but had abstained from Communion at the recommendation of their spiritual father. See Gosudarstvennyi Arkhiv Vladimirskoi Oblasti, f. 560, *op.* 1, *d.* 327, *ll.* 70–77. Similar explanations for semiobservance are given by parishioners in St. Petersburg in 1750 (Gosudarstvennyi Arkhiv Leningradskoi Oblasti, f. 19, *op.* 112, *g.* 1751, *d.* 94).

20. See the 1747 resolution, based on old patriarchal decrees, in "Ukaz Velikogo Gospodina Preosv. Veniamina, episkopa Viatskogo," *Trudy Viatskoi uchenoi arkhivnoi komissii* (1910), vyp. 1, otd. 3, pp. 54–55.

21. N. Rozanov, *Istoriia moskovskogo eparkhial'nogo upravleniia,* 3 vols. in 5 pts. (Moscow, 1869–1871), vol. II, pt. 2, notes 354 and 369. For similar materials, see A. Lebedev, "Primenenie nakazanii v srede dukhovenstva i mirian Belogorodskoi eparkhii v XVIII v.," *Russkaia starina,* 73 (1892), pp. 328–330.

22. *Polnoe sobranie postanovlenii i rasporiazhenii po vedomstvu pravoslavnogo ispovedaniia. Tsarstvovanie Elizavety Petrovny* [hereafter PSPREP], 4 vols. (St. Petersburg, 1899–1911), I, p. 165.

23. RGIA, f. 796, *op.* 37, *g.* 1756, *d.* 520, *l.* 1.

24. RGIA, f. 796, *op.* 48, *g.* 1767, *d.* 322.

25. RGIA, f. 796, *op.* 47, *d.* 399, *ll.* 14 ob.-15.

26. Parfenii (Sopkovskii) and Georgii (Konisskii), *O dolzhnostiakh presviterov prikhodskikh ot slova Bozhiia, sobrannykh pravil i uchitelei tserkvi sostavlennoe* (St. Petersburg, 1776), pp. 151–52.

27. Tikhon (Sokolov), *Sochineniia,* 15 vols. (St. Petersburg, 1825), I, p. 10.

28. Thus the two-volume guide to penance, published on the eve of emancipation, declared that "penance should be not so much a punishment as a treatment against sin." See Platon (Fiveiskii), *Napominanie sviashchenniku ob obiazannostiakh ego pri sovershenii tainstva pokaianiia,* 3d ed. (Moscow, 1896), I, p. 200n.

29. *PSPREP,* IV, p. 1620.

30. RGIA, f. 796, *op.* 61, *g.* 1780, *d.* 123, *ll.* 1–2.

31. For the reiteration that bishops submit full reports punctually, see the Synod's decree of 11 March 1777 in RGIA, f. 796, *op.* 58, *g.* 1777, *d.* 74, *l.* 3.

32. RGIA, f. 796, *op.* 82, *g.* 1801, *d.* 58, *l.* 74–74 ob. (Kazan).

33. For an example of reports on the spiritual state of penitents, see the file on a deacon from Moscow in Rossiiskii Gosudarstvennyi

Istoricheskii Arkhiv g. Moskvy, *f.* 203, *op.* 552, *d.* 105, *l.* 4–4 ob. For an example of a reduced penance because of early and sincere repentance, see the case described in RGIA, *f.* 796, *op.* 82, *g.* 1801, *d.* 68, *l.* 74 ob. For the Synod's general directive to observe this rule, see its decree of 31 December 1849 in RGIA, *f.* 796, *op.* 148, *g.* 1867, *d.* 628, *l.* 3.

34. Sectarians and schismatics, especially those incarcerated in Solovetskii and Spaso-Evfimiev monasteries, generally remained impervious to the conditions of incarceration or blandishments of early release. Some lay sinners also refused to relent. Thus Kiev authorities reported in 1850 that a fifty-year-old noble "does not accept the exhortations to correct his behavior and, because of his stubbornness, contemptuously rejects this." See RGIA, *f.* 796, *op.* 132, *g.* 1851, *d.* 124, *ll.* 174 ob.–175.

35. It is impossible to determine the scale of public penance imposed before the late eighteenth century, when the Church began to require regular and systematic reports from diocesan bishops, but in all likelihood it was significantly greater before the secularization of church lands and peasants in 1764. At the simplest level, secularization had deprived the Church of many monastic institutions, thereby reducing substantially the possibilities for the detention of inveterate sinners. It also meant the abolition of the Church's own security forces, for those monasteries that survived had limited secular staffs—far smaller than the huge complex of lay servitors in earlier times. But perhaps the greatest change was the loss of authority over ecclesiastical peasants. Once constituting a third of all the peasants in Muscovy, Church peasants had been exclusively subject to ecclesiastical courts and therefore vulnerable to their sanctions and penalties, including monastic incarceration. Secularization deprived the Church of that control, however, leaving only the clergy as a group directly subject to its authority and sanctions.

36. In 1841, for example, the Church reported 1,147 penitents in the empire. See *Izvlecheniia iz otcheta ober-prokurora po vedomstvu pravoslavnogo ispovedaniia za 1841 god* (St. Petersburg, 1842), pp. 51–52.

37. RGIA, *f.* 796, *op.* 132, *g.* 1851, *d.* 124.

38. A statistical analysis and examination of individual categories of penance is provided in Gregory L. Freeze, *Church, Society and Religion in Modern Russia* (forthcoming).

39. In the 1840s the number of cases per annum was 9.2 for bestiality, 59.1 for homicide, and 365.9 for theft. V. M. Cheremtnianskii, *Opisanie Orenburgskoi gubernii* (Ufa, 1859), p. 240.

40. Reliable data on illegitimacy are lacking before 1867, but some hints can be gleaned from the episcopal reports about the condition of the population. Thus, although no diocese had more than a dozen penance cases for illegitimacy per annum, the instances of such births were far higher—for example, 1,770 in Smolensk, 2,011 in Voronezh, 561 in Penza, and 184 in Astrakhan (data from the early 1820s in RGIA, *f.* 796,

op. 104, *g.* 1823, *d.* 1367, *ll.* 4–8, 38–39, 88–93, 130–135).

    41. RGIA, *f.* 1281, *op.* 5, *g.* 1851, *d.* 49.

    42. Typical cases involved a peasant woman and a noblewoman from Ekaterinoslav and Mogilev, respectively, in 1831, and a peasant woman from Poltava diocese in 1851 (RGIA, *f.* 796, *op.* 112, *g.* 1831, *d.* 1052a; *f.* 796, *op.* 132, *g.* 1851, *d.* 124, *l.* 232). A woman from Pskov seems to hold the record—*four* illegitimate children—before finally coming under ecclesiastical discipline in 1811 (*f.* 796, *op.* 92, *g.* 1811, *d.* 84, *ll.* 12–13 ob.).

    43. In 1850 Solovetskii monastery held sixteen prisoners, chiefly Old Believers and self-castrating sectarians (*skoptsy*) (RGIA, *f.* 796, *op.* 132, *g.* 1851, *d.* 89). A report from Spaso-Evfimiev monastery in Vladimir diocese listed fourteen convicts (*kolodniki*) as prisoners: four monks, three parish clergy, one merchant, two townsmen, three peasants, and one unidentified (ibid., *op.* 125, *g.* 1844, *d.* 682, *l.* 8–8 ob.). On the latter see "Spisok soslannykh pod nadzorom i strazhu Vladimirskoi gubernii v Suzdale v Spaso-Evfimievskii monastyr' raznogo zvaniia liudei s 1801 goda po 30 noiabria 1836 goda," *Byloe* (1907), no. 8.

    44. That policy, for example, inspired exceptional tolerance for recent converts who failed to fulfill their duties of confession and Communion. Thus in one case the Synod issued this order: "After a public admonition in the [parish] church, the penance is to be performed and the [prescribed] genuflections to be made. But one is to be careful that this spiritual discipline remain without any kind of coercion, and that it be carried out only if the deviants agree of their own free will to fulfill their Christian duties." *Polnoe sobranie postanovlenii i rasporiazhenii po vedomstvu pravoslavnogo ispovedaniia. Tsarstvovanie Imp. Nikolaia Pavlovicha* (St. Petersburg, 1915 [hereafter *PSPRNP*], no. 275. See also RGIA, *f.* 796, *op.* 102, *g.* 1821, *d.* 37, *ll.* 207–208; *op.* 114, *g.* 1833, *d.* 1082, *ll.* 12–17.

    45. RGIA, *f.* 796, *op.* 132, *g.* 1851, *d.* 124, *ll.* 173 ob.–174.

    46. Infanticide, usually involving an illegitimate birth, was difficult to demonstrate forensically and, in most cases, ended with a verdict of "suspected infanticide." To be sure, some of the accused confessed to their crime; for instance, an eighteen-year-old peasant woman from Riazan admitted that "after having been raped by the state peasant Petr Shchepetov and having become pregnant, I gave birth to a live child the week before Easter. Out of fear of my family and out of shame, I cast the child naked through a hole in the ice of a nearby stream." In addition to the thirty blows of the whip administered by state authorities, the woman had to undergo ten years' penance, including one in a convent (RGIA, *f.* 796, *op.* 92, *g.* 1811, *d.* 338, *l.* 7–7 ob.). The perpetrators of infanticide, with rare exceptions, came almost exclusively from the lower social strata.

    47. The statistical precision of this variable must be treated with

some caution: 192 (22.7 percent) of the penitents failed to list their age. Because the failure to list age was the function of diocesan administration, it is unlikely that this missing component affects the age structure of the population in any significant way.

48. See, for instance, the typical complaints in I. S. Belliustin, *A Description of the Clergy in Rural Russia*, ed. and trans. Gregory L. Freeze (Ithaca, N.Y.: Cornell University Press, 1985), pp. 141–153.

49. Thus priests comprised 29.1 percent of the penitents, with deacons and sacristans comprising the balance (18.3 and 52.5 percent, respectively). These proportions differ only slightly from their proportions then in service, with the priests slightly more numerous and the deacons slightly less. For data see Gregory L. Freeze, *The Parish Clergy in Nineteenth-Century Russia: Crisis, Reform, Counter-Reform* (Princeton: Princeton University Press, 1983), p. 462.

50. The order by Emperor Paul was issued on 16 May 1799 and distributed by the Synod shortly afterward. RGIA, *f.* 796, *op.* 80, *g.* 1799, *d.* 394, *ll.* 1–8; *f.* 797, *op.* 1, *d.* 1921.

51. To this should probably be added the four civil officials, evidently nonnoble minor officials who would otherwise have been listed as townsmen or *raznochintsy.*

52. See, for example, the cases cited in Gregory L. Freeze, "The Orthodox Church and Serfdom in Prereform Russia," *Slavic Review,* 48 (1989), pp. 378–379.

53. RGIA, *f.* 796, *op.* 132, *g.* 1851, *d.* 124, *ll.* 178–208. Surprisingly, diocesan authorities made only a nominal effort to force laity to comply, perhaps in part because penance had to be sincere and voluntary, but also because they lacked the means of coercion. Especially after the secularization of Church properties in 1764 and the establishment of a niggardly budget, the Church had to reduce its police forces sharply and to rely upon the voluntary obedience of the laity. To be sure, the bishop could appeal to the state for assistance, especially in cases involving criminals and dangerous sectarian leaders. In the typical case of immorality, however, the bishop had to rely upon voluntary compliance. Thus some reports about penitents indicate that the "government police" bore primary responsibility for delivering the guilty party to the monastery. See, for example, the 1831 case from Mogilev in RGIA, *f.* 112, *op.* 112, *g.* 1831, *d.* 1052a, chast': Mogilev.

54. Gerasim (Nikitinov), *Rassuzhdenie ob epitimiiakh* (Moscow, 1838), pp. 1–2. See also Arkhimandrit Innokentii (Borisov), *Sobranie slov, besedy i rechei na raznye dni i sluchai,* 2 vols. (Kiev, 1836–1837), I, pp. 205–225; Gavriil (Rozanov), *Slovo o taine pokaianiia ili ispovedi tserkovnoi* (Moscow, 1833); Ignatii (Semenov), *O pokaianii. Besedy* (St. Petersburg, 1847).

55. RGIA, *f.* 796, *op.* 135, *g.* 1854, *d.* 2309, *ll.* 2–2 ob.

56. RGIA, *f.* 796, *op.* 99, *g.* 1818, *d.* 72, *l.* 2; see also *f.* 796, *op.* 82, *g.* 1801, *d.* 322, *l.* 1 ob.; *f.* 796, *op.* 122, *g.* 1831, *d.* 1052a, chast': Vladimir.

57. RGIA, *f.* 796, *op.* 98, *g.* 1817, *d.* 845, *ll.* 2–3.

58. For a case of complaints against ecclesiastical authorities in the Vladimir diocese, see RGIA, *f.* 796, *op.* 125, *g.* 1844, *d.* 682, *ll.* 1–20.

59. RGIA, *f.* 797, *op.* 12, *d.* 30107, *ll.* 1–3 (1842 petition).

60. See, for instance, the vociferous complaints from Metropolitan Arsenii (Matseevich) of Rostov in 1759 that state officials were remiss in surrendering transgressors, especially those who had committed adultery. RGIA, *f.* 796, *op.* 40, *g.* 1759, *d.* 56, *l.* 2.

61. RGIA, *f.* 797, *op.* 13, *d.* 32878.

62. RGIA, *f.* 796, *op.* 132, *g.* 1851, *d.* 214, *ll.* 5–6 (memorandum of 27 January 1851). In reply the bishop of Arkhangel'sk, it should be noted, vigorously rejected the governor's claims about this particular case and complained about "the intervention of state authorities in matters of diocesan administration without any valid reasons" (ibid., *ll.* 7–8 ob.).

63. RGIA, *f.* 796, *op.* 132, *g.* 1851, *d.* 911, *l.* 32 ob. (10 November 1851).

64. Filaret (Drozdov), *Polnoe sobranie rezoliutsii,* 3 vols. (Moscow, 1903–1904), II, p. 56, pt. 3.

65. Ibid., I, p. 522.

66. Ibid., I, p. 129. For a specific case from the 1850 list, see the entry for a woman in Perm who was to be released "upon entering into marriage." RGIA, *f.* 796, *op.* 132, *g.* 1851, *d.* 124, *l.* 208.

67. For example, in an 1854 case involving homicide, the Synod prescribed a penance of three years, which was to be reduced by half if the offender proved to be married. RGIA, *f.* 796, *op.* 135, *g.* 1854, *d.* 2308.

68. *PSPRNP,* no. 304. Similar concerns were expressed in the prelates' annual reports; see, for instance, the statements from the bishops of Arkhangel'sk and Nizhnii Novgorod in 1850 in RGIA, *f.* 796, *op.* 132, *g.* 1851, *d.* 2357, *ll.* 8, 169 ob.-170.

69. RGIA, *f.* 796, *op.* 138, *g.* 1857, *d.* 1185, *l.* 1–1 ob.

70. See also the blunt comments by participants at a conference of spiritual elders at Optina Pustyn' in 1854: Otdel Rukopisei Gosudarstvennoi Biblioteki im. V. I. Lenina, *f.* 302, *karton* 3, *d.* 18.

71. RGIA, *f.* 796, *op.* 132, *g.* 1851, *d.* 911, *l.* 4.

72. Thus even Metropolitan Filaret, who applied public penance sparingly and prescribed short terms, took exception to its total abrogation. It was especially needed, he argued, for those who had neglected their duty of confession and Communion for several years, and hence were certain to be indifferent to the entreaties of the parish priest. He also argued that monastic incarceration was useful for those guilty of illicit sexual liaisons (to terminate the relationships) and of manslaughter

(to give "peace to their souls"). Filaret also argued that a brief confinement in the monastery (for instance, to punish those who failed to perform confession and Communion duties) was no great burden, especially since this penance could be performed outside peak periods of agricultural labor. See RGIA, *f.* 796, *op.* 132, *g.* 1851, *d.* 911, *ll.* 32–33.

73. RGIA, *f.* 796, *op.* 135, *g.* 1854, *d.* 2325.

74. For example, the annual reports for 1866 indicate that only 195 laity were currently being held in monasteries. RGIA, *f.* 796, *op.* 148, *g.* 1867, *d.* 1595.

75. Suvorin, *O tserkovnykh nakazaniiakh,* pp. 203–204; RGIA, *f.* 796, *op.* 148, *g.* 1867, *d.* 628, *ll.* 23–40.

76. See Gregory L. Freeze, "Rechristianization of Russia: The Church and Popular Religion, 1750–1850," *Studia Slavica Finlandensia,* 7 (1990), pp. 101–136.

BRENDA MEEHAN

Popular Piety, Local Initiative, and the Founding of Women's Religious Communities in Russia, 1764–1907

*H*istory never repeats itself exactly, but it does offer a sufficient store of arresting parallels and recurring patterns to affirm those who find strength in historical precedents and to discourage those who seek an infinite malleability in life. As we focus on the recovery of religious identity in the former Soviet Union, it is worthwhile to point to an earlier moment in Russian history when popular piety proved triumphant over government regulation, and a core part of the Christian tradition—in this instance the contemplative life—was reaffirmed.

*I*n 1764 things looked bleak for the Orthodox church in Russia. In that year the government confiscated monastic properties, cutting the number of monasteries in Russia by more than half.

The first effort at actual secularization of ecclesiastical estates had been made by Peter III in 1762.[1] When Catherine II succeeded him, she initially repudiated his program, as she did most of his policies, to justify the coup against him that brought her to power. But by 1763 she was moving in a similar direction of asserting state authority over church privilege, and finalized this move with the church reform of February 28, 1764.[2] The manifesto accompanying this reform, which confiscated monastic lands, put them under state control, and gave the church a compensatory budget, was more tactful and self-serving than that of Peter III. In it, Catherine explained that she was acutely conscious of her accountability to God for the "good order" of the church and desirous of freeing the clergy from the burden of property and the cares of the material world; therefore, she was taking upon herself and upon the state the burden of administering church properties. Henceforth, all monastic estates and the serfs attached to them were to become the property of the state. Feudal dues would be rendered to the College of the Economy, and part of the income generated by ecclesiastical properties would be returned to the church in the form of clerical salaries.

A table of organization and a budget issued for the church reflected the state's driving impulse toward rationalization, centralization, and a fiscal economy.

Now that the state had to pay clerical salaries and fund ecclesiastical institutions, the government vigorously eliminated "superfluous" clergy, churches, and monasteries. In 1762, 881 monasteries existed in Russia, including 678 for men and 203 for women. The reform of 1764 reduced the number to 385: 318 men's monasteries and 67 women's monasteries.[3] Smaller monasteries were closed, and monks and nuns, many old and ailing—who had lived and worshipped for decades in monasteries that were now closed—were arbitrarily transferred to larger monasteries in their diocese in order to rationalize resources. In the process, considerable social dislocation occurred; not only was there the problem of relocation to new and strange environments, but many former residents of dissolved monasteries found themselves without an assigned, stipendiary slot in the new budget. Homeless monks and nuns began appearing in provincial towns and in the streets of Moscow and St. Petersburg, begging for food and shelter. Embarrassed by their appearance in the capital cities, Catherine II issued a strong edict, ordering vagabond clergy to return to the diocese from which they had come.[4] In addition, vigorous measures were taken to conscript "superfluous" clergy into the army.[5] It was a bleak moment indeed, and many would have forecast the decline of monasticism in Russia.

Instead, Russia experienced a flowering of monasticism that began in the late eighteenth century, grew steadily throughout the nineteenth century, and continued until the Revolution of 1917. By 1907 there were almost 1,100 monastic communities in Russia, and the number was growing daily.[6] Throughout the nineteenth century, suppressed monasteries had been reopened and, more significantly, new ones had been formed. Between 1764 and 1890, 292 new monastic communities were established, including 95 men's monasteries and 197 women's monasteries.[7] Between 1890 and 1907, another 86 women's religious communities were formed.[8]

Intellectually, the monastic revival began in the second half of the eighteenth century and is associated with the work of Paisii Velichkovskii (1722–1794), whose life of austere asceticism on Mount Athos attracted many Russian and Romanian disciples. Eventually this revival led to the formation of a monastery in Moldavia based on the cenobitic rule of St. Basil. Paisii and his followers undertook the translation into Russian of the writings of the early desert fathers.[9] His most influential work was the translation in 1793 of the *Philokalia*, a collection of spiritual and hesychastic writings that formed a type of inward piety guided by spiritual devotion. This widely read book "provided the spiritual food" for monks and laity in Russia for the next two centuries.[10] Through his writings and the formation of both male and female disciples, who became spiritual guides and monastic superiors, Paisii initiated a contemplative revival that continued until the Russian Revolution and found its greatest expression among spiritual elders of the Optina Pustyn'.[11] Other important figures who stimulated the contemplative revival through lives that combined spiritual intensity and asceticism, and through publication of significant theological and spiritual writings, included St. Tikhon of Zadonsk (1724–1783); Platon, Metropolitan of Moscow (1737–1812); and Filaret, Metropolitan of Moscow (1782–1867).

But the contemplative revival was more than a matter of men and books. It was part of a larger religious awakening that touched the hearts and souls of countless Russians—religious and lay people alike. Its roots were as diverse as the tides of romanticism, idealism, and nationalism that swept across Europe in the wake of the Napoleonic wars that stimulated in Russia a specific Slavophile rejection of Western rationalism and materialism, and an embracing of Russian spirituality and Orthodoxy.[12] At the popular level, it was stimulated by an increase in literacy and an expanding system of colportage that made lives of the saints and devotional literature widely available.[13] And it was fed by modernity itself, by the longing for deeper meaning that the shallowness and rootlessness of modern life often engender, and by a specific anti-urban, anti-noise-and-bustle impulse that made the "sweet silence" of monasticism appealing.[14] But this is the broad picture, the sweeping strokes on the vast canvas of Russian intellectual life. The picture drawn here is composed of minute details, of local color and rich texture that come only from studying the lives of ordinary men and women as they wrestled with both the routine of life and large, often overwhelming forces.

A study of the plight of the dislocated clergy, the homeless monks and nuns displaced or resettled by the harsh church reform of 1764, reveals a grass-roots movement in their support, an anger at the closing of the local monasteries, and a series of petitions from local laymen to the religious authorities expressing particular concern about the fate of elderly and ailing nuns. Several petitions from local laymen offered to support a local convent out of their own resources, or urged that one not be closed until after the death of the elderly nuns living there.

In 1765, twenty-eight merchants and gentry living near the Bolkhovskii Rozhdestvenskii convent sent a petition to the metropolitian of Moscow and the Holy Synod urging that the convent not be closed because it had been built by local gentry and merchants, because the women who lived there were mothers and sisters of the local gentry and merchants, and because these women had contributed to their own support by giving to the convent property they had inherited, "wives from husbands, daughters from fathers, and mothers from their allotment."[15] The tone of the petition clearly indicates a belief on the part of the petitioners that the church property the government had confiscated was family property that had been turned over to the church for the support and sustenance of female relatives. In the end, the petition was granted, in that these women were allowed to live out their days in the local convent, but no new nuns were permitted to be taken in.[16]

In 1766, thirty-seven gentry and merchants from the town of Rylsk offered to support from their own resources nuns living in the local convent, in order to prevent it closing. The government responded by allowing the petitioners to take on the support of the nuns presently living in the convent but forbade the acceptance of any new nuns.[17] These and similar petitions indicate local ties and family connections with the local convents, which served, among other things, as dignified retirement homes for female relatives. The centralizing, rationalizing government made occasional, temporary concessions to these local bonds but continued its long-range policy of consolidating monasteries and limiting the number of stipendiary clergy.

Although the government's restrictions on the number and location of monasteries and clergy applied to both men and women, women responded in a special way by almost immediately forming unofficial religious communities called *zhenskie obshchiny* (women's communities). These communities were self-supporting and presumably met the need for a religious, disciplined, communal way of life and means of support for women who were shut out of official religious "slots" by the restrictive church budget of 1764. The first such community was formed in the town of Arzamas in 1764, on the site of a closed convent.

At the time of the secularization, there were in Arzamas five men's monasteries and two women's monasteries, the Alekseevskii and the Nikolaevskii.[18] By decree, in a provincial town there could be only one third-class women's monastery, which would be chosen according to the condition of the buildings. Because the Alekseevskii monastery was in poor repair, the Nikolaevskii monastery was chosen. The Alekseevskii church was converted into a parish church, and the cloister was suppressed; the nuns were to be transferred to the Nikolaevskii convent. But there proved to be insufficient room for the displaced nuns at Nikolaevskii, and as a result, displaced nuns and would-be nuns gathered on the site of the suppressed convent, living unofficially in the closed cells.[19]

The number of women grew to 270, and in 1777 the local bishop gave his blessing to the community and allowed it to be considered a subsidiary of the official Nikolaevskii convent. In 1842, at a time of increasing supervision of the church by Nicholas I and his appointees, the community was brought under the "protection and supervision" of the central church and state authorities. In 1881 the sisters of the community received permission to wear official garb, and in 1897 the community was transformed into an official convent. During all this time, the community was self-supporting; although it was increasingly supervised by the crown, it received no support from it. It did, however, receive donations of money and land from local supporters. By 1908 the community owned 1,128 *desiatiny* (approx. 3046 acres) of land; ran two hospitals for nuns, a guest house for pilgrims, and a renowned embroidery workshop; and supported 63 nuns and 617 lay sisters.[20]

The evolution of the Arzamas community is typical of the majority of succeeding *zhenskie obshchiny*. It began on the initiative of local women to meet the need for a religiously oriented life and mutual security—a need that could not be legislated away by government decree. Gradually it came under the control, though not the financial support, of church and government authorities, eventually being transformed into an official monastery. It was supported both financially and emotionally by local donors, and in turn it provided services to the local community.[21]

Between 1764 and 1907, 217 *zhenskie obshchiny* were formed.[21] They began as unofficial, autonomous communities, but over time more and more were transformed into official women's monasteries. Of the 156 *zhenskie obshchiny* formed between 1764 and 1894, 67 percent eventually became official convents, and the process accelerated in the second half of the nineteenth century.[22]

Although this essay will focus on the founding of these communities, it is important to note certain ways in which they (and the monasteries into which many of them evolved) differed from traditional monasteries in Russia. Women in *zhenskie obshchiny*, unlike those in monasteries, did not take monastic vows. Although they were expected to be celibate while in the community, they were not permanently bound to the community.[23] Second, *zhenskie obshchiny* and the monasteries that developed from them were organized along communal (cenobitic) lines, in contrast with the idiorhythmic, noncommunal organization of traditional *shtatnye* monasteries. In fact, *zhenskie obshchiny* played an important role in the monastic reform of the nineteenth century through their emphasis on stricter discipline, deeper religious practice, and more communal life.[24]

Two final observations: In contrast with the relatively fewer women's religious institutions that began as monasteries after 1764, *zhenskie obshchiny* seem to have had more humble origins, formed overwhelmingly at local lay initiative in towns and villages. While all men's monasteries formed in the nineteenth century began as monasteries, women's religious institutions typically followed a transitional or semiofficial path from *zhenskie obshchiny* to monasteries.[25] One can only speculate whether this indicated greater autonomy on the part of the women's communities or less willingness on the part of ecclesiastical and government authorities to grant official recognition to women's religious institutions.

The present study focuses on the 217 *zhenskie obshchiny* formed between 1764 and 1907, and examines where and how these communities were formed. The first picture that emerges is that these 217 religious communities are overwhelmingly rural. Of them, 113 originated in villages, 102 in provincial towns, and only 2 in cities. A possible explanation is that cities such as Moscow, St. Petersburg, and Kiev already offered sufficient opportunity for entry into religious life through their existing monasteries, and sufficient social services to the population through myriad private and public charitable and poor-relief agencies.[26] The story of how these communities emerged is a rich record of local initiative and popular piety, a tale best told by looking at the founders of the communities. Among them we find recognizable clusters, such as nuns of suppressed monasteries, women of intense religious experience, widows, local clergy and hierarchs, and people of local communities. The Arzamas Alekseevskaia community, the first *zhenskaia obshchina*, formed by nuns and lay sisters living in the cells of a suppressed monastery, has already been discussed. Another such community was the Arkadievskaia Viazemskaia community in Smolensk, founded in 1780 by tenacious nuns of the suppressed Il'inskii monastery.[27]

But the forming of women's religious communities was sparked by more than tenacity or a desire to hold onto a way of life threatened by government decrees. It was fueled by the religious revival, by a call to spiritual intensity, to the purity and austerity of the early desert fathers, and to the radiance of mystical experience. St. Serafim of Sarov (1759–1833) was a glowing example of the long Eastern tradition of monasticism and asceticism newly made fresh. He was a model for many women who formed religious communities and was a founder of an important women's community.

St. Serafim was a monk, a hermit, and a *podvizhnik* (ascetic). The *podvizhnik* was a spiritual athlete of sorts, an accomplisher of astonishing ascetic feats. The tradition of asceticism went back to the early desert fathers of Egypt and Syria, and was more than an act of renunciation. In its deepest form, it was the act of literalizing symbols, an act of extreme faith in the redemption of the world through Christ, and a return to the wholeness of the Garden of Eden. Sebastian Brock and Susan Harvey, authorities on early Syrian Christianity, have said:

> In its extreme form, this literalizing of symbols led to striking behavior on the part of the Syrian believer. The redeeming work of Christ, the second Adam, had made salvation possible for humanity and brought the promise of a return to Paradise, to the perfect life as it was lived by Adam and Eve before their Fall. In anticipation of that return, and indeed to hasten its coming, some believers adopted a life of stunning physical symbolism: living naked in the wilderness, living on wild fruits and water, living among

the wild beasts, living exposed to the elements, living an uninterrupted life of prayer and devotion to the divine as Adam and Eve had done. They acted out with their bodies the spiritual truth of their faith.[28]

Thus the *podvizhnik* lived at one with God and nature, breaking through the pain of alienation that the Fall represents. Although the *podvizhnik* lived alone, often in silence, there was a "jarring translucence," a radiance and magnetism that drew people to him.[29]

And so it was with St. Serafim. The wonder of his ascetic practice and his long years of silence—over twenty years—drew people seeking his wisdom, his understanding of the divine, his counsel, and his healing. In response to the stream of visitors, and some say in response to a vision of the Virgin Mary, he ended his vow of silence in his late fifties or early sixties, and assumed the role of *starets,* or spiritual elder, another Eastern tradition.[30] He became spiritual counselor to hundreds, including many women living in the vicinity of the Sarov hermitage and many who had settled in the area to be near this revered holy man. Serafim took an active interest in the spiritual development of these women and founded a special community of virgins at Diveevo, based on a strict ascetic rule, alongside an existing community of widows and virgins that had been founded in the late eighteenth century by Agafeia Melgunova, the wife of a colonel.[31] Diveevo became a famous women's religious community renowned for its spiritual intensity and discipline; many of the women who lived there became influential religious figures in their own right.

One such figure was Blessed Natal'ia, a renowned *podvizhnitsa* and *staritsa* who had lived in the Serafimo-Diveevo cloister from 1848 and helped to form the Meliavskaia Teplovskaia women's community in the late nineteenth century.[32] Natal'ia had been a pilgrim before entering Diveevo, and initially had difficulty adjusting to monastic rule. She lived a solitary life, prayed constantly, read the Psalter all night, ate sparingly, and was indifferent to all kinds of weather, dressing lightly whether in rain or frost. The intensity of her ascetic practice and the simplicity of her manner drew the local people to her. They sought her blessings and her advice, and she soon developed a reputation as a wise *staritsa*. A contemporary reminisced, "Natasha possessed the gift of counsel. Her speech was direct, clear, not allegorical. Her wisdom and erudition were great, and she never lost her perspicacity."[33] Although in her youth she had been considered a holy fool, in maturity she was honored as a spiritual elder. The number of visitors seeking her counsel, and of women wishing to serve as postulants under her, grew to such an extent that it became a problem for the monastery. As a result, toward the end of her life, Natal'ia planned the creation of a separate women's community at Meliavskaia that opened in 1900.

The life of the hermit Anastasia Semenovna Logacheva (1809–1875) is a similar story of growth from *podvizhnitsa* to *staritsa* and to the inspiration for a women's religious community in her honor.[34] Anastasia was born to peasants living on crown property. When she was eight, her father was drafted; her mother and younger sister joined him, leaving Anastasia feeling like an orphan in her uncle's large family. She became a loner at an early age, going into the woods for long periods of time, finding comfort in the quiet and in her devotion to the Mother of God. She stayed in the woods for longer and longer periods of time and began ascetic tests. When she was seventeen, she went to see Serafim of Sarov, having heard that he would not refuse anyone guidance on salvation and the life of a hermit. St. Serafim advised her to continue to pray ardently to the Mother of God. A few years later she journeyed to see him again, and he advised her to go on a pilgrimage to Kiev.

Finally, shortly before the death of Serafim, Anastasia visited a third time, seeking his blessing on undertaking the life of a hermit and a *podvizhnitsa*. She received his blessing, but evidently she was advised first to support her elderly and incapacitated parents. During this time, she provided a livelihood for her parents and herself by reading the Psalter for the deceased, spinning, and doing odd jobs. After her parents' death, she gave away everything she had and began the austere life of a religious hermit. But she, too, in her withdrawal from the world, became a radiant light, attracting the troubled and the searching. A contemporary of hers, reflecting on this paradox, commented, "The world doesn't love pious and good people, but sometimes it seeks out, marvels at the ascetic feats of, and seeks counsel from those very people when they withdraw from the world. And so it was with Nastas'iushka; people from the local settlements began to come to her, to seek her holy prayers, to seek her counsel in the difficulties of life, and for several, to seek instruction in how to be saved and how to pray."[35]

Because of the number of people seeking her advice and wanting to live near her to take up a similar life, including three women who already lived in huts near her and a peasant man who wanted to live the same way, Anastasia decided that it was necessary to build a house, but to do this required the permission of the local crown authority, because the woods to which she had retired was crown property. This led to an investigation of her request. Not only was it refused, but she was told that she would have to leave her hermitage. After her eviction, she wandered for a while, went on a pilgrimage to Jerusalem, and eventually settled in the new Nikolaevskii women's monastery in Tomsk province, where she was tonsured, became the mother superior, and died in 1875.

After Anastasia's death, at the initiative of local peasants and with the permission of the tsar, who ceded five *desiatiny* (13.5 acres) of land, an almshouse was opened in her honor on the spot where she had lived as a hermit. In 1899, the almshouse was transformed into the Znamenskaia

Kurikhinskaia women's community.[36] Other women's communities that began as clusters of women drawn to a locally renowned holy man or woman were the Troitskaia Odigitrievskaia Zosimova, formed around the *starets* Zosima in 1826; Ivanovskaia Kazanovskaia Sezenovskaia, formed around the hermit Ioann Ivanovich in 1840; Toplovskaia Paraskevskaia, formed around the Bulgarian hermit maiden Konstantina in 1858; and Shamordinskaia Kazanskaia, formed in 1884 by Amvrosii, the famous *starets* of Optina Pustyn'.[37] (Amvrosii was a model for the character Father Zosima in Dostoevsky's *The Brothers Karamazov*. Both Dostoevsky and Tolstoy visited Optina, and Tolstoy's sister, Mariia, was a nun at the Shamordino community founded by Amvrosii.)[38]

Women's communities also grew out of a religious intensity based on personal experience, such as a miraculous healing or delivery from a cat-astrophic event. The Troitskaia Tikhonovskaia Zadonskaia women's community was formed from a wayfarers' home built in the 1830s by the artisanal maiden Matriona Naumovna Popova, who had been miracu-lously cured of a serious illness at the grave of St. Tikhon of Zadonsk. In thanksgiving she formed a society, the Tikhonovskoe Sisters of Mercy, to minister to the pilgrims who gathered there.[39]

Widows comprised another noticeable cluster among the founders of *zhenskie obshchiny*, having formed over twenty communities. They in-cluded women of all classes, although sources are best for aristocratic women and the resources available to them were greatest. The first and most prominent of such communities was Spaso-Borodinskaia, formed by Margarita Mikhailovna Tuchkova, née Naryshkina, the widow of General Tuchkov, who was killed at the Battle of Borodino in 1812.[40] Grief stricken by her loss, Tuchkova vowed to build a church in honor of her husband on the spot where he and so many other brave Russians had fallen. Determined, indefatigable, and well connected, she eventually re-ceived permission for the construction of the church and a donation of ten thousand rubles from the tsar. But it was difficult in the beginning, and Tuchkova had to sell property and jewelry to realize her project. Dur-ing the years of construction, she traveled back and forth between the construction site and her house in Moscow, where she was supervising the education of her son.

While in Borodino, Tuchkova lived in a small house described as a "hermit's hut," and her reputation for piety and almsgiving drew people to the spot. One day, when traveling through a neighboring village, she came upon a beaten, trembling woman lying in a cart. Upon inquiry, she found out that the woman's husband was a notorious drunkard who reg-ularly beat and terrorized his wife and two daughters. Tuchkova was de-termined to provide protection and shelter for these women, and insisted on getting the permission of the local official to remove the women from the village. Out of the shelter she built for them at Borodino gradually grew the Spaso-Borodinskaia *zhenskaia obshchina*. After the tragic death of her son in 1826, Tuchkova settled there permanently, and the community of poor and homeless women began to grow. In 1833 it was officially recognized as a *zhenskaia obshchina* by the church and government authorities; in 1838 the community was elevated to a monastery, and Tuchkova, having been tonsured and given the monastic name Mariia, was appointed abbess. In 1877, the monastery had over 200 sisters. By 1807, there were an abbess, 50 nuns, and 195 lay sisters (*poslushnitsy*); a parish school for 30 girls; a small hospital; and an almshouse for elderly women.[41]

The founder of the Anosino-Boriso-Glebskaia community was Princess Evdokiia Meshcherskaia, born Tiutcheva, aunt of the famous Russian poet F. I. Tiutchev.[42] Born in 1774, in 1796 she married Prince Boris Ivanovich Meshcherskii, who died three months after their wedding and left her pregnant. Meshcherskaia retired to her estate of Anosino to raise her daughter and lead a pious life. During her daughter's youth, she built a stone church at Anosino; in 1821, in honor of her deceased husband, she built an almshouse, which formed the basis for a women's religious community. In 1823 the community was raised to a women's communal monastery, and Meshcherskaia, having fulfilled her responsibilities to her daughter, was tonsured and received the monastic name of Evgeniia. According to an 1877 source, there were at the monastery an almshouse, a hospital for nuns, and a "clean and comfortable" inn for pilgrims.[43] In 1907 there were an abbess and 118 nuns and lay sisters.[44]

Such communities inspired other women to think of forming religious communities on their estates. For example, after the death of her husband, Anna Gavrilovna Golovina, née Princess Gagarina, dreamed of building on the ancient Golovin estate of Novospasskoe a women's community modeled after that of Spaso-Borodinskaia.[45] Her son supported her in this plan, and together they donated 108 *desiatiny* (292 acres) of land, a mill that earned up to five hundred rubles a year, and a stone house in Moscow that grossed fifteen hundred rubles a year income. In 1852 the community, known as Spaso-Vlakhernskaia, was officially recognized by state and ecclesiastical authorities; and in 1856, shortly before her death, Golovina was tonsured, having earned a wide reputation as a philanthropist and a spiritual elder. In 1907, the community, which had been raised to a monastery in 1861, consisted of an abbess, thirty-eight nuns, and two hundred lay sisters, and ran a hospital for sisters of the cloister and an inn for pilgrims.[46]

Aleksandra Filippovna Shmakova, founder of the Troitskaia Tvorozhkovskaia women's community, was born into a noble family in St. Petersburg, educated at the Smol'nyi Institute, and married in 1824 to Karl Andreevich Fon Roze, a wealthy Lutheran nobleman.[47] Her father and mother were unusually pious, and she developed an early distaste for the vanities of aristocratic social life, preferring the quiet of a chapel to the whirl of a ballroom. After the death of her only daughter, she and her husband became increasingly devout. After his conversion to Orthodoxy, they bought the secluded, deserted estate of Tvorozhkovo, realizing that its woods, lake, and distance from other estates would make it an ideal spot for a monastery some day. They agreed that if Karl died first, Aleksandra would build a women's religious community and retire to it.

When Karl Andreevich died in 1858, Aleksandra Filippovna sought to establish a women's religious community at Tvorozhkovo at her own expense, but was refused permission by the metropolitan because there was a parish church nearby. In the meantime she lived quietly and ascetically, earning a reputation for charity among the local poor. With the appointment of a new metropolitan in 1861, permission was given; and plans began in earnest for a women's community, which necessitated the building of a wooden house and chapel for the sisters. Aleksandra Filippovna pledged the money from the sale of her house in St. Petersburg and prayed that pious women would begin to gather. By the time of the official establishment of the community in 1865, there were about fifteen women at Tvorozhkovo; by 1872, there were twenty-six women: Aleksandra Filippovna, who had been tonsured and taken the name Angelina; two widows of government officials; a woman from the merchantry; a woman from the clerical estate; eight women from the lower townspeople (*meshchanki*); and thirteen women from the peasantry.[48] By 1873 the widows had opened an orphanage for girls of the clerical estate and an almshouse for six elderly women.[49]

A final example of a women's community founded by an aristocratic widow is the Razritovskaia Troitskaia Pokrovskaia, which was formed in 1900 by Princess Aleksandra Vasil'evna Golitsyna, widow of a vice admiral, on her estate in Chernigov province.[50]

But widows of all social classes participated in this phenomenon, indicating a long Russian tradition of entering the monastic life at midlife, after one had fulfilled one's obligation to spouse and children.[51] Women of all social classes wished to retire in their widowhood to a contemplative life, and founding religious communities made this possible. Among this varied group of founders there are widows of officers, such as the widow of Major General Gauzen, who founded the community of Rozhdestvo-Bogoroditskaia on her estate in 1865, and the widow of Captain Egorov, who founded the community of Vvedenskaia Kievskaia in Kiev in 1878; widows of government officials, such as Ol'ga Aleksandrovna Vinogradova, widow of a collegiate secretary, who founded the community of Iletskaia Nikolaevskaia in 1892, and Sofiia Muromtseva, widow of a state councillor, who gave land and money for the creation of the community of Sofiiskaia in 1903; widows of merchants, such as

Pelagaia Popova, who donated land for the Panovskaia Troitskaia community in Saratov province in 1881; widows of artisans and tradesmen, such as Paraskeva Razguliaeva, widow of a *meshchanin* from Samara, who founded the community of Pokrovskaia on her property in 1898; and widows of peasants, such as Marfa Dmitrieva, who formed the hostel that developed into the women's community of Malaia Pitsa in Nizhegorod.[52]

The story of the founding of the women's community of Krestovozdvizhenskaia Ierusalimskaia attests to the pivotal role of the widow of the merchant Savatiugin, and to the intriguing ties between city and village formed through a shared faith. In the village of Pakhro, about thirty versts (twenty miles) from Moscow, there was a pious, pilgrim-loving priest who had living in his parish a certain Ivan Stepanovich, who was considered by some to be a holy fool and by others a sage. This Ivan Stepanovich was known to Metropolitan Filaret of Moscow, who regarded him kindly, and to many families in Moscow, including a pious merchant family by the name of Savatiugin. Shortly after the death of Savatiugin, Ivan Stepanovich came to his widow and asked her for thirty rubles. He explained that there was in the village of Pakhro a small group of women who gathered at the home of the parish priest and perpetually read the Psalter, and with this donation they would remember Savatiugina's deceased husband eternally in their prayers.

When Tsar Nicholas I died in 1855 and people were urged to remember him through the perpetual reading of the Psalter, the group of women at Pakhro grew. Savatiugina decided to retire there, and in 1856 donated a house that was used as an almshouse and for the reading of the Psalter. In 1865 this almshouse was changed to a *zhenskaia obshchina*. Savatiugina supported the community, and by 1870 it had grown so large—over seventy sisters—that it was decided to move the community to the village of Lukino. In 1873, the widow Savatiugina was tonsured, taking the monastic name Pavla. By 1877 there were over one hundred sisters and a school for thirty girls.[53]

Local clergy and hierarchs formed a fourth cluster of founders of women's religious communities, although usually if a community began at the initiative of a bishop, it began as an official monastery rather than following the semiofficial route from *zhenskaia obshchina* to monastery.[54] The two examples of *obshchiny* founded by bishops were both in "border" areas, that is, areas where the church was interested in the spread of Orthodoxy. These communities were the Ioanno-Marinskaia community in Stavropol', founded in 1847 by Ieremei, first bishop of the Caucasus; and the Bogoroditskaia community in Lesna, founded in 1885 by Leontii, bishop of Kholmsko-Warsaw, in order to fight the dominant Catholic-Uniate influence in the area.[55] To that end, Leontii planned a school for girls as an integral part of the community at Lesna and appointed as its first mother superior Countess Evgeniia Borisovna Efimovskaia (1890–

1925), in religious life Ekaterina, who was "the ablest Russian woman theologian of her time" and an advocate of the restoration of the diaconate for women.[56]

At the parish level, local priests occasionally encouraged the creation of *zhenskie obshchiny* as a way of organizing a local school, almshouse, or orphanage. In 1866 the parish priest Zosimov, along with the tradesman Chebanenko, donated land for the creation of Tikhvinskaia Ekaterinoslavskaia women's community, which opened a school for girls and an almshouse.[57] In 1881 Vasilii A. Golubev, parish priest in the village of Tavolzhanka, Voronezh province, donated 600 *desiatiny* (1,620 acres) of land for the creation of the Kazanskaia women's community, which ran a parish school, an almshouse for old women, an orphanage for girls of the clerical estate, and a wayfarers' hostel.[58]

In some cases, *zhenskie obshchiny* developed as spin-offs of existing monasteries, either at the initiative or with the permission of monastic superiors. This was the case with the Vladychne-Pokrovskaia community, established in the city of Moscow in 1869 by Mitrofaniia (1825–1898), abbess of the Vladychnyi monastery in Serpukhov.[59] Born Baroness Rozen', Mitrofaniia was a woman of startling energy who vigorously fostered at Serpukhov four strands of contemporary Russian monasticism: the contemplative and cenobitic, economic self-sufficiency, the restoration of buildings and icons, and social service and charitable work. Spiritually, Mitrofaniia introduced into the monastery ascetic and monastic reforms initiated by Paisii Velichkovskii and encouraged by her patron, Metropolitan Filaret. In addition she encouraged publication of the works of the desert fathers and wrote an article on St. Pachomius, considered the founder of Eastern cenobitic monasticism.[60]

Economically, Mitrofaniia expanded the resources of the monastery, disdaining begging and collections, and encouraging the development of an apiary, fishery, kiln, and embroidery and textile workshops. She even entered some of the monastery's products in the St. Petersburg Manufacturing Exhibition of 1870.[61] A skilled icon painter, Mitrofaniia opened a workshop for icon painting and restoration, and she devoted considerable energy to the restoration of monastic buildings.[62] Philanthropically, Mitrofaniia was best known for her medical work. A trained *fel'dsher* (paramedic), she established a large hospital and apothecary at Serpukhov, and intended the women's religious community that she established in Moscow to provide similar medical care.[63] This community was transformed in 1870 into a community of sisters of mercy, under the direct patronage of the empress. Reflecting the stamp of its founder and the needs of society, the Moscow Vladychne-Pokrovskaia community by 1907 was running an orphanage for girls, a school, a training course for paramedics, a clinic and pharmacy, an embroidery workshop, and a home for elderly nuns and sisters.[64]

The needs of society, particularly of rural Russia, become apparent in analyzing the final cluster of founders and donors of women's religious communities—ordinary men and women of villages and towns. Before examining the profile of these founders and donors, it is important to look at the functional role of the *zhenskie obshchiny* and the institutional base from which these societies were most likely to spring. Functionally, *zhenskie obshchiny* were almost universally associated with shelters for women who were homeless, elderly, and widowed—"familyless" women, as the records of the Holy Synod say again and again.[65] These shelters for women were often combined with shelters, orphanages, and schools, particularly for poor and orphaned girls. Again, the records are a barometer of special needs, sometimes indicating a particular concern for poor and orphaned girls of the clerical estate, and sometimes showing a direct response to tragedies created by war, such as the shelters formed for orphans of "fallen soldiers" of the Turkish War, or again in 1904–1906, for orphans of the Russo-Japanese War.[66] They also frequently provided infirmaries, hospitals, and wayfarers' hostels—an important function in a country increasingly given to mobility, migration, and pilgrimage.

Religiously, the presence of a *zhenskaia obshchina* in a town or village meant the presence of a church and the possibility for prayers and services, particularly prayers for the dead. Often the construction of a church was the point at which an unofficial gathering of women became officially recognized by ecclesiastical and civil authorities as a *zhenskaia obshchina*. Thus there is an evolutionary path, particularly in the second half of the nineteenth century, from the creation of an almshouse to the establishment of a *zhenskaia obshchina* that occurred with the building of a church and securing of sufficient funds or land to support the community. At least thirty-six of the *zhenskie obshchiny* in this study began as almshouses. Conversely, women's religious communities often sprang up around existing parish churches, particularly graveyard (*kladbishche*) churches. Here women gathered for the preparation of Communion bread and for the reading of the Psalter—a crucial way of remembering the dead and an important function provided by pious women for the local community.

When we realize, then, the range of services, social and spiritual, that local women's religious communities provided, it is understandable that they were supported by men and women of all social classes, from nobles (*pomeshchiki*) to peasants. This study is based on information on the founding donors for 67 of the 113 village *zhenskie obshchiny* formed between 1764 and 1907, and for 65 of the 102 town *zhenskie obshchiny*. The social origins of the founding donors of *zhenskie obshchiny* in villages were nineteen nobles, thirteen merchants, thirteen peasants, twelve local citizens, eleven military personnel, nine civil officials, five clergy, and three tradespeople (*meshchane*). We have sufficient data to know that thirty-one of these were men and forty-nine women. Women were classified according to the social status of their husbands or, if single, according to that of their fathers. Noble women, the local *pomeshchitsy,* formed the largest group of donors, but support in the form of money and land came from women of all social groups.

For example, the Troitskaia Novaia community was established in 1874 with the resources of Varentsova, a local gentry woman who donated for the support of the *obshchina* and the almshouse for elderly women built at the *obshchina* a wooden house, five outbuildings, 430 *desiatiny* (1,161 acres) of land, and four thousand rubles, while a soldier's wife, Irina Lazareva, founded the Spasskaia Zelenogorskaia community in the first quarter of the nineteenth century as a shelter for orphans.[67] Other examples of piety and charity at the village level include the merchant Afanasii Torpov, who donated 470 *desiatiny* (1,269 acres) of land, a water mill, and ten thousand rubles, and pledged to build at his own expense a church and all the necessary buildings for an almshouse and an *obshchina* in the village of Pososhka;[68] Count V. Kapnist and his wife, who in 1885 helped to establish at the local church of Bogoroditsi-Rozhdestvenskaia an *obshchina* with a hospital, a school, and an almshouse, and whose donations to the *obshchina* included a revered icon of the Mother of God that attracted a large number of pilgrims;[69] and the peasant woman Ol'neva, who together with several anonymous philanthropists, in 1877 donated twenty-two thousand rubles and 138 *desiatiny* (373 acres) of land for the establishment of an *obshchina* in the village of Median.[70]

The view from the towns shows a similar dynamic of local initiative, piety, charity, and shared cultural values that cut across class lines. The founding donors for *zhenskie obshchiny* in the towns numbered twenty-two from the merchantry, sixteen from the local citizens, twelve from the tradespeople, eleven from the clergy, nine from the peasantry, six from civil officialdom, four from the military, and four from the nobility. Where the gender of the donor is clear, thirty-four were men and thirty-eight women.

The community of Pokrovskaia was founded around 1800 in the town of Ardatov by *meshchanka* Vasilisa Dmitrievna Poliukhova, who with three single women settled around the local church and occupied themselves with the baking of Communion bread.[71] The Orskaia community was established in 1888 with a school for girls by tradeswomen Anna Arzamastseva and Efimiia Shuvalova, and twelve other women "zealous of a pious life."[72] The Kazanskaia Bogoroditskaia community was founded in the town of Bugul'mo in 1879 by the peasant woman Matiushkina, who gave a house with a garden in the town and 300 *desiatiny* (810 acres) of land, and the merchant Stakhev, who donated thirty-one thousand rubles.[73]

In the towns more than in the villages, multiple donors contributed to the establishment of a women's religious community. In 1835 the Tikhvinskaia Bogoroditskaia community in Buzuluka was founded by a peasant woman, Ovsiannikova, and in 1847 it was "brought under the protection" of the ecclesiastical and civil authorities upon the deeding to it of 111 *desiatiny* (300 acres) of land donated by citizens of the town.[74] In 1866, the Volskaia Vladimirskaia community, with an attached almshouse, was established in the town of Volgsko through the ceding to it of land by the town society (*gorodskoe obshchestvo*), through capital amounting to 24,032 rubles donated by *meshchanka* Leont'eva, and through acquiring parcels of land.[75] In 1868, in the town of Bezhetska, a women's religious community was established with a school and an orphanage; for the use of the community the brothers Kruikov donated 50 *desiatiny* (135 acres) of land, tradesman Arkhipov gave a two-story wooden house with land near the town, and the merchant Nevrotin donated 15 *desiatiny* (41 acres) of land and indicated his willingness to build a brick house.[76] In 1872 in the town of Vyshnyi-Volochek, Prince Putiatin built a two-story stone structure with a church and three wooden buildings on stone foundations, and gave land totaling 276 *desiatiny* (745 acres) for the founding of a women's religious community with a hospital. In addition, Rykachev, a member of the local gentry, gave 109 *desiatiny* (294 acres) of land, and in 1885 Hereditary Honorary Citizen Sivokhin donated the ancient Greek icon of the Mother of God, named Andronikova, which was transferred from St. Petersburg to the community.[77] In 1877, in the interests of establishing a women's religious community with a school for Cheremiss girls, the town society of Kozmodem'iansk in Kazan province ceded a parcel of land, the merchant Zubov gave two houses and three thousand rubles, and Cheremiss peasants gave seventy-seven hundred rubles.[78]

A close examination of the origins of women's religious communities in the towns and villages yields a clear picture of repeated examples of local initiative, popular piety, and charitable work. In the Russian context, it is worth drawing attention to this local initiative. The common cultural and historiographical image of Russia is of a society long ruled from the center through a chain of imperial and bureaucratic edicts falling on a phlegmatic population. One sees instead energetic individuals, local initiative, and grass-roots organization. What motivated these people? What impelled the founding of so many women's religious communities in Russia in the nineteenth and early twentieth centuries?

It is presumptuous to speak for the voiceless dead. One can only speculate and point to large issues, the dynamic intermingling of high and low culture, exalting spiritual ideas, and raw social dislocation. Russia in the nineteenth century experienced both a spiritual revival and a social and economic upheaval; both fed the growth of women's religious communities.

The social upheaval caused by modernization, urbanization, and industrialization meant for rural Russia an intense period of out-migration, a massive exodus of peasants into the cities. In Russia this out-migration assumed a particular pattern, in that men formed the overwhelming bulk of those leaving the villages and moving into the new industrial labor force. It was typical for men to marry before setting out for the cities, leaving a wife behind to maintain a share in the household land allotment. But the long-range effect of male out-migration was to increase the number of "familyless" women and widows in the rural areas. Male migrant laborers suffered higher mortality rates than did males in the villages because of poverty, disease, and harsh labor conditions in the cities. For this reason, the number of widows was abnormally high in areas with high out-migration rates. For example, in Kostroma province, where the majority of men had left to work in St. Petersburg, of sixty-one peasant households in four villages studied in 1891, there were twenty-six widows ranging in age from twenty-two to one hundred, and only two widowers; and in 1906 a participant at the Ninth Annual Congress of Kostroma Physicians reported that while one would normally expect 120 old women for every 100 old men, in certain areas of Kostroma, there were 212 or even 286 old women for every 100 old men.[79]

It is possible that women's religious communities, composed of women who ministered overwhelmingly to elderly and to "familyless" women, were a particular, though by no means sufficient, response to the dislocation caused by migrations and modernization. Autonomy and self-development may also have played a role: a detailed analysis of the archival records of one community, Sviato-Troitskaia Tvorozhkovskaia in St. Petersburg diocese, indicates that in the second half of the nineteenth century the community was overwhelmingly composed of peasant women, that these women had higher literacy rates than other rural women, and that they enjoyed areas of autonomy and opportunities for the holding of positions of considerable authority.[80]

Spiritually, the formation of women's religious communities testifies to popular piety, to a deep expression of religious faith by those who founded them, those who entered them, and those who supported them. Those who entered women's religious communities found the possibility for an increased intensity in their experience of God in an environment supportive of retreat from the world in order to turn to the divine. Theologically, this was a returning to the core of Christianity, the contemplative tradition, and yet it was combined with a deep compassion for the world and ministering to the poor, the homeless, the sick, the elderly, and the young. Those who supported a community gained the opportunity for piety and charity. Everyone in a local community found the opportunity for liturgy and prayer, especially prayer for the dead. And finally, for the more searching, for the spiritual and physical pilgrims of the world, there was an opportunity for spiritual direction and guidance in the religious community.

All of this was spontaneous, genuine, and local. It laughed in the face of government regulations, and it turned a bleak century of bureaucratization and centralization into a surprising era of religious vitality.

NOTES

SOURCE: This essay originally appeared in an earlier version under the same title in *St. Vladimir's Theological Quarterly*, 30, no. 2 (1986).

ACKNOWLEDGMENTS: The research and writing of this essay have been supported at various stages by the Academy of Sciences of the USSR, the International Research and Exchanges Board, the Kennan Institute of the Woodrow Wilson International Center for Scholars, the National Endowment for the Humanities, the National Humanities Center, and the University of Rochester. The author gratefully acknowledges this support.

1. *Polnoe sobranie postanovlenii i rasporiazhenii po vedomstvu pravoslavnogo ispovedaniia* (hereafter *PSPR*), *Tsarstvovanie gosudaria imperatora Petra Fedorovicha*, no. 175, February 16, 1762.

2. *PSPR, Tsarstvovanie imperatritsy Ekateriny Alekseevny*, no. 167, February 28, 1764.

3. V. V. Zverinskii, *Materialy dlia istoriko-topograficheskogo issledovaniia o pravoslavnykh monastyriakh v rossiiskoi imperii*, vol. 1 (St. Petersburg, 1890), p. xi.

4. *PSPR, Tsarstvovanie imperatritsy Ekateriny Alekseevny*, no. 212, November 12, 1764.

5. Gregory L. Freeze, *The Russian Levites: Parish Clergy in the Eighteenth Century* (Cambridge, Mass.: Harvard University Press, 1977), p. 40.

6. L. I. Denisov, *Pravoslavnye monastyri rossiiskoi imperii. Polnyi spisok vsekh 1105 nyne sushchestvuiushikh v 75 guberniiakh i oblastiakh Rossii (i 2 inostrannykh gosudarstvakh) muzhskikh i zhenskikh monastyrei, arkhiereiskikh domov i zhenskikh obshchin* (Moscow, 1908), p. ix.

7. This is the author's compilation of data in Zverinskii, 1, pp. xviii, 1–17.

8. This is the author's compilation of data from Denisov.

9. Sergii Chetverikov, *Starets Paisii Velichkovskii: His Life, Teaching, and Influence on Orthodox Monasticism*, trans. V. Lickwar (Belmont, Mass.: Nordland Publishing Co., 1980).

10. "Velitchkovsky, Paissy," *New Catholic Encyclopedia*, vol. 14 (New York: McGraw Hill, 1967), p. 593.

11. Ibid.; Chetverikov, pp. 285–322.

12. James H. Billington, *The Icon and the Axe: An Interpretive History of Russian Culture* (New York: Knopf, 1966), pp. 269–328; and Nicholas Riasanovsky, *Russia and the West in the Teaching of the Slavophiles* (Gloucester, Mass.: Peter Smith, 1965).

13. On the expansion of literacy see Jeffrey Brooks, *When Russia Learned to Read: Literacy and Popular Literature, 1861–1917* (Princeton: Princeton University Press, 1985). On colportage see Stephen Batalden, "Colportage and the Dissemination of Holy Scripture in Late Imperial Russia," in *California Slavic Studies (Christianity and the Eastern Slavs)*, pt. 2 of 3 vols. (Berkeley: University of California, 1993). Nikolai Astaf'ev, *Obshchestvo dlia rasprostraneniia sv. Pisaniia v Rossii 1863–1893: Ocherk ego proiskhozhdeniia i deiatel'nosti* (St. Petersburg, 1895); and the annual reports of the British and Foreign Bible Society.

14. The expression "sweet silence" of Metropolitan Platon of Moscow (1737–1812) was quoted in Robert Nichols, "Metropolitan Filaret of Moscow and the Awakening of Orthodoxy" (Ph.D. diss., University of Washington, 1972), p. 29.

15. *PSPR, Tsarstvovanie imperatritsy Ekateriny Alekseevny*, no. 250, July 22, 1765.

16. Ibid.

17. Ibid., no. 370, August 22, 1766.

18. N. Shchegol'kov, *Arzamasskii Nikolaevskii obshchezhitel'nyi zhenskii monastyr': Istoriia ego i opisanie* (Arzamas, 1903), p. 15.

19. Ibid., pp. 15–16; I. N. Chetyrkin, *Istoriko-statisticheskoe opisanie arzamasskoi Alekseevskoi zhenskoi obshchiny* (Nizhnii Novgorod, 1887), p. 23.

20. Denisov, pp. 551–553.

21. This is the author's compilation based on data from Zverinskii and Denisov.

22. "Monashestvo," in *Entsiklopedicheskii slovar'*, vol. 38 (St. Petersburg, 1898), p. 730.

23. "Zhenskie obshchiny v nizhegorodskoi gubernii," *Zhurnal ministerstva vnutrennikh del*, no. 19 (1847), p. 275.

24. See Brenda Meehan-Waters, "Metropolitan Filaret (Drozdov) and the Reform of Russian Women's Monastic Communities," *Russian Review* (Summer 1991), pp. 310–323.

25. See Zverinskii, 1, pp. xviii, 5–8, for a list of the 95 men's monasteries; see pp. xviii, 4–17, for a list of the 28 men's monasteries that became women's monasteries, a list of 38 new women's monasteries, and a list of 131 *zhenskie obshchiny*, of which 79 eventually became monasteries, formed between 1772 and 1890. The author's observation of the differences in their origins is based on an analysis of the data in Zverinskii's 294 pages.

26. For an excellent discussion of charitable services in Russia see Adele Lindenmeyr, "Public Poor Relief and Private Charity in Late Imperial Russia" (Ph.D. diss., Princeton University, 1980).

27. Zverinskii, 1, p. 78; and Denisov, p. 780.

28. Sebastian P. Brock and Susan Ashbrook Harvey, *Holy Women of the Syrian Orient* (Berkeley: University of California Press, 1987), p. xiv.

29. Ibid., p. xviii, for the phrase "jarring translucence" in relation to ascetic practice.

30. "Zhenskie obshchiny v nizhegorodskoi gubernii," pp. 279–281; Zverinskii, 1, p. 135; Denisov, pp. 544–547; "Serafim of Sarov," in *The Modern Encyclopedia of Russian and Soviet History*, no. 34 (Gulf Breeze: Academic International Press, 1983), pp. 23–24.

31. Denisov, pp. 544–545; for a hagiographic life of Mel'gunova (in religious life Aleksandra), see "Abbess Alexandra, Foundress of the Diveevo Convent," *Orthodox Life* 3 (1983), pp. 21–32.

32. V. Tenishchev, *Novoustroiaemaia Meliavskaia (Teplovskaia) zhenskaia obitel' v ardatovskom uezde nizhegorodskoi gubernii* (Ardatov, 1902).

33. Ibid., p. 16.

34. A. Priklonskii, *Zhizn' pustynnitsy Anastasii (Semenovny Logachevoi), vposledstvii monakhini Afanasii, i vozniknovenie na meste eia podvigov zhenskoi obshchiny* (Moscow, 1902), p. 11. For a fuller discussion, see Brenda Meehan-Waters, "The Authority of Holiness: Women Ascetics and Spiritual Elders in Nineteenth-Century Russia," in *God's Servants: Church, Nation and State in Russia and Ukraine*, ed. Geoffrey A. Hosking (London: MacMillan, 1990), pp. 38–51; and Brenda Meehan, *Holy Women of Russia* (San Francisco: Harper Collins, 1993).

35. Priklonskii, p. 11.

36. Denisov, p. 550.

37. On Troitskaia Odigitrievskaia Zosimova, see Zverinskii, 1, p. 265; and Denisov, p. 514; Pimen, "Vospominaniia arkhimandrita Pimena, nastoiatelia Nikolaevskogo monastyria, chto na Ugreshe,"*Chteniia v Imperatorskom obshchestve istorii i drevnostei rossiiskikh pri Moskovskom Universitete*, no. 1 (1877), p. 295; on Ivanovskaia Kazanovskaia Sezenovskaia, see Zverinskii, 1, p. 151; and Denisov, p. 814; on Toplovskaia Paraskevskaia, see Denisov, p. 798; and E. S. Gorchakova, *Opisanie toplovskogo obshchezhitel'nogo monastyria sv. prepodobnomuchenitsy Paraskevy v Krymu* (Moscow, 1885), pp. 5–7; on Shamordinskaia Kazanskaia, see Zverinskii, 1, p. 159; Denisov, p. 286; and John B. Dunlop, *Starets Amvrosy, Model for Dostoevsky's Starets Zosima* (Belmont, Mass.: Nordland Publishing Co., 1972), pp. 98–99.

38. Dunlop, *Starets Amvrosy*, pp. 60–61.

39. Zverinskii, 1, p. 259; Denisov, pp. 184–185; *Tserkovnye vedomosti*, no. 42 (1888), pp. 63–65.

40. E. V. Novosil'tseva (pseud. T. Tolycheva), *Spaso-Borodinskii mo-*

nastyr' i ego osnovatel'nitsa. (*Posviashchaetsia vsem pochitaiushchim pamiat'*
Margarity Mikhailovny Tuchkovoi), 3d ed. (Moscow, 1889), pp. 16–28.

41. Pimen, p. 295; Denisov, pp. 520–522.

42. "Igumen'ia Evdokiia, osnovatel'nitsa Boriso-Glebo-Anosina
obshchezhitel'nogo devichi'ia monastyria," *Chteniia v Imperatorskom Obshchestve istorii i drevnostei rossiiskikh pri moskovskom universitete,* no. 2
(1876), pp. i–iii; Pimen, pp. 288–292.

43. Pimen, p. 292.

44. Denisov, p. 519.

45. Pimen, pp. 300–303.

46. Denisov, p. 518.

47. *Monakhinia Angelina (v mire Aleksandra Filippovna Fon-Roze) osnovatel'nitsa i stroitel'nitsa sviato-troitskoi tvorozhkovskoi zhenskoi obshchiny
vozvedennoi v monastyr' s naimenovaniem ego Sviato-Troitskim obshchezhitel-
'nym zhenskim monastyrem* (St. Petersburg, 1888).

48. Ibid., pp. 151–152.

49. Ibid., pp. 101–102.

50. Denisov, pp. 911–912.

51. The Russian Orthodox tradition of entry into monastic life in
midlife was reinforced by the Spiritual Regulation of 1721, a pivotal Petrine reform, which made clear the state's regulation of church affairs and
skepticism concerning the contemplative, monastic life. So that subjects
should not flee the obligations of this world, entrance for men was
strictly limited, and women were not permitted to take the veil until the
age of fifty. It was assumed that nuns would be widows who had already
fulfilled their obligations as wives and mothers. In the event that a young
girl should "desire to remain a young virgin with the intention of taking
monastic orders," she was scrupulously supervised and made to "remain
without orders until she is sixty, or at least fifty, years old." *The Spiritual
Regulation of Peter the Great,* Alexander V. Muller, trans. and ed. (Seattle:
University of Washington Press, 1972), pp. 79–80. For the Russian text,
see *Polnoe sobranie zakonov rossiiskoi imperii s 1649 goda,* lst ser., no. 6 (St.
Petersburg, 1836), p. 3718. These regulations were somewhat modified
in the nineteenth century; a man could be tonsured at the age of thirty,
or twenty-five if he had theological schooling, but a woman had to wait
until she was forty. *PSPR, Tsarstvovanie gosudaria imperatora Nikolaia I,*
no. 430, June 17, 1832.

52. On the Rozhdestvo-Bogoroditskaia see Zverinskii, 1, p. 219;
and Denisov, p. 779; on the Vvedenskaia Kievskaia, see Zverinskii, 1, p.
111; on the Iletskaia Nikolaevskaia see Denisov, p. 626; on the Sofiiskaia
see Denisov, p. 726; and Zverinskii, 1, p. 199; on Panovskaia Troitskaia
see Denisov, pp. 758–759; on Pokrovskaia see Denisov, p. 626; on
Malaia Pitsa Skorbiashchenskaia see Zverinskii, 1, p. 232; and Denisov,
p. 541.

53. Pimen, pp. 303–307.

54. For the thirty-eight women's monasteries that were formed as official monasteries between 1772 and 1890, see Zverinskii.

55. On Ioanno Marinskaia, see Zverinskii, 1, p. 157; Denisov, p. 782. On Bogoroditskaia, see Zverinskii, 1, p. 91; Denisov, p. 785.

56. Nicholas Zernov, *The Russians and Their Church* (London, 1945), p. 151.

57. Zverinskii, 1, p. 254.

58. Denisov, p. 187.

59. V. N. Andreev, *Zhizn' i deiatel'nost' Baronessy Rozen' v monashestve Igumeni Mitrofanii* (St. Petersburg, 1876).

60. Ibid., pp. 89–105.

61. Ibid., p. 125.

62. Ibid., p. 52.

63. Ibid., pp. 50–51.

64. Denisov, p. 511.

65. See, for example, *Tserkovnye vedomosti*, no. 42 (1888), p. 207.

66. Examples of *zhenskie obshchiny* with shelters and schools for poor and orphaned girls of the clerical estate include Arkadievskaia Viazemskaia (Zverinskii, 1, p. 78), Dmitrievskaia Milostova Bogoroditskaia (Zverinskii, 1, p. 135), and Tikhvinskaia Bogoroditskaia (Denisov, p. 650). Examples of *zhenskie obshchiny* with shelters for orphans of the Russo-Turkish War include Nikonovskaia Sushkinskaia (Zverinskii, 1, p. 196), Pokrovskaia Balashovskaia (Zverinskii, 1, p. 207), and Troitskaia Dmitrievskaia (Zverinskii, 1, p. 262). An example of a *zhenskaia obshchina* with a shelter for orphans of the Russo-Japanese war is Sv. Ravnoapostol'naia Nina, founded in 1906 (Denisov, p. 949).

67. On the Troitskaia Novaia, see Zverinskii, 1, p. 262; and Denisov, p. 949; on the Spasskaia Zelenogorskaia, see Zverinskii, 1, p. 249; and Denisov, p. 542.

68. Zverinskii, 1, p. 210; Denisov, p. 642.

69. Zverinskii, 1, p. 90.

70. Zverinskii, 1, p. 205; Denisov, p. 767.

71. Zverinskii, 1, p. 206; Denisov, p. 543.

72. Zverinskii, 1, p. 199.

73. Ibid.

74. Zverinskii, 1, p. 258; Denisov, p. 736.

75. Zverinskii, 1, p. 119.

76. Ibid., 1, p. 84.

77. Ibid., 1, p. 159.

78. Ibid., 1, p. 271.

79. Barbara Alpern Engel, "The Woman's Side: Male Outmigration and the Family Economy in Kostroma Province," *Slavic Review* (Summer 1986), p. 267.

80. See Brenda Meehan-Waters, "To Save Oneself: Russian Peasant Women and the Development of Women's Religious Communities in Pre-Revolutionary Russia," in *Russian Peasant Women,* ed. Beatrice Farnsworth and Lynne Viola (New York: Oxford University Press, 1992), pp. 122–133.

The Schism and Cultural Conflict in the Seventeenth Century

Translated by Stephen Batalden

T he schism of the Russian church in the middle of the seventeenth century was among the most tragic events in Russian
history and was the most tragic event in the history of the Russian church. The schism was caused by the reforms of Patriarch Nikon.
These reforms divided the Great Russian population into two antagonistic groups—Old Believers who refused to accept the innovations introduced by the patriarch and followers of Nikon.

It is remarkable that this schism, unlike all other schisms in Christianity, had nothing to do with dogmatic controversy. Rather, it had semiotic
and philological foundations, for the schism was based on a cultural conflict. These cultural, semiotic, and philological differences, highlighted in
the controversy over the church reforms, were comprehended essentially
as theological differences, despite the fact that there was no independent
scholarly discipline of theology in medieval Rus'. Nevertheless, everything could in principle be understood in theological terms. In this controversy over texts, not only the content but also the form could be
understood as a manifestation of divine truth, as a direct witness of God.
This conjunction of form and content was an extension of the same attitude toward the sacred sign expressed in the veneration of icons.

The schism was provoked by the change in some rituals in the church
service and by the correction of church books. The schism began in 1653,
when a new edition of the Psalter was published. In the 1653 Psalter,
references were deleted that had been quite conspicuous in preceding editions. They concerned, in particular, the two-fingered sign of the cross
and prostration.[1] Prior to Lent of 1653, an epistle of the patriarch, distributed to churches, had established the three-fingered sign of the cross
and the reducing of prostration during the reading of the Lenten prayer
of St. Ephrem of Syria.[2] There followed a correction of almost all the
liturgical books, most important of which was the corrected service book
published in 1655. In all these changes, the Nikonian reforms were concerned not with content or dogmatics but with form. Nonetheless, they
provoked an unusually sharp reaction, for form and content were virtually identified in the traditional cultural consciousness.

A characteristic example of these reforms was the change in the form-ing of fingers to make the sign of the cross: the two-fingered configu-ration was changed to a three-fingered one. In essence there was no difference, for in each case both the idea of the Trinity and the idea of duality (the double nature of Christ as divine and human) were ex-pressed. Previously, the idea of the Trinity had been expressed by bring-ing together the thumb, the little finger and the fourth finger, while at the same time expressing God's dual nature by bringing together the in-dex and the middle fingers. According to the new manner, the Trinity was expressed by bringing together the thumb, index and middle fingers, while God's dual nature was expressed by the fourth finger and little fin-ger. And it cannot be said that some fingers were considered semiotically more important than others. Thus, from the point of view of the ex-pressed content, there was no difference whatsoever. Nevertheless, it was precisely this innovation in the ritual that served to launch the schism. The two-fingered sign of the cross became the symbol of adhering to the old ritual. The mass of self-immolations that followed demonstrated the fidelity to that principle. When in 1666, the Orthodox All-Church Council was convened with the participation of eastern Orthodox patri-archs (Paisios of Alexandria and Makarios of Antioch), it defended Ni-kon's innovations. In front of this court of patriarchs, the dissenting archpriest Lazar proposed that the court turn to divine judgment to find out which ritual was authentic and truly Orthodox. "Allow me to pro-ceed to the divine fate in the fire," he announced. "If I burn, it means that the new ritual is good; if, however, I survive, it means that the old ritual is truly the Orthodox ritual."[3] The patriarchs would not agree to such a trial. Instead, on 1 April 1682, on orders from Moscow, the archpriest Lazar, as well as the archpriest Avvakum, the deacon Fedor, and the monk Epifanii were burned at the stake in Pustozersk for adhering to the old ritual. Divine judgment had been replaced by a human court, and a voluntary test of faith by compulsory execution.

The example of the finger configuration was particularly telling, for it clearly demonstrated the purely semiotic nature of the conflict. Both modes of finger configuration were semantically identical. Still, each side stubbornly insisted on its own rectitude. At the same time, the viewpoint of Old Believers was essentially different from that of the new ritualists.

Old Believers declared that their rituals were the only correct ones. In saying this, they were referring to tradition, to the mystical experience of preceding generations, including that of Russian saints, who had been practicing these rituals for centuries and in this way confirmed their ef-ficacy and power.[4]

For the new ritualists the main point was their cultural orientation. They were oriented toward the Greeks, striving to make Russian rites conform to the Greek rites. Hence, Patriarch Nikon, whose liturgical reforms provoked the schism and who so resolutely insisted on the correction of church books, could nevertheless allow the usage of old church books in some individual cases, albeit as an exception. Later, Patriarch Ioakim, an active supporter of the Nikonian reforms, could declare that it was not so important, after all, how one made the sign of the cross— what was important was to obey the regulations of the church authorities. However, such an attitude was characteristic only of the cultural elite. The vast majority of the new ritualists in the second half of the seventeenth century held the same ideology as the Old Believers. Therefore, among new ritualists, unlike the cultural elite, it was possible to encounter the notion that the old way of finger configuration was absolutely incorrect, just as the Old Believers considered the new way absolutely incorrect. It was possible for the Nikonians to regard ritual as a sort of accepted convention, while the Old Believers always proceeded from the assumption that the forms they defended were unconditionally correct. Thus, the semiotic conflict became manifest in an altogether different approach toward the sacred sign.

The same difference was also revealed with regard to language. As noted, the schism was, to a significant degree, provoked by the correction of church books. In some cases the correction was of textual character; that is, the text was revised and made to correspond to the Greek texts. In most cases, however, the corrections were of a purely formal linguistic character. It was simply the form that was subject to correction. The language was changed in aspects that had nothing to do with content. Thus, for example, the spelling and accentation in church books was altered, and the construction of possessive adjectives was changed to the equivalent construction of the genitive case. All this called forth sharp protests. Deacon Fedor, one of the Old Believer leaders and an associate of Archpriest Avvakum, declared, "It behooves all of us Orthodox Christians to die for one *az* [i.e., for one letter *a*], which this cursed enemy [Patriarch Nikon] threw out of the Creed." The question here concerned the exclusion of the conjunction *a* (but) in the Creed. In the original wording it was *rozhdenna, a ne sotvorenna* (born *but* not created), but under the new wording it read, *rozhdenna, ne sotvorenna* (born, not created).[5] Fedor actually died for his Creed, accepting a martyr's death at the stake in Pustozersk along with Avvakum, Epifanii, and Lazar.

Unlike the Reformation in the West, it was not the opposition between the bookish language and the vernacular that was at stake. Indeed, both Old Believer and Nikonian books were rendered in Church Slavonic, and both parties recognized Church Slavonic as the only possible language for Russian church books. The attitude toward language, however, was drastically different between old and new ritualists. In other words, the conflict revealed underlying differences in their treatment of the sacred sign—one conventional, the other unconventional.[6]

Language, generally speaking, can be understood as a means of communication or as a means of expressing certain information irrespective of the act of communication. The former notion stresses the process of transmitting information, while the latter accentuates the manner of expression. Church Slavonic traditionally was understood as a means of expressing divinely revealed truth. Such a view assumed, necessarily, a nonconventional approach to the linguistic sign. In this case it was the linguistic form that was especially important, and the linguistic form was not set in opposition to content.

If language is regarded as a medium of communication, the linguistic behavior is evaluated in pragmatic terms. The linguistic behavior is good if the communication is efficient. In such cases, it is the perception of the subject for whom the transmitted information is intended that is significant. Indeed, one and the same content can be expressed in various ways. Different means of expression may be equally appropriate in relation to the transmitted content, but one method of expression may prove to be more successful in some particular respect. This presupposes a rational conception of the text as an object critically apprehended by the subject. The given text is understood then as being possible but not obligatory. That is, it is a realization of one of the potentially possible means of transmitting some inherent content that, in principle, is independent of a given text.

Thus, in one case what is at stake is the problem of the correctness of expression, while in the other there is the problem of efficiency (the intelligibility, or the impact upon the addressee). In the first instance, the content is what must be expressed, while in the second case, the content is what must be interpreted. In the first case it is necessary to find an adequate means of expression, while in the second case it is necessary to find an adequate means of interpretation. In the former, one goes from the meaning to the text, while in the latter one goes from the text to the meaning.

Obviously, the stated functions of a language (communicative and significative) correspond to the roles of the speaker and the listener in discourse. If I am told something, it is important that, first of all, I understand and master the content. I am not responsible for the form; it is not mine. In principle, it makes no difference to me. If, however, I am the one who speaks, then it is important that I express the content as best I can; my task is to fit meaning into form. For me, content does not exist outside of expression. It is psychologically important to choose the correct, most adequate means of expression. Consequently, indifference to form may, in this case, mean indifference to content. We might otherwise assume that language always acts as a means of communication. In the case of sacred text, however, the communication appears as that between

God and man. God is the sender. He sends us the text, and we receive it. The relationship between God as the creator of a divinely revealed text and the text itself makes the text unconventional. At the same time, the relationship between the individual (as the receiving subject) and the text defines the problems of perception, posing thereby the conventional attitude toward the linguistic sign.

Old Believers preserved the attitude toward the sacred sign that was characteristic of Muscovy. Followers of the new rituals were influenced by the Polish baroque through Ukrainian culture. Hence, the conflict between Old Believers and the followers of the new rituals reflected a conflict between Eastern and Western cultural traditions.

The conflict of Muscovite and Ukrainian cultural traditions preceded the schism, for it began in the first half of the seventeenth century, after the Time of Troubles, but especially came to characterize the middle of the century. For example, in 1627 a Ukrainian priest, Kirill Trankvillion Stavrovetski, came to Muscovy in order to publish his *Didactic Gospel* (a collection of sermons). The book was in Church Slavonic, but since Kirill was Ukrainian, the spelling was Ukrainian. The language of the book was thus a Ukrainian version of Church Slavonic. The Muscovite authorities asked two recognized Moscow book correctors—Hegumen Il'ia and Ivan Nasedka (the latter known for his participation in the revision of the grammar of Meletii Smotritskii) to review the book. The Moscow reviewers were sharply negative in their reaction to the writings of Kirill Trankvillion, particularly his unusual spelling. For example, their attention was drawn to the form of the possessive adjective derived from the name of Christ (Khristov*i*, as opposed to Khristov*y*, that is, Christ's), written according to the spelling then current in Ukrainian (when the letter *i* renders the phoneme *y*). "Tell me, oh adversary," they addressed Kirill Trankvillion, "whose speech is this? These are Christ's words [*sut' slovesa Khristovi*]. And if these are Christ's words, why have you changed so much as a letter?" (Golubtsov, 1890, p. 552). The Muscovite reviewers perceived the incorrect form as certain proof of Kirill Trankvillion's non-Orthodoxy, that is, evidence that the whole text in question did not come from God. Consequently, the style of the book—its *style,* not its content—was judged heretical and the book was solemnly burned "because of its heretical style" (Golubtsov, 1890, p. 565; Zabelin, 1872–1873, II, p. 487; Kharlampovich, 1914, p. 111; AMG, 1890–1891, I, pp. 224–225, no. 201).

The same reaction was caused by the new grammatical forms introduced by the adherents of Patriarch Nikon. Again, reference was to the change of form, a change that did not affect content. For example, in the Creed the new form of the genitive plural was introduced, the construction of the verb with the dative case was changed to an equivalent construction with the genitive, and the short form of an adjective was transformed into the full form (for example, *nas radi cheloviek* changed to *nas radi cheloviekov; suditi zhivym i mertvym* changed to *suditi zhivykh i mertvykh; edinu sviatuiu sobornuiu i apostol'skuiu tserkov'* changed to *edinuiu sviatuiu sobornuiu i apostol'skuiu tserkov'*). In his consideration of such emendations, the monk Avraamii concluded in his petition of 1678 (citing the work of Maksim Grek and the Catechism of Lavrentii Zizanii), "And from this, the theologians have established, great heresy arises in the Church. For it is written that actually by one single letter of the alphabet heresy comes into being . . . and those doing such things are subject to anathema" (Subbotin, 1875–1890, VII, pp. 319–320).[7]

Similarly, Avraamii protested the change of the exclamation *vo vieki viekom* to *vo vieki viekov* in the Nikonian books (Barskov, 1912, p. 159). The meaning remained the same, but the form of the dative plural (with the meaning of the genitive) was replaced by the genitive plural. Archpriest Lazar, another leader of the Old Believers, wrote in the 1660s, "It is printed in the new books, in all the prayers and in all the parts of the *lectio solemnis*, 'now and forever through all eternity [*nynie i prisno i vo vieki viekov*].' These words are heretical" (see Lazar's "Rospis' v krattse," Subbotin, 1875–1890, IV, p. 200).[8] Archpriest Avvakum also wrote about the use of the form *viekov* instead of *viekom*, "It is a small letter, but it contains great heresy" (Avvakum, 1927, col. 465).[9] Avvakum spoke in exactly the same terms about the form for the word "amen," which appeared in corrected texts as *amin:* "We find *amin'* in the old books and *amin* in the new ones. Small as is this letter, great is the heresy it creates" (see Avvakum's "Poslanie k neizvestnym," in Borozdin, 1898, supp., p. 42).

Thus, it was not only content but form as well that was recognized as heretical. Not only could a concrete text with some definite meaning contain heresy but language itself as a device for expressing various meanings could also be heretical.[10]

It is entirely natural, then, that the slightest error in the pronunciation of sacred texts, such as a nondistinction between the letters *e* and *ie* (*jat*), which are very close in pronunciation and were not distinguished in everyday speech, was immediately corrected during the church service (a phenomenon that still takes place among Old Believers— Selishchev, 1920, p. 16; Uspensky, 1971, p. 45). In a mid-seventeenth- century pronunciation manual, a selection of typical reading errors, particularly those showing incorrect stress, ended with the following important conclusion: "It is horrible, brethren, not only to pronounce this, but even to think it" (Buslaev, 1861, col. 1088). The correlation of incorrect form of expression with incorrect content came across with vivid clarity in these words. The attitude of copyists toward misspellings of sacred texts was practically the same. In Russian penitential books there was a special prayer for scribes seeking absolution. It included the passage "I have sinned in copying the Divine Scriptures of the Holy Apostles and Holy Fathers of my own free will and by my own misunderstanding, and not as it was written" (Gorskii and Nevostruev, 1855– 1917, III, 1, p. 219; see also Petukhov, 1888, pp. 45–46; Almazov, 1894, III, p. 210, 216; Nikol'skii, 1896, pp. 58, 62; Ognev, 1880, p. 9). The copyist's position was more difficult, however, inasmuch as he was supposed to correct errors in the text he was copying. Among the typical penitential replies at confession was also the following: "I am a sinner, having copied books without correcting them" (Almazov, 1894, III, p. 238; Petukhov, 1888, p. 45). It was understood that one should correct books, but in the right way.[11]

Such an attitude toward error in written or oral speech was not at all characteristic of the Catholic West (see Mathiesen, 1972, pp. 48–49). In the West an involuntary error was in no way associated with a distortion of content and thus was not viewed as a sin. At the same time, the Russian word for error was derived from the word "sin" (*pogreshnost'*, from *grekh*). No less indicative were the differing attitudes on this matter in Muscovite Rus' and in Ukraine. In his preface to the published Prayer Book of 1646, Peter Mohyla emphasized that any errors or mistakes occurring in the ecclesiastical books were "in no way harmful to salvation, for they do not affect the number, power, matter, form, and content of the Holy Sacraments" (Titov, 1916–1918, p. 268, supp., p. 371).

Thus, not only the thought or belief but also the very form—in other words, the symbolic embodiment of the thought—could be seen as heretical. As a matter of principle, form and content were identified, and any deviation from the correct marking could effect a change in content. In any case, form was not indifferent to the content.

Basically, words of the sacred language functioned in these circumstances just as proper names do. Indeed, proper names are specifically characterized by a direct and unequivocal association of signifier and signified: A change in the form of the name is usually connected with another referent—that is, an altered form is naturally understood to be another name (Jakobson and Halle, 1962, pp. 464–467; Jakobson, 1971, p. 131). It was practically the same with the words of sacred language.

Church Slavonic was understood in Rus' not simply as a possible vehicle for transmitting information but first and foremost as a system for the symbolic presentation of the Orthodox confession—that is, as an icon of Orthodoxy. Such an understanding found its theological justification in a special Orthodox conception of language already elaborated on Greek soil but receiving its broadest dissemination in Muscovite Rus'.[12] According to this teaching, the soul (*psyche*), the word (*logos*), and the mind (*nous*) constituted an undivided unit that was a manifestation of the Holy Trinity. Speech was born twice. First, it was born in an incomprehensible way in one's soul.[13] Then it was born in the body—that is, materially incarnate in the body—just as God the Son was first born in a mystical way by God the Father and then made incarnate through the human body of the Virgin Mary (Mathiesen, 1972, pp. 28–29). Correspondingly, true faith presupposed a correct mode of expression.

This approach led to a negative attitude toward other languages, inasmuch as they were associated with alien (non-Orthodox) confessions. In particular, Latin was perceived as a symbol of Catholic belief (as a sort of icon of Catholicism), and Tatar was associated with Islam. Thus, Tatar and Latin were considered impure languages that defiled those who spoke them. When in the middle of the seventeenth century Patriarch Makarios of Antioch came to Moscow, he was especially warned that he "never speak in Turkish." "God forbid," said Tsar Aleksei Mikhailovich, "that such a holy man defile his mouth and tongue by such impure speech" (Pavel Aleppskii, 1896–1900, III, pp. 20–21). The same kind of attitude existed toward Latin. "Satan wholeheartedly loves Latin," affirmed Ivan Vishenskii in "Zachapka mudrago latynnika z glupym rusinom" (Ivan Vishenskii, 1955, p. 194). Patriarch Nikon would make the same argument against the Greek metropolitan of Gaza, Paisios Ligarides. When Metropolitan Paisios started disputing with Nikon in Latin, Nikon exclaimed, "O cunning slave, I judge by your lips that you are not Orthodox, for you befoul us with Latin" (Gibbenet, 1882–1884, II, p. 61, n. 11, p. 436).[14]

Latin was perceived as a paradigmatically heretical language that, by its own nature, distorted the content of Christian teaching.[15] It was assumed to be impossible to speak Latin and remain Orthodox, and vice versa. To be Orthodox, one had to accept Orthodox means of expression. In other words, one needed to use Greek or Church Slavonic.[16] This attitude toward Latin found expression in the following verse by a seventeenth- century writer thought to be Ivan Nasedka:

> Catholics praise their Latin writing most,
> They say it is the wisest,
> Alas, say we: nothing more evil is there than Latin,
> No saint created it,
> But it was created by pagan and unbaptized Hellenes.
>
> Our writing by a saint created
> Is like a flower from the herbs collected,
> And given to the Bulgars and us, the Slavs,
> That every Christian soul be led by the Lord's command.
> (Bylinin and Grikhin, 1987, p. 378)[17]

It was not surprising, therefore, that when Kievan monks appeared in Moscow to teach Latin in the 1650s (shortly before the schism), they provoked strong protest. For example, Luk'ian Timofeevich Golosov, future head of the Posolskii Prikaz, said that "he who studies Latin will stray from the right path," adding not without pride that he "does not know Latin, for many are the heresies in it."[18] Similarly, a priest named Stepan, who was studying Latin with Arsenii the Greek, was repeatedly told by his friends and relatives to "stop studying Latin, since it is bad; but they did not say just what was so bad about it." The priest ultimately stopped studying Latin and destroyed all his papers. Meanwhile, according to one account from 1649, the Moscow priest Foma received the following advice from his sexton, Konstantin Ivanov, regarding the appeals of the priest's spiritual children to be allowed to study Latin in Kiev: "Do not let them, for God's sake," said Konstantin, "for the Lord will count it against your soul" (Kapterev, 1913, pp. 145–146, note 1).[19]

In the second half of the seventeenth century and the beginning of the eighteenth century, following the schism of the Russian church, the attitude toward Latin caused heated arguments among the followers of the new ritual, between the Great Russian and southwest Russian parties (the so-called Grecophiles and the Latinophiles). In these arguments a major role was assigned to linguistic questions because the arguments concerned the possibility of transmitting Orthodox teaching via Latin. Arguing against the Chudov monk Evfimii, Sil'vester Medvedev noted in his book, *Manna khleba zhivotnago* (1687), that he found the reverence for Greek strange, "as if God put such power into that language that no one could write heresy in it." Medvedev asked, "If the Gospel and the Books of the Apostles were translated correctly from Latin books, should we trust them or not?" (Prozorovskii, 1896, pp. 528, 519). In 1704, Gavriil Dometskii argued with the monk Evfimii in a similar way (Iakhontov, 1883, p. 88; Smentsovskii, 1899, p. 335). In this argument one can clearly see the principal differences in the attitude toward language itself. For one side, language existed simply to communicate a thought, but for the other side it became first and foremost the means for expressing God's revealed truth. In one case linguistic expression became something conventional, but in the other case it became intertwined with the content itself.

Evfimii and other Grecophiles came forward with linguistic treatises that confirmed the non-Orthodoxy of Latin—that is, of the language as such, not of texts written in the language. Their conclusion was that it was harmful to study Latin. Evfimii devoted to this question his "Considerations on Whether It Is More Useful for Us to Study Grammar and Rhetoric . . . or, Not Studying Such Sophisticated Things, to Please God in Simplicity . . . and on Which Language It Is More Needful and Useful for Us Slavs to Study—Latin or Greek" (1684–1685). As a reproach to the Latin language he pointed out that in Latin the sacred names sound corrupted: "The saving name of the very Son of God, *Iisus,* they pronounce *Iezus;* and the holy names they pronounce as *Mikhael', Daniel', Izrael', Izmael', Ieruzalem,* and *Gregor.* Worst of all, the Holy Martyr *Iov* is shamefully called *Iob* [i.e., fucked]" (Smentsovskii, 1899, supp. p. XV).[20] Evfimii stated that studying Latin would lead one to break with Orthodoxy: "Those who have studied Latin almost all became Uniates, rarely remaining Orthodox" (Smentsovskii, 1899, supp. p. XXV). The same idea was conveyed in an analogous treatise, written at the same time: "An Argument Briefly Presented, if Greek Language and Learning Are Much More Necessary Than Latin, What Use Is Latin to the Slavs?"[21] The following argument was offered here for why the Orthodox faith was being "harmed" by Latin: "And while the Belorussians have taken to Latin simply because of the absence of Greek studies (except for L'vov, where Greek is taught), it is worth mentioning that some Jesuit contaminants are still to be found, both in those who do not join the Uniates, and in those who do" (Kapterev, 1889, pp. 96, 94).[22]

Arguing with Gavriil Dometskii, the Chudov archdeacon Damaskin stated in 1704, "If a teacher of the church knows only Latin, he cannot be called a true son of the Eastern Church" (Iakhontov, 1883, pp. 88–89). In 1705, the same Damaskin wrote to Metropolitan Iov of Novgorod:

> If you wish to take pleasure in the Holy Scripture and the many other divine books, it will be well pleasing for you to find Greek translators and scribes. Having witnessed this glorious wonder, you will understand how complete the Greek writing is. We have no need of the Latinizers whatsoever. We can do mightily without them. They flatter us in vain. The Lord has not sent them to us, but Satan—and for seduction, not for improvement. (Obraztsov, 1865, p. 94; cf. Iakhontov, 1883, *passim*)

Thus, the Latin language, in addition to the Latin teachings, was being linked directly with the devil. As written in the anonymous Old Believer composition of 1710, probably composed by Kuz'ma Andreev, the devilish essence of Tsar Peter I, who was perceived as the Antichrist, was made manifest in the fact that he signed his name in Latin: "Just as in transforming the name of Jesus the devil presents a different Jesus, so the newly applied Latin name of Peter points to a hellish devil presiding over and through him."[23] So, just as one letter added to the name *Isus* resulted in a different *Iisus,* not Christ but Antichrist,[24] so the Latin name in place of the name *Petr* revealed the devil hidden with the bearer of that name (Smirnov, 1909, pp. 691–692).[25] Even in the eighteenth century, Tatishchev wrote in his *Razgovor dvukh priiatelei o pol'ze nauki i uchilishch* (1730s) that many people think that "learning of foreign languages leads to sin" (Tatishchev, 1979, p. 99).[26] In turn, the adherents of Latin accused their opponents of ignorance and darkness. The opponents of Latin somehow seemed to accept such blame, however, declaring that it was more useful "to please God in simplicity" than to study grammar, rhetoric, and such subjects.

Not coincidentally, according to Kotoshikhin, the tsar's children were not taught foreign languages, undoubtedly because it was considered confessionally risky (Kotoshikhin, 1906, p. 17).[27] Moreover, that attitude toward studying foreign languages remained even after the establishment of the Slavonic-Greek-Latin Academy, which originally was intended to teach Greek, Latin, and Polish, no doubt having the schools of Ukraine as a prototype (DRV, 1788–1791, VI, p. 411).[28] Nevertheless, Polish was not taught there, and the teaching of Latin was quickly dropped. The Likhud brothers, founders of the Academy who taught Latin, were exiled, and Latin was not taught at the Academy until July 1701, when Peter I issued a special decree to commence the "study of Latin" (Smirnov, 1855, pp. 34, 39, 80; DRV 1788–1791, XVI, p. 302; Alekseev, 1862, p. 88).[29] The same situation prevailed in 1598, when Boris Godunov decided to establish a university and to invite teachers from Germany and other countries to lecture in it. The clergy resisted, saying that differences in language could bring differences in faith (Karamzin, 1892, XI, p. 53; Ustrialov, 1859, I, p. 18).[30]

Especially telling in this context was later evidence from Antiokh Kantemir (in the notes to the first edition of his first satire), who recorded that "not once, but many times, have we heard these words, that, as soon as we started using foreign languages and customs, our crops failed" (Kantemir, 1867–1868, I, p. 198). Thus, it was supposed that studying foreign languages caused the earth's wrath.

In these and similar testimonies, one can hear the characteristic belief that it was impossible to resort to foreign means of expression while staying within the limits of one's own ideology. In particular, it was impossible to speak such "unorthodox" languages as Tatar (perceived as the means of expression of Islam) or Latin (perceived as the means of expression of Catholicism) while remaining pure in relation to Orthodoxy. Quite consistent on this matter was the opinion of Fedor Polikarpov, who maintained (see his "Uveshchatel'noe izveshchenie i prestezhenie," which opens his *Leksikon treiazychnyi*, 1704) that knowledge of Church Slavonic allowed foreigners to become pious and that foreigners who came to Russia needed to be taught this language so that they would turn to Orthodoxy (Polikarpov, 1704, leaf 6 of first pagination).[31]

Thus, languages and semiotic modes of expression in general could be Orthodox and non-Orthodox. In the extreme they could even be heretical, and these heretical languages in the abstract could be contrasted to the "angelic language" that Archpriest Avvakum referred to when he discussed the issue of studying foreign languages. Avvakum was negatively inclined even to the study of Greek, because he believed that the Greeks were flawed in their Orthodoxy. Addressing Tsar Aleksei Mikhailovich, Avvakum wrote:

> I know your mind. You can speak many languages, but what is the use? Take a good, deep breath and say in Russian, "Lord, have mercy on me, a poor sinner," and abandon "Kyrie Eleison." You, Mikhailovich, are Russian, not Greek. Speak your natural tongue. Do not demean it in church, at home and in your sayings. We should speak the way Christ has taught us, as it is befitting to do. God loves us no less than he loves the Greeks. He has granted us letters in our language from St. Cyril and his brother. What more do we want? The angel tongue? No, it will not be given us until the final resurrection. (Avvakum, 1927, para. 475)[32]

The angelic language is the language of heavenly discourse; it could not be used on earth ("it will not be given us until the final resurrection"). But the Church Slavonic language, according to those Slavonic scribes, led to God. In the preface to the service and prayer book written by Dionisii Zobninovskii in the 1630s, we find stated, "If one reads books correctly, and another listens attentively, then both converse with God" (Gosudarstvennaia Biblioteka im. Lenina, Div. of Manuscripts, fond 163, *delo* 182, leaf 2 ob.). In his *Knizhka*, Ivan Vishenskii wrote that "the Slavonic . . . is the most fruitful of all languages, and the most beloved to God, because . . . by simple, diligent reading . . . it leads to God" (Ivan Vishenskii, 1955, p. 23).[33]

No less demonstrative was the assertion of Slavonic bookmen that it was absolutely impossible to lie in the Church Slavonic language, precisely because it was the means of expressing divinely revealed truth. Thus, in the words of Ivan Vishenskii, "in the Slavonic language, falsehood and the wiles of the devil . . . can have no place." That is why the devil could not abide this language and struggled with it. Church Slavonic was declared "sacred" and "saving" because it was "founded and built on the rightness and truth of God's law, and defended by it."[34] Accordingly, declared Vishenskii, "One who desires salvation, or wishes to draw nigh to the saints, without attaining the simplicity and truth of the humble Slavonic language, will attain neither salvation, nor sanctification" ("Zachapka mudrago latynnika z glupym rusinom," Ivan Vishenskii, 1955, pp. 192, 195). Ivan Vishenskii, who came from Ukraine, nevertheless affirmed the Great Russian concept of the Church Slavonic language, and it is understandable that his writings survived primarily in Old Believer manuscripts (Goldblatt, 1991).[35]

If different languages are equal in relation to the content being expressed—equal in the sense that different modes of expression of the same content are possible—then the content appears distanced from the form because it exists by itself and, in principle, does not depend on form. In the opposite case, the form and the content appear intrinsically and immediately interrelated, and there is no content outside some particular expression—that is, content is embodied in form. If the content is abstracted from the form, transmission of the immanent content suggests some conventional rules of expression. Such are the grammatical rules—they enable us, in particular, to translate from one language into another (and it is assumed in this case that the meaning remains constant).

Grammatical rules, however, are necessarily conventional because they open the opportunity to play with meaning or even to construct a new meaning. As a matter of fact, grammar sets out the rules for the composition of the text—*any* text in a given language, without regard to its content. These rules allow for meaning to be manipulated and, thereby, for the world to be modeled. This accounts for the protests against grammars that are typical both for Russian medieval bookmen and for Old Believers (see Uspensky, 1988).

The Nikonian correctors based their revisions upon the grammar of Meletii Smotritskii, and they routinely referred to grammatical rules (see Siromakha, 1979). Meanwhile, for Old Believers, reference to some kinds of rules could in no way serve as a foundation for correcting the divinely revealed text.

According to the medieval notion, the world was a book—that is, a text containing divine meaning in itself. The symbol of the world was a book and not a system of rules, a text and not a model. While grammar gave a particular model of the world, like any model it allowed for the creation of texts that were demonstrably false in their content. Such a notion, even in the West, during the Middle Ages would have associated Latin grammar with the devil, since it could teach people to decline the word *God* in the plural, even though God was surely one. Thus, the use of grammatical rules could create the notion of many gods and, therefore, lead to heresy (see, in particular, the considerations of Petrus Damianus, Migne, CXLV, col. 695). As Gregory the Great wrote, "It is indecent to surrender the words of heavenly revelation to the rules of Donatus" ("indignum vehementer existimo, ut verba coelestis oraculi restringam sub regulis Donati," Migne, LVXX, col. 516).

In much the same way, Old Believers justified their protests against grammar. Thus, for example, the monk Savvatii in his petition to Tsar Aleksei Mikhailovich (1660s) protested the actions of Nikon's correctors, who, when addressing God, consistently changed the second person singular in the aorist form *byst'* to *byl esi* in order to avoid the homonymy of the second- and third-person singular in conjugations of the past tense.[36] According to Savvatii, "These correctors know nothing of grammar, and are wont to define God through their shallow grammar in the past tense, and to ascribe a person to the terrible, ineffable Godhead, where it is not fitting" (*Tri chelobitnye...*, 1862, pp. 22–23). In other words, Savvatii blamed the Nikonian correctors for the fact that they subordinated God's image to a conventional grammatical scheme. The presentation of time and person became conditioned by considerations of grammar.

In contrast, the followers of the new ritual emphasized the conventional character of any expression, of any grammatical form. Characteristic of this view were the arguments of Simeon Polotskii and Archpriest Lazar. Lazar chided Nikon's followers for the fact that in their books it was written that "no one does not believe that Jesus has risen." Lazar responded to this statement by saying, "That is a great source of temptation, for we all believe."[37] Answering this reproach, Simeon Polotskii justified the correctness of the phrase by pointing to the grammatical rules: "That no one does not believe indeed means that everyone believes." Polotskii then advised his opponent to "go learn to deal with grammar first" (Simeon Polotskii, 1667, pp. 100ob.–101; see Subbotin, 1875–1890, IV, pp. 214–215). Simeon Polotskii derived this from Latin grammar, where a double negative makes a positive, whereas in Slavic languages double negation normally emphasizes negation. We know that Polotskii studied Church Slavonic by using Latin grammar—indeed, he drew together Church Slavonic and Latin as bookish languages (Uspensky, 1983, p. 114; also Uspensky, 1987, p. 213). It seems that the followers of the new rituals realized this game of meanings, but it was important for them to destroy the fetishism of form. Meanwhile, from the point of view of Old Believers, such a game of meanings was, in principle, unacceptable.

This explains the protests of the Old Believers against grammar, and also against rhetoric and philosophy. As Archpriest Avvakum taught in his *Kniga tolkovanii,* "Seek neither rhetoric, nor philosophy, nor eloquence, but live according to the right and true word" (Avvakum, 1927, cols. 547–548). In the same manner, Avvakum addressed F. M. Rtishchev: "Christ . . . didn't teach dialectics or rhetoric, for a rhetor and a philosopher cannot be Christian. . . . God reveals the mysteries of Christ to Christians through the Holy Spirit, not through external wisdom" (Demkova, 1974, pp. 388–389). Accordingly, in a letter to one of his spiritual daughters, Avvakum offered the following admonition:

> Evdokeia, Evdokeia, why dost thou not drive the demon of pride from thee? Thou seekest lofty knowledge, from which people fall like leaves, not nourished by God. . . . O foolish, foolish, most foolish one. Why do you, a crow, need a high perch. For grammar and rhetoric one needs the mind of St. Basil the Great, St. John Chrysostom and St. Athanasius of Alexandria. What was needed of both philosophy and dialectics was taken into the church, and what was not was shoveled into a heap of rubbish. Who do

you think you are, O child without strength. No, enough! If you were near
me I would tear out your hair for all that grammar of yours! (Avvakum,
1979, pp. 227–228)

Grammar, rhetoric, dialectics, and philosophy were perceived as one single complex of knowledge—they all appeared as a variety of external wisdom that did not lead to faith but rather led away from it. Thus, the
correcting of sacred texts in accordance with grammatical rules was considered an improper, seductive matter.

At the same time, if language is understood as a means of communication, then it is important to establish certain rules for conveying information— that is, a system that provides for adequate understanding of
content. The system in question would be that conventional code uniting
the sender and receiver of a message. Then it is important to have grammatical rules; the sender and receiver must have the same idea of grammar, and this has to be the basis for their linguistic activity. In this view,
the orientation toward grammar is a necessary condition for using language rightly.

Characteristically, the practice of confession for deaf-mutes in the Russian church was changed after the reforms of Patriarch Nikon. Before,
church procedure emanated from the need of a deaf-mute coming to
church for confession to demonstrate repentance. It was understood that
his coming demonstrated his willingness to confess. Accordingly, the
priest absolved him of his sins and allowed him to receive the Lord's Sacrament (similar to the practice used during the so-called deaf confession,
when administering the sacrament to an unconscious or sick person on
his deathbed). There was no actual communication in this case.[38] From
the second half of the seventeenth century, priests became obliged to
communicate with such a person by gesticulation (Almazov, 1894, II, pp.
22–24, 444–449). Obviously, this manifested a new attitude toward language as a means of communication. The existence of one or another
method of conveying information was perceived as a necessary condition
of communication. This demand to use gestures in such cases apparently
originated in Ukrainian and Belorussian liturgical practices.[39]

The difference in the perception of language before and after the
schism was especially obvious in the attitude expressed toward metaphorical, figurative usage of language. In early Russian spiritual instructions,
one can find direct indications of the sinfulness of such use. Thus, for
instance, we find in Russian penitential books a rule forbidding the expression *dozhd' idet* ("it's raining," or, literally, "the rain goes"). For this,
one was supposed to receive a penance of a hundred prostrations ("Whoever says '*dozhd' idet*' should prostrate oneself a hundred times"—see
Smirnov, 1913, supp. p. 30, no. 30; also p. 154, no. 23; p. 305, art. "e";

p. 185, n. 4). Nevertheless, this was a common idiom, and it was practically impossible to avoid it and escape the sin. Obviously, this phrase was associated with pagan ideas suggesting the personification of acts of nature. Thus, metaphor in this instance actualized pagan beliefs. In the end, using words in their figurative meaning contributed to deviation from Christianity and, consequently, promoted a tendency toward heresy. Here again, modes of expression could themselves be considered non-Orthodox.

Examples of a similar attitude toward metaphorical usage were not at all unusual. There was a special treatise, for instance, asserting that it was wrong to call one another "the sun of righteousness." No mortal beings should be named in such a way, including tsars: "Heed this, beloved brethren, that you never call one another 'the sun of righteousness.' You cannot call by this name an earthly king or an earthly lord, since it is the Lord's name, not appropriate to one who is mortal" (*Let. rus. lit.*, 1859–1863, V, pt. III, pp. 90–93). The expression *solntse pravednoe (sol justitiae)* was used in connection with God (see Malachi 4:2), and by no means could it be used in connection with mortals.[40] Nevertheless, the tsar could sometimes be called by this name, especially after the schism. The first sovereign who was called this was the False Dmitrii (Zhivov and Uspensky, 1987, p. 57). Here, perhaps, was an example of the attitude in southwestern Rus' toward linguistic signs, whereby it was possible to justify the use of sacred language in a figurative sense. In exactly the same way Archpriest Avvakum protested calling the tsars holy. He wrote angrily in his interpretation of the Psalter: "Now they [the Nikonians] have placed things in disorder. They identify a living person as a saint. Thus, in their *Pomiannik* it is written, 'let us pray for the holy sovereign lord tsar' [*pomolimsia o derzhavnom sviatom gosudare tsare*]" (Avvakum, 1927, cols. 465–466). Indeed, starting in the second half of the seventeenth century, sacred appellations for tsars became quite customary.

The attitude toward figurative use of linguistic signs—and, first of all, toward words and expressions with a sacred meaning—changed completely after the schism. In this, the opinions of the Old Believers and the followers of the new rituals differed dramatically. These differing attitudes toward metaphor reflected a difference in cultural traditions between Muscovite and southwestern Rus'. As a result, the same texts could function in different modes. Depending upon the position of the reader, texts could be understood either literally or figuratively. This difference in understanding sometimes caused fierce arguments and resulted in real cultural conflicts (see more detailed treatment in Zhivov and Uspensky, 1983).

An example of this was the argument between the Old Believer Nikita Dobrynin, bearer of the traditional Muscovite attitude toward texts, and

Simeon Polotskii, representative of the new, baroque culture. The subject of their argument was the phrase *Tebe sobesieduiut zviezdy* ("the stars converse with You"), found in the address to God in one of the prayers for the sacrament of baptism in the Nikonian edition of the Prayer Book. In the pre-Nikonian version it had read *Tebe moliatsia zviezdy* ("the stars pray to You"). According to Nikita Dobrynin, such a text should be understood literally. In Nikita's opinion, stars were angels, and angels could only pray to God. They could not converse with God because of their subordinate position. As Dobrynin put it, "The angels are not enthroned with God, but only the Son and the Holy Spirit are. . . . And nowhere can it be found in Scripture that the stars are God's interlocutors" (Rumiantsev, 1916, supp., pp. 339, 258). Answering these arguments, Simeon Polotskii wrote:

> The point here is not about having a communication by tongue or by intellect. The stars have neither mouths, nor minds. They are inanimate objects. . . . As the prayer says, "The sun sings to you; the moon glorifies you." All these words are used here metaphorically. . . . These phrases are not meaningless, but, to reasonable people, beautiful and pleasing. However, to mindless Nikita and his cohorts these references are but seductions. (Simeon Polotskii, 1667, pp. 55–56ob)

Thus, Simeon Polotskii directly demonstrated the possibility of two perceptions of the same text. In this example it is clear how the new concept of a linguistic sign was connected to metaphorical usage.

In the very same way Stefan Iavorskii later justified the necessity of understanding words in their figurative meaning. Furthermore, he considered it possible to approach Holy Scripture in the same way. He argued that the appellation *vselenskii* (ecumenical) in the title of the patriarch of Constantinople did not mean "owning the universe [ecumene]." Iavorskii wrote, "It is a well-known fact that the word *vselennaia* [ecumene] does not always apply to all places in the world, but sometimes refers in a metaphorical way to many places or to a considerable part of the world."[41] He provided examples from the Bible where the word *vselennaia* (universe or ecumene) could not be understood in any literal way. Quoting a phrase from the Gospels, "a decree went out from Caesar Augustus that *all the world* should be registered [Luke 2:1]," Stefan Iavorskii reasoned, "Is all the universe with its inhabitants, countries, towns, kingdoms, etc., under the rule of Caesar Augustus? By no means. For the recently acquired New World, the Indian Kingdom, the Great Tartaria, and many other places did not know of his rule." Iavorskii found other examples of this kind and drew the same conclusion (Gosudarstvennyi Istoricheskii Muzei, Uvar. 1728/378/588, leaf 2ob.-3; Zhivov, forthcoming, 1993).

Thus, the representatives of the Ukrainian tradition in southwestern

Rus' separated the word from its content, making possible the use of a word in its figurative meaning (*tropicheskim razumom*). For Stefan Iavorskii, the text of the Gospel was not, in and of itself, the truth (*glagoly tochiiu, a ne samaia istinna*); the contents of the text were the truth. Therefore, the text came to be open to various interpretations and the truth was determined through correct interpretation—this determined the importance of philological exegesis in a post-Renaissance world view.

In contrast, for the followers of the Great Russian tradition, the Gospels and all of Holy Scripture were God's revealed text, and as such constituted truth, in and of itself. In principle, this did not depend upon a grasp of the subject. Sacred form and sacred content could not, in essence, be divided. One implied the other. From this point of view, truth was connected not with proper interpretation but with the right reproduction of the text.

With the acceptance of Western baroque culture in Russia there appeared the possibility of a twofold reading of one and the same text. What could be understood as a figurative form of speech by some readers could be understood in a literal sense by others. This conflict deepened with time and became especially evident during the period of Peter the Great. When Feofan Prokopovich, for example, unexpectedly confronted Peter during an all-night drinking spree, the former Kievan Academy rector uttered the words of the festal anthem, "Behold, the bridegroom cometh in the night [*Se zhenikh griadet vo polunoshchi*]" (Golikov, 1807, pp. 422–423; Nartov, 1891, p. 73). In such a setting, what some could interpret as metaphorical image, others would find blasphemous. From Peter's time on, this conflict could be thought of as a contrast between Russia and the West, between conservative tradition and innovation. A conventional understanding of the linguistic sign was consciously being planted in Russia as an element of enlightened culture.[42] At the same time, for the followers of traditional culture—and, first of all, for Old Believers—the notion that words changed their meaning, depending upon the context, remained unacceptable.

In this consideration of attitudes toward the linguistic sign, the schism was first and foremost reflected in problems of language. It is in the sphere of language that the semiotic conflict between two cultural traditions was most explicitly revealed. However, this conflict between a conventional and nonconventional understanding of signs also became evident outside the sphere of language. Indeed, the same conflict was evident in the attitude toward visual signs. In icon painting of the second half of the seventeenth century there appeared naturalistic images and illusory effects such as the use of perspective and chiaroscuro, all of which affected perception and, consequently, suggested a conventional approach to signs—in particular to visual symbols. Characteristically, this new manner of icon painting was called *friazhskaia* (literally, Frankish), meaning Western, and it evoked sharp protests from Old Believers. For instance, the Archpriest Avvakum said in his *Beseda o ikonnom pisanii* (Conversation on Icon Painting) that icon painters of the new school depicted saints as living beings, as was done in Western painting:

> They paint the image of Immanuel the Saviour with a swollen face, red mouth, curly hair, fat arms and hands, plump fingers, legs and thighs—all his body fat and bloated, like a foreigner, only without the sword on his thigh. And all is painted in a carnal way, for the heretics love the fat of the flesh. . . . But, our theologians teach us that Christ has a subtle fineness of bearing. . . . And, that dirty dog Nikon, the enemy, has designed it so that one should paint the saints as though they are living, and arrange everything in a Frankish, foreign way. (Avvakum, 1927, cols. 282–283)[43]

Avvakum uttered the same view in his *Beseda o vneshnei mudrosti* (Conversation on External Wisdom): "Look at the sacred icons and behold the saints, how the good icon painters depict their image. The face, the arms, the legs exhausted by fasting, and all their subtle feelings overcome by grief. But you, today, have changed their image and paint them the way you look yourselves, with fat bellies and faces, and with arms and legs like pillars" (Avvakum, 1927, col. 291). It is possible to find an analogous protest against *odebelivaniia ploti* (the fattening of the flesh) in Andrei Denisov's *Pomorskie otvety* (answer 50, article 20), wherein we read: "The contemporary icon painters do not draw icons from the old sacred prototypes of Greek and Russian miracle-working images, but from rational conjurings. They fatten the body of Christ the Saviour, and the saints . . . not according to the ancient sacred icons, but according to the pictures published in Latin and other printed Bibles [i.e., printed engravings], and those painted on canvases" (1884, p. 183). Accordingly, Old Believers refused to venerate the new icons, because from their point of view, living people, and not saints, were represented in them. As the Rostov tailor Sila Bogdashko declared to Metropolitan Iona of Rostov in 1657, "You are portraying your own faces, and your services are no longer services, but games" (Rumiantseva, 1990, p. 31). All these quotations have as their point the naturalism of representation, which in principle is uncharacteristic of icon painting.

A typologically analogous phenomenon could be observed at the same time in the realm of church singing, wherein traditional singing in unison was transformed into singing in parts. The intention was that some external effect would be generated. Especially significant in this respect was the transition from multiple-voiced singing (*mnogoglasie*) to the single voice (*edinoglasie*), and from a traditionally intoned vowel singing (*khomovoe penie*) to singing according to the written text (*narechnoe penie*).

The practice of singing in many voices (*mnogoglasie*) presupposed the conducting at one and the same place of several services—that is, the pronunciation of several chants simultaneously.[44] The appearance of this practice was made necessary by the desire to pronounce all texts prescribed by church regulation. It was understandable that such a practice did little to aid in the reception of these texts. *Khomovoe* singing contrasted with *narechnoe* singing. In *khomovoe* singing the sounds *o* and *e* appeared as substitutes for etymological "jers" (reduced vowels). This was true in both the strong and the weak phonetic positions, where the sounds had long disappeared.[45] For example, the words *Khristos"*, *S"pas"*, and *d'nes'* were formerly pronounced in singing as *Khristoso, Sopaso,* and *denese,* since there were reduced vowels in these words at an earlier time. This pronunciation naturally made it very difficult to comprehend the text.

In the middle of the seventeenth century, singing in *mnogoglasie* was replaced by singing in *edinoglasie*. At the same time *khomovoe* singing was changed to *narechnoe* singing, that is, the pronunciation of words in church singing ceased to differ from the pronunciation in reading. This evoked sharp criticism, and it is particularly significant that both these transitions in church singing came to be joined in the larger cultural perception (see, for example, Rogov, 1973, pp. 81, 87–91).[46] Indeed, both reforms in church singing were very much connected. The transition from *mnogoglasie* to *edinoglasie* and the transition from *khomovoe* to *narechnoe* singing were essentially brought about by a new orientation toward understanding, an orientation suggestive of a conventional attitude toward sacred symbol. In both instances, with respect to the church service, one can see the transition from an internal to an external point of view.

In reality, under the conditions of *mnogoglasie* what was really important was to pronounce (reproduce) the sacred text, regardless of how well this text could be understood by those in the church. The church service was understood as communion with God, not with humankind, and consequently its real importance lay in the objective meaning of voiced text, as distinct from the subjectivity of its external perception. The church service addressed God, and this circumstance alone eliminated the difficulties of communication. In modern usage, there was intended an ideal channel of communication—and there obviously was to be no technical difficulty while communicating with God! Meanwhile, the transition to *edinoglasie* singing and reading was undoubtedly tied to the fact that the worship service had become oriented not only toward God but also toward the person standing in the church.[47] This circumstance, quite naturally, called attention to and exacerbated the problem of communication, shifting the focus to the reception of the service.

Quite identical was the transition from *khomovoe* singing to a much more easily understood *narechnoe* singing. In this sense, both transitions came to be treated as a variant of one and the same dilemma. Both *kho-movoe* singing and *mnogoglasie* were equated in the seventeenth century, although in reality they were two different phenomena. It is quite possible that with the elimination of *khomovoe* singing, all kinds of glossolalic elements present in earlier church singing vanished (see Metallov, 1912, p. 122; Smolenskii, 1901, p. 98). In a sense, both *khomovoe* singing and *mnogoglasie* can be regarded as a kind of glossolalia—that is, as text that is apprehended more by God than by man. For an external audience would have been unable to understand it.

Just as the language of church service was likened to the language of angels, the archetypal form of sacred language (compare the words of Avvakum quoted above), so church singing was likened to "angelic-voiced singing." According to Orthodox conceptions, during the service the church was considered an earthly heaven, a temporary embodiment of God's kingdom.[48] By extension, church singing could be likened to an angelic doxology and the singers themselves to angels. This notion was explicitly expressed in the *Kheruvimskaia pesn'* (The Song of the Cherubs) that begins the Orthodox Liturgy of the Faithful.[49] Glossolalic singing elements could be identified directly with the exultation of the heavenly hosts.[50] The idea of angelic-voiced singing inspired by the Holy Spirit was not compatible with conventional modes of expression, which one way or another were oriented toward perception.[51]

Finally, the conflict between conventional and unconventional understandings of signs also revealed itself during this same period in the theatrical sphere. Thus, the theatrical performances on sacred topics put on in Moscow during the time of Tsar Aleksei Mikhailovich were perceived by Old Believers as blasphemy. They rejected in principle the conditional character of theatrical depiction. Archpriest Avvakum directly blamed the tsar as the initiator and organizer of these performances, indicating that in doing so, he was equating himself with God. Comparing Aleksei Mikhailovich to Nebuchadnezzar, who considered himself equal to God ("I am the Lord. Who is equal to me? Only the Father in Heaven. He rules in heaven; I on earth"), Avvakum said, "Today similar things occur. A peasant, having been costumed as the Archangel Michael and having found himself in a palace, was asked, 'who are you and from where have you come'? He answered, 'I am the captain of the Lord's power. I was sent to you, great lord.' This is how he was infected, possessed by Satan's power, the archangel of darkness. He was ruined both in body and soul" (Avvakum, 1927, col. 466).

From Avvakum's point of view, both the person who depicted Archangel Michael and the tsar who participated in that performance destroyed their souls. Thus, the anonymous Old Believer "Appeal from a Spiritual Son to His Confessor" (1676) declared the death of Aleksei

Mikhailovich. The addressee of the appeal, perhaps the Archpriest Avva-kum, tied the sickness and death of the tsar particularly to the fact that, using sacred themes, he "entertained himself with all manner of amuse-ments and plays":

> Utterly shocking were the plays they performed—like those about the cre-ation of the world, the Flood, the events before and during the life of Christ, His miracles, etc. [reference here is to the theatrical scenes from the Old and New Testaments]. . . . And all was against the letter [*pisma*, i.e., Holy Scripture]. . . . This is what was performed in these plays—the cru-cifixion of Christ, his burial, his descent into Hades and his ascension into Heaven. And even the non-Orthodox were surprised by these plays and said, "There are in our countries such plays, called comedies, but not among very many of the confessions." How strange and frightening it is to hear that a simple peasant in Christ's image is nailed to a cross, a crown of thorns is put on his head, and a bladder with blood is hidden under his armpit so that he bleeds between the ribs when stabbed. Moreover, instead of the image of the Virgin, a foreign damsel with loose hair weeps; and instead of John the Theologian being summoned, the body of Christ is handed over to a young beardless man. (Bubnov and Demkova, 1981, 143)

The obvious reference here was to the theatrical mystery depicting Christ's passion. This kind of performance was accepted at the Mohyla Academy in Kiev and from there found its way to Moscow. The perfor-mance had its origin in the Polish Jesuit theater. The Old Believer atti-tude toward the theatrical performance of sacred themes resembled their attitude toward the use of metaphor in sacred texts.

In all these cases one can clearly see an unconventional attitude toward the sacred sign typical of traditional Russian culture as preserved among Old Believers. Theirs is the experience of the sacred sign as of something unconditioned and indeterminate, not dependent upon observers for its existence. With such an understanding, if one manipulates these signs, plays with them, endows them with new meaning, places them in a new order, it happens only in the world of appearances. For, in reality, there is a deeper tie between the sacred sign and its significance, and humanity becomes but a toy in the hands of otherworldly forces. In this con-text, performances of sacred themes, as pious as they might seem, are diabolical plots. Broadly speaking, the same can be said of all signs in-fused with sacred content when used as conditional, conventional modes of expression.

NOTES

1. It should be pointed out that the Psalter was not only a liturgical book but an instructional guide as well, for it was used particularly to

study language. Therefore, editions of the Psalter were normally accompanied by instructive lessons.

2. This prayer ("Lord and master of my life. . ."), which is regularly read during Lent, has special significance in the Orthodox service.

3. At the base of Lazar's suggestion there apparently rested the practice of burning heretics at the stake. His death at the stake symbolically would signify that he was a heretic. Being confident in his rectitude, Lazar reckoned that the Lord would not permit this to happen.

4. In this the Old Believers preserved the older Greek finger configuration that had been changed by the Greeks themselves. The two-fingered sign of the cross was practiced in Byzantium at the time of the baptism of Rus' and was borrowed together with other Christian rituals by the Russians (Kapterev, 1913, pp. 73ff., 231ff.; Golubinskii, 1905, pp. 158ff.; Sobolevskii, 1909, pp. 4–6). Thus, historically the matter was really that of the opposition of the older to the new Greek rite. In the actual consciousness of that time, however, the opposition was perceived as that of the Russian and Greek traditions.

5. This correction may be looked upon as both a textological and a linguistic key. The Nikonian version corresponds verbatim to the Greek text of the Creed, and thus the absence of a conjunction in the corrected Church Slavonic text is justified by the absence of a conjunction in the original Greek text. On the other hand, Nikon's opponents considered that in Church Slavonic, in contrast with the Greek language, there could not be an asyndetic combination of homogeneous parts of the sentence, for asyndesis, in their opinion, assumed either hypotaxis or contiguity. Consequently, the elimination of the conjunction, according to Old Believers, essentially changed the meaning of the Creed (see Mathiesen, 1972, pp. 45–46; Uspensky, 1987, pp. 314–316).

6. Just as in the controversy of the iconoclasts and icon worshipers, there was not so much a difference of attitude toward the icon as such as there was a difference of attitude toward the sacred sign.

7. The innovations discussed by Avraamii in a number of cases were not included in the final Nikonian edition of the Creed—that is, they reflect an interim stage of correction.

8. See the answer of Simeon Polotskii in *Zhezl' pravleniia* (Simeon Polotskii, 1667, leaf 151).

9. See Avvakum's *Poslanie k neizvestnym* (Borozdin, 1898, supp., p. 42) and the petition of Nikita Dobrynin (Subbotin, 1875–1890, IV, pp. 138, 152; Rumiantsev, 1916, pp. 462, 466–467, 495, and supp. pp. 340, 354). As a result, the use of one or another form—the genitive or the dative case— could be interpreted generally as a diagnostic sign of the truth or falsehood of the corresponding text. Thus, Andrei Denisov in his polemical letters sought to repudiate the evidence of several early printed books of Ukraine precisely because of the use of *vo vieki viekov,*

and not *vo vieki viekom* (Smirnov, 1909a, p. 195). Two hundred years later, for the very same reason, participants at the first council of Pomorskie Old Believers doubted the authenticity of the musical texts from the epoch of Ivan the Terrible (Deianiia, 1909, p. 63, second pagination).

10. The characteristic justification for the impossibility of any would-be deviations from the canonical form of the sacred text was contained in the answers of the Old Believers of the Nizhnii-Novgorod region, responding in 1719 to the questions of the Nizhegorod and Alator Archbishop Pitirim (the so-called "Pitirim" or "Kerzhen" or "D'iakonov" answers [*D'iakonovy otvety*]—authorship of which is attributed to Andrei Denisov; see *Kerzhenskie otvety,* 1906).

11. For the typical relationship of the early Russian scribe to his transcribed text, see the manuscripts of Arsenii Glukhoi, particularly the revealing introduction to his transcribed Canon of 1616 (Ilarii and Arsenii, 1878–1879, II).

12. See, in particular, such works as the treatise concerning the eight parts of speech, "Beseda o uchenii gramote," Iosif Volotskii's "Prosvetitel'," and Zinovii Otenskii's "Istiny pokazanie k voprosivshim o novom uchenii" (Jagic, 1896, pp. 40–41, 47, 362, 385–388; Sukhomlinov, 1908, p. 352; Dmitrieva, 1979, pp. 210, 224, 241, 251, 264; Subbotin, 1875–1890, VIII, p. 219).

13. In this same regard, there is the widely held notion of thought as the sound of the heart (Toporov, 1973, pp. 140–141).

14. Nikon conveys these words in his counterarguments to S. L. Streshnev (see Nikon, 1861, p. 490). According to Paisii Ligarid, Nikon refused to listen to his speech in Latin and announced that Latin was a "cursed" language of pagans (Makarii, 1857–1883, XII, pp. 451–453). See also the description of this incident by Nicolaas Witsen (1966–1967, pp. 209, 446).

15. According to Witsen, Russians used to say that "Latin is a heretical language because God does not speak in this language" (Witsen, 1966–1967, p. 446). This declaration should perhaps more precisely be understood to mean that Latin does not adequately convey Christ's teaching.

16. For the contrast of Greek and Church Slavonic, on the one side, and Latin, on the other, see Zakharii Kopystenskii's preface (1623) to his translation of John Chrysostom's interpretation of the epistles of the apostle Paul. Greek and Church Slavonic are recognized as languages that adequately express Orthodox theological thought, while Latin, in the opinion of Kopystenskii, is not able to convey such content (see Titov, 1916–1918, supp., p. 74).

17. Arguments regarding the superiority of Church Slavonic over Latin go back to the tale of the monk Khrabr, *O pismenekh,* a particularly popular work among Russian readers between the fifteenth and

seventeenth centuries. See note 35 below.

18. It is curious that further on, the same Luk'ian Golosov became famous for his knowledge of Latin (see Witsen, 1966–1967, pp. 176–177, 211, 221; Reitenfel's, 1905, pp. 98–99). Reitenfel's points out that knowledge of Latin brought Golosov "a lot of worry and misfortune" (p. 160). From 1653, Luk'ian Golosov was a sexton in the patriarch's office. Thus, he was serving directly under Nikon. In the 1680s he wrote poems in the spirit of Simeon Polotskii. It seems that he undoubtedly became, in the end, a follower of Nikon's cultural reforms (see Bogoiavlenskii, 1946, p. 247; Veselovskii, 1975, pp. 122–123; Panchenko, 1973, pp. 110–111).

19. These quotations have come down to us from the *Delo po donosu chernetsa Saula na boiar Ivana Vasil'evicha Zasetskogo . . . chto oni k nemu v kel'iu prikhodili i proeretichestvo govorili*. On this affair, see Solov'ev, 1962–1966, V, pp. 491–492; Makarii, 1857–1883. XI, pp. 134–136; Kharlampovich, 1914, pp. 135–136. See also in this connection the petition of Stefan Vonifat'ev (10 October 1650) asking that Ivan Zaretskii and his friends from the Greek-Latin school be sent to monasteries for refusing to study Latin (Rumiantsev, 1916, p. 35).

20. For the later Westernized (Latinized) pronunciation of the name Iov, see the late-eighteenth-century poem of Ia. V. Kniazhnin, *Popugai* (Kniazhnin, 1961, pp. 710–711).

21. Regarding possible authorship of this tract, there are various opinions. Usually the names of the monk Evfimii and Nikolai Spafarii have been mentioned (see Kapterev, 1889, pp. 69–98; Mirkovich, 1878, p. 31; Brailovskii, 1889, pp. 280–281; Smentsovskii, 1899, p. 32; Mikhailovskii, 1900, pp. 4–11; Florovskii, 1949, p. 123).

22. In this latter composition there is noted, among other things, the particular danger of Latin as a first foreign language. Acquaintance with Latin apparently could not harm one who already knew Greek (Kapterev, 1889, p. 96). The thought that one should not know Latin without first knowing Greek was also expressed by the Likhud brothers in *Akos* in 1687 (Prozorovskii, 1896, pp. 562–563; Smentsovskii, 1899, pp. 274–275), as well as later by the Chudov archdeacon Damaskin in his objection to the composition of Gavriil Dometskii in 1704 (Obraztsov, 1865, p. 91).

23. Peter signed his name "Petrus" (Petros) or "Piter." Regarding Peter the Great as Antichrist, see Uspensky, 1976a.

24. The new form, *Iisus* (instead of the old form *Isus*), adopted during the patriarchate of Nikon, could be regarded by Old Believers as the title for the Antichrist (see Smirnov, 1898; Uspensky, 1989, p. 214).

25. See in this regard the affair regarding a written agreement with Satan (1725). The agreement was written in blood and "in the Latin dialect" (Peretts, 1907, pp. 37–39). Witsen (1966–1967, p. 444) reports

on the occasion when a person who knew Latin and owned a globe was accused of sorcery and beaten with a whip. In the same manner Old Believers reacted to the title "emperor" that Peter the Great adopted in 1721. In 1855, the Old Believer I. M. Ermakov testified, "I do not consider [the newly crowned] Aleksandr Nikolaevich an emperor, but a tsar. . . . The title 'emperor' was taken by Peter the Great from the impious and satanic Roman pope" (Kel'siev, 1860–1862, I, p. 220).

26. For Sumarokov's observations on Latin and Greek in the reign of Peter the Great, see his *Slovo pokhval'noe o Gosudare Imperatore Petre Velikom* (1787, II, pp. 222–223).

27. In the diary of S. Maskevich there is the record (under the year 1611) of the boyar Fedor Golovin, who secretly studied Latin and German. Golovin told Maskevich "that he had a brother who had a strong predilection for foreign languages, but was unable to study them. In order to do so, he secretly kept at his house a German who lived in Moscow. He also found a Pole who knew Latin. Both of them would come secretly to him dressed in Russian clothes, lock themselves in the room and together read Latin and German books" (Ustrialov, 1859, I, pp. 55–56).

28. In the *Privilegiia* of the Academy collected in 1682–1685 and entrusted to the regent Tsarina Sofiia Alekseevna in January 1685, study of foreign languages was strictly regarded. Under penalty of confiscation of private property, it was forbidden to study languages on one's own (DRV, 1788–1791, VI, p. 409). Thus, studying foreign languages, even with the establishment of special schools for that purpose, continued to be regarded as a dangerous matter requiring extreme precautions.

29. According to Georgius David, in 1686 the Jesuit Ioannes Schmid was in danger of exile because he taught boyars' children Latin (David, 1965, p. 46). Similarly, Fedor Polikarpov, who in 1701 published a Slavonic-Greek-Latin primer, considered it important to include a special warning to the reader, despite the fact that the primer was composed under Peter the Great's directive (Polikarpov, 1701, preface, leaf 3ob.).

30. This is perhaps the same episode Samuel Collins had in mind when he stated that in 1560 the school for Latin language studies was established in Moscow, only to be destroyed by the Moscow clergy (Kollinz, 1846, p. 1). Collins in any case is mistaken on the date.

31. It is impossible not to recall in this connection the verse of Mandel'shtam regarding the study of foreign languages: "Do not tempt foreign dialects, but try to forget them. . ." [*Ne iskushai chuzhikh narechii, no postaraisia ikh zabyt'*]. Mandel'shtam's poem is dedicated, on the whole, to another theme, but it is remarkable that this poet, who is so sensitive to language, introduces religious terminology here, using to good effect precisely the religious connotations of this theme. He uses

the verb "to tempt" (*iskushat'*), but every temptation comes from the devil. Mandel'shtam's image is very traditional, corresponding to that tradition according to which language study is, indeed, a sinful seduction, leading away from God's revealed word.

32. Referring to the "natural Russian language," Avvakum has in mind Church Slavonic, which he does not set in opposition to spoken Russian. Indeed, the phrase from the prayerful Church Slavonic address, "Lord, have mercy upon me, a sinner" [*Gospodi, pomilui mia grieshnago!*], also is used in Russian. The identification of Church Slavonic as "Russian" is quite usual for Great Russian bookmen.

33. Unusually descriptive in this sense is the book *Rafli,* which was really a fortune-telling and astrological guide composed in 1579 by Ivan Rykov (*Uchenie raflem, siirech' sviattsam raznym strannym, prevedeno po slovenskomu iazyku*). The compiler of this book totally understands the pagan origins of the teaching described in it, but he also is aware of the fact that this teaching is being blessed by the Slavonic language in which it is embodied. Describing the procedure of fortune-telling by ancient pagan sages, Ivan Rykov translates pagan terms into Slavonic, suggesting to his reader that pagan wisdom is, in effect, sanctioned by the church when rendered in Slavonic (Turilov and Chernetsov, 1985, pp. 299, 303, 308, 309). It was, in this sense, entirely logical that citations from Holy Scripture and the prayer book be incorporated into what, by origin, was a pagan text.

34. In just the same way Church Slavonic literacy could be called "sacred," "the Lord's," or "divine" in popular *byliny,* traditional Russian heroic poems (Markov, 1901, pp. 256, 269, 297).

35. It was important in this matter that, like the Moscow bookmen, Ivan Vishenskii could set off Church Slavonic not only against Latin but also against Greek (Ivan Vishenskii, 1955, p. 24). The view that Church Slavonic was more sacred than Greek goes back to a well-known treatise by Khrabr, *O pismenekh.* Khrabr's argument focused on the point that Greek was created by pagans but Church Slavonic by the sainted apostles Cyril and Methodius. Russian authors appealed to this argument quite often. Thus, Epifanii the Wise, in his *Zhitie Stefana Permskogo,* maintains with Khrabr that Slavonic writing is most honorable, more than Greek (Kushelev-Bezborodko, 1860–1862, IV, p. 153). This opinion takes on special meaning after the Florentine union (1439) and the subsequent fall of Constantinople (1453), when Russians began to think that Greeks were corrupted in their faith. For the fall of the Byzantine Empire came to be viewed precisely as punishment for the act of treason toward Orthodoxy (see Uspensky, forthcoming 1993). In the original Russian collection, known under the title *Skazanie o slavianskoi pis'mennosti,* which became part of the *Tolkovaia Paleia* of 1494, Russian writing, along with Russian faith, was considered divinely revealed and independent of Greek

mediation (see Mareš, 1963, pp. 174–175). The fact that Church Slavonic biblical texts were translated by saints served Zinovii Otenskii as an argument against the corrections of the *Simvol very* proposed by Maksim Grek (Zinovii Otenskii, 1863, pp. 961–967). Echoes of the work of Khrabr are often found in the writings of Old Believer authors—in particular, in the appeals of the monk Savvatii or of Archpriest Avvakum to Tsar Aleksei Mikhailovich (Uspensky, 1987, pp. 233–234).

36. The forms of the second and third persons singular coincide in the paradigms of the aorist and imperfective, and thus the form *byst'* can mean both "you were" and "he was." For that reason, the Nikonian correctors introduced the perfective form (of the type *byl esi*) as a form for the second person. The same principle of avoiding homonymy reverberated in the grammatical tradition of the sixteenth and seventeenth centuries. This is particularly seen in the work of Maksim Grek and in the grammar of Meletii Smotritskii, both of whom were followed by the Nikonian correctors (see Uspensky, 1987, p. 151).

37. See also the petition of the monk Antonii to Tsar Aleksi Mikhailovich (Subbotin, 1875–1890, VIII, p. 116). There is the following phrase in one of the illuminations from an edited publication of the *Shestodnev: Iako Khristos voskrese, nikto zhe da ne vieruet* (Shestodnev, 1660, leaf 248ob.; Shestodnev, 1663, leaf 259ob.).

38. See, in this same regard, the instruction of Metropolitan Fotii to Pskov priests in the first half of the fifteenth century (RFA, 1986–1988, III, p. 500). One must bear in mind that in Russian liturgical practice, confession and receipt of the sacrament of the Eucharist are directly connected. In other words, the receipt of God's sacrament implies having made a confession. Accordingly, in Russian prayer books of the sixteenth and first half of the seventeenth centuries, there are special articles such as "Permission to the Mute and Deaf" or "Order How to Confess the Deaf or Mute Person Who Is Unable to Answer for Himself" (Almazov, 1894, III, pp. 8–9 of second pagination). A similar article exists in the printed Moscow Prayer Book of 1639 but is already missing in the Prayer Book of 1651.

39. See, in this regard, the Prayer Book of Peter Mohyla of 1646 (Almazov, 1894, II, p. 446).

40. In just the same way it was not acceptable during baptism to name someone *Iisus* in honor of Christ or *Mariia* in honor of the Mother of God, and likewise unacceptable to give the names of the most honored saints (Uspensky, 1989, pp. 39–40).

41. Iavorskii uses the expression *tropicheskii razum* to refer to this metaphorical or figurative use of language. The expression *tropicheskii razum* draws semantically from the Latin calque *sensum tropicum*.

42. In 1704, on the occasion of the conquest of Livonia, when a triumphal entry of Petr into Moscow was arranged, Iosif Turoboiskii,

dean of the Moscow Slavonic-Greek-Latin Academy, who compiled the description of this ceremony, specifically explained that this ceremony, despite its wide use of religious symbols, had no religious significance. Turoboiskii emphasized the metaphorical nature of the images used and insisted in general on the necessity and lawfulness of a metaphorical approach to meaning. In doing so he pointed to the existence of metaphors in Holy Scripture (Grebeniuk, 1979, pp. 154–155).

43. To be fair, it must be clarified that Nikon himself was against the new manner of icon painting. He did not consider such images to be icons and ordered them to be destroyed or repainted (see, in particular, the testimony of Pavel Aleppskii, 1894–1900, III, pp. 136–137). For Nikon, the icons were "not painted according to fatherly tradition," and were in the form of Catholic paintings (see Gibbenet, 1882–1884, II, pp. 473–475; Gibbenet, 1882–1884, I, p. 20; Solov'ev, 1962–1966, V, pp. 619–630). As can be seen, the position of Nikon on this matter does not differ from that of Avvakum. Thus, Nikon's approach to the visual symbol was different from his position with respect to the linguistic sign.

44. *Mnogoglasie* as a liturgical term pertaining to the church service should not be confused with the purely musical term *mnogogolosie* (polyphony).

45. Until the twelfth century, "jers" (the hard and soft signs) in Russian were pronounced as special reduced vowels. Later, significant restructuring of the phonetic system occurred, such that in certain positions (the so-called strong syllables) the hard and soft signs were transformed into vowels of full formation. Thus, in the strong syllables, the hard sign was transformed into *o* and the soft sign into *e*. In other positions (in the so-called weak syllables), the sounds disappeared. This process, which started in the spoken language, impacted church reading. Meanwhile, in church singing, this vocalization of reduced vowels could, in principle, be noticed in all syllables, both strong and weak. This was conditioned by the conservatism of church songs. In the spoken language, the dropping of the hard and soft signs in weak syllables reduced the number of syllables. But in the choral tradition, where reducing the number of syllables would lead to distortion of the melodic line, the vowels were retained. The result was the separation of the choral tradition from church reading. In practice, the very same words came to be pronounced differently in reading than in singing (Uspensky, 1988a).

46. For declarations against *edinoglasie,* see Belokurov, 1894; Kapterev, 1908; "Rassprosnye rechi . . . ," 1861, pp. 394–395. For declarations against *narechnoe* singing, see Uspensky, 1971, pp. LXVII–LXIX.

47. Not coincidentally, it was during that same period, particularly in the second half of the twelfth century, that the sermon was introduced (see Uspensky, 1987, pp. 282–283; Shliapkin, 1891, pp. 103, 108; Nikol'skii, 1901, pp. 4–5).

48. This Orthodox view of the church carried with it ramifications for behavior in church. There are numerous references to this view of the church as the embodiment of God's kingdom. See, for example, the epistle of Kirill Belozerskii to Prince Andrei Dmitrievich Mozhaiskii at the beginning of the fifteenth century (Buslaev, 1861, col. 930). On behavior in church, see, for example, the instruction of the Stoglav Sobor of 1551 (Stoglav, 1890, p. 160).

49. We constantly find comparison of church singing with heavenly singing in the works of Byzantine authors—for example, Maximos the Confessor or John Chrysostom. Angel singing stands here as the archetype of the singing intoned during the worship service. The relationship of church and angelic singing corresponds, then, to the relationship of image and original form in iconographic depiction (see Vladyshevskaia, 1990).

50. Thus, inserted syllables—*na-ne-na* (so-called *anenaiki*)—sometimes get special interpretation among Old Believer singers, who think that here the speech of the Mother of God is being depicted. In particular, the *anenaiki* of the Assumption hymn of praise is interpreted as the exultation of the Mother of God (Uspensky, 1971, p. LXX). Much the same interpretation is found in Greek singing (Voznesenskii, 1895–1896, I, p. 103; Preobrazhenskii, 1924, p. 37).

51. This orientation of early church art toward God, not human beings, is also seen in architecture (see Ioffe, 1944, pp. 238–239; Uspensky, 1976b, p. 38). This has not always been taken into consideration by restorers whose work may arise out of new aesthetic principles. Thus, restorers of the Dmitrovskii Sobor in Vladimir in 1837–1839 eliminated additions to that church on the grounds that these additions were located on the outside walls of the main building of the temple and therefore were not able to be perceived. Meanwhile, recent research has shown that these additions were constructed more or less simultaneously with the main building (Voronin, 1961–1962, I, pp. 420–421). The circumstance that certain images were not readily accessible for perception did not, evidently, trouble the ancient artist. His primary interest was not in perception but in expression. The very fact of the existence of the image already had an objective meaning, one that was in principle independent of its perception.

REFERENCES

Alekseev, 1862. Alekseev, F. "Iz istorii nashikh dukhovnykh shkol," *Pravoslavnoe obozrenie* (oktiabr' 1862).

Almazov, I–III. Almazov, A. I. *Tainaia ispoved' v pravoslavnoi vostochnoi tserkvi: Opyt vneshnei istorii. Issledovanie preimushchestvenno po rukopisiam.* T. I–III. Odessa, 1894.

AMG, I–III. *Akty moskovskogo gosudarstva, izdannye imperatorskoiu aka-demieiu nauk.* T. I–III. Spb., 1890–1891.

Antonii, 1899. *Kniga Palomnik: Skazanie mest sviatykh vo Tsaregrade An-toniia Arkhiepiskopa Novgorodskogo v 1200 godu.* Ed. Kh. M. Loparev. In *Pravoslavnyi palestinskii sbornik,* T. XVII, vyp. 3 (51), 1899.

Avvakum, 1927. *Pamiatniki istorii staroobriadchestva,* kn. 1, vyp. 1 ("Soch-ineniia protopopa Avvakuma"). L., 1927 (*Russkaia istoricheskaia bib-lioteka,* T. XXXIX). Avvakum, 1979. *Zhitie protopopa Avvakuma, im samim napisannoe, i drugie ego sochineniia.* Irkutsk, 1979.

Barskov, 1912. Barskov, Ia. L. *Pamiatniki pervykh let russkogo staroobriad-chestva.* Spb., 1912.

Belokurov, 1894. [Belokurov, S. A.]. "Deianie moskovskogo tserkovnogo sobora 1649 goda (Vopros o edinoglasii v 1649–1651 gg.)," *Chteniia obshchestva istorii i drevnostei rossiiskikh,* kn. 4, 1894.

Bogoiavlenskii, 1946. Bogoiavlenskii, S. K. *Prikaznye sud'i XVII veka.* M.-L., 1946.

Borozdin, 1898. Borozdin, A. K. *Protopop Avvakum: Ocherk iz istorii umstvennoi zhizni russkogo obshchestva v XVII veke.* Spb., 1898.

Brailovskii, 1889. Brailovskii, S. "Otnosheniia chudovskogo inoka Evgimiia k Simeonu Polotskomu i Sil'vestru Medvedevu (Stran-ichka iz istorii prosveshcheniia v XVII stoletii)," *Russkii filolo-gicheskii vestnik,* no. 4, 1889.

Bubnov and Demkova, 1981. Bubnov, N. Iu., and N. S. Demkova. "Vnov' naidennoe poslanie iz Moskvy v Pustozersk 'Vozveshchenie ot syna dukhovnogo ko ottsu dukhovnomu' i otvet protopopa Avvakuma (1676 g.)," *Trudy otdela drevnei russkoi literatury,* T. XXXVI, 1981.

Buslaev, 1861. Buslaev, F. *Istoricheskaia khristomatiia tserkovnoslavianskogo i drevnerusskogo iazykov.* M., 1861.

Bylinin and Grikhin, 1987. Bylinin, V. K., and V. A. Grikhin, compilers and commentators. *Satira XI–XVII vekov* ("Sokrovishcha drevnerusskoi literatury"). M., 1987.

David, 1965. David, Georgius, S. J. *Status modernus Magnae Russiae seu Moscoviae* (1690). Edited with intro. and explanatory index by A. V. Florovskij (*Slavistic Printings and Reprintings,* vol. LIV). London-The Hague-Paris, 1965.

Deianiia, 1909. *Deianiia pervago vserossiiskago sobora khristian-pomortsev, priemliushchikh brak, proiskhodivshago v tsarstvuiushchem grade Moskve v leto ot sotvoreniia mira 7417 v dni s 1 po 12.* M., 1909.

Demkova, 1974. Demkova, N. S. "Iz istorii rannei staroobriadcheskoi lit-eratury," *Trudy otdela drevnerusskoi literatury.* T. XXVIII, 1974.

Dmitrieva, 1979. Dmitrieva, R. P., ed. *Povest' o Petre i Fevronii.* L., 1979.

DRV, I–XX. *Drevniaia rossiiskaia vivliofika, soderzhashchaia v sebe Sobranie drevnostei rossiiskikh, do istorii, geografii i genealogii rossiiskiia kasaiu-*

shchikhsia, izdannaia Nikolaem Novikovym. 2d ed. Ch. I–XX. M., 1788–1791.

Florovskii, 1949. Florovskii, A. "Chudovskii inok Evfimii: Odin iz poslednikh pobornikov 'grecheskogo ucheniia' v Moskve v kontse XVII veka," *Slavia,* 1949, nos. 1–2.

Gibbenet, I–II. Gibbenet, N. *Istoricheskoe issledovanie dela patriarkha Nikona.* Ch. I–II. Spb., 1882–1884.

Goldblatt, 1991. Goldblatt, N. "On the Reception of Ivan Vyšenskyj's Writings among the Old Believers." *Harvard Ukrainian Studies,* vol. XV, 1991, no. 3–4.

Golikov, 1807. Golikov, I. I. *Anekdoty, kasaiushchiesia do Gosudaria Imperatora Petra Velikogo.* 3d ed. M., 1807.

Golubinskii, 1905. Golubinskii, E. "K nashei polemike s staroobriadtsami (Dopolneniia i popravki k polemike otnositel'no obshchei ee postanovki i otnositel'no glavneishikh chastnykh punktov raznoglasiia mezhdu nami i staroobriadtsami)," *Chteniia obshchestva istorii i drevnostei rossiiskikh,* kn. 3, 1905. Golubtsov, 1890. G[olubtso]v, A. "Sud'ba Evangeliia uchitel'nogo Kirilla Trankvilliona-Stavrovetskogo," *Chteniia v obshchestve liubitelei dukhovnogo prosveshcheniia,* no. 4, 1890.

Gorskii and Nevostruev, I–III. Gorskii, A. V., and K. I. Nevostruev. *Opisanie slavianskikh rukopisei moskovskoi sinodal'noi biblioteki.* Otd. I–III. M., 1855–1917.

Grebeniuk, 1979. Grebeniuk, V. P., ed. *Panegiricheskaia literatura petrovskogo vremeni.* M., 1879.

Iakhontov, 1883. Iakhontov, I. K. *Ierodiakon Damaskin, russkii polemist XVII veka.* Spb., 1883.

Ilarii and Arsenii, I–III. [Ieromonakh Ilarii i ieromonakh Arsenii]. *Opisanie slavianskikh rukopisei biblioteki sviato-troitskoi sergievoi lavry.* Ch. I–III. M., 1878–1879.

Ioffe, 1944. Ioffe, I. I. "Russkii renessans," *Uchenye zapiski Leningradskogo Gosudarstvennogo Universiteta,* Seriia filologicheskikh nauk, vyp. 9, 1944.

Ivan Vishenskii, 1955. Ivan Vishenskii. *Sochineniia.* Edited, with commentary by I. P. Eremin. M. - L., 1955.

Jagic, 1896. Jagic, V., comp. and ed. *Codex slovenicus rerum grammaticarum (Razsuzhdeniia iuzhnoslavianskoi i russkoi stariny o tserkovnoslavianskom iazyke).* Petropoli, 1896.

Jakobson, 1971. Jakobson, R. "Shifters, Verbal Categories, and the Russian Verb," in Roman Jakobson, *Selected Writings,* II: *Word and Language.* The Hague-Paris, 1971.

Jakobson and Halle, 1962. Jakobson, R., and M. Halle. "Phonology and Phonetics." In Roman Jakobson, *Selected Writings,* I: *Phonological Studies.* 'S-Gravenhage, 1962.

138   BORIS A. USPENSKY

Kantemir, I–II. Kantemir, A. D. *Sochineniia, pis'ma i izbrannye perevody* (*C portretom avtora, so stat'eiu o Kantemire i s primechaniiami V. Ia. Stoiunina*). Ed. P. A. Efremov. T. I–II. Spb., 1867–1868.

Kapterev, I–II. Kapterev, N. F. *Patriarkh Nikon i Tsar' Aleksei Mikhailovich.* T. I–II. Sergiev Posad, 1909–1912. Reprint from *Bogoslovskii Vestnik,* 1908–1911.

Kapterev, 1889. Kapterev, N. F. "O greko-latinskikh shkolakh v Moskve v XVII veke do otkrytiia Slaviano-Greko-Latinskoi Akademii." In *Godichnyi akt v Moskovskoi Dukhovnoi Akademii 1-ogo oktiabria 1889 goda.* M., 1889.

Kapterev, 1892. Kapterev, N. F. "Suzhdenie bol'shogo moskovskogo sobora 1667 goda o vlasti tsarskoi i patriarshei (K voprosu o preobrazovanii vyshego tserkovnogo upravleniia Petrom Velikim)," *Bogoslovskii vestnik* (oktiabr' 1892).

Kapterev, 1908. Kapterev, N. F. "Bor'ba kruzhka revnitelei blagochestiia s patriarkhom Iosifom po voprosu o edinoglasii," *Bogoslovskii vestnik* (aprel' 1908).

Kapterev, 1913. Kapterev, N. F. *Patriarkh Nikon i ego protivniki v dele ispravleniia tserkovnykh obriadov: Vremia patriarshestva Nikona* (S prilozheniem: "Otvet professoru Subbotinu"). 2d ed. Sergiev Posad, 1913.

Karamzin, I–XII. Karamzin, N. M. *Istoriia gosudarstva rossiiskogo.* Tt. I–XII. Spb., 1892.

Kel'siev, I–IV. *Sbornik pravitel'stvennykh svedenii o raskol'nikakh, sostavlennyi V. Kel'sievym.* Vyp. I–IV. London, 1860–1862.

Kerzhenskie otvety, 1906. *Otvety Aleksandra diakona (na Kerzhentse), podannye Nizhegorodskomu episkopu Pitirimu v 1819 [1719] godu.* [Nizhnii Novgorod, 1906] (Prilozhenie k zhurnalu *Staroobriadets,* 1906).

Kharlampovich, 1914. Kharlampovich, K. V. *Malorossiiskoe vliianie na velikorusskuiu tserkovnuiu zhizn'.* T. I. Kazan', 1914.

Kniazhnin, 1961. Kniazhnin, Ia. B. *Izbrannye proizvedeniia.* Edited, with an introduction and commentary by L. I. Kulakova (*Biblioteka poeta,* bolshaia seriia). L., 1961.

Kollinz, 1846. Kollinz, S. "Nyneshnee sostoianie Rossii, izlozhennoe v pis'me k drugu, zhivushchemu v Londone (Perevod s angliiskogo Petra Kireevskogo s izd. 1671 g.)," *Chteniia obshchestva istorii i drevnostei rossiiskikh,* kn. 1, 1846.

Kotoshikhin, 1906. Kotoshikhin, Grigorii. *O Rossii v tsarstvovanie Alekseia Mikhailovicha.* 4th ed. Spb., 1906.

Kushelev-Bezborodko, I–IV. *Pamiatniki starinnoi russkoi literatury, izdavaemye Grigoriem Kushelevym-Bezborodko.* Vyp. I–IV. Spb., 1860–1862.

Let. rus. lit., I–IV. *Letopisi russkoi literatury i drevnosti.* Edited by N. S.

Tikhonravov. T. I–IV. M., 1859–1863.

Lileev, 1880. Lileev, M. I. "Opisanie rukopisei, khraniashchikhsia v biblioteke Chernigovskoi dukhovnoi seminarii." Spb., 1880. Reprint from *Pamiatniki drevnei pis'mennosti*, T. 6.

Lotman and Uspensky, 1973. "Mif-imia-kul'tura," *Trudy po znakovym sistemam*. Vol. VI, Tartu, 1973 (*Uchenye zapiski Tartuskogo universiteta*, vyp. 308).

Makarii, I–XII. Makarii (Bulgakov). *Istoriia russkoi tserkvi*. T. I–XII. Spb., 1857–1883.

Maresh, 1963. Maresh, V. F. "Skazanie o slavianskoi pis'mennosti (po spisku Pushkinskogo doma AN SSSR)," *Trudy otdela drevne-russkoi literatury*, T. XIX, 1963.

Markov, 1901. Markov, A. V. *Belomorskie byliny*. M., 1901.

Mathiesen, 1972. Mathiesen, Robert Christian. "The Inflectional Morphology of the Synodal Church Slavonic Verb." Ph. D. Diss. Columbia University, 1972.

Metallov, 1912. Metallov, V. M. *Bogosluzhebnoe penie russkoi tserkvi v period domongol'skii po istoricheskim, arkheologicheskim i paleograficheskim dannym*. M., 1912 (*Zapiski imp. moskovskogo arkheologicheskogo instituta*, T. XXVI).

Migne, I–CCXXI. Migne, J. P., ed. *Patrologiae cursus completus*. Series latina. T. I–CCXXI. Paris, 1844–1864.

Mikhailovskii, 1900. Mikhailovskii, I. N. "O nekotorykh anonimnykh proizvedeniiakh russkoi literatury kontsa XVII i nachala XVIII stoletiia." In *Sbornik istoriko-filologicheskogo obshchestva pri Institute kn. Bezborodko v Nezhine*, T. III. Nezhin, 1900.

Mirkovich, 1878. Mirkovich, G. "O shkolakh i prosveshchenii v patriarshii period," *Zhurnal ministerstva narodnogo prosveshcheniia* (iiul' 1878).

Nartov, 1891. Maikov, L. N., ed. *Rasskazy Nartova o Petre Velikom*. Spb., 1891.

Nikol'skii, 1896. Nikol'skii, K. *Materialy dlia istorii ispravleniia bogosluzhebnykh knig: Ob ispravlenii Ustava tserkovnogo v 1682 godu i mesiachnykh Minei v 1689–1691 gg*. Spb., 1896.

Nikol'skii, 1901. Nikol'skii, N. K. *Istoricheskie osobennosti v postanovke tserkovno-uchitel'skogo dela v Moskovskoi Rusi (XV–XVII vv.) i ikh znachenie dlia sovremennoi gomiletiki*. Spb., 1901.

Nikon, 1861. "Mnenie patriarkha Nikona ob Ulozhenii i proch. (iz otvetov boiarinu Streshnevu)," *Zapiski otdeleniia russkoi i slavianskoi arkheologii imperatorskogo russkogo arkheologicheskogo obshchestva*. T. II. Spb., 1861.

Nikon, 1982. *Patriarch Nikon on Church and State: Nikon's "Refutation"* ["Vozrazhenie ili razorenie smirennago nikona, Bozhieiu milostiiu patriarkha, protivo voprosov boiarina Simeona Streshneva, ezhe

napisa Gazskomu mitropolitu Paisiiu Likaridiusu i na otvetu
Paisiovy"]. Edited, with introduction and notes by Valerie A. Tu-
mins and George Vernadsky. Berlin, New York, Amsterdam, 1982
(Slahvistic Printings and Reprintings, vol. CCC).

Obraztsov, 1865. Obraztsov, I. "Arkhimandrit Gavriil Dometskii i ierodiakon Damaskin," *Dukhovnaia beseda*, nos. 1–3, 1865.

Ognev, 1880. Ognev, V. *Stranitsy iz istorii knigi na Rusi.* Viatka, 1880.

Panchenko, 1973. Panchenko, A. M. *Russkaia stikhotvornaia kul'tura
XVII veka.* L., 1973.

Pavel Aleppskii, I–IV. "Puteshestvie antiokhiiskogo patriarkha Makariia
v Rossiiu v polovine XVII veka, opisannoe ego synom, arkhi-
diakonom Pavlom Aleppskim (Perevod s arabskogo G. Murkosa),"
Chteniia obshchestva istorii i drevnostei rossiiskikh, kn. 4, 1896; kn. 4,
1897; kn. 3–4, 1898; kn. 2, 1900.

Peretts, 1907. Peretts, V. N. "Iz istorii starinnoi russkoi povesti, I–XIII,"
Universitetskie izvestiia, nos. 8–9, 1907.

Petukhov, 1888. Petukhov, Evgenii. *Serapion Vladimirskii, russkii propoved-
nik XIII veka.* Spb., 1888 (*Zapiski istoriko-filologicheskogo fakul'teta
S.-Peterburgskogo Un-ta*, ch. XVII).

Polikarpov, 1701. [Polikarpov, Fedor]. *Bukvar' slavenskimi, grecheskimi,
rimskimi pismeny, ouchitisia khotiashchym i liubomudrie v polzu dushe-
spasitelnuiu obresti tshchashchymsia.* M., 1701.

Polikarpov, 1704. [Polikarpov, Fedor]. *Lexikon treiazychnyi, sirech' rechenii
slavenskikh, ellinogrecheskikh i latinskikh sokrovishche . . .* M., 1704.

Polotskii, 1667. [Simeon Polotskii]. *Zhezl pravleniia: na pravitel'stvo
myslennago stada pravoslavnorossiiskiia tserkve. Outverzheniia: vo
utverzhenie koleblilushchikhsia vo vere. Nakazaniia: v' nakazanie ne-
pokorivykh ovets. Kazneniia: na porazhenie zhestokovyinykh i khishchnykh
volkov, na stado Khristovo napadaiushchikh.* M., 1667.

Pomorskie otvety. *Pomorskie otvety.* Manuilovskii Nikol'skii Monastyr',
1884.

Preobrazhenskii, 1924. Preobrazhenskii, A. V. *Kul'tovaia muzyka v Rossii*
(*Russkaia muzyka*, vyp. II). L., 1924.

Prozorovskii, 1896. Prozorovskii, A. "Sil'vestr Medvedev, ego zhizn' i deiatel'nost'," *Chteniia obshchestva istorii i drevnostei rossiiskikh*, 1896,
kn. 2–4.

Rassprosnye rechi . . . "Rassprosnye rechi o edinoglasii (1651 goda),"
*Zapiski otdeleniia russkoi i slavianskoi arkheologii imperatorskogo
russkogo arkheologicheskogo obshchestva.* T. II. Spb., 1861.

Reitenfel's, 1905. Reitenfel's, Iakov. *Skazaniia svetleishemu gertsogu tos-
kanskomu Koz'me Tret'emu o Moskovii (Paduia 1680).* Trans. into
Russian from the Latin by A. I. Stankevich. M., 1905.

RFA, I–IV. *Russkii feodal'nyi arkhiv XIV - pervoi treti XVI veka.* Vyp. I–
IV. M., 1986–1988.

Rogov, 1973. Rogov, A. I., comp. and trans. *Muzykal'naia estetika Rossii XI XVIII vekov*. M., 1973.

Rumiantsev, 1916. Rumiantsev, Ivan. *Nikita Konstantinov Dobrynin* (*"Pustosviat"*): *Istoriko-kriticheskii ocherk*. Sergiev Posad, 1916.

Rumiantseva, 1986. Rumiantseva, V. S. *Narodnoe antitserkovnoe dvizhenie v Rossii v XVII veke*. M., 1986.

Rumiantseva, 1990. Rumiantseva, V. S., comp. *Dokumenty Razriadnogo, Posol'skogo, Novgorodskogo i Tainogo prikazov v gorodakh Rossii 1654–1684gg*. M., 1990.

Selishchev, 1920. Selishchev, A. M. *Zabaikal'skie staroobriadtsy: Semeiskie*. Irkutsk, 1920.

Shestodnev, 1660. *Shestodnev*. M., 1660.

Shestodnev, 1663. *Shestodnev*. M., 1663.

Shliapkin, 1891. Shliapkin, I. A. *Sv. Dimitrii Rostovskii i ego vremia* ("Zapiski istoriko-filologicheskogo fakul'teta Sankt-Peterburgskogo un-ta," ch. XXIV). Spb., 1891.

Siromakha, 1979. Siromakha, V. G. "Iazykovye predstavleniia knizhnikov Moskovskoi Rusi vtoroi poloviny XVII v. i 'Grammatika' M. Smotritskogo," *Vestnik moskovskogo universiteta*, Series 9: *Filologiia*, no. 1, 1979.

Smentsovskii, 1899. Smentsovskii, M. *Brat'ia Likhudy: Opyt issledovaniia po istorii tserkovnogo prosveshcheniia i tserkovnoi zhizni kontsa XVII i nachala XVIII vekov*. Spb., 1899.

Smirnov, 1855. Smirnov, Sergei. *Istoriia Moskovskoi Slaviano-Greko-Latinskoi Akademii*. M., 1855.

Smirnov, 1895. Smirnov, P. S. *Istoriia russkogo raskola staroobriadstva*. 2d ed. Spb., 1895.

Smirnov, 1898. Smirnov, P. S. *Vnutrennie voprosy v raskole v XVII veke: Issledovanie iz nachal'noi istorii raskola po vnov' otkrytym pamiatnikam, izdannym i rukopisnym*. Spb., 1898.

Smirnov, 1909. Smirnov, P. S. "Perepiska raskol'nicheskikh deiatelei nachala XVIII veka," *Khristianskoe chtenie*, nos. 1–3, 1909.

Smirnov, 1909a. Smirnov, P. S. "Vzgliad raskola na perezhivaemoe vremia v pervoi chetverti XVIII veka," *Khristianskoe chtenie*, no. 5, 1909.

Smirnov, 1913. Smirnov, S. "Drevnerusskii dukhovnik: Issledovanie po istorii tserkovnogo byta," *Chteniia obshchestva istorii i drevnostei rossiiskikh*, 1912–1914.

Smolenskii, 1901. Smolenskii, St. *O drevnerusskikh pevcheskikh notatsiiakh* ("Pamiatniki drevnei pis'mennosti i iskusstva," CXLV). Spb., 1901.

Smolenskii, 1910. Smolenskii, S. V. *Musikiiskaia grammatika Nikolaia Diletskogo*. Spb., 1910.

Sobolevskii, 1909. Sobolevskii, A. I. "Dvuperstie, suguboe alliluiia i khozhdenie posolon' s istoricheskoi tochki zreniia." In *Trudy tret'ego oblastnogo istoriko-arkheologicheskogo s"ezda, byvshego v g. Vladimire 20–26 iiunia 1906 g.* Vladimir, 1909.

Solov'ev, I–XV. Solov'ev, S. M. *Istoriia Rossii s drevneishikh vremen.* kn. I XV. M., 1962–1966.

Stoglav, 1890. *Tsar'skiia voprosy i sobornyia otvety o mnogorazlichnykh tserkovnykh chinekh (Stoglav).* M., 1890.

Subbotin, I–IX. Subbotin, N. I., ed. *Materialy dlia istorii raskola za pervoe vremia ego sushchestvovaniia.* T. I–IX. M., 1875–1890.

Sukhomlinov, 1908. Sukhomlinov, M. I. *Issledovaniia po drevnei russkoi literature.* Spb., 1908.

Sumarokov, I–X. Sumarokov, A. P. *Polnoe sobranie vsekh sochinenii v stikhakh proze.* Collected and edited by Nikolai Novikov. 2d ed. M., 1787.

Tatishchev, 1979. Tatishchev, V. N. *Izbrannye proizvedeniia.* Ed. by S. N. Valk. L., 1979.

Titov, 1916–1918. Titov, Feodor. *Tipografiia Kievo-Pecherskoi lavry: Istoricheskii ocherk, 1606–1616–1916 gg.* T. I. Kiev, 1916; Prilozhenie k pervomu tomu (Kiev, 1918).

Toporov, 1973. Toporov, V. N. "O dvukh praslavianskikh terminakh iz oblasti drevnego prava v sviazi s indoevropeiskimi sootvetstviiami." In *Strukturno-tipologicheskie issledovaniia v oblasti grammatiki slavianskikh iazykov.* M., 1973.

Tri chelobitnye... Kozhanchikov, D. E., ed. *Tri chelobitnye: Spravshchika Savvatiia, Savvy Romanova i monakhov Solovetskogo monastyria (Tri pamiatnika iz pervonachal'noi istorii staroobriadstva).* Spb., 1862.

Turilov and Chernetsov, 1985. Turilov, A. A., and A. V. Chernetsov. "Otrechennaia kniga Rafli," *Trudy otdela drevnerusskoi literatury,* T. XL. 1985.

Uspenskii, 1969. Uspenskii, B. A. *Iz istorii russkikh kanonicheskikh imen (Istoriia udareniia v kanonicheskikh imenakh sobstvennykh v ikh otnoshenii k russkim literaturnym i razgovornym formam).* M., 1969.

Uspenskii, 1971. Uspenskii, B. A. *Knizhnoe proiznoshenie v Rossii (Opyt istoricheskogo issledovaniia).* Doctoral Disseration, Moscow University, 1971 [typescript].

Uspenskii, 1976. Uspenskii, B. A. *Historia sub specie semioticae: Kul'turnoe nasledie Drevnei Rusi (Istoki, stanovlenie, traditsii).* M., 1976.

Uspenskii, 1976a. Uspensky, Boris. *The Semiotics of the Russian Icon.* Lisse, The Netherlands, 1976.

Uspenskii, 1983. Uspenskii, B. A. "Iazykovaia situatsiia Kievskoi Rusi i ee znachenie dlia istorii russkogo literaturnogo iazyka." In *IX Mezhdunarodnyi s"ezd slavistov: Doklady.* M., 1983.

Uspenskii, 1987. Uspenskii, B. A. *Istoriia russkogo literaturnogo iazyka (XI XVII vv.).* Munich, 1987 ("Sagners Slavistische Sammlung," Bd. 12).

Uspenskii, 1988. Uspenskii, B. A. "Otnoshenie k grammatike i ritorike v Drevnei Rusi (XVI–XVII vv.)." In *Literatura i iskusstvo v sisteme kul'tury.* M., 1988.

Uspenskii, 1988a. Uspenskii, B. A. "Russkoe knizhnoe proiznoshenie XI–XII vv. i ego sviaz' s iuzhnoslavianskoi traditsiei (Chtenie erov)." In *Aktual'nye problemy slavianskogo iazykoznaniia.* M., 1988.

Uspenskii, 1989. Uspenskii, B. A. "Iazykovaia situatsiia i iazykovoe soznanie v Moskovskoi Rusi: Vospriiatie tserkovnoslavianskogo i russkogo iazyka." In *Vizantiia i Rus'* (*Pamiati Very Dmitrievny Likhachevoi, 1937–1981*). M., 1989.

Uspenskii, forthcoming. Uspenskii, B. A. "Vospriiatie istorii v drevnei Rusi i kontseptsiia "Moskva - Tretii Rim," forthcoming.

Ustrialov, I–II. [Ustrialov, N.]. *Skazaniia sovremennikov o Dimitrii Samozvantse.* 3d ed. Ch. I–II. Spb., 1859.

Veselovskii, 1975. Veselovskii. *D'iaki i pod'iachie XV–XVII vv.* M., 1975.

Vladyshevskaia, 1990. Vladyshevskaia, T. F. Bogodukhnovennoe angeloglasnoe penie v sisteme srednevekovoi muzykal'noi kul'tury: Evoliutsiia idei." In *Mekhanizmy kul'tury,* M., 1990.

Voronin, I–II. Voronin, N. N. *Zodchestvo severo-vostochnoi rusi XII–XV vekov.* T. I–II. M., 1961–1962.

Voznesenskii, I–II. Voznesenskii, Ioann. *O penii v pravoslavnykh tserkvakh grecheskogo vostoka s drevneishikh do novykh vremen: S prilozheniem vizantiiskogo tserkovnogo osmoglasiia.* Ch. I–II. Kostroma, 1895–1896.

Witsen, 1966–1967. Witsen, Nicolaas. "Moscovische reyse 1664–1665," *Journaal en aentekeningen.* Uitgegeven door Th. J. G. Locher en P. de Buck, deel I–III. 'S-Gravenhague, 1966–1967 (*Werken uitgegeven door de Linschoten-Vereeniging,* LXVI–LXVIII), continuous pagination in all three numbers.

Zabelin, I–II. Zabelin, I. E. *Opyty izucheniia russkikh drevnostei i istorii.* Ch. I–II. M., 1872–1873.

Zhivov, forthcoming. Zhivov, V. M. "Neizvestnoe sochinenie mitropolita Stefana Iavorskogo kak pamiatnik tserkovnoi mysli epokhi petrovskikh preobrazovanii," forthcoming.

Zhivov and Uspensky, 1983. Zivov, V. M., and B. A. Uspensky. "Zur Spezifik des Barock in Russland (Das Verfahren der Aquivokation in der russischen en Poesie des 18. Jahrhunderts)." In *Slavische Barockliteratur,* II: *Gedenksschrift für Dmitrij Tschizewskij.* Munich, 1983 (*Forum slavicum,* Bd. 54).

Zhivov and Uspensky, 1987. Zhivov, V. M., and B. A. Uspensky. "Tsar' i Bog: Semioticheskie aspekty sakralizatsii monarkha v Rossii." In *Iazyki kul'tury i problemy perevodimosti.* M., 1987.

Zinovii Otenskii, 1863. Zinovii [Otenskii]. *Istiny pokazanie k voprosivshim o novom uchenii* (Supplement to the journal, *Pravoslavnyi sobesednik*). Kazan', 1863.

Interpreting the Fate of Old Believer Communities in the Eighteenth and Nineteenth Centuries

*I*nterpreting the history of Old Belief presents many challenges. Apart from the inherent complexity of the movement—if we can use so neat a label—historians must wrestle with the ideological assumptions and loyalties of earlier generations of scholars and publicists; for their writings in large measure still shape our varied understandings of the Old Believers' aspirations and our explanations of their fate.

In his brilliant essay "The Old Believers and the New Religion," Michael Cherniavsky argued that literature on Old Belief falls into two basic categories, both well-established by the end of the nineteenth century: the monographs and source publications of Eastern Orthodox church historians and the writings of the populists. The former, he argued, viewed Old Belief as a rebellion against the authority of the Russian Orthodox church arising from "ignorance and obscurantism, the mistaking of ritual for substance."[1] Within this framework, Orthodox scholars published editions and studies of Old Believer writings on issues of theology, liturgy, and canon law that remain indispensable to scholars of the movement.[2]

The populists saw Old Belief not primarily as a rebellion against ecclesiastical authority but as an expression of the social and political protest of the lower classes of the Russian Empire, stated, to be sure, in the ideological coin of the realm, the language of Eastern Orthodox Christianity. Beginning with A. P. Shchapov, populist writers concentrated on the geographical spread and social composition of the adherents of Old Belief, the ways in which they structured their economic and social life, their relations with the imperial government, and the periodic revolts against its authority.[3] Understandably the populist tradition retains its appeal in Russia and abroad. The radicals of the mid-nineteenth century first drew attention to the connection between devotion to Old Belief and regional loyalties in the European north—the Urals and Siberia and the Cossack lands—and underlined the fact that the overwhelming majority of the movement's adherents were peasants or merchants. Moreover, the populists gave close attention to the explicit and implicit ways in which the Old Believers' words and actions constituted a radical critique of the government and social order of imperial Russia. As they wrestle with these issues, all living scholars are Shchapov's heirs.

At the same time, the populist mode of explanation has distinct limitations. As we listen to the Old Believers speak through their elaborate "book culture" and their autobiographical statements, they remind us that, in spite of their biases, the ecclesiastical historians were also partly correct. To judge by their manuscript books, the Old Believers spent a great deal of time and energy creating a rigorous and satisfying system of worship and attempting to solve a bewildering array of canonical and theological problems that arose from their peculiar position as Eastern Orthodox Christians alienated from the system of authority of the official Orthodox Church. In the first years of the twentieth century and again in recent decades, archaeographers have collected thousands of manuscripts on these themes from all corners of Russia.

The populist tradition contains other traps as well. Since its adherents regard Old Belief as an expression of the latent radicalism of the masses, they tend to undervalue the more conservative tendencies in the movement. Priestly Old Believers (*popovtsy*) often seem less significant or authentic than the priestless (*bezpopovtsy*). Old Believers who reluctantly made their peace with the imperial authorities appear less admirable than radicals who held out to the bitter end.[4] Similarly, the populist system of values tends to give greater moral weight to peasant Old Believers than to the merchants and other townspeople who played leading roles in the movement's later history. Taken together, these ideological commitments and emotional attachments produce a neat—and misleading—pattern of historical evolution. The first generation of Old Believers established a tradition of resolute opposition to official church, state, and society; as time passed, more and more of their heirs made their peace with the demands of the government and the realities of everyday life, leaving the defense of the tradition of militancy to groups like the *stranniki* (wanderers) on the radical fringe of the movement. Yet the history of the major Old Believer communities of the eighteenth and nineteenth centuries suggests that reality was a good deal more complicated.

Since Cherniavsky wrote in 1966, a number of scholars have attempted to find a creative middle ground between the two traditional models.[5] In a book that is only now receiving the recognition it deserves, Serge Zenkovsky argued that the Old Believer movement grew out of and embodied a striving for religious renewal, a desire to rekindle the devotion of clergy and laypeople to the worship and way of life of Russian Orthodoxy.[6] With the recovery of religious identity, Zenkovsky's work is available to readers in the former Soviet Union where, by definition, most discussion of the meaning of Old Belief will take place.

In recent years, many Russian scholars have also attempted to transcend the old dichotomies in the recovery of religious identity. I. V. Pozdeeva and her associates at Moscow University are attempting to reconstruct traditional Russian spiritual and material culture through detailed multidisciplinary study of an isolated region in the upper Kama Valley.[7] Like their fellow archaeographers in other centers, the Moscow group has assembled a remarkable collection of old printed books and manuscripts, preserved or written by the Old Believers, as well as other objects. At the same time, the approach of the Moscow group raises significant questions. As critics have suggested, Pozdeeva tends to equate the book culture of the Old Believers, the central focus of her own studies, with traditional Russian culture as a whole. Moreover, working in a peasant setting that would have delighted the populists, she concentrates on the "core" of traditional spiritual culture—the same liturgical, theological, and devotional texts around which the ecclesiastical historians of the nineteenth century built their studies.[8]

In a very different vein, the groups of scholars in Novosibirsk and Ekaterinburg approach the Old Believers as one manifestation of the ideology and culture of the peasants, industrial workers, and merchants of the Urals and Siberia. In this respect, they remain heirs of the populist tradition. At the same time, they give careful attention to the ideological implications of the texts they study and, in connecting them to the social milieu from which they came, succeed, in considerable measure, in avoiding the teleological and moralizing tendencies of earlier populism.[9]

The proponents of all three of these approaches recognize that, as Cherniavsky put it, "the *Raskol* [Schism] developed and expressed its ideology in the language of religion" and that "this theological or religious language, like all language, possessed a logic of its own."[10] In spite of their obvious differences, all serious contemporary scholars of Old Belief have accepted the task of studying this language, the convictions it expressed, and the ways in which it shaped the modes of thought and manner of life of the believers who used it. Recent work indicates, moreover, that while "This language is not ours today . . . ," it is less remote from us than Cherniavsky implied.[11]

Comprehending this language demands further work on a number of problems. First, we must continue the efforts of the ecclesiastical historians in analyzing, editing, and publishing the most important liturgical, historical, and polemical works of the Old Believers. Second, following the populists' lead, historians of Old Belief must continue their explorations of the complex interconnection between the liturgical practices and the ideological and theological convictions of the various groups that constituted the movement, and the social origins of those groups' leaders and adherents.

Finally, we must address the dilemmas familiar to historians of "popular religion" or "popular culture" in early modern Europe. As it survives into the twentieth century, Old Belief poses these issues in particularly vexing form. Contemporary ethnographers and archaeographers encounter cultural systems, now preserved mainly among peasants and the urban working class, in which liturgical texts and elaborate, archaic polemical and devotional writings serve as a unifying element and a link with tradition. What these texts mean to the men and women who read, copy, and preserve them remains, in some measure, a mystery. Has that meaning changed from one generation to another? How do the language and messages of these texts fit into the fabric of daily life and the attitudes of the bearers of these traditions? We have much work ahead.

The history of the most important Old Believer communities offers yet another vantage point from which to study the movement without succumbing to the extremes of either nineteenth-century tradition. Yet this subject has received relatively little attention, particularly in recent years.[12] The sole exception is the Vyg community, the most important center of priestless Old Belief from the first years of the eighteenth century until the reign of Catherine II, and an important cultural and organizational force until the officials and gendarmes of Nicholas I finally destroyed it in the 1850s.[13] In addition, some recent historians of industrial development and urban life in the late eighteenth and nineteenth centuries have discussed the Old Believer centers in Moscow that suddenly became prominent in the reign of Catherine II.[14] Otherwise, pre-Revolution Russian publications—ecclesiastical and populist—still provide the most useful information on the later history of Old Belief and of the communities that served as its lighthouses.

In spite of the paucity of scholarly research on these issues, several general patterns of historical development are clear and familiar. First, from the very beginning, Old Belief brought together under one banner a wide variety of regional, social, and cultural forces.[15] Over time, the movement became ever more divided and diverse.[16] In particular, the priestless groups in which each man and woman was, by default, his or her own priest repeatedly quarreled and broke apart over canonical or liturgical issues. At the same time, all of the main groups that made up the movement shared a number of characteristics, among them the urge to establish quasi-monastic communities as sources of leadership and authority for their adherents.

The pattern of continuous fragmentation had an ambiguous impact on the historical fate of the Old Believers. The divisions within the movement prevented—and still prevent—the Old Believers from addressing the outside world with a single voice. At the same time, the lack of a single organizational structure, combined with their tradition of individual and local initiative and their networks of personal contacts, has made them extremely flexible and resilient in the face of persecution.

Second, the most important Old Believer communities were very complex organizational structures that combined features of monastic and lay styles of life.[17] Moreover, given their size and visibility, the principal Old Believer communities developed complex and shifting relationships with the imperial government and the increasingly secular society beyond their walls. Most of them—Vyg and the Moscow and St. Petersburg communities, for example—had little choice but to reach a modus vivendi with the imperial authority and endure the bitter attacks of their more radical brothers and sisters for their accommodation with the powers of the Antichrist.[18] At the same time, these increasingly respectable communities remained highly ambivalent toward the imperial authorities.[19] In their practical dealings with officialdom, their conduct was profoundly manipulative.[20]

As recent archaeographers have emphasized, the principal Old Believer communities served as focal points of a complex and sophisticated cultural system—or systems. Vyg not only produced a number of the classic texts defending the "old faith" but also, through its scriptoria and workshops, served as a veritable publishing house.[21] The distinctive and elegant manuscripts from Vyg became the treasured possessions of Old Believers throughout the Russian Empire.[22] Vyg also produced large numbers of icons and other devotional objects for the scattered Old Believer communities of the empire. In the late eighteenth and early nineteenth centuries, the Moscow centers likewise distributed liturgical books and icons to their adherents throughout Russia.[23]

Finally, as visible centers of a movement of opposition within an absolute monarchy, the main Old Believer communities depended for their survival on the willingness of the state to tolerate their continued existence. From the beginning of the movement's history until the relatively tolerant reigns of Catherine II (1762–1795) and Alexander I (1801–1825), government and official church took the initiative on most important issues and the Old Believers reacted to their policies. The unavoidably but frustratingly passive stance of their leaders toward the powers of this world helps to explain why, in the course of Old Believer history, many individuals and small groups took extraordinary measures to provoke confrontation with the agents of the imperial government.

In the last years of Alexander's reign and especially under the regime of Nicholas I (1825–1855), the relations between the Old Believers and the state became considerably more complicated. The Old Believers continued to see themselves as victims of governmental repression. From the perspective of the imperial government and the official Orthodox church, however, Old Belief was a powerful subversive force, actively proselytizing among the Orthodox population with promises of both spiritual and material reward, and building its own religious and social institutions to undermine the established order in church and state.[24]

Since the existence of the most important communities depended on the inefficiency, venality, repression, or tolerance of the government and its agents, we would do well to review the changes of imperial policy toward religious dissent. The general outlines of that policy are well known. In the last half of the seventeenth century, the Russian state and the official church attempted to destroy the conservative opposition to recent changes in liturgy, church governance, administrative practice, legal and social relations, and high culture. At first haphazard, the crusade against Old Belief became a war of extermination during the regency of Sophia. The decree of December 1684 made it plain that any Old Believers who did not submit to the discipline of the official church were to be destroyed.[25] Left with no other means to defend their convictions, thousands of Old Believers fled beyond the borders of the empire or escaped this world altogether through self-immolation.

Peter I's policies toward the Old Believers were far more complex. In the early years of his reign, mobilizing the nation for war with Sweden occupied all of his energies. Under these conditions, he treated the Old Believers pragmatically, tolerating communities like Vyg that could contribute to the war effort.[26]

At the same time, Peter savagely defended the honor of his office. His secret agents ferreted out all critics of the regime, Old Believers or not, and subjected them to unspeakable tortures.[27] Moreover, as the years passed, Peter increasingly became aware that Old Belief inevitably included a dimension of political opposition, and that even the most respectable individuals and communities could not be trusted entirely. Accordingly, he took steps to isolate Old Believers from the rest of the population by decreeing that they register with the government; wear beards, old-fashioned clothes, and an identifying medal; and pay double the usual capitation tax for this dubious privilege.[28] His government also supported the missionary campaign of the official church, designed to win ordinary Old Believers back to the fold by exposing their leaders' ignorance in a series of obligatory public debates. Under these conditions, the main concentrations of Old Believers underwent different fates. The Vyg community met the challenges and thrived. At the other extreme, the Kerzhenets settlements in the Nizhnii Novgorod region succumbed to the pressure of officials and missionaries, and their inhabitants scattered.

Peter's odd combination of tolerance and repression remained the norm through the middle decades of the eighteenth century. If anything, the regime of Empress Anna attempted to apply his legislation more rigorously than he himself had done, and added the requirement that the Old Believers provide military recruits along with the rest of the population.[29] Her government and that of Elizabeth remained sensitive to any evidence that the Old Believers did not recognize the legitimacy of their rule. Accordingly, when an informer revealed that the members of the Vyg community did not pray for the monarch during their worship, the government launched an extensive investigation. With the existence of their community at stake, the leaders of Vyg capitulated and agreed to pray for the ruler—a decision that infuriated a number of their most militant followers, led by Elder Filipp, who seceded to form their own communities and carry on the struggle against the power of the Antichrist.[30]

The reigns of Peter III and Catherine II were a veritable golden age of Old Belief. Acting on the Enlightenment notion that religious toleration was both morally sound and practically useful, the two monarchs drastically changed official policy toward religious dissenters. In his brief reign, Peter ordered officials to halt the persecution of Old Believers and invited the inhabitants of the refugee communities in Vetka, just across the Polish border, to return to the empire. After seizing the throne, Catherine systematically repealed earlier punitive legislation and allowed Old Believers to live and worship openly as long as they did not directly challenge her power or commonly accepted standards of morality.[31] Accordingly, older Old Believer communities thrived, and large and vital centers of the movement emerged in Moscow and St. Petersburg. Indeed, given their central location, size, wealth, and extensive charitable activities, the Preobrazhenskoe and Rogozhskoe Kladbishcha in Moscow soon became the institutional hubs of the movement throughout the empire.[32]

The reign of Nicholas I brought unmitigated disaster to the Old Believers' quasi-monastic communities. Although the emperor's policy toward other adherents of the movement was inconsistent, he and his officials hounded the main Old Believer centers mercilessly.[33] First to feel the pressure were the Irgiz communities near Saratov, home of the descendants of former residents of Vetka who had returned to Russia. The local governor, Prince A. B. Golitsyn, forced their leaders to accept the authority of the hierarchy of the official church (the so-called *edinoverie*), then closed the unofficial monasteries and convents and dispersed their inhabitants.[34] In the last, most repressive years of Nicholas's reign, the main Old Believer centers in Moscow and St. Petersburg suffered a parallel fate. Local officials dispersed the monks and nuns who lived in them, took over the management of their charitable activities, and converted the chapels to official Orthodoxy (the *edinoverie*).[35]

The final agony of Vyg, already in decline, was particularly painful. The local representatives of the imperial bureaucracy, particularly Prince A. V. Dashkov, subjected the community to unremitting pressure through a combination of bureaucratic pedantry and brutal insensitivity. At his most heavy-handed, for example, he ordered a midwife to examine the nuns of the Leksa convent to determine which of them were virgins. One by one, the community lost its rights, its lands, and many of its people, who were repatriated to their native villages, to be replaced by poor non–Old Believer peasants from another part of the country. At the height of "Mamai's devastation," officials knocked down all but one of the chapels in the settlements and made it an Orthodox church.[36]

The zeal with which Nicholas and his officials dogged the Old Believer communities appears puzzling at first glance. In hindsight, the centers of the old faith appear to have provided useful social services to the community and, at worst, to have threatened no one. Why, then, were they persecuted with such doggedness? Part of the answer probably lies in the eagerness of ambitious officials to overfulfill their bureaucratic norms in carrying out a policy of which Nicholas I himself clearly approved.

Much more was involved, however. Going to such trouble to destroy the Old Believer communities indicated that the government found them subversive. And, in the perfect autocracy of Nicholas I, subversive they were. First of all, as self-established settlements that, in various combinations, included features of monasteries and lay settlements, the Old Believer centers did not fit any bureaucratic pigeonhole, ecclesiastical or secular. Moreover, in a supreme act of defiance, the priestly Old Believers, after many futile attempts, succeeded in 1846 in establishing their own hierarchy at Belaia Krinitsa, on Austrian territory.[37] By creating their own institutions, then, the Old Believers challenged the neat administrative categories of the empire.

Second, instead of gradually disappearing with the passing of time, as earlier rulers had hoped, the Old Believers appeared to be growing steadily in numbers in the first decades of the nineteenth century. According to one view, the Old Believer population of the empire reached its highest point before the mid-nineteenth century in the 1820s.[38] The extent to which the apparent increase in numbers reflected the conversion of adherents of official Orthodoxy or simply the increasingly open allegiance of previously secret Old Believers is hard to determine. Without question, agents of the government and the official church believed that conversions from Orthodoxy accounted for the phenomenon. In addition, as the secular and ecclesiastical administrations improved their recordkeeping, officials became increasingly aware of the large number of *poluraskolniki*, Old Believers who masqueraded as members of the official Orthodox Church in order to avoid the sanctions against open adherents of the old faith.[39]

In other ways as well, they threatened the emperor's beloved ideals of Orthodoxy, autocracy, and nationality. The actions and reactions of officials indicate some of the features of Old Believer life that particularly shocked them. Simply by existing, of course, they challenged the monopoly of the official Orthodox church. Moreover, even the most respectable Old Believers continued to question the legitimacy of the imperial power. Nearly a century after agreeing to pray for the monarch, the people of Vyg still refused to use the epithet *blagovernyi* (right-believing) in connection with the present ruler because he was obviously not truly Orthodox.[40] Even more startling was the discovery, in 1820, that the Preobrazhenskoe settlement had a portrait of the reigning monarch, Alexander I, as Antichrist with horns, a tail, and the number 666 on his forehead.[41]

That was not all. Remarking on the strength of Old Belief in the northwestern borderlands of the empire, near Vyg, Nicholas made the following revealing comments: "the main foundation of their life is willfulness and debauchery. Therefore it is necessary to strengthen local surveillance, build communications, and provide means for the poor class of inhabitants to get sustenance in order to weaken the sectarians' influence over them."[42] Again and again, official documents note the relative prosperity of the Old Believer communities and repeat the conviction that their wealth allowed them to win converts from the official church.[43] That the Old Believers' hard work, frugality, and good business sense might benefit the empire never occurred to Nicholas and his officials.

The persistent accusations of debauchery and sexual license strike a particularly strange chord to anyone familiar with the history or contemporary style of life of the Old Believers. Apart from its capacity to shock the uninformed, the charge reflected the determination of Nicholas's government and the church to regularize family life and make it conform to traditional Christian teaching and contemporary standards of respectability.[44] Since many of the priestless refused to marry in the official church and, lacking priests, had no sacrament of marriage within their own communities, they founded families without benefit of clergy. This long-established practice offended the moral and canonical sensibilities of the Orthodox hierarchy and subverted their attempts to enforce their rigid definition of Christian marriage. Indeed, in the opinion of contemporaries, the Old Believers' more practical and flexible attitude toward marriage drew new adherents away from the official church.[45]

No less subversive of propriety and social order was the prominent role of women in Old Belief.[46] In 1852, a government report noted that the Preobrazhenskoe Kladbishche had, as regular residents, 628 women and 110 men.[47] In the central monastery and convent of the Vyg community, the census of 1836 recorded 71 men, many of them old, and 522 women.[48] Although men held the most important positions of leadership, the Old Believer communities increasingly resembled unofficial convents that provided pious women with institutional support and a way of life distinct from society's usual expectations. From this quiet subversion, I would argue, arose the suspicion that the unofficial nuns of Old Belief led hypocritical and debauched lives.

In the unequal struggle with the Old Believer communities, the imperial government inevitably emerged the victor. The great age of the quasi-monastic communities was over, even though the lure of the monastic vocation lived on and still attracts some Old Believers, particularly women.[49] The destruction or crippling of its most visible centers did not destroy the movement, however. With the resilience they had shown so many times before, the guardians of the old faith regrouped and consolidated their ranks in a semilegal situation that lasted, with a few exceptions, until the movement emerged strong and well organized to take advantage of the opportunities created by the Revolution of 1905.[50]

Our story, of course, has no end. The Old Believers are alive and well, in the former Soviet Union and abroad. And historians have only begun to re-create and understand the past of which many Old Believers themselves are only dimly aware. One part of the task of re-creation and comprehension is the study of the history of the Old Believer communities— and, more broadly, of the institutional and social development of the movement as a whole. This approach offers many opportunities to study the language of faith and its implications in concrete political and social settings without falling into either extreme of nineteenth-century historiography. Moreover, such study helps us to understand the problems and prospects that Old Believers face in our own day. For if the history of their communities in the eighteenth and nineteenth centuries teaches us anything, it reminds us that during the recovery of religious identity in Russia, the Old Believers' fate will depend not only on their own faithfulness and ingenuity but also on the policies of the government under whose rule they live.

NOTES

1. Michael Cherniavsky, "The Old Believers and the New Religion," *Slavic Review* 25 (1966), pp. 1–39, see p. 2.

2. Outstanding examples are N. Subbotin, ed., *Materialy dlia istorii raskola za pervoe vremia ego sushchestvovaniia*, 9 vols. (Moscow, 1874– 1890); and the monographs of P. S. Smirnov, especially *Vnutrennie voprosy v raskole v XVII veke* (St. Petersburg, 1898) and *Spory i razdeleniia v russkom raskole v pervoi chetverti XVIII veka* (St. Petersburg, 1909).

3. A. P. Shchapov, "Russkii raskol staroobriadstva, razsmatrivaemyi v sviazi s vnutrennim sostoianiem russkoi tserkvi i grazhdanstvennosti v XVII veke i v pervoi polovine XVIII" and "Zemstvo i raskol," in his *Sochineniia*, 3 vols. (St. Petersburg, 1906), 1, pp. 173–579. Numerous later books and articles continue the populist tradition. One good and useful example is V. V. Andreev, *Raskol i ego znachenie v narodnoi russkoi istorii* (St. Petersburg, 1870).

4. This assumption runs through N. S. Gur'ianova's excellent monograph, *Krest'ianskii antimonarkhicheskii protest v staroobriadcheskoi eskhatologicheskoi literature perioda pozdnego feodalizma* (Novosibirsk, 1988).

5. An earlier work, Pierre Pascal, *Avvakum et les débuts du raskol* (Paris, 1938; repr. The Hague, 1963), is still the best study of the origins and early history of Old Belief in any language.

6. S. Zen'kovskii, *Russkoe staroobriadchestvo* (Munich, 1970).

7. See I. V. Pozdeeva, "Kompleksnye arkheograficheskie ekspeditsii. Tseli, metodika, printsipy organizatsii," *Istoriia SSSR* (1978), no. 2, pp. 103–115; and "Zadachi i osobennosti raboty ekspeditsii, sobiraiushchikh pamiatniki kirillovskoi knizhnosti," *Arkheograficheskii ezhegodnik za 1977 god* (Moscow, 1978), pp. 56–61. The most impressive collection of articles by members of the Moscow group is *Russkie pis'mennye i ustnye traditsii i dukhovnaia kul'tura* (Moscow, 1982).

8. A. A. Amosov, V. P. Budaragin, V. V. Morozov, and R. G. Pikhoia, "O nekotorykh problemakh polevoi arkheografii (v poriadke obsuzhdeniia)," in *Obshchestvenno-politicheskaia mysl' dorevoliutsionnogo Urala* (Sverdlovsk, 1983), pp. 5–19. Pozdeeva and her associates appear to proceed on the assumption that Old Russian culture—the "core" of which she speaks—was a single, unchanging system.

9. See, for example, N. N. Pokrovskii, *Antifeodal'nyi protest Uralo-sibirskikh krest'ian staroobriadtsev v XVIII v.* (Novosibirsk, 1974); R. G. Pikhoia, *Obshchestvenno-politicheskaia mysl' trudiashchikhsia Urala (konets XVII–XVIII vv.)* (Sverdlovsk, 1987); and the numerous collections of essays published by both centers.

10. Cherniavsky, "Old Believers," p. 5.

11. Ibid. Cherniavsky's remarkable reconstruction of the Old Believers' "political theology" would appear to contradict his more general statements.

12. Manfred Hildermeier's study "Alter Glaube und neue Welt: Zur Sozialgeschichte des Raskol im 18. und 19. Jahrhundert," *Jahrbücher für Geschichte Osteuropas* 38 (1990), pp. 372–398, 504–525, a broad, thoughtful survey of the social history of Old Belief, and the sequel, "Alter Glaube und Mobilität. Bemerkungen zur Verbreitung und sozialen Struktur des Raskol im früindustriellen Russland (1760–1860)," *Jahrbücher für Geschichte Osteuropas* 39 (1991), pp. 321–338, do much to fill this gap.

13. Robert O. Crummey, *The Old Believers and the World of Antichrist: The Vyg Community and the Russian State, 1694–1855* (Madison, Wis., 1970). See also P. G. Liubomirov, *Vygoretskoe obshchezhitel'stvo* (Moscow-Saratov, 1942); and D. Ostrovskii, *Vygovskaia pustyn' i eia znachenie v istorii staroobriadcheskago raskola* (Petrozavodsk, 1914). The role of Vyg as a center of Old Believer polemical writing and copying makes its history unusually accessible to scholars. Historians make particularly extensive use of Ivan Filippov's *Istoriia Vygovskoi pustyni* (St. Petersburg, 1862). As the more recent studies of N. V. Ponyrko, N. S. Gur'ianova, and E. M. Iukhimenko make clear, scholars can still find

valuable new materials in the manuscript tradition of the community. See, for example, N. V. Ponyrko, "Uchebniki ritoriki na Vygu," *Trudy Otdela drevnerusskoi literatury* 36 (1981), pp. 154–162; Ponyrko and V. P. Budaragin, "Avtografy vygovskikh pisatelei," *Drevnerusskaia knizhnost'. Po materialam Pushkinskogo Doma* (Leningrad, 1985), pp. 174–200; N. S. Gur'ianova, "Pomorskie istoricheskie sochineniia XVIII v.," *Istochniki po istorii obshchestvennoi mysli i kul'tury epokhi pozdnego feodalizma* (Novosibirsk, 1988), pp. 92–102; "'Zhitie' Ivana Filippova," *Khristianstvo i tserkov' v Rossii feodal'nogo perioda (materialy)* (Novosibirsk, 1989), pp. 227–253; "Dopolnenie k 'Istorii Vygovskoi staroobriadcheskoi pustyni' I. Filippova," *Publitsistika i istoricheskie sochineniia perioda feodalizma* (Novosibirsk, 1989), pp. 221–245; "Problema istoricheskogo povestvovaniia v interpretatsii pisatelei vygovskoi literaturnoi shkoly," *Izvestiia SO AN SSSR. Istoriia, filosofiia i filologiia*, vyp. 3 (1991), pp. 14–18; "Dukhovnye zaveshchaniia vygovskikh bol'shakov," *Traditsionnaia dukhovnaia i material'naia kul'tura russkikh staroobriadcheskikh poselenii v stranakh Evropy, Azii i Ameriki* (Novosibirsk, 1992), pp. 96–102; E. M. Iukhimenko, "'Vinograd Rossiiskii' Semena Denisova (tekstologicheskii analiz)," *Drevnerusskaia literatura. Istochnikovedenie* (Leningrad, 1984), pp. 247–266; "Vnov' naidennye pis'ma Semena Denisova," *Trudy Otdela drevnerusskoi literatury* 44 (1990), pp. 409–421; "'Istoriia o ottsakh i stradal'tsakh solovetskikh' Semena Denisova—pamiatnik vygovskoi literaturnoi shkoly pervoi poloviny XVIII v.," *Traditsionnaia dukhovnaia i material'naia kul'tura russkikh staroobriadcheskikh poselenii v stranakh Evropy, Azii i Ameriki* (Novosibirsk, 1992), pp. 107–113.

14. For example, P. G. Ryndziunskii, "Staroobriadcheskaia organizatsiia v usloviiakh razvitiia promyshlennogo kapitalizma," *Voprosy istorii religii i ateizma* 1 (1950), pp. 188–248; and his *Gorodskoe grazhdanstvo doreformennoi Rossii* (Moscow, 1958); Manfred Hildermeier, *Bürgertum und Stadt in Russland 1760–1870: Rechtliche Lage und soziale Struktur* (Cologne, 1986); and William L. Blackwell, *The Beginnings of Russian Industrialization, 1800–1862* (Princeton, N.J., 1962).

15. Georg Michels's studies make this point with particular force. See his article, "The Solovki Uprising: Religion and Revolt in Northern Russia," *Russian Review* 51 (1992), pp. 1–15.

16. Were it not for the arbitrary boundaries drawn by the secular and ecclesiastical authorities of imperial Russia, it would be extremely difficult, in many cases, to determine who was an Old Believer and who was not.

17. See Crummey, *Old Believers;* Hildermeier, "Alter Glaube und neue Welt," pp. 383–386; and the articles of L. K. Kuandykov, especially "Razvitie obshchezhitel'nogo ustava v Vygovskoi staroobriadcheskoi obshchine v pervoi treti XVIII v," in *Issledovaniia po istorii obshchestvennogo soznaniia epokhi feodalizma v Rossii* (Novosibirsk, 1984), pp. 51–63, and

"Vygovskie sochineniia ustavnogo kharaktera vtoroi poloving *xviii* v." in *Istochniki po istorii russkogo obshchestvennogo soznaniia perioda feodalizma* (Novosibirsk, 1986), pp. 120–130. Some of the populist historians of earlier times took pains to minimize the monastic features of the main Old Believer communities. For their part, the leaders and spokesmen of Vyg stressed, both in their polemical statements and in the rules of the community, that the Vyg and Leksa settlements were monasteries, heirs of the great monastic corporations of the Russian church, above all, Solovki.

18. In practice, like other Christians who completely reject the powers of this world, the most radical Old Believers discovered that, in order to deal with the practicalities of life, they needed the help of less militant sympathizers who continued to live more or less normal lives "in the world."

19. Cherniavsky, "Old Believers," and Gur'ianova, *Krest'ianskii antimonarkhicheskii protest*, both stress this point.

20. The history of Vyg provides many examples. After its reluctant commitment to pray for the ruler, the leaders of Vyg wrote a number of letters to reigning Empresses in a tone of extreme humility and gratitude. At roughly the same time the community's polemicists justified the decision to pray for the ruler with the argument that earlier Christians had prayed for heretical or pagan monarchs!

21. See, for example, the comments of N. Iu. Bubnov in his dissertation, "Staroobriadcheskaia kniga v Rossii vo vtoroi polovine XVII v." (Leningrad, 1989). The most popular works written in Vyg were *Pomorskie otvety* (Ural'sk, 1911), by Andrei and Semen Denisov, and Semen Denisov's two martyrologies, *Vinograd rossiiskii* (Moscow, 1906) and the "Istoriia o ottsekh i stradal'tsakh solovetskikh," in G. V. Esipov, *Raskol'nich'i dela XVIII st.,* 2 vols. (Moscow, 1863), 2, pp. 1–55.

22. See, for example, Abby Smith and Vladimir Budaragin, *Living Traditions of Russian Faith. Books & Manuscripts of the Old Believers* (Washington, D.C., 1990), esp. pp. 27–33.

23. Ryndziunskii, "Staroobriadcheskaia organizatsiia," pp. 222–223.

24. See, for example, P. I. Mel'nikov [Andrei Pecherskii], "Ocherki popovshchiny," in his *Polnoe sobranie sochinenii,* 7 vols. (St. Petersburg, 1909), 7, pp. 3–375, here pp. 204–209. The same attitudes inform N. V. Varadinov, *Istoriia Ministerstva vnutrennykh del,* vol. 8 (St. Petersburg, 1863), a valuable compendium of official reports on the activities of Old Believers and sectarians.

25. *Polnoe sobranie zakonov Rossiiskoi Imperii* [hereafter *PSZ*], sobranie pervoe, 45 vols. (St. Petersburg, 1830–1843), 2, pp. 647–650 (no. 1102). See also Crummey, *Old Believers,* pp. 39–47; and Lindsey

Hughes, *Sophia, Regent of Russia 1657–1704* (New Haven and London, 1990), pp. 121–124.

26. Crummey, *Old Believers,* pp. 167–170.

27. See Cherniavsky, "Old Believers." A number of the cases of lèse majesty involving Old Believers are described in detail in Esipov, *Raskol'nich'i dela.*

28. Among the most important laws on Old Belief are *PSZ* 5, p. 166 (no. 2991), 5, p. 200 (no. 2996), 5, p. 590 (no. 3232); 6, pp. 641–642 (no. 3944) and 6, pp. 678–681 (no. 4009). See also A. Sinaiskii, *Otnoshenie russkoi tserkovnoi vlasti k raskolu staroobriadchestva v pervye gody sinodal'nago upravleniia pri Petre Velikom (1721–25)* (St. Petersburg, 1895).

29. B. V. Titlinov, *Pravitel'stvo Imperatritsy Anny Ioannovny v ego otnosheniiakh k delam pravoslavnoi tserkvi* (Vilnius, 1905), pp. 418–429.

30. Crummey, *Old Believers,* pp. 159–183.

31. Ibid., pp. 194–197.

32. On the Moscow communities, see Ryndziunskii, "Staroobriadcheskaia organizatsiia"; Mel'nikov, "Ocherki popovshchiny"; N. Popov, ed., "Materialy dlia istorii bezpopovshchinskikh soglasii v Moskve: 1. Fedosievtsev Preobrazhenskago Kladbishcha," *Chteniia v Imperatorskom Obshchestve istorii i drevnostei rossiiskikh pri Moskovskom Universitete* [hereafter *ChOIDR*) (1869), bk. 2, pp. 71–174; and *Sbornik dlia istorii staroobriadchestva,* vol. 1 (Moscow, 1864). There is an extensive literature on the Moscow and St. Petersburg communities in prerevolutionary Russian ecclesiastical periodicals.

33. Nicholas's government assiduously collected information on Old Believer activities and interpreted their findings in the most unflattering light. See Varadinov, *Istoriia,* vol. 8; and A. A. Titov, ed., "Dnevnye dozornye zapisi o Moskovskikh raskol'nikakh," *ChOIDR* (1885), bk. 2, pt. 5, pp. 1–40; bk. 3, pt. 5, pp. 41–80; bk. 4, pt. 5, pp. 81–120; (1886), bk. 1, pt. 5, pp. 123–192; (1892), bk. 1, pt. 1, pp. 1–98; bk. 2, pt. 1, pp. 99–251.

34. N. Sokolov, *Raskol v Saratovskom krae* (Saratov, 1888), pp. 275–329, 373–401, 412–421.

35. V. Vasil'ev, "Organizatsiia i samoupravlenie Feodosievskoi obshchiny na Preobrazhenskom Kladbishche v Moskve," *Khristianskoe chtenie* (1887), pp. 568–615, see pp. 604–615; "Iz istorii Rogozhskago Kladbishcha," *Bratskoe Slovo* (1891), pt. 2, pp. 448–466; V. Nil'skii, "Raskol v Peterburge: Molennaia Kostsova v Volkovskoe Fedoseevskoe Kladbishche," *Istina* 55 (1877), pp. 1–68, see pp. 42–56; and "Malookhtenskoe pomorskoe kladbishche v Peterburge," *Istina* 42 (1875), pp. 61–88, see pp. 84–87.

36. Crummey, *Old Believers,* pp. 203–218. On the later history of Vyg, see I. A. Shafranov, "Vygoretskoe staroobriadcheskoe

obshchezhitel'stvo v kontse XVIII i v pervoi polovine XIX v.," *Russkoe Bogatstvo* (1893), no. 10, pp. 171–199; no. 11, pp. 58–98. The most important source on the last years of the community is the Vyg chronicle, different versions of which have been published as *Staropomorskii letopisets* (Moscow, 1913 [?]); and "Kratkoe letoschislenie nastoiashchago veka," *Bratskoe slovo* (1888), bk. 1, no. 10, pp. 793–815.

37. For a convenient summary of this episode, see P. S. Smirnov, *Istoriia russkago raskola staroobriadchestva* (St. Petersburg, 1895), pp. 145–159.

38. Mel'nikov, "Schislenie raskol'nikov," *Polnoe sobranie sochinenii,* 7, pp. 384–409, see p. 391. See also Hildermeier, "Alter Glaube und Mobilität"; and Gregory L. Freeze, "The Rechristianization of Russia: The Church and Popular Religion, 1750–1850," *Studia Slavica Finlandensia* 7 (1990), pp. 101–136, here pp. 107–108.

39. On this phenomenon, see Gregory L. Freeze, "The Wages of Sin: The Decline of Public Penance in Imperial Russia," in this volume.

40. Shafranov, "Vygoretskoe . . . obshchezhitel'stvo," no. 10, p. 191.

41. V. I. Kel'siev, *Sbornik pravitel'stvennykh svedenii o raskol'nikakh,* 4 vols. (London, 1860–1862), 1, p. 43. The government had other reasons to suspect the Old Believers of disloyalty. At the height of the Crimean War, its leaders were acutely aware that the Old Believer communities had close ties with their coreligionists in two enemy states, Austria-Hungary and Turkey. Wartime tension helps to explain why Nicholas's government persecuted the dissenters with particular savagery in the early 1850s.

42. Quoted by Shafranov, "Vygoretskoe . . . obshchezhitel'stvo," no. 11, pp. 62–63.

43. In a very similar vein, Hildermeier's "Alter Glaube und Mobilität" argues that the Old Believers won many converts in the first decades of the nineteenth century because their countersociety offered ordinary Russians far better opportunities for economic prosperity and upward social mobility than did the rest of society.

44. Gregory L. Freeze, "Bringing Order to the Russian Family: Marriage and Divorce in Imperial Russia, 1760–1860," *Journal of Modern History* 62 (1990), pp. 709–746, see pp. 737, 746.

45. As Freeze felicitously puts it, "Old Belief represented not only the old rites but also the old rights—that is, not only old rituals but also the old freedom in making and unmaking familial bonds" (ibid., p. 746).

46. It is instructive to compare the status and role of women in Old Belief with the position of the leaders and members of the unofficial women's monastic communities within the Orthodox church. See Brenda Meehan, *Holy Women of Russia* (San Francisco: Harper Collins, 1993).

47. Vasil'ev, "Organizatsiia," p. 607.

48. Crummey, *Old Believers,* p. 206.

49. See, for example, the remarkable story of a contemporary Old Believer nun, A. Lebedev, "Taezhnyi prosvet: Kak ia ezdil k Agaf'e Lykovoi," *Tserkov'* no. 0 [sic](1990), pp. 26–32 (published as *Rodina* no. 9 [1990]) and no. 1 (1992), pp. 34–41.

50. See Peter Waldron, "Religious Reform after 1905: Old Believers and the Orthodox Church," *Oxford Slavonic Papers* 20 (1987), pp. 111–139. The history of Old Belief between 1855 and 1917 is particularly in need of serious study and analysis. Roy R. Robson, "Old Believers in a Modern World: Symbol, Ritual and Community, 1904–14" (unpublished Ph.D. dissertation, Boston College, 1992) is an important first step in this direction.

An Architecture of Change

Old Believer Liturgical Spaces in Late Imperial Russia

*I*mperial edicts of 1905 and 1906, which offered Old Believers first the right to freedom of conscience and then better defined their position within the Russian Empire, occurred in a period of unprecedented social and cultural change. The Old Believers, emerging from their previous shadowy legality, used these newfound legal rights as a catalyst to inaugurate their own silver age in fin-de-siècle Russia. In doing so, they sought to integrate their own views with the emerging modern society, culture, and politics of the period.[1] This attempt at integration was realized in the construction of many Old Believer religious buildings between 1905 and 1917.

The history of old ritualist liturgical spaces illustrates the paradoxical nature of the Old Belief in this period.[2] How the Old Believers juggled legal issues, design and construction, and the symbolism of their liturgical spaces gives clues to the way in which the Old Belief tried to integrate the mandate of religious tradition into changing Russian society. The nature of Old Believer religious ideology also placed particular importance on the physical building as a symbol and focus of ritual life. Liturgical spaces therefore commented symbolically on both religious and social activities that occurred in them, especially on the social organization of the community.

Although Old Believers resided throughout the Russian Empire, analysis of Russian architecture has just recently begun to include their contributions.[3] Previously, texts either did not mention Old Believers at all or placed them only in the context of the Russian North, associating them with ancient wooden architectural forms indigenous to that part of the empire. Old Believers sometimes have been credited with maintaining traditional Russian building design and practices long after other parts of the empire accepted Western innovations. While, for example, I. E. Grabar's famous history of Russian architecture did not include Old Believer buildings, a later study has claimed that "the style of wooden architecture did not change over the centuries and later examples, particularly in the north where many conservative Old Believers settled after the schism in the 1650s, are based on ancient models."[4]

A more recent work, written by a noted restorer of the Kizhi complex of wooden churches, has invested Old Believers with immense responsibility: "It was the Old Believers who defended and preserved the traditional way of life, the art and above all the churches of medieval Russia. They were the only effective resistance to the formidably overwhelming power of the state."[5] This analysis, although exaggerated, correctly linked Old Believer architecture with the group's political situation.

Scholarly preoccupation with north Russian conservatism presents a chicken-and-egg problem for the study of Old Believer liturgical spaces. While Old Believers did enjoy a measure of freedom to maintain the old ways in the North, the region's conservatism was both a product of and a guiding hand in Old Believer life. The Vyg community, the most famous Old Believer monastery in the far North, did provide a focus for cultural as well as religious life. To claim, however, that "the demise of the Old Believer movement spelt the end of wooden church construction"[6] with the destruction of Vyg in 1864 misjudges the death of both the Old Belief and Russian traditional architecture. Instead, the happy union of social conservatism and Old Belief combined to keep traditional church design and symbolism intact there throughout the imperial period and beyond.

Robert Crummey's work on the Vyg community, the most reliable analysis of northern Russian Old Belief, has noted the cultural influence of Old Believers in the far North. An independent peasantry in the North—"stable, industrious, and often isolated from the outside world"—provided a complement to the culture of the Old Belief. Such influence, Crummey continues, has been long-lived: "Soviet scholars have uncovered literary and artistic treasures, lovingly preserved by the inhabitants of remote northern villages whose cultural life still preserves traces of the influence of Vyg and its offshoots."[7] The problem with studying Vyg's influence on architecture, however, is that it was an anomaly, not the rule: in other parts of the empire the Old Believers needed to build more circumspectly than in the autonomous North.

SACRED BUILDING AND STATE AUTHORITY

Both the imperial government and the Russian Orthodox church understood the importance of the focus provided by a place of worship, and at first outlawed Old Believer buildings outright. Failing that, authorities endeavored to license and to restrict temple design and construction. Catherine II, however, granted Old Believers relative freedom of worship and association, including the right to build temples. Paul and Alexander I also treated the Old Believers liberally on this issue. Under Nicholas I, however, the building or restoration of chapels was forbidden once again, leaving many buildings to disintegrate or to be sealed shut.

The reign of Alexander II inaugurated an amelioration of the Old

Believer plight. An *ukaz* of 16 August 1864 gave Old Believers the right to repair decrepit chapels and other structures, so long as the outside did not resemble a Russian Orthodox church.[8] Alexander III's *ukaz* of 3 May 1883, however, ended the more laissez-faire attitude of the state during the reign of Alexander II. It granted the Old Believers more leniency in terms of passports and legal status, but it forbade any open show of Old Believer religious life.[9] By curtailing the building or renovation of chapels or churches, among other things, the government again hoped to keep the Old Believers from luring members of the Russian Orthodox church into schism through competitive manifestations of faith. This law became the bedrock for state actions regarding the Old Believers until the promulgation of the manifesto of religious toleration in 1905. Under the terms of the 1883 law, no renovation, construction, nor public display of the old ritual was acceptable without express permission from the Ministry of the Interior. That ministry in turn was supposed to work in consort with the Holy Synod. In reality, however, the two groups fought bitterly about the Old Believers as well as other issues.

This system of bureaucracy made building and restoring religious structures next to impossible for Old Believers. Those who petitioned the government on this issue before the 1905–1906 reforms sometimes received approval from local or provincial authorities and sometimes even from the Ministry of Internal Affairs. If, however, proposals to use a home as a prayer house or to reconstruct a dilapidated chapel were forwarded to the religious authorities, the request was almost always denied.[10] These cases effectively undercut what little freedom the 1883 statute had given to Old Believers. The Minister of Internal Affairs himself questioned the church's attitudes on this issue:

> Only in rare cases do the religious authorities recognize as proper the petitions of the schismatics for permission to open new prayer houses, on the grounds that each new house of prayer not only helps to strengthen the Schism, but also makes missionary preaching more difficult. . . . The protests of the bishops against the opening of prayer houses proceed generally from the view that this is dangerous for Orthodoxy and produces disaffection among the believing—but if such protests are recognized to the extent of refusing the petitions of schismatics, then nowhere and never can new prayer houses be opened.[11]

Despite the attitude taken by Church officials (and taking advantage of the disagreement between bureaucracies), some Old Believer communities did build or restore their temples of worship. Industrial centers in the Urals often had Old Believer chapels on their grounds, although frequently they were in poor repair, and industrialists of the Moscow region built them as well.[12]

The promulgation of the 1905 and 1906 laws transformed the legal situation on this subject. From then on, Old Believers were free (according to the law) to restore, to build, and to open their own temples. Some imperial or Church officials tried, however, to undercut the new situation on a local level. In Kazan during 1906, a missionary priest purportedly told Old Believers, "Your life and death are in my hands. I may want to allow [renovation of your church], I may not want to."[13] The priest's attitude, as reported in an Old Believer journal, did not reflect the "new thinking" about reconstructing Old Believer liturgical buildings. It did, however, hint at the importance placed on such projects by the Old Believers themselves. The priest understood that corporate worship—the life and death of an Old Believer community—depended on a suitable space. Many Old Believer journals noted resistance to the new legal situation; while in retrospect it would seem natural that the old regime would guard its prerogatives, it infuriated the zealous Old Believers. "And this," complained one, "after 17 April!" (in respect to the 1905 manifesto on religious toleration).[14]

Despite these early efforts to hinder the restoration of churches and prayer houses, Old Believers took on the task with gusto. In previous generations the faithful many times had to pray in a makeshift chapel—often one room of a peasant house—and now they looked forward to building a more substantial focal point for their liturgical life. The process of building was undoubtedly helped by the Old Believer tradition of mutual aid. A system of financial support was in place before the call went out for money with which to build. While calls for construction support sometimes appeared in the Old Believer press, the local community generally supported the temple financially. The wealth of Old Believer merchants and industrialists has been noted many times, but even the poorest Old Believer villages usually had provisions for mutual aid,[15] and the traditions of almsgiving and financial support for coreligionists were long and distinguished among the Old Believers.[16] One Russian Orthodox bishop sniffed that "unquestionably the most attractive, tempting side of schism consists of the material mutual aid among schismatics."[17]

Community organization through autonomous local units also aided the building of these structures, since an organized group of Old Believers often existed before a liturgical space could be built. The organization of the Old Believers created a membership, leadership, and financial structure just waiting for the chance to build a chapel or church. The "community structure of management in religious matters," complained one Russian Orthodox church bishop, "in which every member of the community holds a rightful voice in discussion of religious activities," provided a cornerstone of Old Believer appeal.[18] He also noted the accessibility of Old Believer clergy to their flocks. Within such communities lay members could find an engaged religious life.[19] When, therefore, the legal situation changed in 1905, Old Believers were in a position to exploit their new status, and began to build temples almost immediately. W. C. Brumfield has noted that Old Believers had "already established the principle of local initiative in construction of churches" before such grass-roots support existed on a large scale in the dominant church.[20]

As leaders of the Russian Orthodox church suspected, the 1905 and 1906 laws on the freedom of conscience did provide inroads for Old Believers to propagate the old faith. Although the substantial Pokrovskii Cathedral in Moscow held the seat of the Belokrinitsa metropolitan, the Belokrinitsy continued to build in the city, including one church costing more than two hundred thousand rubles.[21] The Pomortsy, in another case, convened their 1909 all-Russian conference in a newly constructed Moscow temple—the first in the city to be built specifically by the sect. The expansion of the Belokrinitsy and the presence of a major new Pomortsy temple in Moscow clearly illustrated the Old Believers' growing visibility as a legitimate form of Orthodoxy. In all, at least fifteen new Old Believer liturgical buildings were constructed between 1905 and 1917, not counting private devotional chapels.[22] The Russian Orthodox church, ever jealous of its position of prominence, noted the Old Believer building boom even in small towns and villages, and worried that many new structures were "magnificent and grand."[23] On the national level, Russian Orthodox leaders sought to curb Old Believer influence by using their political power to keep Old Believers from using the word "church," arguing that such a term could be used only by true Orthodox, which, in their opinion, the Old Believers were not. The government noted, however, that Old Believers usually used the word "temple" instead of "church," and this provided reasonable differentiation between their and Russian Orthodox structures.[24]

Notwithstanding outside pressures, interest in temple building found an outlet in the Old Believer press, often through short articles from regional correspondents. Old Believer magazines fanned excitement over these projects by producing longer descriptions, pictures, and photographs of the structures as they sprang up around Russia. Good examples of such articles could be seen in practically every issue of all Old Believer journals, sometimes including detailed descriptions of church design and cost as aids for other communities. This construction boom continued well into the second decade of the twentieth century: on the eve of World War I, for example, Old Believers were still opening large and ornate temples.[25]

The Old Believers prided themselves on their new liturgical buildings, saying that constructing them was one proof of the Old Belief's vitality.[26] Old Believer writers, moreover, began to see the opening and maintenance of liturgical buildings to be a central civil right, especially the freedom from having temples closed "by caprice," as they had been during previous generations.[27] One journal succinctly connected the growth of a church building to the life of the old ritual itself, calling the opening of a new temple in Arkhangelsk "The Celebration of the Old Belief."[28]

TRADITION, INNOVATION, AND DESIGN

When (as during the reign of Catherine the Great) Old Believers before 1905 had received the opportunity to build as they wished, some remarkable temple exteriors resulted. Preobrazhenskoe, a major center of priestless religious life, had constructed a "gothic chapel" in 1805 (Figure 1), following the more traditional (yet also highly adorned) Nikol'skaia Chapel of 1784 (Figure 2) and preceding the return to traditional form in the Krestovozdvizhenskii Chapel in 1811 (Figure 3). These structures, designed by F. K. Sokolov, were built during the period of toleration that coincided with the creation of the Preobrazhenskoe community. Their exteriors provide a clue to the form of priestless chapels that might have sprung up had there been no official persecution.[29]

The Rogozhskoe cemetery cathedral, built later than the Preobrazhenskoe complex by the Belokrinitsa *popovtsy* congregation in Moscow, provided the other significant pre-1905 exception to the plain exterior usually legislated by imperial authorities. The Cathedral of the Pokrov Mother of God, centerpiece for the Belokrinitsa hierarchy, enclosed a traditional interior with neoclassical Greco-Roman pilasters and columns. The foreign-inspired exterior of the Pokrov cathedral was complemented after 1905 by a highly traditional Russian bell tower church situated next to it. In short, the necessity and desire to mold into the society of the day influenced priestly Old Believer temple design to the point of using a neoclassical motif (Figure 4). That the *popovtsy* Old Believers maintained a closer link to greater Russian society than their *bespopovtsy* counterparts is illustrated in the classical aspects of their building.

Although (whenever possible) they were ambitious builders of church structures, Old Believers after 1905 found themselves without a clear external design tradition. In legislating how the exterior of an Old Believer temple had to appear but ignoring the interior, previous centuries of imperial law had fostered a dichotomous relationship between the outside of an Old Believer structure and its inside design. This phenomenon created a curious aspect of Old Believer buildings—while tradition mandated a strict interpretation of liturgical space indoors, the outside of Old Believer buildings varied in light of legal problems, local conditions, and regional aesthetic. Since Old Believers bowed under the constraints of these legal issues until 1905, their liturgical spaces had to conform to standards imposed by those unsympathetic to their religious ideology. To make matters worse, legislation generally prohibited any outward signs

Figure 1. "Gothic Chapel" at Preobrazhenskoe Cemetery. *Courtesy of the Center of Traditional Russian Culture.*

Figure 2.   Nikol'skaia Chapel at Preobrazhenskoe Cemetery.

of Orthodoxy on Old Believer buildings (bell towers, crosses, and the like), and thereby forced them to blend into the style prevalent in a given geographic area. This situation was highly symbolic for Old Believers—while maintaining tradition within the community (as shown by the largely unchanged interior design) the faithful often needed to fit their lives into the fabric of local society, echoing the unobtrusive exterior of their temples. For the *poluraskol'niki*, moreover, who followed the old

Figure 3.   Krestodvizhenskii Chapel at Preobrazhenskoe Cemetery.

Figure 4.   Pokrov Cathedral at Rogozhskoe Cemetery.

rituals but did not register with the government as Old Believers, the plain exterior of Old Believer temples harmonized with their own interior belief masked by outward indifference to the old ritual.

At the time of the 1905 reforms, therefore, traditions of exterior church design that had been lost to many Old Believers had to be consciously recalled and revived. Old Believers had by this point largely accepted the idea that a building's exterior did not have to mirror its interior traditions. This freed the designers of post-1905 edifices to combine the traditions of the Russian North and of Muscovite architecture with the building materials and aesthetic of *art moderne*. In a very real way, after 1905 "everything old was new again": Old Believer renewal of medieval forms was heralded as an innovation in architectural design.

The simplicity of line and lack of ornament in many buildings, for example, recalled the many years of Old Believer construction under persecution in combination with a modern aesthetic sensibility. What is more, expanded exposure of its architecture accompanied an upsurge in interest in the Old Belief in general. Brumfield has noted that the architectural press commented positively on the designs of new Old Believer churches, and that Old Believers helped to fuel a fin-de-siècle renaissance in traditional architectural design: "Much that is innovative in Russian church architecture at the beginning of the twentieth century can be attributed to Old Believer communities."[30] Another writer has explained it this way: "It was certainly not [the Old Believers'] intention to return to the Orthodox forms of the State religion, and for this reason their architects attempted to suggest in their churches not only the Orthodox character of the Old Believers' faith and its relation to Byzantine and Russian history, but also their long exile in the north."[31] It seemed a paradox that the Old Belief—an ultratraditional form of Orthodoxy—appeared better able to make itself relevant to the new political and cultural age than the more "modernized" Russian Orthodox church. Freedom after years of persecution, combined with localized organization of Old Believer communities, created an atmosphere of great vitality in the Old Belief that was missing in the established Church. This liveliness found its outlet in both the number and the design of Old Believer liturgical buildings constructed from 1905 to 1917.

The Pomortsy temple dedicated to the Resurrection, constructed in Moscow in 1909, exemplifies this link between traditional Russian symbols and a modern aesthetic (Figure 5). Its "beautiful external appearance, and the richness of its internal finishing, make it among the most remarkable church structures in the city of Moscow," claimed the Old Believer magazine *Zlatostrui*.[32] One could easily identify typical elements of ancient Russian style—pitched roof, front bell tower, and onion domes—but the construction technique and simplified lines of the chapel gave it an appearance that straddled tradition and modernity. This design, by I. Bondarenko, concretely illustrated the situation facing Pomortsy after the edict of toleration: although their historical strength and leadership came from the far North, where they promoted a life detached from the rest of society, the Pomortsy spread throughout the empire. In more cosmopolitan environments, the faithful began to break down the walls between them and outside society that had been second nature in the North. The new Pomortsy temple in Moscow thereby symbolized the group's need to fit its religious sensibility into modern conditions while retaining the traditions of its elders. (This stylistic decision differed only a little from that made by the Belokrinitsy a century earlier, when that community decided to follow the vogue for classical construction; it took the Pomortsy another century, however, to arrive at such a point.)

Figure 5.   Voskresenie Temple of the Pomortsy. *Courtesy of Penguin Books.*

In this, like other Old Believer temples, the dramatically new design and building techniques on the exterior of the temple enclosed a highly traditional worship space. Although, for example, the building was constructed in part of reinforced concrete, its interior design and furnishings

Figure 6. Pokrov Church of the Belokrinitsy. *Courtesy of the University of California Press.*

retained traditional motifs.[33] Such a mixture confirmed the Old Believer willingness to interpret ancient building exteriors in light of contemporary conditions while retaining the interior elements in highly traditional form. The Pokrov church built by the Belokrinitsy also returned to traditional forms, including a semidetached bell tower and traditional roof and dome design (Figure 6). The new bell tower at the Pokrovskii Cathedral recalled traditional Muscovite themes as well. These, like other symbols of Old Believer life, declared that not only were Old Believers true Russian Christians but also that they—not the established Russian Orthodox church—were heirs to the Russian religious birthright. In their use of traditional design the Old Believers both attempted to "rework traditional forms in the spirit of a new age"[34] and to claim their place as the only vital, true Russian Orthodox.

IZBA, TEMPLE, AND THE COMMUNAL LIFE

As architectural historians have noted, Old Believer buildings in the North and Siberia never had to bifurcate exterior and interior designs. This was due to the greater autonomy granted to the old ritual in such sparsely populated regions, and provided examples for post-1905 architectural design in the rest of the empire. In these geographic areas, Old Believers followed architectural traditions that guaranteed their reputa-

tion as conservators of ancient styles and techniques. Here, more insu-
lated from political and social influences than their coreligionists
elsewhere, Old Believers held to simple, traditional designs handed down
through generations. To this end, Old Believer temples in the far North
and Siberia made their most basic point of reference the traditional *izba*
(hut) structure of the Russian peasantry.

Elements of *izba* design had informed Russian church architecture
from the baptism of Rus' onward. Although most prevalent in the
wooden churches of the North (notably some of those now preserved in
the Kizhi complex), *izba* influence was seen in stone churches as well. A
nineteenth-century analyst recognized that the ancient form of wooden
church architecture in Russia resembled a "simple *izba*." He claimed that
"this form of church diffused northwest of Moscow and reached to the
Olonets province [in the north] and the Ural Mountains [in the south],
and hence moved through all of the area of the Novgorod coloniza-
tion."[35] Another interpretive venture has explained that "just as the
tri-partate plan of the *izba* is repeated in the palaces of the Russian aristocracy, so it dominates the design of the [ancient] Orthodox church,
whose liturgical function also called for three different areas."[36] The *izba*
consisted of a series of rectangular cells placed end to end, almost always
constructed of wood. The central cell (*klet*) contained the main, heated
living area—also called the *izba*—and another storage room and passage-
way might be added. The underlying structure of three rectangular cells
arranged linearly could be enlarged or contracted as necessary. Atop the
cells was a wooden roof, of either pitched or tent construction.

This living arrangement, while hardly a sophisticated design, provided
a number of benefits. The cells could be easily and quickly constructed
from rough-hewn timbers, and could be modified for specific purposes.
In addition, the *izba* enveloped myriad activities of the family. Like other
premodern people, Russian folk spent their indoor life mostly in one
large room, instead of a number of small chambers (as would be the case
in bourgeois culture). Privacy was inconsistent with the *izba*, which encouraged a communal life for its inhabitants. All the family lived together, regardless of age or place in the family structure.

Northern Russian Old Believer structures can be stylistically compared with the Church of Lazarii Muromskii (Figure 7), believed to be
the oldest extant example of Russian wooden architecture, or the Chapel
of the Archangel Michael, both now in the Kizhi complex on Lake
Onega. Churches like Lazarii Muromskii provided the basis for later Old
Believer design. In northern Russia, as one Russian scholar has explained, the religious space was often built with just two cells, creating a
chapel instead of a sanctified church.[37] Priestless Old Believers (the dominant sect in the North) borrowed freely from chapels of this design that
"were to be found in hamlets and, like memorial crosses, in places with a

Figure 7.   Church of Lazarii Muromskii at the Kizhi complex of wooden churches. *Courtesy of Harry N. Abrams.*

special spiritual significance, where a pious Christian might want to make the sign of the cross. . . . The main difference [between them] was that a church had an iconostasis but a chapel had neither iconostasis nor sanctuary, and its interior was modest and simple."[38] An ethnographic study of Bukhtarminskie (Tomsk province) Old Believers, published in 1930, claims that priestless chapels built there and in Kazakhstan were nothing more than *izby* with added bell towers, and that they resembled wooden churches of the Russian North, thousands of miles away.[39] The Siberian Old Believer bell tower design was apparently similar even to those built of stone in Pskov and Novgorod.

Izba design harmonizes with the Old Believer symbolism of the temple. Its design and function follow that of the *izba* because it, too, transforms a group of individuals into a cohesive whole—an Old Believer community. The need for communal prayer, added to the necessity for

Old Believers often to pray in a converted room of a home, maintained the linkage between *izba* as home and *izba* as prayer house. As can be seen in its design, the temple was an integral part of Old Believer life, a true house of prayer for their communities: the Old Believer temple literally housed the community. A related analysis of Old Believers has shown that the home could be seen as a chapel, just as the chapel could be seen as a home: "Despite its ordinary appearance, the home is considered a place of elevated ritual status. If one sees a genuine church as a reflection of heaven, and the local chapel as the reflection of a church, then the home may well be understood as a reflection of the chapel. It is the lowest link in the chain connecting God with His followers and the past with the present."[40]

Thus the relationship between home and chapel, between *izba* design and temple design, was an explicit one for the Old Believers. For in the temple, as in the home, the communal needs of the faithful weighed more heavily than the desires of any one individual. Leaders of the Pomortsy, for instance, in 1909 consciously refused to dictate the exterior design of a temple, saying that both Old Russian church style and the style of a "simple house" were acceptable forms.[41]

Communal prayer, as opposed to private devotion, was particularly important to the Old Believers. In their liturgical life they maintained practices that helped bond believers into a single voice of prayer: "in one thought, and accord, and love of union."[42] Physically rigorous worship, uniformity in ritual activity, and an emphasis on ritual discipline created an atmosphere that promoted communal unity in prayer.

The imperative for communal prayer made the temple a central symbol for Old Believer spirituality. Early in the Old Believer experience, for example, the Vyg community placed its chapels (one for men and one for women) in the geographic center of the community, spiritual and architectural foci for the *pustyn'* (hermitage) (Figure 8).[43] Old Believers built on this tradition after 1905 to construct buildings that could disseminate their view of prayerful life throughout the empire. From the temple, which enclosed the community at prayer, radiated the organizational theme of the Old Believer community. One Old Believer monk explained it this way: "The temple must be, for Christians, a visible, real means of unification among themselves—a symbol of unity. In them must flow together thoughts of all people in one general anthem of prayer and unbroken brotherly union, never hostile, spiteful, wrathful, envious, hateful, or disdainful. As one . . . all must be encircled with peace, accord, unity of spirit, and love."[44] In other words, the symbolism of the liturgical space reinforced the communal relationship between Old Believers and reminded them that, in the process of prayer, all Old Believers were spiritually joined together, regardless of social position.[45]

The traditional interior of Old Believer temples, little changed over the

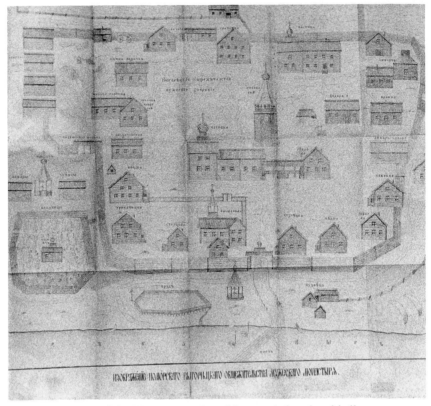

Figure 8.   View of the Vyg community with central chapel and bell tower.

centuries, followed the interior floor plan of the *izba* church: a series of squares or rectangles oriented west to east. In the far west of the structure stood the vestibule (Figure 9, no. 1), known in Russian as the *trapeza* and identified most closely in the western European churches with the narthex. This part of the structure might be compared with the porch room of the *izba,* and served some of the same functions—as entry and social meeting area. In *bespopovtsy* chapels especially, the vestibule also functioned as a buffer between the profane and the holy, sometimes even between men and women. Visitors might stand in the vestibule;[46] it might be used to accommodate an overflow from the nave; or those performing a penance might stand there during the service or make low bows to ask community forgiveness. By the late imperial period, the narthex had often been lost in Russian Orthodox church design, but was revived for Old Believer buildings of the period.

The plan of an Old Believer religious space made sense in relation to its religious function: priestless Old Believers, for example, said the Or-

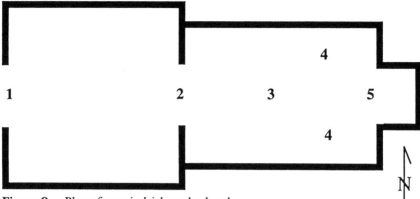

Figure 9.   Plan of a typical *izba*-style church.

thodox "entrance prayers" twice—first as cleansing after contact with the
outside world, and again to begin the liturgical services.[47] If a person
arrived after prayers had begun, he or she did not join the congregation
in the nave until after reciting the prayers at the narthex. In this way, the
back of the building acted as a filter between the profane and the sacred
and marked the passage from secular to sacred space and time, from concerns of the world to those of the divine.[48]

Sometimes temples were built as one large cell, transforming the vestibule into the western portion of the building. The *trapeza* could therefore be integrated into the nave as a congregation grew or as a separate
porch or meeting area was built, leaving one large room demarcated by
railings or steps instead of walls. While in a way commingling the sacred
and profane areas, even single-room chapels did not forsake the basic dynamic of internal design: churchgoers entered at the west end of the
building, blessing themselves when crossing into the nave itself (Figure
9, no. 2).

The combination of vestibule and nave into one large room, generally
undifferentiated, was one adaptation of traditional *izba* design. It symbolized the slow acceptance by some Old Believers of society's status quo,
of the commingling of sacred and profane, of the unclean outside world
with the ritually cleansed Old Believer community. That is, while remaining true to a distinction between the community and the outside world,
some Old Believers began to accept a liturgical building that blurred
the differentiation between the community of Believers and the outside
world, often thought of as the province of Antichrist.

The next cell eastward from the vestibule was the temple's body, or
nave (Figure 9, no. 3). Here the congregation celebrated the services,
and its walls held icons or biblical inscriptions. Traditional form called
for the room to be divided in half, west to east, with women standing on

the north side and men on the south. Wooden benches hugged the out-side walls of the chapel or were in rows across the nave. A few chapels hid the sexes from each other's view by drawing a curtain down the center. This occurred especially in Old Believer monasteries, where the segrega-tion by sex was of special importance.[49] The practice had many varia-tions: in Wojonow, Poland, for example, there was no separation by sex.[50] In Pogorzelec, Russian Poland, in the early twentieth century, the oldest men stood at the front of the chapel, and the oldest women stood in the back. Then, in varying degrees, younger men and women stood closer to the middle of the nave.[51] (A close modification of this pattern remains today in Oregon and Alaska *bespopovtsy* chapels, where men tend to cluster at the front and women toward the rear; women there are called to help celebrate the divine service only when there is a shortage of men.) Such patterns may have reflected the size of a community: small groups may have been more lenient in this regard than large ones. These differences also illustrate variations in custom by geographic region.

In the front of the nave, sometimes divided by a small screen, railing, or step (but clearly still part of the central cell) stood the *kliros* (choir), in the tradition of ancient Russian Orthodox churches (Figure 9, no. 4).[52] A choir area physically connected to the altar and the nave helped to in-tegrate the congregation into a communal liturgical experience. This front-and-sides position in wooden churches was described by nineteenth-century architectural historians, and had occurred in seventeenth-century parish and monumental structures—the Cathedral of the Trinity in Ser-geer Posad is a pertinent example.[53] The Russian Orthodox church later changed this design, however, and often moved the choir behind and above the nave; thus a Western-style choir loft separated the *kliros* from the rest of the church. This redefined the choir's function as an indepen-dent part of the sacred service; its members were no longer on the same plane as the rest of the congregation. Old Believers, on the other hand, revived the ancient design on a large scale with their building boom in the late imperial years.

Russian Orthodoxy had also embraced polyphonal singing, eschewed by the Old Believers. Polyphony, while liturgically acceptable, helped to defeat the theory of communal worship central to the Old Believer ex-perience. First, it undercut the symbolism of singing in monophony—one sound as if from one voice. Further, polyphonal singing became ever more intricate and Westernized, reinforcing the physical separation of the choir from the congregation in the nave through the need for specialized musical training. (By the late imperial period even the great Russian sym-phonic composers—Tchaikovsky, Rimsky-Korsakov, and others—wrote for Russian Orthodox choirs.) The Russian Orthodox church choir thereby became increasingly professional and remote from the rest of the congregation. In this way the ideal of communal worship also became remote when compared with the Old Belief, in which the choir was linked to monophonic *znamenyi raspev* (chant by signs) and placed in the nave itself.[54]

At this point, beyond the *kliros,* design of priestly and priestless temples diverged. For the priestly Old Believers, an iconostasis (usually of carved wood) stood in front of the choir area, as in any Orthodox church. In a priestless chapel, however, the east wall usually served as a sort of wall-iconostasis, as opposed to a free-standing structure. According to Orthodox tradition, the iconostasis screened the sanctuary from the nave. In a priestless church, however, there was no consecrated altar. As a result, the *bespopovtsy* built chapels without sanctuaries, transforming the east wall into the iconostasis, thus following the design of ancient Russian wayside chapels. Even so, the iconostasis/front wall preserved a standardized organization: an icon of Christ enthroned was in the middle, flanked by those of saints and the Holy Family; underneath there usually was a row of major feast icons, then icons of all-saints, lesser holidays, and others. A few chapels had royal and deacons' doors, albeit without an altar behind them.[55]

Some analyses have noted an oral tradition that the *bespopovtsy* refused to hang icons on the wall—an accepted Orthodox practice—as blasphemy to the holy images. Instead, priestless Old Believers built shelves and stood their icons upon them. Not all sources have supported this claim, but interior views of priestless buildings often show such an arrangement. Quite possibly the tradition of placing icons on shelves grew out of the transitory nature of Old Believer parishes in the early schism. Ancient icons, so revered by Old Believers, would have been lost to the persecuting forces of church and state had they been permanently affixed to a wall. Icons standing on a shelf could be easily removed for hiding or taken with the faithful on their flight from persecution. This tradition lived on after the legalization of the Old Belief, symbolizing (like the plain exterior of Old Believer temples) the inconstant legal position of the Old Belief in Russia before 1905. In some post-1905 buildings built by wealthy congregations, however, traditional iconostases were built of wood and placed along the east wall of the chapel. These proclaimed a permanency theretofore only rarely seen in Old Believer buildings.[56]

If priestless temples must be understood as an extension of the ever-malleable *izba* design, the easternmost cell made not only theological but also architectural sense. A sanctuary, after all, contained the altar consecrated by a priest and signified the tomb of Christ wherein transubstantiation of bread and wine took place. Since the *bespopovtsy* were without a priesthood, there could be no altar, and thus no sanctuary.[57] In place of a consecrated altar, a table holding a cross and Gospel stood in the front-center of a priestless chapel, always in the main cell but sometimes raised a step (Figure 9, no. 5). This Gospel table imaginatively combined the elements of a lectern and an altar table.[58]

To understand the Gospel table's function, some explanation of Orthodox worship is in order. The full-rite Orthodox liturgy—lost to the *bespopovtsy*—consisted of two sections: the Liturgy of the Word and the Liturgy of the Gifts. The crowning point of the Liturgy of the Word came at the Little Entry, wherein the clergy brought the Gospel from the altar to the front of the royal doors and presented it to the congregation. At this point a deacon or priest read the appointed Gospel selection of the day, setting the book on a movable lectern.[59]

Since the Liturgy of the Gifts was theologically impossible for the priestless Old Believers, the cycle had to end with the reading of the Gospel. Thus, instead of a portable lectern (that no longer needed to be moved for the Great Entry), the Gospel table took on the permanence traditionally reserved for the altar table. This surrogate altar provided the focus for the interior in the same way as an altar inside the sanctuary of a priestly church. In the priestless tradition the Gospel table became a permanent fixture at the east end of the nave, at the same relative position as the lectern. Here, before the Gospel, the preceptor would bow to the assembled community to ask forgiveness, then proclaim the Word of God.

Much might be made of this creation of a substitute altar used for the Gospel instead of the Eucharist. Indeed, Old Believers earned the reputation as lovers of holy books that predated Nikonian reforms. Old Believers read, handled, and collected books with adoration, and were widely believed to be more highly literate than the average Russian.[60] Old Believers' love for books and their high literacy rate (among other factors) have led scholars to claim that the development of the Old Belief was analogous to the Protestant Reformation in western Europe. In this model, the preeminence of the written word in the priestless temples could be construed as the symbolic elevation of the Gospels above the holy mysteries. Creation of a permanent Gospel table instead of the altar table might then be seen as replacing the Body and Blood of Christ with the Word of God, much as in the Protestant tradition.[61]

The argument, although faulty, does reveal some facets of the Old Belief. It would, for example, dovetail conveniently with the Old Believers' well-known love for books. Unlike the Protestant tradition, however, that held the Bible as the single source of divine exposition, Old Believers revered books *themselves* as vessels of tradition and thus as keys to salvation. A common priestless attitude (this one held even into the late twentieth century) stated that religious questions were not open for debate: "You have Holy-Books—you open the books and there is your answer."[62] More often than not, liturgical and polemical texts received the same ad-

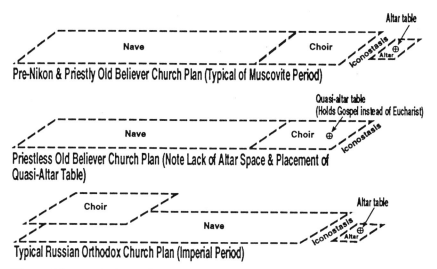

Figure 10.   Typical use of liturgical spaces.

oration by Old Believers as the Gospels, a clear difference from the teaching of Martin Luther.

Rather than a move toward Protestantism, the creation of a permanent Gospel table in the place of a sanctified altar symbolized the incomplete nature of priestless Orthodoxy. Old Believers did not try to create a new religion, or even a new religious sensibility. Instead, they believed that they were maintaining, as fully as possible, the traditions of Orthodoxy as it developed in premodern Russia. Thus, in the spiritual desert created by the loss of the priesthood, the *bespopovtsy* needed to provide both a central focus for their chapels and to establish that the reading of the Gospel was the culminating liturgical act available to them. In that light, the written Word provided not innovation but the means to transmit the piety of Old Rus' to succeeding generations.

As Figure 10 shows, the entire interior space of Old Believer liturgical buildings maintained a tradition that emphasized the unity of community members. The priestly Old Believers continued the traditional floor plans of Russian churches. This included an integrated choir and the retention of a single physical level for all worshipers. It was the priestless groups, however, that most obviously stated the unity of members through their design. In the *bespopovtsy* tradition, both the spiritual father and the equivalent of the altar area had to be moved into the nave of the building, since the separate altar area did not exist. The organization of Old Believer communities was realized every time it gathered to pray. In these buildings, the preceptor (not a cleric) acted as a lay leader of the congregation, and thus stood within it.

Many priestless Old Believers placed special significance on the eastern end of the chapel, especially between the Gospel table and front wall, following the tradition of a sacred altar space found in priestly churches. An ethnographic study of Masurian Old Believers has described this phenomenon among some contemporary faithful, but the tradition existed at the turn of the century as well:

> A certain nostalgia for the sanctuary appears in terms used to describe their chapel by those people deprived of the Eucharist. Thus the wall which carries the icons is called by them the "iconostasis," and the space between it and the stands to which only those who celebrate the religious ceremony have access is, always according to their terminology, the "holy of holies." In the absence of an altar the two designations are obviously improper.[63]

The "obvious" impropriety of this nomenclature makes sense, however, in terms of the priestless Old Believers' desire to retain all facets of Orthodoxy available to them. Much as joining the functions of lectern and altar, Old Believers needed to make some areas in their buildings the foci for communal worship—many communities even retained the term *pristol'* for their surrogate altar.

Not all communities maintained these linguistic distinctions. Some, for example, believed that some spaces were particularly holy areas but did not use the terminology described above. Its use, however, provided legitimization of priestless chapels as true houses of worship and a link to the piety of Old Rus', whose traditions the Old Believers struggled to maintain. In this as in other facets of their sacred design, the Old Believers showed themselves to be an integral and vital part of Russian culture, not a schism or sidetrack from it. The Old Believers' vision of themselves as heirs was borne out in the outpouring of construction after 1905: temples recalled the most traditional Russian designs set within modern conditions, illustrating that the Old Belief was neither a radical departure from Orthodoxy nor a Protestant statement against it, but a living and vital remnant of traditional Christianity. At the same time, the basic plan of Old Believer liturgical spaces reinforced the central role for a community of believers in the life of the church. Identity and salvation were not to be found through faith in a personal savior but, rather, in communitarian songs of repentance and praise.

NOTES

1. By this period Old Believers had, in general, crystallized their sectarian organization into a number of separate groups. The major difference between them remained the question of a sanctified priesthood, which split the Old Belief into the *popovtsy* (priestly) and *bespopovtsy*

(priestless) groups. Among the former, the Belokrinitsa hierarchy (also known as the "Austrian Hierarchy") was the dominant group in this period; among the latter, the Pomortsy had the most adherents and influence. In general, the priestly Old Believers accepted a closer relationship with greater Russian society than any of the priestless groups, who counseled that anti-Christian influences still reigned in Russian society. Even the most strict *bespopovtsy,* however, found it necessary to redefine their place in Russian society after the legalization of their religion.

2. Terms such as "church," "chapel," and "prayer house" are not synonymous in the case of the Old Believers. In traditional Orthodox nomenclature, chapels and prayer houses did not have a consecrated altar. These therefore are the most precise terms to use for priestless liturgical buildings. Churches, also called "temples," in the strictest sense had consecrated altars, and designated only priestly structures. By the late imperial period, however, the Old Believers had begun to call any major liturgical structure a "temple," regardless of whether it had a consecrated altar. Thus in the Preobrazhenskoe priestless complex, the Krestovozdvizhenskii and Nikol'skaia buildings were designated *khram* (temple) and the cemetery building *chasovnia* (chapel), although none of the structures housed a consecrated altar. In general, therefore, the more important and structurally impressive priestless buildings were designated as "temple," while smaller ones were called "chapels" or "prayer houses." All priestly buildings were called either "church" or, more regularly, "temple."

3. See *Vsepoddanneishii otchet ober-prokurora sviateishego sinoda po vedomstvu pravoslavnogo ispovedaniia za 1910 god* (St. Petersburg, 1913), p. 154, which noted that Old Belief existed in every province.

4. See I. E. Grabar, *Istoriia russkoi arkhitektury,* 4 vols. (Moscow, 1909–1915); and Kathleen Berton, *Moscow: An Architectural History* (London: Macmillan, 1977), p. 38.

5. Alexander Opolonikov and Yelena Opolonikova, *The Wooden Architecture of Russia: Houses, Fortifications, Churches* (New York: Harry N. Abrams, 1989), p. 23.

6. Ibid., p. 24.

7. Robert O. Crummey, *Old Believers and the World of Antichrist* (Madison: University of Wisconsin Press, 1970), p. 131.

8. *Polnoe sobranie zakonov Rossiiskoi imperii,* second series, 55 vols. (St. Petersburg, 1830–1884), 39: 41199. Hereafter cited as *PSZ.*

9. *PSZ,* third series, 28 vols. (St. Petersburg, 1911), 3: 1545.

10. J. S. Curtiss, *Church and State in Russia: The Last Years of the Empire, 1900–1917* (New York: Columbia University Press, 1940), pp. 141 ff. See also V. I. Iasevich-Borodaevskaia, *Bor'ba za veru* (St. Petersburg, 1912), pp. 601–602.

11. Rossiskyi Gosudarstvennyi Istoricheskii Arkhiv SSSR,

Ministerstvo Vnutrennikh Del', Dep. Obshchikh Del, *delo* 29, *ll.* 6–13, cited in Curtiss, p. 144.

12. See, for example, N. N., "Glavneishie tsentry sovremennogo raskola," *Khristainskoe chtenie* (1890), no. 1–2, pp. 163–164.

13. See "Po gorodam i vesam: Koz'modem'iansk (Kazan gub.)," *Staroobriadets* (1906), no. 4, p. 209.

14. Ibid. See also "O staroobriadcheskom kolokol'nom zvone," *Staroobriadets* (1906), no. 4, pp. 206–208. Later analysis of imperial policy on Old Believer temples can be found in "O staroobriadcheskikh khramakh," *Tserkov'* (1914), no. 2, pp. 44–45.

15. K. P. Gorbunov, "Sredi raskol'nikov iuzhnogo urala (iz dnevnika turista)," *Istoricheskii vestnik* (1888), no. 12, p. 711. Ethel Dunn, "A Slavophile Looks at the Raskol and the Sects," *Slavonic and East European Review,* 44 (1964), p. 171, quotes Ivan Aksakov's comment on the general well-being of Old Believers a generation earlier:

> The Great Russian raskolnik population [in Starodub] is sharply distinguished, courageous, industrious; they are mature and large, but somewhat rough in appearance.... It would be unpleasant to meet them at night, in the forest. But, on the other hand, I have never seen anywhere stouter, more satisfied, fatter women, all white and fleshy, the real type of Russian beauty; and in fact they would be very beautiful if they were not so obese.

16. "O staroobriadcheskom bogadel'nom dome v Sudislave (1828)," *Russkii arkhiv* (1884), no. 3, pp. 37–54, gives an account of an early almshouse built by the Old Believers. It was a large and prosperous affair, with capital of three hundred thousand rubles, acquired as early as 1812. The project housed up to two hundred people.

17. *Vsepoddanneishii otchet ober-prokurora sviateishego sinoda K. Pobedonostseva po vedomstvu pravoslavnogo ispovedaniia za 1890 i 1891 gody* (St. Petersburg, 1893), p. 191.

18. *Vsepoddanneishii otchet . . . za 1910 god,* p. 159.

19. See, for example, *Vsepoddanneishii otchet . . . za 1890 i 1891 gody,* pp. 188ff., for the reasons given to explain the "steadiness of schism."

20. William Craft Brumfield, "The 'New Style' and the Revival of Orthodox Church Architecture, 1900–1914," in William C. Brumfield and Milos M. Velimirovic, eds., *Christianity and the Arts in Russia* (New York: Cambridge University Press, 1991), p. 117.

21. "Novyi staroobriadcheskii khram v Moskve," *Zlatostrui* (1911–1912), no. 5, p. 53.

22. Brumfield, p. 112.

23. *Vsepoddanneishii otchet . . . za 1910 god,* p. 157.

24. See Peter Waldron, "Religious Reform After 1905: Old Believ-

ers and the Orthodox Church," *Oxford Slavonic Papers* 20 (1987), p. 128.

25. See V. Kh., "Osviashchenie khrama v s. Zueve," *Shchit very* (1914), no. 1, pp. 87–103, for a particularly lengthy description of the building of a Pomortsy temple. Also see V. Filippov, "Torzhestvo osviashcheniia khrama," *Shchit very* (1913), nos. 2–3, pp. 254–263.

26. K. Shvetsov, "Vozrazdaiushchaiasia Rossiia," in "Sel'skoe khoziaistvo," *Zlatostrui* (1912–1913), no. 1, p. 83.

27. See, for example, A. Kuznetsov, "Obshchiny i ikh razvitie," *Ural'skii staroobriadets* (1915), no. 2, p. 19.

28. Aleksandr Modolov, "Torzhestvo staroveriia," *Shchit very* (1912), no. 4, pp. 354–357; nos. 5–6, pp. 485–498.

29. The Preobrazhenskoe complex is being partially renovated as the Center for Traditional Russian Culture. My thanks to Director I. K. Rusakovskii for his aid in preparing this analysis.

30. Brumfield, p. 109.

31. George Heard Hamilton, *The Art and Architecture of Russia* (New York: Penguin Books, 1983), p. 409.

32. "Pervyi v Moskve khram staroobriadtsev pomortsev brachnogo soglasiia," *Zlatostrui* (1910), no. 4, p. 56.

33. Brumfield, p. 110, also notes that the interior of the church was much less distinctive than the exterior.

34. Ibid.

35. Lev Vladimirovich Dal', "Drevniia dereviannyia tserkvi v Rossii," *Zodchii: Arkhitekturnyi i khudozhestvenno-tekhnicheskii zhurnal* (1875), no. 6, p. 78.

36. Hubert Faensen, Vladimir Ivanov, and Klaus G. Beyer, *Early Russian Architecture* (London: Paul Elek, 1972), p. 40.

37. V. P. Ofinskii, *Dereviannoe zodchestvo karelii* (Leningrad: Izdatel'stvo Literatury po Stroitel'stvu, 1972), p. 56.

38. Opolonikov and Opolonikova, p. 157.

39. Akademiia Nauk SSSR, *Bukhtarminskie staroobriadtsy* (Leningrad: Akademiia Nauk SSSR, 1930), pp. 305–311.

40. David Z. Scheffel, *In the Shadow of Antichrist: The Old Believers of Alberta* (Peterborough, Ontario: Broadview Press, 1991), p. 164.

41. *Ulozhenie pervogo vserossiiskogo sobora khristian-pomortsev* (Moscow: Moskovskaia Staroobriadcheskaia Knigopechatnia, 1909), fol. 15. In general the Pomortsy did not dictate exterior design. See, for example, "Sooruzhenie ili remont khrama," *Shchit very* (1916), no. 4, p. 167.

42. Iosif Volotskii, as quoted in "Otvety redaktsii," *Ural'skii staroobriadets* (1916), no. 3, pp. 21–22.

43. See the maps of the Vyg community in I. Filippov's important *Istoriia vygovskoi staroobriadcheskoi pustyni* (St. Petersburg, 1862).

44. Sviashchenno-inok Serapion, "Khram i molitva," *Tserkov'* (1914), no. 25, p. 594.

45. The democratic as well as the unifying nature of the temple was noted in Modolov, p. 486.

46. Although at times welcome to attend services, non–Old Believer visitors could not participate in liturgical celebrations. See "Otvety redaktsii," *Zlatostrui* (1910–1911), no. 12, p. 67.

47. Bows were to be made whenever one entered the building, were repeated at the beginning and end of the service, and were prescribed for the entrance and departure from one's home.

48. A technologically elaborate message system, with lights to call the pastor back to the narthex, was developed in some places so that the community preceptor would be alerted to come and lead prayers for latecomers.

49. Crummey, p. 64.

50. Bernard Marchadier, "Les vieux-croyants de Wojonow," *Cahiers du monde russe et soviétique* 18 (1977), p. 442.

51. This arrangement served to segregate the eldest, but let the youngest parishioners watch after themselves in the middle of the church. Thus a young woman and man could stand rather close to each other during the service, making the chapel a social center during long services.

52. A seventeenth-century precedent for this step design can be found in a wooden church at Kopotna, near Moscow. See *Drevnosti: Trudy komissii po sokhraneniiu drevnikh pamiatnikov imperatorskogo moskovskogo arkheologicheskogo obshchestva* (Moscow, 1907), fol. XVI. See also David Buxton, *The Wooden Churches of Eastern Europe: An Introductory Survey* (London: Cambridge University Press, 1981), p. 44.

53. See Dal', p. 78.

54. Traditional Old Believer liturgical singing, like church design, found new life after 1905. Touring choirs performed with great success and journals devoted especially to singing began to complement the many articles in the general Old Believer press. See, for example, *Tserkovnoe penie*, which, as part of the Belokrinitsa journal *Staroobriadcheskoe mysl'*, included articles on the cultural importance of the old rite singing, its place in Old Believer history, and technical articles regarding the method and pedagogy of the old chant, as well as polemics against "many-voiced" or "Italianate" singing.

55. The Nikol'skaia chapel at Preobrazhenskoe cemetery is a pertinent example.

56. There is also a more practical reason for icons being stood on shelves. In poor communities Old Believers would often lend family-owned icons to the temple when it did not own enough. This in turn sacramentalized the family icon and reinforced the relationship between home and temple. The Russian Orthodox church banned this custom in the eighteenth century because many icons were judged to be of substandard quality.

57. When segments of *bespopovtsy* communities decided to receive the full sacramental life (most notably in the diaspora communities of Pennsylvania, Oregon, and Alaska), they maintained their tradition of a front icon wall instead of an icon screen. This persistent tradition—perhaps reinforced by the cost of tearing down a wall to build a screen during the change from priestless to priestly—has given Old Believer churches in these communities a distinct design; since the iconostasis is a wall, there is no space between it and the ceiling. The altar, instead of being a section screened from the nave, is a completely different room. In design and practice, congregations that accepted priesthood "rebuilt" an altar on the front end of the chapel, converting it to a church. This convention remained faithful to the concept of adding or subtracting *izba* cells as necessary.

58. This phenomenon has been noted by Scheffel even among twentieth-century Old Believers in Alberta, Canada. See Scheffel, p. 134.

59. Examples of these, also used by Old Believers, can be found in "Drevne-russkaia utvar i mebel," *Zodchii* (1879), fol. 18, no. 6.

60. Eugeniusz Iwaniec, *Z dziejow staroobrzedowcow na zemiach polskich xvii–xx w.* (Warsaw: Wydawnictwo Naukowe, 1977), p. 280. Scheffel, pp. 104–116, describes this in detail.

61. See James Billington, *The Icon and the Axe: An Interpretive Study of Russian Culture* (New York: Random House, 1966), pp. 193ff. An early proponent of this view was Albert F. Heard, in his *The Russian Church and Russian Dissent* (New York: Harper & Brothers, 1887; repr., New York: AMS Press, 1971). Brumfield, p. 110, makes a similar comment in regard to Old Believer architecture, saying that "the functional, relatively austere design of the interior . . . resembled more closely the simplicity of a Protestant meeting house than the usual Orthodox Church."

62. "Minutes of Russian Old Believers' Conference," Erie, Pa., 2 September 1984, pp. 1–2.

63. Marchadier, p. 442.

Part Two

Confessional and National Identity in the Orthodox World

The Third Rebirth of the Ukrainian Autocephalous Orthodox Church and the Religious Situation in Ukraine, 1989–1991

Since 1988 the religious situation for Eastern Christians has changed more radically in Ukraine than in any other area of the former Soviet Union. Until the millennium celebrations and the delayed beginning of perestroika and glasnost in Ukraine, the Russian Orthodox church (ROC) was the only Eastern Christian institution with legally recognized congregations in Ukraine. By August 24, 1991, when Ukraine declared independence, the Ukrainian Catholic church (UCC), the Ukrainian branch of the Moscow Patriarchate, and the Ukrainian Autocephalous Orthodox church (UAOC) maintained competing organizations with legally registered parishes.

Descending from the Union of Brest of 1596, the UCC, formerly known as the Uniate or the Greek Catholic church, had been the dominant church among Eastern Christian believers in Galicia and Transcarpathia until these areas were annexed to the Soviet Union during World War II. The Soviet authorities forcibly liquidated the UCC and incorporated it into the ROC. Despite decades of persecution, an underground church had been maintained and a considerable portion of the ostensibly Russian Orthodox clergy and believers continued to be loyal to the Union of Brest. Galicia and Transcarpathia were especially important for the ROC in Ukraine because they contained almost half its parishes, and generally the best organized ones.

Organized under the leadership of the Metropolitan of Kiev as the Exarch of Ukraine, the ROC had controlled the Orthodox of Ukraine since the transfer of the Metropolitanate of Kiev from the jurisdiction of the Patriarchate of Moscow in 1685–1686. Despite short-term concessions to aspirations for Ukrainian religious autonomy in 1918 and during World War II, the ROC had succeeded in maintaining itself as a unified, centralized institution.

Although the UAOC sees itself as the heir of the Kiev Metropolitanate as it existed before its incorporation into the ROC, its more modern institutional antecedents are the Ukrainian Autocephalist Orthodox church, formed out of the Ukrainian church movement in 1921, and the Ukrainian Autocephalous Orthodox church, established in 1942 during the German occupation of Ukraine. The first combined aspirations for an independent Ukrainian church with a movement for radical religious reform. The establishment of a hierarchy without consecration by bishops led to its appellation as "self-consecrators." The UAOC, liquidated under pressure from the Soviet authorities in the 1930s, survived among Ukrainian communities abroad. Revived in Ukraine in 1942, its hierarchy was consecrated in the traditional manner and was more conservative in its theology and adherence to traditional Orthodox canons than its predecessor. Destroyed by the return of the Soviet authorities, the UAOC of 1942 came to play a dominant role in Ukrainian Orthodox communities abroad.

As was universally expected, the abating of active persecution led to the reemergence of the UCC from the underground in the western Ukrainian regions of Galicia and Transcarpathia.[1] With the defeat of the Communist party in the three Galician oblasts in March 1990, the UCC no longer faced local government opposition to reclaiming the churches that it had possessed before 1946, so that by 1991 Archbishop Major of Lviv, Cardinal Myroslav Liubachivs'kyi, who returned from exile in Rome, headed about two thousand Uniate congregations. Although the Ukrainian Exarchate of the Moscow Patriarchate lost hundreds of congregations and churches to the Ukrainian Catholics, the ROC benefited from the new religious policies by receiving permission to establish new congregations and to take over hundreds of church edifices. The renaming of the Exarchate as the Ukrainian Orthodox church (UOC) and the granting of broad autonomy by the Patriarchate in 1990 were more unexpected.[2] Nevertheless, the most unexpected event on the Ukrainian religious scene was the rapid development of the UAOC following the declaration by the first parish in August 1989 that it was breaking with the Moscow Patriarchate.[3]

Unlike the UCC, which had maintained a continuous underground organization after 1946, and the UOC, which merely assumed the institutions of the Moscow Patriarchate, the UAOC had to establish its structure in entirety. Other than mentions in the dissident literature and the activities of Father Vasyl' Romaniuk, who affirmed his allegiance to the UAOC, no organized movement to reestablish the UAOC existed as late as 1988.[4] Yet students of Ukrainian church history realized that relenting of political repression and a Ukrainian cultural revival had twice before stimulated the establishment of the UAOC in the twentieth century.[5] Even they could hardly have predicted how rapidly it would regenerate.

The failure of the Moscow Patriarchate to learn from the lessons of

1917–1921 and 1942, the two earlier establishments of the UAOC, and to make concessions to Ukrainian ecclesiastical aspirations was fundamental to the rebirth of the UAOC.[6] Even though in the 1970s and 1980s over 50 percent of the parishes of the Patriarchate were in Ukraine, with 25 percent in the nationally conscious western Ukraine, the ROC permitted very few Ukrainian elements.[7] Indeed in the Brezhnev-Suslov years, when the Soviet government embarked on more intensive Russification, including the attempt to form one "East Slavic nation," the church removed some of the concessions it had made to Ukrainians in ritual and assignment of cadres. Its Russian-language seminaries, including the one in Ukraine, did not teach the Ukrainian language and culture, much less examine specifically Ukrainian spiritual and ecclesiastical traditions.

Despite the decree of autonomy proclaimed in 1918 and the titles of Exarch and Exarchate, the church in Ukraine was fully subsumed into the ROC. The ROC remained the only Russian imperial structure in the Soviet period, since it did not adjust in name or structure to the recasting of the Russian Empire as the Soviet Union, except for its loss of the Georgian church. The church in some way mitigated this affiliation by using the term *Rus'ka Pravoslavna Tserkva* (Rus' Orthodox church) in Ukrainian instead of *Rosiis'ka Pravoslavna Tserkva* (Russian Orthodox church). It did so to evoke Kievan or Old Rus', though in nineteenth- and early twentieth-century west Ukrainian usage, the term would mean "Ukrainian," excluding Russians. In fact, in contemporary usage even in western Ukraine, the term *Rus'ka* had come to signify "Russian," and the church was perceived as such. In practical terms, the church used Russian pronunciation of Church Slavonic everywhere but in Galicia and Transcarpathia, and Russian as the language of preaching in urban areas and even at times in rural areas outside western Ukraine. In liturgy, music, architecture, and iconography, it adhered to norms that were portrayed as Orthodox but were in fact imperial Russian. Its historical and cultural self-conception was as an all-Russian Orthodox church, so much so that it emphasized the traditions of the church of Muscovy to the neglect of those of the Kiev Metropolitanate. The major features distinguishing the Exarchate from the general ROC, aside from its greater density of parishes and numbers of vocations, were that it devoted greater attention to anti-Uniate polemics and that in the former Uniate regions priests were permitted to incorporate some local religious and artistic traditions. Nevertheless, with the greater mixing of cadres and the striving for "pure Orthodox practices," even these were concessions under pressure.

An interview with Patriarch Aleksii published in *Literaturnaia gazeta* on November 28, 1990, most clearly demonstrated the degree of alienation of the leadership of the ROC from Ukrainian religious aspirations. By then the new patriarch had traveled twice to Ukraine.[8] In the summer, he had to answer requests by clergymen gathered at the Pochaiv Monastery that autocephaly be granted to the church in Ukraine as a way of saving Orthodoxy's position.[9] In the fall he had come to Kiev to grant the church autonomy instead, and had been confronted by large crowds of believers and Ukrainian activists objecting to the Russian patriarch's use of St. Sophia Cathedral of Kiev, which until its closure in the early 1930s had belonged to the UAOC.[10] Still, in describing the situation in Ukraine, the patriarch said:

> Relating to the so-called Ukrainian autocephalists—these people wish to see in Christ not their Lord and Judge, but an ally. An ally in political struggle. Two thousand years ago people also treated Christ as a political figure: some placed hope in Him as a political leader, others feared Him also as a dangerous political criminal. And as a result together they crucified Him. . . . The subordination of church interests to political interest, the transformation of the church into an instrument of politics, always constitutes violence on the faith and the church, always leads the church to Golgotha.

Given the traditional relation of the ROC to the Russian Empire and the Soviet Union, the patriarch argued from a position of weakness. His church's active agitation for a Soviet All-Union treaty demonstrated that no such break had occurred even in 1990. Just as significant was the patriarch's interpretation of the religious situation:

> If the Ukrainian autocephalists could clearly explain in what way unity with the Russian church hinders the act of their spiritual salvation and in what way they would be spiritually richer dividing themselves off from their Russian brothers, I would attempt to understand them. In the Ukrainian Church there are its own specific complications [*slozhnosti*], its own traditions. Knowing of this, we granted it independence [*nezavisimost'*] and autonomy [*samostoiatel'nost'*] in matters of administration.

As of November 1990 the patriarch had not tried to understand the autocephalists' position, and his mention of "specific complications" rang truer than that of "its own traditions" in explaining why autonomy had been granted to a newly named "Ukrainian Orthodox" church in late 1990.

That the newly elected patriarch had not yet considered the autocephalists' views and did not seem to have reflected deeply on the traditions of a UOC can hardly be surprising when one examines how late the concept of a UOC emerged among the leaders of the Exarchate in Ukraine. In the early 1980s, even in writing for the Ukrainian diaspora, which belonged in large part to Ukrainian Orthodox churches, leaders of the Exarchate would go no further than entitling their works "Orthodoxy in Ukraine," with the accompanying assertion that the Exarchate was an inseparable part of the ROC.[11] Accounts of the history of Orthodoxy, far from discussing the evolution of a Ukrainian Orthodox tradition or of the Kiev Metropolitanate, concentrated on Muscovy-Russia in the fifteenth to seventeenth centuries, viewing the period of clear and stable separation of the metropolitanates of Kiev and Muscovy (1458–1686) as negative, and examining events in Ukraine only episodically. Writing "On the Question of the History of the Kiev Metropolitanate" after the proclamation of the UOC, Metropolitan Filaret Denysenko did not depict the history of a continuously developing ecclesiastical tradition but confined himself to answering the autocephalist views of specific incidents (such as "The separation of the Rus'ka Pravoslavna Tserkva into two metropolitanates" [fifteenth century], "The Reunification of the Kiev Metropolitanate with the Moscow Patriarchate" [1685–1686], and above all the events of the twentieth century and the rise of the UAOC) without diverging from usual interpretations or admitting that the policies of the ROC in any way erred on Ukrainian issues.[12]

In general, the Moscow Patriarchate belatedly reacted to Ukrainian religious and national aspirations. Deeply imbued, even in Ukraine, with its identity as the ROC and devoid of any conceptualization of a legitimate Ukrainian ecclesiastical culture, the church leadership was ill-prepared for responding to the renewed autocephalist movement or for establishing a Ukrainian Orthodox church. Linguistically Russified in eastern Ukraine and immersed in Russian ecclesiastical and secular culture, many of the clergy lacked both the knowledge and the desire to respond to the Ukrainian national revival. Since in 1990 the autocephalists won over clergy and believers in western Ukraine and the intelligentsia throughout Ukraine, the Moscow Patriarchate lost its component most attuned to Ukrainian aspirations.[13] At the same time, its leaders became more suspicious of Ukrainian issues as promoting schism and more dependent on maintaining the old political order to buttress their position.[14]

If the Moscow Patriarchate provided an environment conducive to the rebirth of the UAOC, the national revival in Ukraine cultivated knowledge and reverence toward the UAOC. In the renewal of Ukrainian culture and national awareness in the 1980s, attention focused on the 1920s. Although the original intention may have been to rehabilitate the Ukrainian national Communists in order to legitimize Soviet Ukrainian patriotism, the renewal soon expanded into a return to the Ukrainian cultural flowering. This period, frequently called the "Executed Renaissance," ended with the Stalinist pogrom of the Ukrainian intelligentsia and the man-made famine of 1932–1933. As the focus shifted to the study of the noncommunist element of the revival and the process of Ukrainianization of the masses, intellectuals paid more attention to the role of the UAOC. With increased discussion of Stalinist crimes, the accusations against the

UAOC at the show trials of the League for Liberation of the Ukraine in 1930 and the ruthless persecution and destruction of the church and its leaders in the 1930s gave it authority as a national institution and an aura of martyrdom.[15]

The general Ukrainian historical and cultural renewal also made the Ukrainian intelligentsia more favorable to the UAOC and the traditions and views it had espoused. As the Soviet interpretation of Kiev Rus' as the cradle of the "Old Rus' nationality" that spawned the three "fraternal" East Slavic nations was questioned, the ROC's principal theoretical underpinning was challenged. When historians and political leaders could once again discuss Russification in the nineteenth-century Russian Empire, they inevitably condemned the ROC's role as a major proponent and instrument of these policies. The most important impetus for the Ukrainian national revival to take interest in religious affairs and in the UAOC was its focus on the "Cossack Age," the sixteenth to eighteenth centuries, as the source of Ukrainian identity. Not only was the period one in which religious affairs were central, but it was one in which the Kiev Metropolitanate had been separate from the church in Muscovy (entirely until 1686) and in which Ukrainian religious culture—literary, artistic, and musical—was quite distinct from Russian. The UAOC had revived these traditions in the 1920s while the ROC had largely suppressed them. The Ukrainian cultural revival and growth of historical consciousness inevitably led even those distant from church affairs to view the UAOC positively and the ROC negatively.[16]

The UAOC revived so rapidly because it had survived outside the Soviet Union and churches in the West could serve as models, financial supporters, and sources of literature and cadres. The history of Ukrainian Orthodox churches in the West has involved the complex evolution of a number of organizations, reflecting religious developments in Ukraine and conditions in the countries of settlement.[17] By the 1980s the great majority of Ukrainian Orthodox belonged to three metropolitanates—the UAOC (Europe, South America, Australia), the Ukrainian Orthodox Church of the United States of America, and the Ukrainian Orthodox Church of Canada—which though administratively separate, considered themselves in spiritual unity as one church. With about three hundred thousand believers, four hundred churches, two hundred priests, and two seminaries, the three metropolitanates constituted both a significant component of the Orthodox diaspora and a major institution in Ukrainian community life. In Canada, the Ukranian Orthodox church was the largest Orthodox jurisdiction, while in the United States the church center in South Bound Brook, New Jersey, with its memorial church, museum, archive, seminary, cultural center, and Ukrainian national cemetery, served as a focal point for the Ukrainian diaspora.

Metropolitan Mstyslav Skrypnyk closely linked the metropolitanates of

the UAOC and the Ukranian Orthodox church in the United States because he served as metropolitan of both. Bishops who traced their apostolic succession to the UAOC revived in 1942 or to the interwar Polish
Orthodox church led the three metropolitanates. That most Orthodox
jurisdictions did not recognize the Ukrainian Orthodox churches or admit their hierarchs to the Standing Conference of Orthodox Bishops
(North America) merely served to reinforce their Ukrainian identity,
since they were not drawn into discussions to abolish ethnic allegiances in
the interests of Orthodox unity. In particular, Metropolitan Mstyslav remained dedicated to ensuring that the church in the West would be prepared for its mission in Ukraine. In his very person—as nephew of the
head of state of the Ukrainian National Republic of 1919, Symon Petli-
ura; as participant in the struggle for Ukrainian independence of 1917–
1921; as political leader of Ukrainians in Poland in the interwar period;
and as bishop consecrated in Kiev in 1942—he embodied the strivings
for Ukrainian religious and national rights.[18]

Perestroika and glasnost permitted the Ukrainian Orthodox churches
in the West to influence the religious situation in Ukraine. Visits and
family contacts made more and more believers and clergy in Ukraine
aware of the Ukrainian Orthodox churches in the West. Suspension of
radio jamming permitted more of Ukraine's population to listen to the
churches' religious programs. The end to customs' seizures of religious
literature allowed a massive program of propaganda to be undertaken, in
which the Ukranian Orthodox Church of Canada dispatched hundreds
of thousands of books and pamphlets. As early as 1977, Father Vasyl'
Romaniuk had recognized the authority of Metropolitan Mstyslav, who
held the title of Metropolitan of Kiev. When the former Russian Orthodox Bishop Ioan Bodnarchuk accepted the leadership of the autocephalists in the fall of 1989, he recognized the authority of Metropolitan
Mstyslav. The First Council of the UAOC in June 1990 elected Mstyslav
"Patriarch of Kiev and All Ukraine," and in the fall the ninety-two-year-
old hierarch was finally granted a Soviet visa and installed in Kiev.

An important factor explaining the rapid rebirth of the UAOC was its
ability to find mass support in Galicia. Before World War II only a few
Orthodox parishes existed in Galicia. The forcible nature of the area's
"conversion" to Orthodoxy in 1946 and the heroic struggle of the underground Ukrainian Catholics had led many western Ukrainians to assume
that with the end of persecution and the legalization of the church almost
all believers and parishes would return to the UCC. Although the migration of east Ukrainians and Russians to western Ukraine after World
War II meant that the Eastern Christians in Galicia were no longer
homogeneously western Ukrainians, the greater incidence of religious
practice of the native Galicians ensured that they were the vast majority
of believers and a majority of the clergy. Nevertheless, a considerable

segment of the Galician population has chosen to remain Orthodox, and most of these have broken with the Moscow Patriarchate and joined the UAOC.[19]

Traditionally the Ukrainian or Greek Catholic church had been divided between "Westernizers" and "Easternizers." The latter resisted the latinization of the church, in part because it was associated with polonization, and a segment had always been pro-Orthodox. In the decades after World War II, part of the clergy who had undergone forcible conversion in 1946 accepted their affiliation with Orthodoxy, in particular if they had traditionally been Easternizers. Their numbers increased as more and more of the clergy studied in the seminaries of the Moscow Patriarchate. The Vatican's *Ostpolitik* under Pope Paul VI had profoundly disillusioned some believers, who consequently lost their devotion to the papacy. During the early 1980s, the Soviet authorities had discussed the possibility of recognizing a UCC that would break with Rome; and some believers, despairing of ever gaining recognition otherwise, had entertained this idea. In many ways, the UAOC embodied this concept of a Ukrainian church not affiliated with the Moscow Patriarchate or with Rome. Also, because a faction of the underground church censured those who had attended the churches of the Moscow Patriarchate in the years of persecution, some clergy and believers found a return to the UCC humiliating.

By 1989, the activities of the UCC greatly increased as it emerged from the underground and as the Soviet policy of denying religious freedom in western Ukraine became increasingly untenable for domestic and international reasons. Resentment against the Soviet regime and Russification surfaced powerfully in an area where the Moscow Patriarchate was viewed as intrinsically part of both. Facing the indifference and even hostility of the Patriarchate and the Exarchate to Ukrainian religious and national aspirations, those clergy who wished to remain Orthodox and retain their congregations realized that only an autocephalous Ukranian Orthodox church could do so.[20]

The events and motivations of the establishment of the UAOC in Galicia remain the subject of great controversy. Father Volodymyr Iarema and the parish of Sts. Peter and Paul in Lviv declared their adherence to the UAOC on August 19, 1989, a few months before the Ukrainian Catholics took control of the Transfiguration church in the same city. Certainly the clergy who began to declare their allegiance to the UAOC were motivated by a desire to keep their congregations from passing over to the UCC. Some Ukrainian Catholics have claimed that the KGB had a hand in the movement, as a means of hindering the UCC and sowing discord in the Ukrainian national movement. In fact, some priests may have been compromised by the KGB and have realized that they had little future in the restored UCC. Allegations have centered on the person of

Bishop (now Metropolitan) Ioan Bodnarchuk, formerly Russian Orthodox bishop of Zhytomyr, who took over leadership of the newly forming
UAOC in late October 1989.

In 1990 the UAOC increased so rapidly in Galicia that by the end of
the year about 1,000 parishes had formed. This contrasts with the much
slower growth of the church in other regions, where by early 1991 about
150 parishes existed.[21] With functioning parishes and church buildings,
the UAOC in Galicia became the stronghold for religious and organizational activities. Seminaries were formed in Lviv and Ternopil', and
youth groups and brotherhoods were organized in the three Galician
eparchies.[22] Contacts with the Ukrainian Orthodox churches abroad also
assisted the UAOC in making inroads in Galicia, since the majority of
Ukrainian Orthodox believers in Canada and at least a plurality in the
United States are descended from Galician immigrants. The church also
benefited from anti-Polish sentiments in western Ukraine, in particular
suspicions of the Polish Roman Catholic church and revanchist circles.[23]
Here the attraction of the church was as much freedom from the Vatican
led by a Polish Pope as independence from Moscow.

By 1991 the UAOC had achieved sufficient stability as an institution
to ensure that it would continue to play a major role in Ukrainian reli-
gious affairs. In addition to the patriarch elected at the council of June
1990, the church had a metropolitan of Galicia in Lviv, and bishops for
Ternopil', Ivano-Frankivs'k, Rivne (with an assistant in Dubno), Luts'k,
Chernivtsi, Uzhhorod, Bila Tserkva, Sumy, Mykolaiv, Kamianets'-
Podil's'kyi, and Dnipropetrovs'k. Of the bishops the most renowned
was Volodymyr of Bila Tserkva, formerly the political prisoner Father
Vasyl' Romaniuk, who had responsibilities for mission work in eastern
Ukraine. In Kiev the church had four parishes and had established a central administration, although the patriarchal chancery was still housed in
the Hotel Ukraina. The Galician eparchies had a considerable network of
organizations. In other areas the Brotherhood of St. Andrew, with leadership provided by the Kiev chapter, spearheaded missionary work. In
1991, over three hundred delegates from brotherhoods throughout
Ukraine attended the second congress of the organization.[24] The UAOC
had also established an active press, with newspapers such as *Nasha vira
pravoslav'ia* (initially ten thousand press run) and journals such as *Tserkva
i zhyttia* and numerous local bulletins. Several Ukrainian intellectuals of
note worked in the church as activists; most significantly, Ievhen Sverstiuk, literary critic and former political prisoner, served as editor of *Nasha
vira pravoslav'ia*.

The great prominence that the church had assumed in Ukrainian civic
and cultural life stemmed to a considerable degree from the active leadership of Patriarch Mstyslav. After his arrival in October 1990, despite his
age, he tirelessly traveled throughout Ukraine, from Lviv in the west

to Kharkiv in the east. He paid great attention to pastoral affairs and to ensuring that the church served at the numerous national and cultural commemorations that have become so common throughout Ukraine. Through his action—such as meeting the material needs of the victims of the Chernobyl catastrophe; his press conference with the Kiev soccer club Dynamo, which pledged to assist him in rebuilding St. Michael's Monastery; and his appearance before hundreds of thousands gathered at Beresteckho to commemorate the Cossacks who died there in 1651—Patriarch Mstyslav brought great visibility to the church, and with it recognition as a national institution.[25]

Despite the great achievements of the UAOC, it remained a very inchoate institution. Not only did the patriarch not receive a permanent residence and administrative offices, he did not yet have a well-established chancery. The UOC and the Communist party press tried to undermine his authority by charging that he had collaborated with the Germans during World War II. Lines of authority among the hierarchs were not clearly established, especially the powers of Metropolitan Ioan of Galicia (who went on a leave for medical treatment in the United States) and of Bishop Antonii of Rivne, who served as patriarchal exarch before Patriarch Mstyslav's arrival and continued to organize church activities in Kiev. The division of functions between the Brotherhood of St. Andrew, which took such a great role in the organizing of the church in eastern Ukraine, and the hierarchy was not clear-cut. Outside of Galicia, the eparchies often had only a few parishes (for instance, Rivne, six parishes, but only four registered in March 1991;[26] Kamianets'-Podil'skyi, three parishes as of June 1991).[27] The church suffered from a critical shortage of clergy, and priests such as Father Iurii Boiko in Kiev had to travel ceaselessly to provide services to the UAOC congregations and to ensure that the church sanctified the numerous commemorations of the victims of the famine of 1932–1933 and Ukrainian cultural events.[28]

To a great degree the actions of the civil authorities determined the situation of the church. They registered congregations, disposed of church buildings, and controlled movement in and out of (and at sometimes within) Ukraine. While political pluralism and assertion of the primacy of government institutions over Communist party organizations came to many regions and levels of government in Ukraine, the hard-line Communist faction that opposed the UAOC still ruled substantial areas of the republic, particularly in the east and in rural areas. In eastern Ukraine only in large cities such as Kiev and Kharkiv were there sufficient members of the democratic opposition and the reform Communists to give the UAOC at least a hearing. Although the parliament also had significant similar factions, the registration of congregations and the assigning of buildings were settled at the oblast and municipality level. Patriarch Mstyslav's meetings with Leonid Kravchuk, chairman of the

Supreme Soviet, and Vitold Fokin, prime minister, at least signaled that after years of persecution followed by harassment, the government of the republic viewed the UAOC as a legitimate institution. But at the local level the old-guard Communists fiercely opposed the UAOC, resorting to physical attacks, defamation, harassment, and overt preferential treatment of the UOC. Frequently, groups organized jointly by the Communists and the UOC carried out violence and intimidation.[29] The triumph of Rukh and the democratic opposition in Galicia placed the UAOC in a much better position than in other areas, but certain elements of the new government were antagonistic to the UAOC and favored the UCC, though given a choice between the UAOC and the UOC, their preference was the former.

The Moscow Patriarchate and the UOC were the major opponents of the UAOC. During his visit to Ukraine, Patriarch Aleksii even went so far as to counsel the municipal government of Zhytomyr against giving a church building to the UAOC.[30] Metropolitan Filaret and the hierarchs of the UOC launched an ongoing campaign against the UAOC, including attacks on the person of Patriarch Mstyslav and accusations that the UAOC is somehow Uniate. The UOC, with nineteen eparchies and more than five thousand parishes, was an imposing foe.[31] Although the number of parishes was somewhat inflated because those it claimed in Galicia were virtually extinct as believers defected to the UAOC and the UCC, the UOC expanded significantly in eastern Ukraine.[32] Indeed, the challenge of the UAOC has in some ways assisted the UOC in expanding, since in cities such as Chernihiv and Dnipropetrovs'k the local authorities hastened to hand over closed churches to the UOC to avoid having to approve requests by the UAOC.[33] This was similar to the Communist authorities' policies in Galicia in 1988, when they handed over hundreds of closed churches to the Russian Orthodox church to prevent Ukrainian Catholics from using them.[34] Nevertheless, the dependence of the UOC on the Communist authorities ever more opened it up to accusations that it was "the Ukrainian [or Russian] Orthodox church supporting the platform of the Communist Party of the Soviet Union." Given the growing anticommunist feeling in Ukraine, the UOC was undermining its long-term position for short-term advantage.

In its competition with the UOC, the UAOC faced an opponent ever more conscious of its need to deal with Ukrainian issues. Well into 1990, the UAOC had great opportunities because it challenged a Russian, not a Ukrainian, Orthodox church. With its change of name, the Exarchate sought to adjust to the Ukrainian national and political revival, above all the declaration of sovereignty of July 16, 1990.[35] The UAOC's insistence on the continued Russian nature of what it frequently termed the "so-called UOC" testified to the Exarchate's successes in partially defusing its alienation from Ukrainian aspirations. Initially the UAOC had no real competition in sanctifying events such as commemorations of the famine of 1932–1933 and celebrations of Cossack and national holidays because the Exarchate, and later the UOC, avoided what it saw as nationalist and anti-Soviet events. By 1991, the UOC ever more openly sought to take part and even to monopolize Ukrainian patriotic events. By May 1991 it not only took part in ceremonies honoring Taras Shevchenko but, with the compliance of the local Kaniv authorities, it blocked Patriarch Mstyslav from conducting services at the monument in the city by holding services from 8:00 in the morning to 8:00 in the evening.[36]

In this new role the UOC faced certain obstacles. As recently as 1989 its clergy had blessed the ceremonies celebrating the anniversary of the "Reunification of Ukraine with Russia," and in early 1991 its clergy had advocated voting "yes" on the All-Union treaty.[37] Consequently its sincerity in participating in Ukrainian events was questioned.[38] By the same token it possessed few nationally conscious and culturally educated cadres, and many of its clergy remained ardently Russian in language and world view. The fact that the new seminary in Kiev taught only one subject in Ukrainian, except for language and literature, demonstrated how far the church's practices were from the goals of the Ukrainian national movement.[39] Numerous charges were made that the Exarchate of the ROC, now the UOC, had destroyed Ukrainian art and desecrated monuments to Ukrainian national heroes in the churches it had been given.[40] The person and intentions of Metropolitan Filaret were especially objects of opprobrium and suspicion. Still, the church tried to make the necessary accommodations to the new situation. In 1991 it transferred the bishop of Chernivtsi to Russia because he did not speak Ukrainian.[41] Metropolitan Filaret tried to counter charges of the Russified nature of the church by arguing the church has two versions of Church Slavonic, "western" and "eastern," without mentioning that the eastern is identical with the Russian version.[42] The church adopted more Ukrainian elements, but it still insisted that it was linked to universal Orthodoxy through the Moscow Patriarch, that the preservation of the Soviet Union was positive, and that the church in Ukraine was multinational.[43] In fact, it had to consider the consequences of any Ukrainianization because it feared losing Russian supporters who might defect to the Russian Orthodox Church Abroad.

The UAOC also faced a regional challenge in Galicia, the UCC. In Galicia, everywhere but in the northeastern section of Ternopil' oblast near the Pochaiv Monastery, which belonged to Volhynia before World War II, the UAOC was the predominant Orthodox group. In its initial phases the UAOC was primarily the creation of clergymen who wished to remain Orthodox and to retain their parishes for Orthodoxy. Because the clergy were primarily western Ukrainians and the churches functioned as Ukrainian institutions, with Ukrainian as the language of preaching, the Ukrainian version of Church Slavonic, and Ukrainian liturgical traditions, this shift could be accomplished merely by accepting Ukrainian as the liturgical language.

The formation of the UAOC entirely changed the religious situation in Galicia. The Orthodox-Catholic four-part commission established by the Vatican and the Moscow Patriarchate in the fall of 1989 to adjudicate church properties, including representatives of the Vatican, the UCC, the Moscow Patriarchate, and the Exarchate, quickly became irrelevant, in part because it did not include the major Orthodox group in the region. Although this somewhat simplified the position of the Vatican, which wished to keep good relations with the Moscow Patriarchate, the situation gave the UAOC, which had been excluded from the commission, the occasion to maintain that the Vatican and the UCC preferred to deal with the Moscow Patriarchate instead of with the UAOC, and that the UAOC could defend the religious interests of the Ukrainian people against foreign intrusions from Moscow and Rome better than the UCC could. The Vatican's lack of links to the UAOC made intergroup ecclesiastical relations primarily a matter of local UCC and UAOC relations, in which the UCC clergy and intelligentsia bitterly condemned the UAOC as divisive and as possibly KGB inspired. In cities, church buildings could be apportioned to the two churches, but in small towns and villages sharp conflicts emerged for the one edifice, with shared usage often increasing the friction, while withdrawal of the minority to erect a new church resulted in financial burdens for the community.[44] The UAOC was in a better situation than the UOC because the latter could be associated with the forcible dissolution of the UCC in 1946 and with the Moscow Patriarchate's takeover of its buildings and properties. Still, Ukrainian Catholics who believed that the UCC should recover all the assets it possessed in 1946 expressed considerable resentment toward the UAOC.

Cultural, social, and personal issues often determined choices between two churches of similar liturgical practices and Ukrainian patriotic sentiments. Ukrainian Catholics emphasized the patriotic activities of the Ukrainian Greek Catholic church in the nineteenth and twentieth centuries, the heroic struggle of the UCC in the underground, and the identification of Orthodoxy with Russia as reasons for opting for the UCC. Ukrainian Autocephalous Orthodox concentrated on Orthodoxy as the "Cossack faith," the use of force in organizing and propagating the Union of Brest, the identification of Catholicism and the Union with Poland, and the advantages of the UAOC as an independent church under neither Rome nor Moscow.[45] In many cases attitudes toward the village priest, as well as social and family allegiances, determined choices, particularly when villages were divided on the religious issue, and heated debate and violence took place. After the democratic opposition came to power in March 1990, the UAOC, the smaller of the institutions, charged that not only did it suffer violence from the Catholic majority but it was also discriminated against by the government.

By 1991 the religious conflict in Galicia seemed to be subsiding somewhat.[46] As opinion polls were taken and churches were assigned, factions had less reason to continue confrontation. The "losers" began to direct their attention to finding other facilities and building churches. The Ukrainian Catholics came to realize that their vision of prewar Galicia, with a homogeneous Ukrainian Catholic society and possession of all church properties held in 1946, did not correspond to the reality of 1991. The Ukrainian Autocephalous Orthodox understood that as a religious minority they had to come to an accommodation with the majority. The increasing activities of the UAOC outside of Galicia won approval from Ukrainian patriots among the Uniates, who saw the development of the church in eastern Ukraine as positive for the Ukrainian cause. Ukrainian Autocephalist Orthodox from outside Galicia, such as Ievhen Sverstiuk, strove to calm the religious strife. The commitment of the UCC and the UAOC to Ukrainian culture and independence brought them together, if only for tactical reasons. Patriarch Mstyslav Skrypnyk and Archbishop Major Myroslav Liubachivs'kyi took over leadership of the churches, bringing with them the experience of the Ukrainian diaspora, where the two churches had worked out a modus vivendi. Antagonism and frictions still existed. Despite ostensible declarations of their desire to meet, the leaders of the two churches did not meet in Ukraine.

One of the greatest problems that the UAOC faced was its relationship with the Orthodox world. The UAOC established under the leadership of Metropolitan Vasyl' Lypkivs'kyi in 1921 could not be recognized by other Orthodox churches because of its radical canons, especially its consecration of bishops without participation of existing bishops. The UAOC formed in 1942 ensured that the church had bishops consecrated in the traditional manner, but in the short period that it existed in Ukraine, it did not receive recognition by other Orthodox churches. The newly restored UAOC sought to secure recognition in the Orthodox Oecumene, but it faced formidable problems.

With its decentralized structure and its lack of the elaborated procedures of the Catholic church, the Orthodox church does not have clearly established procedures for the institution of autocephaly or of patriarchate, as the modern history of the church in areas such as the Balkans has shown. Generally, political events have determined the evolution of ecclesiastical structures. Crucial to the situation of the church in Ukraine is the question of which Orthodox church exercises legitimate ecclesiastical authority. The Moscow Patriarchate asserted that it had that right, and that in its granting of autonomy to the UOC in 1990, it had full authority in its own ecclesiastical province. As recently as 1924, however, the

Ecumenical Patriarchate had charged that the Moscow Patriarchate's absorption of the Kiev Metropolitanate in 1685–1686 was uncanonical, thereby claiming the continued subordination of the Kiev Metropolitanate to the Patriarchate of Constantinople. The reestablishment of the UAOC must be placed in the context of the rivalry of Moscow and Constantinople. In recent times this tension has resulted in Moscow's recognition of an autocephalous church in North America, an act that Constantinople views as illegitimate, and in the refusal of the Patriarch of Constantinople to attend the Moscow celebrations of the millennium of Christianity in Rus'.

The UAOC asserted that the claims of the Patriarchate of Moscow to the Metropolitanate of Kiev are illegitimate because Kiev is the mother church of Moscow and the acts of 1685–1686 were uncanonical. Although the leaders of the UAOC acted on their own in reestablishing their church, they hoped for recognition from Constantinople. The first parish of the UAOC, Sts. Peter and Paul, asked for Patriarch Demetrios's protection until a UAOC hierarchy could be established, and the church council in Kiev in June 1990 addressed an appeal to the Patriarchate.

The Moscow Patriarchate and the UOC actively sought Constantinople's support against the autocephalists. While the diplomatic initiatives and the agreements are not fully public, the Moscow Patriarchate had considerable success. In early 1990, a Constantinopolitan delegation called the autocephalist issue an internal matter of the Moscow Patriarchate, and in early 1991 the Constantinople Patriarchate censured the autocephalist movement in a statement.[47] A delegation from the Patriarch of Constantinople to Kiev in July 1991 displayed support for the UOC by joint services and met with officials of the Ukrainian government.[48] No answers were issued to the UAOC's appeals. The Ecumenical Patriarchate, however, appeared not to be fully supportive of Moscow. It was rumored to have chastised its 1990 delegation for going too far, and its statement of 1991 contained an ambiguous allusion to its recognition of the authority of the Moscow Patriarchate on the basis of a council of 1593, which set borders excluding the Metropolitanate of Kiev.[49]

The situation of the Orthodox and Ukrainian diasporas, above all in North America, influenced the relation of the UAOC to the Orthodox world.[50] In 1970 the Patriarchate of Moscow recognized the Russian Orthodox Greek Catholic Metropolia as the Orthodox Church of America, basing its authority on the Russian church's mission to North America and its control over Orthodox believers until the Revolution. The Patriarchate of Constantinople and other eastern patriarchates condemned this act as illegitimate, with Constantinople arguing that canons gave it primary authority in lands where no fully constituted Orthodox churches existed. Constantinople's dependence, above all financial, on the Greek Archdiocese of North and South America must have played a role in its adamancy, as did the fact that the Greek church is the largest Orthodox group in North America. In practice, this situation made Constantinople and the Greek Orthodox Archdiocese allies of the Ukrainian Orthodox Church in the United States and the Ukrainian Orthodox Church of Canada, which favored retention of cultural traditions, and historically opposed the Moscow Patriarchate and the transformed Russian Metropolia. Although the Constantinople Patriarchate and the Greek Archdiocese did not officially recognize the two Ukrainian churches and maintained a Ukrainian group (the Ukrainian Orthodox Church of America) under their direct authority, they lent a more sympathetic ear to the Ukrainians' aspirations and cultivated closer contacts. Metropolitan Mstyslav pursued this policy of rapprochement without conceding the principle of autocephaly for the UAOC in the West or the international unity of the Ukranian Orthodox churches.

Canada presented a special question because the Ukranian Orthodox Church of Canada was the largest and best organized Orthodox group. Desiring to enter the general Orthodox community, the leaders of the Ukrainian Orthodox Church of Canada negotiated an agreement with the patriarchate that established intercommunion but maintained its traditional organization and autonomy. Although a Ukrainian Orthodox council in Canada approved the agreement in 1989, the exact nature of the relationship remained unclear.[51] In particular, just how the church was in intercommunion with Constantinople while retaining its links with its sister Ukrainian Orthodox metropolitanates and the UAOC in Ukraine, which it supported, remained uncertain. It would seem that the rebirth of the UAOC in Ukraine came unexpectedly, at a time when the Canadian church's negotiations with Constantinople were well advanced. With the increasing involvement of Ukrainian Canadians in their ancestral homeland and the rebirth of UAOC, the Canadian church found its relations with Constantinople and Kiev difficult to balance. On the other hand, the Ukrainian Orthodox Church of Canada could use its new relation to secure Constantinople's support for Orthodox Ukrainians and to argue the UAOC's case before the Ecumenical Patriarchate.[52]

The UAOC faced great obstacles in obtaining recognition in the Orthodox world. As had been the experience of the UCC at times when it sought the Vatican's support, the desire to maintain good relations with the large and powerful Moscow Patriarchate influenced the policies of churches outside the Soviet Union. The eastern patriarchates and other autocephalous churches confronted even more difficult issues in choosing between the UAOC and the larger UOC. Adhering to the principle that the church should have only one bishop in one locality—a principle breached in many areas of the world—they viewed the existence of two hierarchies in Ukraine negatively. In addition, they were suspicious of the legacy of the UAOC, above all its break with traditional canons in 1921, as well as certain current practices of conciliar governance. Even the consecration of the present church hierarchy was questioned by some Orthodox.[53] Most Orthodox churches looked askance at UAOC's proclamation of a patriarchate. The Orthodox churches were also extremely antagonistic to Uniates, so that they viewed any cooperation of the UAOC with the UCC negatively, even if solely for reasons of national unity. Nevertheless, resentment in the Orthodox world about many of the actions of the Patriarchate of Moscow, as well as the traditional claims of the Patriarchate of Constantinople to Ukraine, favored a hearing for the UAOC.

Political and cultural factors, as well as ecclesiastical developments, influenced the situation of the UAOC. The church was identified with the forces favoring real Ukrainian statehood. The relation of the UAOC and political groups was quite complex. The church generated considerable support in eastern Ukraine because it was associated with democratic and anticommunist groups. Therefore, the UAOC faced a quandary because it was attempting to set up an institutional structure under a Communist-dominated government. With the appearance of "sovereignty Communists" and the evolution of Leonid Kravchuk toward Ukrainian statist policies, the church faced a dilemma. Patriarch Mstyslav was involved in the difficult diplomacy of seeking the government's support, especially in changing the policies of hard-line Communist local governments against the UAOC. The "sovereignty Communists" sought legitimacy among Ukrainian patriots from the UAOC. At the commemoration of the Battle of Berestechko in June 1991, Patriarch Mstyslav went so far as to defend Kravchuk from protestors in the democratic camp who viewed the presence of the former party ideologue as a desecration.[54] Therefore, the church had to tread a fine line of obtaining concessions from the government and supporting its movement toward sovereignty without alienating its core support from Rukh and the anticommunists.

Cultural change and the Ukrainian national revival also presented the UAOC with opportunities and challenges. The growth of Ukrainian national consciousness stimulated the rebirth of the church, especially in eastern Ukraine. In many areas the activists of the Society for the Ukrainian Language and the UAOC worked closely, and many members of the often secularized intelligentsia were drawn to the church as a preserver of Ukrainian spiritual and national traditions.[55] Yet as the national awakening broadened, especially as schools and government institutions propagated the Ukrainian language, the relative role of the church was less important.

The UAOC inherited an ecclesiastical tradition that both shaped the church and provided it strengths and weaknesses. The church of the 1920s had developed principles of autocephaly, Ukrainianization, separation of church and state, conciliar rule, and Christianization of life that Bohdan Bociurkiw has described as a program for modernization.[56] In general, these traditions stood the church in good stead in Ukraine during the early 1990s, for many of the characteristics of the ROC against which the Ukrainian church movement was formed at the beginning of the twentieth century still remained. Autocephaly and Ukrainianization obviously corresponded in the religious sphere to growing political and cultural movements in Ukraine. Conciliarism provided for the active involvement of the laity at a time when the bishops of the Moscow Patriarchate had compromised their hierarchically ruled church. Separation of church and state gave the UAOC a dynamism that was lacking in the Moscow Patriarchate and UOC, which still turned to the state as the proper protector of the church and executor of their decisions. Christianization of life mandated an active evangelization program in which the church engaged in cultural, social, and political movements.

But if the UAOC legacy left the church considerable strengths as an ecclesiastical entity, it also left it weaknesses. Some merely reflected the fact that the UAOC had been able to develop in Ukraine only for short periods of time and could not resolve all problems. Not all liturgical books are available in Ukrainian, catechetical literature is insufficient, and theological works have rarely been translated. In the 1920s the UAOC was above all involved in the organization of parishes and local structures. This was once again the case in 1989–1991, but with its establishment of seminaries and eparchy structures, the UAOC had to develop further its own theological and ecclesiastical traditions. The relation of the UAOC to the Orthodox tradition and the existing Orthodox Oecumene was an especially difficult issue. The UAOC declared its wish to adhere to these, but it had embarked on reforms that are not generally accepted. While the present UAOC did not go back to the radical canons of 1921, it also did not publicly criticize that church or its leader, Metropolitan Vasyl' Lypkivs'kyi. However, many clergy of the UOC hesitated to join the UAOC unless it received full recognition from other Orthodox churches.[57]

The UAOC also faced the problem of whether it would define itself as the church of the Ukrainians or the territorial church of Ukraine. Certainly, the Orthodox world found the existence of two Orthodox churches in an ancient Orthodox land troubling. If it wished to assume the role of a territorial church, the UAOC had to integrate the Russian population of Ukraine, a difficult task, given its specific Ukrainian character.[58]

The demise of Soviet totalitarianism and communist ideology resulted in the reemerging of long-suppressed political, cultural, and religious movements. In that context it was not unexpected that Ukraine, which has so long been a zone of competition between Uniatism and Orthodoxy, and between Russian and Ukrainian Orthodoxy, should once again emerge as a region of conflict. Soviet policies decimated religious institutions and impeded the development of religious thought. However, as communism and Soviet rule were discredited, religion gained greater authority and religious institutions became more prominent. In some cases, reassertion of cultural and national values contributed to this greater prominence of churches. In Ukraine, Soviet rule had merely exacerbated religious conflicts. Through its support of Russian Orthodoxy against the UAOC and the UCC, the Soviet government had left the Ukrainian churches bereft of institutions but had given them a greater moral authority. The situation in 1989–1991 also differed from that of earlier periods, in that the Ukrainian lands were all in one state and Ukrainians were more intermixed than they had ever been. Therefore, the largely political divide between Orthodox and Uniate that existed from the late eighteenth century to World War II had broken down.

The breakdown of the Soviet order had permitted the division of the Orthodox in Ukraine. The outcome of the religious competition in Ukraine was not yet certain when the proclamation of Ukrainian independence on August 24, 1991, created an entirely new political context for the religious situation. The rebirth of the UAOC had preceded the emergence of Ukrainian independent statehood and had already split Orthodox believers before the political situation changed to favor some sort of autocephaly for Ukrainian Orthodox believers. For the new state, this divide of Orthodox believers was a cause for concern because it engendered religious conflict and Ukrainian-Russian tension at a time when the government desired civic peace and support from religious believers. For the UAOC, the emergence of an independent Ukraine with an important, if not dominant, control by the old Communist elite meant that central and local authorities were often the former opponents of the UAOC and closely allied to the UOC. By challenging the established authorities, both ecclesiastical and secular, the reborn UAOC of 1989–1991 had created a complex crisis in the religious and political affairs of the new Ukrainian state.

APPENDIX

The failed coup of August 19–21, 1991, in the Soviet Union, the proclamation of Ukrainian independence of August 24, 1991, and the referendum of December 1, 1991, that brought international recognition of the Ukrainian state considerably changed the religious situation. However, the shift of the former Communist party apparatus in Ukraine to a pro-independence position and the election of Leonid Kravchuk, former Communist party ideological secretary, as president meant that these changes were not as favorable to the UAOC as might be expected. As of

January 1, 1992, the church had 1,619 parishes, of which 1,490 were officially registered. It still was much smaller than the UOC, which had 5,473 parishes; and it remained concentrated in Galicia, where 1,453 parishes existed. It was, however, gaining a greater institutional presence in the oblasts near Galicia (Rivne, 32 parishes; Volyn', 14 parishes; Khmelnytsky, 28 parishes; and Chernivtsi, 14 parishes). With a patriarch, 15 eparchies, and 4 theological seminaries, the UAOC established the structures to become a major religious body throughout Ukraine.[59]

The new political situation influenced the UAOC and the UOC and their mutual relations. The continued absence of Patriarch Mstyslav for health and other reasons, as well as his age and unclear status as a foreign national, hindered the formation of clear lines of authority in the church. In particular, conflicts with Metropolitan Ioan increased so much that Ioan was transferred to the Zhytomyr eparchy. In February 1992 Ioan broke with Patriarch Mstyslav and was expelled from the UAOC. The UAOC continued to seek acceptance in the Orthodox world, and in May dispatched a delegation led by Patriarch Mstyslav to Constantinople, where it secured a promise that the Patriarch of Constantinople would send a delegation to investigate the status of the UAOC.

The UOC underwent ever greater change. In 1991 Bishop Ioanafan of Pereiaslav, press secretary of the UOC, publicly denounced Metropolitan Filaret for his immoral life. He was forced to recant; the Metropolitan accused Ioanafan of contacts with the UAOC and had him defrocked. Responding to the new political situation in Ukraine, Metropolitan Filaret led a *sobor* (council) of the UOC on November 1–3, 1991, that requested autocephaly from the Moscow Patriarchate. Ultimately four bishops refused to sign this request, and the matter developed into a power struggle that centered on opposition to Metropolitan Filaret. In addition to requesting autocephaly, Metropolitan Filaret antagonized the Moscow Patriarchate by seeking direct lines of contact to the Constantinople Patriarchate.

By the time a bishops' synod of the ROC met in Moscow on April 1–3, 1992, to consider the request for autocephaly, tensions had increased between Ukraine and Russia, and the Ukrainian government had become more active in seeking religious support for Ukrainian statehood. The synod fully supported Filaret's opponents, and the Metropolitan was forced to issue a statement that he would request the synod of the UOC to relieve him of his responsibilities and to elect a successor. The hierarchs of the ROC also tabled the issue of autocephaly to the next particular synod. (No exact date was set for its convocation.)[60]

On his return to Ukraine, Filaret announced that he would not abide by the promise that he had made under duress. He was called before an ecclesiastical court in Moscow and ultimately deprived of all episcopal and priestly functions. A synod of bishops of the UOC, held in May at

Kharkiv, elected Metropolitan Volodymyr of Rostov and Novocherkask as his successor. Although Filaret received the support of the Ukrainian government, which refused to recognize the legality of a synod held without the Metropolitan, he lost support of almost all bishops and most clergy. As Filaret's position weakened, he sought accommodation with the UAOC. With government officials urging negotiation, UAOC administrator Metropolitan Antonii met in June 1992 with Filaret and his followers. They formed by merger the Ukrainian Orthodox Church—Kiev Patriarchate (UOC-KP), naming Mstyslav as patriarch and Filaret as deputy. Not a party to the talks, Mstyslav, though conciliatory, refused to bless the merger. In the ensuing confusion, UOAC followers tended to view Filaret negatively, yet most clergy and UAOC bishops, except in Galicia, accepted the merger as a means of ensuring a viable autocephalous church.

At its October 1992 church council, which Mstyslav refused to attend, the UOC-KP found itself in the awkward position of recognizing Patriarch Mstyslav, but suspending his administrative authority. Upon Mstyslav's death in June 1993 the UOC-KP declared Archbishop Volodymyr (Romaniuk) its *locum tenens,* and called an all Ukrainian Orthodox church council for October 1993.

Whether the new UOC-KP can succeed the UAOC remains in doubt, as does the status of UAOC parishes rejecting merger. Neither group has been recognized by other Orthodox churches, and, except for Galicia, the Ukrainian Orthodox Church—Moscow Patriarchate remains the largest Orthodox church in Ukraine.

NOTES

1. For a recent discussion of the positions of the UCC, see Bohdan Bociurkiw, "The Ukrainian Catholic Church in the USSR Under Gorbachev," *Problems of Communism,* 39, no. 6 (November–December 1990), pp. 1–19. On January 1, 1991, 1,912 Ukrainian Catholic parishes were registered and 89 had applied for registration ("Über 10.000 staatlich regestierte religiöse Gemeinden derzeit in der Ukraine—ukrainische katholische Kirche verfügt über 1.912 Gemeinden," *Informationsdienst Osteuropäisches Christentum* [Munich], no. 9–10/91 [May 1991], p. 32).

2. The documentation on the granting of a new status to the UOC in October 1990 and the report of a press conference with Metropolitan Filaret are in *Pravoslavnyi visnyk* (Kiev), no. 1 (January 1991), pp. 2–13. "Ukrainian Orthodox church" was approved as an alternative official name of the Ukrainian Exarchate at a hierarchs' council of the ROC on 30–31 January 1990 (*Pravoslavnyi visnyk,* no. 5 [May 1990], pp. 29–30, translated from *Moskovskii tserkovnyi vestnik,* no. 4 [1990]).

3. A specialist on Soviet religious affairs and a keen observer of Ukraine, Gerd Stricker, described the movement for the UAOC as something that only émigré Ukrainians had believed in ("Ist die Ukrainische Kirche zugelassen? Unklarheiten nach Gorbachevs Besuch im Vatikan," *Glaube in der 2 Welt*, 18, no. 1 [1990], p. 23).

4. See Vasyl' Romaniuk, *A Voice in the Wilderness: Letters, Appeals, Essays*, trans. and ed. Jurij Dobczansky (Wheaton, Ill., 1980), p. 45. On the situation of Ukrainian Orthodoxy in the early 1980s, see Frank E. Sysyn, "The Ukrainian Orthodox Question in the USSR," *Religion in Communist Lands*, 11, no. 3 (Winter 1983), pp. 251–263, repr., with emendations, in the booklet *The Ukrainian Orthodox Question in the USSR* (Cambridge, Mass., 1987). The first initiative group for the restoration of the UAOC appeared in February 1989. See Bohdan Nahaylo, "Initiative Group Seeks Renewal of Ukrainian Orthodox Church," *Ukrainian Weekly* (Jersey City), 58, no. 10 (5 March 1989), p. 1.

5. In 1980 Bohdan Bociurkiw wrote: "But behind the facade of the 'monolithic unity' of the regime and the Russian Church, Ukrainization remains a very much alive, if suppressed, idea and an unfulfilled popular aspiration." See "Ukrainization Movements within the Russian Orthodox Church, and the Ukrainian Autocephalous Orthodox Church," *Harvard Ukrainian Studies*, 3–4 (1979–1980), p. 111.

6. Some recent writings of the Moscow Patriarchate and the UOC have admitted that the striving for "pure Orthodox" practices alienated the population of Western Ukraine. See Oleksandr Makarov, "Bii na stupeniakh viry," *Pravoslavnyi visnyk*, no. 3 (1990), p. 24, translated from *Moskovskii tserkovnyi vestnik*, no. 17 (December 1989).

7. See B. R. Bociurkiw, "The Orthodox Church and the Soviet Regime in the Ukraine, 1953–1971," *Canadian Slavonic Papers*, 14, no. 2 (Summer 1972), pp. 193–194, 196.

8. *Literaturnaia gazeta* (Moscow), no. 48 (28 November 1990), p. 9.

9. See the report by Valery Lyubatsky, "Where Is the Split?" *News from Ukraine*, (Kiev), no. 37 (1990), pp. 1, 7.

10. For the UOC's version of the conflict over Patriarch Aleksii's service in St. Sophia's cathedral, see "Zoltyi homin Sofii," *Pravoslavnyi visnyk*, no. 1 (1991), pp. 15–16; also see V. Andriievsky, "Shche raz pro podii bilia Sofiia," *Radians'ka Ukraina*, no. 20 (29 January 1991), p. 3. For another version from parliamentarians, see L. Taniuk and Z. Duma, "Konfliktu mohlo b ne buty. Vysnovky Komisii z pytan' kultury ta dukhovnoho vidrodzhennia z pryvodu podii v Kyievi 28 zhovtnia 1990 roku," *Kul'tura i zhyttia* (Kiev), no. 49 (9 December 1990), p. 7.

11. See, for example, Archbishop Makariy, *The Eastern Orthodox Church in the Ukraine* (Kiev, 1980), reviewed by Frank E. Sysyn in *Religion in Communist Lands*, 14, no. 1 (Spring 1986), pp. 73–76. Even in his address to the council electing a patriarch on 7 June 1990, Metro-

politan Filaret did not mention a "Ukrainian Orthodox" church or any desire for its autonomy (*Pravoslavnyi visnyk*, no. 9 [1990], pp. 13–17). In an interview in 1989 he described the merits of the early seventeenth-century Russian Orthodox Patriarch Ergomen in the liberation of the "Fatherland," despite the fact that Ukraine was not part of the Russian state in 1612 and Ukrainians were fighting for their state, the Polish-Lithuanian Commonwealth, against Muscovy. See H. Chornomors'kyi, " 'Ne ubyi' ne oznachaie 'ne zakhysty,' " *Pravoslavnyi visnyk*, no. 7 (1989), p. 29, translated from *Sovetskii patriot* (9 April 1989). As late as May 9, 1989, Metropolitan Filaret argued that a UOC was unnecessary. Questioned on the issue of the UAOC, he replied "And our church, as is known from history, does everything for the union of peoples. Therefore it is against autocephaly." See "Za iednist' i perebudovu," *Pravoslavnyi visnyk*, no. 8 (1989), p. 22, reprinted from *Radians'ka Ukraina*.

12. Metropolitan Filaret, "Do pytannia pro istoriiu Kyivs'koi mytropolii," *Pravoslavnyi visnyk*, no. 2 (1991), pp. 37–49; no. 3 (1991), pp. 38–49; no. 4 (1991), pp. 44–52. For another history of the Kiev Metropolitanate, which views the "union" of 1685–1686 as positive, see Archpriest Mykola Novosad, "Moskovs'kyi patriarkhat i Kyivs'ka mytropoliia," *Pravoslavnyi visnyk*, no. 8 (1990), pp. 31–34.

13. The importance of western Ukraine in advocating Ukrainization can be seen in an article by Archpriest Sozont Chobych of the L'viv eparchy. See "I tserkvy torkhnylasia perebudova," *Pravoslavnyi visnyk*, no. 2 (1990), pp. 25–26.

14. For the UOC's conflict with *Rukh*, see Metropolitan Filaret, "Liudy, bud'te oberezhnymy!" *Pravoslavnyi visnyk*, no. 5 (1990), pp. 26–27.

15. On the increasing information on the UAOC in the publications of the intelligentsia, see Fedir Turchenko and Oleksander Ihnaiusha, "Ukrains'ka avtokefal'na tserkva," *Vitchyzna*, no. 12 (December 1989), pp. 166–175. For an example of the Ukrainian intelligentsia's reaction to the UAOC in its inital stages, see V. Stel'makh, "Druhe voskresinnia," *Kul'tura i zhyttia* (Kiev), no. 25 (24 June 1990), p. 7. For the increasing interest in Metropolitan Lypkivs'kyi, see the reprinting of his works in *Slovo* (Kiev), no. 21 (November 1990), p. 8.

16. For a criticism of the role of the ROC in Ukrainian history, see Anatolii Shcherbatiuk, "Rosiis'ke pravoslav'ia," *Za vil'nu Ukrainu* (Lviv) (October 1990), p. 2.

17. For a discussion of Ukrainian Orthodox churches in the West, see Frank E. Sysyn, "The Ukrainian Orthodox Churches and the Ukrainian Diaspora," *Vitrazh* (Great Britain), 11 (June 1980), pp. 16–25. Also see Paul Yuzyk, *The Ukrainian Greek Orthodox Church of Canada, 1918–1951* (Ottawa, 1981).

18. See "Biohrafiia Sviatiishoho patriarkha Kyivs'koho i vsiei

Ukrainy Mstyslava," *Nasha vira pravoslav'ia* (Kiev), no. 7 (October 1990), p. 7.

19. In the statistics of registered parishes as of January 1, 1990, in "Über 10.000 staatlich regestierte Gemeinden," the UAOC had 791 parishes and the UOC 734 parishes in Galicia, though the number of UAOC parishes was undoubtedly higher because some of the 128 UAOC parishes seeking registration must have been in Galicia.

20. See the report by Valery Lyubatsky in *News from Ukraine,* no. 37 (1990), pp. 1, 7. The petitioners called for deposing Metropolitan Filaret and stated: "If the upper crust of the Russian Orthodox Church again displays its inability to make decisions for the benefit of Orthodoxy as it was before, we consider it our Christian and pastoral duty to decide independently." Father Viktor, church dean of Striy, said: "We must be grateful, as we are still existing only due to autocephaly. . . . Autocephaly supporters save both us and the very idea of Orthodoxy."

21. After his visit in Ukraine, Archpriest S. Iarmus reported that of the 1,300 parishes of the UAOC, 250 are in eastern Ukraine. See S. Iarmus, "Dukhovyi obraz narodu Ukrainy. Vrazhennia z vidvidyn Ukrainy:27 travnia–9 chervnia 1991," *Visnyk* (Winnipeg), no. 7 (1991), p. 3.

22. On the activities of the Galician brotherhoods, see "Z zhyttia L'vivs'koho molodizhnoho bratstva," *Blahovisnyk vidrodzhennia Ukrains'koi Aftokefal'noi Pravoslavnoi Tserkvy* (Chicago), no. 15 (1 August 1991), pp. 5–6 (hereafter *Blahovisnyk vidrodzhennia*). In March 1991 a conference of brotherhoods in the Ivano-Frankivs'k oblast drew 394 delegates. See *Blahovisnyk vidrodzhennia,* no. 7 (April 1991), p. 5.

23. The UAOC points out that numerous churches have been returned to the Poles in Galicia without securing similar action for the Ukrainians in Poland. See *Blahovisnyk vidrodzhennia,* no. 9 (1 May 1991), p. 7. Suspicion also appears in literature in the West. Archpriest S. Iarmus points to the subordination of the Roman Catholic hierarchy in Ukraine to Warsaw as the result of negotiations between John Paul II and Gorbachev, and writes that one must conclude that their policy is "Paralyze Galicia and western Ukraine and you simultaneously paralyze all Ukraine!" See S. Iarmus, "Dukhovyi obraz narody Ukrainy," *Visnyk,* no. 7 (1991), p. 3.

24. On the activities of the brotherhood, see the speech by Serhii Makarenko at its second conference, February 9–10, 1991, in *Blahovisnyk vidrodzhennia,* no. 6 (17 March 1991), pp. 3–4. For information on the second conference, see Iaryna Tymoshenko, "Vidbulasia konferentsiia vseukrains'koho bratstva," *Ukrainski visti* (Detroit), no. 8 (24 February 1991), p. 1.

25. On his activities for the victims of Chernobyl, see *Blahovisnyk vidrodzhennia,* no. 9 (1 May 1991), p. 2. On Patriarch Mstyslav's plan to

rebuild the ancient Ukrainian church, destroyed by the Soviet authorities in 1934–1935, and his meeting with the soccer clubs, see *Blahovisnyk vidrodzhennia*, no. 11 (1 June 1991), pp. 1–2. On the events at Berestechko, see Marta Kolomayets, "Battle of Berestechko, Glorious Kozak Legacy Recalled by Thousands," *Ukrainian Weekly*, 59, no. 26 (30 June 1991), pp. 1–3. For an example of the respect in which he was held by the Ukrainian intelligentsia, see the article on St. Andrew's Church by Oles' Bilodid and Larysa Kozlovs'ka, "Pervozvanna," *Ukraina* (Kiev), no. 48 (December 1990). They describe his celebration of a Ukrainian-language liturgy in the church in the following manner: "And is it not a good sign—the holy place is not empty. The word of God sounded there in the Ukrainian language from the lips of His Holiness Metropolitan Mstyslav, head of the Ukrainian Autocephalous Church, a person of legendary fate, who underwent all the tortures and sufferings of the Ukrainian revolutionary chaos, malevolence, and wildness and remained alive, because he had God in his heart and finally began to serve Him."

26. In March 1991, Bishop Antonii said that the Rivne eparchy had six parishes. He also gave statistics for Galicia somewhat different from other sources: Lviv oblast, four hundred parishes; Ivano-Frankivs'k, more than three hundred; Ternopil', two hundred. See "Rozum peremozhe emotsii," *Visti z Ukrainy* (Kiev), no. 13 (March 1991), p. 6.

27. Information from the bishop.

28. See the interview with Father Boiko in *Blahovisnyk vidrodzhennia*, no. 14 (16 July 1991), pp. 5–6; no. 15 (1 August 1991), pp. 7–8.

29. *Blahovisnyk vidrodzhennia* contains numerous reports of the persecution of the UAOC—for example, no. 3 (3 February 1991), p. 2 (Chernihiv); no. 5 (3 March 1991), pp. 6–7 (Svitlovods'k); no. 10 (16 May 1991), p. 2 (Zaporizhzhia); no. 12 (16 May 1991), pp. 3–4 (Chernihiv); no. 12 (16 May 1991), p. 8 (Kirovohrad); no. 13 (1 July 1991), p. 4 (Kherson, Mykolaiv, Dnipropetrovs'k, and Kirovohrad oblasts). For an account of the local authorities' campaign against the UAOC in the village of Mytkiv in Chernivtsi oblast, see "Repetytsiia pered referendumom," *Chas* (Chernivtsi), no. 7 (21) (15 February 1991), p. 3.

30. See the account of Patriarch Aleksii's trip by Valery Lyubatsky in *News from Ukraine*, no. 37 (1990), pp. 1, 7.

31. At the time of the proclamation of the autonomy of the UOC, nineteen hierarchs signed the statement. Only in eastern Ukraine did the eparchies include more than one oblast (e.g., Kirovhrad and Mykolaiv, Donets'k and Luhans'k, Odessa and Kherson). See *Pravoslavnyi visnyk*, no. 1 (1991), p. 9. Since then at least one eparchy has been divided.

32. Of the 5,031 parishes of the UOC registered on January 1, 1991, 1,181 were in the traditional Uniate areas of Galicia and Transcarpathia. A further 1,160 were in Bukovyna and Volhynia, areas annexed to

the Soviet Union during and after World War II. Of the 2,690 churches in pre-1939 Soviet Ukraine, 973 were in the three central Ukrainian oblasts of Zhytomyr, Vynnytsia, and Khmel'nyts'kyi. The further east and south, the fewer the registered religious communities in general. Crimea had only 40 parishes, and Luhans'k oblast' had only 92. Still, the UOC had greatly expanded its network of parishes in pre-1939 Soviet Ukrainian territories, and in Bukovyna and Volhynia ("Über 10.000 staatlich regestierte religiöse Gemeinden"). Despite the growth in the east, the losses in the west resulted in an actual decline of parishes in the former exarchate from 5,700 in February 1990 (Archpriest Sozont Chobych, "I tserkvy torknulasia perebudova," *Pravoslavnyi visnyk,* no. 2 [1991], p. 26).

33. In Chernihiv, an oblast controlled by a particularly reactionary Communist party, numerous historic churches were handed over to the UOC. The UOC removed the sarcophagus of Prince Mstyslav Volodymyrovich Khorobryi from the Savior Cathedral. See Vasyl' Chepurnyi, "Chas rozkydaty kaminnia?" *Nasha vira pravoslav'ia* (Kiev), no. 2 (10) (1991), p. 5. The UAOC parish of Dnipropetrovs'k has had a history of attacks on its members, long-term refusal to register the community, and, after the community was registered, refusal to give it a church building, whereas the civil authorities gave a number of buildings to the UOC, which had nine churches in the city. The UAOC requested the Transfiguration Cathedral, currently used as a museum of religion. See *Blahovisnyk vidrodzhennia,* no. 15 (1 August 1991), pp. 3–4. On the community's persecution and its campaign for the Transfiguration Cathedral, see *Preobrazhens'kyi sobor, Vydania Pravoslavnoi Tserkvy Preobrazhenks'koho Katedral'noho Soboru* (Dnipropetrovs'k), no. 1 (April 1991). The Communist party press in Dnipropetrovs'k carried on a scurrilous campaign against the community and Patriarch Mstyslav. See "Chy vse sviate pid ianhol's'kymy krylamy," *Zoria* (Dnipropetrovs'k) (11 June 1991), p. 1.

34. Bohdan Bociurkiw estimated that over seven hundred closed, formerly Ukrainian Catholic churches were handed over to the Russian Orthodox church beginning in the fall of 1988. See "The Ukrainian Catholic Church in the USSR Under Gorbachev," p. 10.

35. For all its insistence that political factors should not determine religious affairs, the Exarchate followed political changes in its policies. Ukrainian was introduced into the Odessa seminary as a reaction to the declaration of Ukrainian as the state language. See "Sozdan synod Ukrainskoi pravoslavnoi tserkvy," *Pravda Ukrainy* (Kiev), no. 34 (10 February 1990), p. 4.

36. For the events at Kaniv on May 22, 1991, see the account by L. Taniuk and Z. Duma, "Khto zh rozpaliuie vorozhnechu?" *Kul'tura i zhyttia,* no. 26 (29 June 1991), p. 2; see also "Rosiis'ka Pravoslavna Tserkva ne dopustyla Patriiarkha Mstyslava do mohyly Shevchenka,"

Ukrains'ki visti, no. 22 (2 June 1991), p. 1.

37. See the account and photographs in *Visti z Ukrainy*, no. 6 (1990), p. 4. Bishop Ioanafan of Pereiaslav took part in this event, which was in fact a rally for the Union treaty. The Exarchate of the ROC and the UOC have a tradition of supporting centralization and viewing the Russian Empire and the Soviet Union, not Ukraine, as the Fatherland. See, for example, the interview of H. Chornomorskyi with Metropolitan Filaret, "Ne ubyi' ne oznachaie 'ne zakhysty,' " p. 30.

38. As late as 1990, Metropolitan Filaret still condemned use of the Ukrainian national colors, blue and yellow. See "Ne sotvorit' gorst' pepla," *Pravda Ukrainy*, no. 1 (1 January 1990), p. 3. In 1989, he maintained: "Speaking about our nation [*nash narod*], I have in mind all the nations of our country.... We must all care for our multinational culture." See "Liudyna povynna buty bezsmertnoiu," *Pam'iatnyky Ukrainy* (Kiev), no. 2 (1989), p. 12. In general the leaders of the UOC merely rejected the contention that the ROC promoted Russification. For one of the few admissions, albeit with apologetics, see the interview with Bishop Evfymii of Mukachiv and Uzhhorod in *Molod' Ukrainy* (Kiev), (23 May 1991). He merely admits that in eastern Ukraine, "The church fell under the pressure of Russification.... But one should not condemn the church—oppressed and persecuted."

39. For an account of the atmosphere of Russian chauvinism at the Kiev Theological Seminary, see the open letter to Metropolitan Filaret by seven seminarians of June 8, 1990, *Za vil'nu Ukrainu*, no. 61 (23 September 1990), p. 2.

40. A major debate surrounds the UOC's actions at the Kiev Caves monastery. See Iurii Horban', "Lavra b'ie na spolokh," *Nasha vira pravoslav'ia*, no. 1(19) (January 1991), p. 4. For the church's actions in Chernihiv, see L. Fesenko, "Vidrodzhennia chy znyshchennia? Pro problemy zberezhennia kul'tovykh pam'iatok," *Robitnycha hazeta* (Kiev), no. 15 (23 January 1991), p. 3. Also see "Sim zapytan' mytropolytu Filaretu vid redaktsii hazety *Nasha vira pravoslav'ia*," *Nasha vira pravoslav'ia* (December 1990), p. 2.

41. On the replacement of Bishop Antonii, see *Blahovisnyk vidrodzhennia*, no. 4 (17 February 1991), p. 8.

42. Metropolitan Filaret proposed this theory in a press conference on October 29, 1990. See *Pravoslavnyi visnyk*, no. 1 (1991), p. 12. The frequent assertions by the UAOC and Ukrainian cultural groups that the UOC services are in Russian in fact means Church Slavonic with Russian pronunciation. In the pastoral message of Metropolitan Filaret and the hierarchy, he defended the primacy of Church Slavonic with the grudging comment, "There is no official document that would ban the use of the native language during the liturgy." See *Pravoslavnyi visnyk*, no. 1 (1991), p. 8.

43. For a criticism of the lack of new thinking in the UOC, see "Mytropolyt Filaret poza chasom," *Nasha vira pravoslav'ia,* no. 7 (October 1990), p. 4.

44. On conflict in Galicia, see "Boli mizhkonfesiinoho konfliktu," *Blahovisnyk vidrodzhennia,* no. 9 (1 May 1991), pp. 6–8. For UAOC protests against the government authorities, see *Za vil'nu Ukrainu,* no. 16 (21 July 1990), p. 1. For a discussion of the conflicts and social divisions in Turka, see Iaroslav Hevrych, "Konflikty vynnykaiut' postiino . . . ," *Za vil'nu Ukrainu,* no. 57 (18 September 1990), p. 2.

45. For the opposing visions of Ukrainian church history, see Ivan Paslavs'kyi, "Mizh skhodom is zakhodom," and Father Volodymyr Iarema, "Nasha Ukrains'ka tserkva, abo chyi my dity," under the rubric "Boh i Ukraina," *Dzvin* (L'viv), no. 10 (1990), pp. 100–110.

46. For Ievhen Sverstiuk's role in calming the UCC-UAOC conflict, see his "Kolonka redaktora," *Nasha vira pravoslav'ia,* no. 2(10) (1991), pp. 2–3. For Patriarch Mstyslav's attempts to calm the religious situation, see his interview with Anzhelika Tatomyr, "Za dukhovnu iednist' Ukrainy," *Za vil'nu Ukrainu,* no. 90 (7 November 1990), p. 1.

47. For the letter of Patriarch Demetrios II to Patriarch Aleksii, January 10, 1991, condemning the "movement of autocephalists," see *Informator: Vydaie Students'ka T-vo, Bohoslovs'koho fakul'tetu Kolegii Sv. Andreia* (Winnipeg), no. 5 (May–August 1991), p. 3.

48. Tass reported that on July 26–27, Metropolitan Bartholomey of Chalcedon led a delegation visiting Metropolitan Filaret and Prime Minister Vitold Fokin. For the UAOC's interpretation of the visit, see "RPTs vlashtovuie pravokatsii," *Svoboda,* 98, no. 148 (6 August 1991), p. 1.

49. This is the interpretation of the Ukrainian Orthodox Church of Canada; see *Informator,* no. 5 (May–August 1991), p. 3.

50. This problem is discussed in Frank E. Sysyn, "The Ukrainian Orthodox Churches and the Ukrainian Diaspora," pp. 22–24.

51. For the documents on the relationship between the Patriarchate of Constantinople and the Ukrainian Orthodox Church of Canada, see *Ridna niva: Kalendar na rik 1991* (Winnipeg), pp. 115–119.

52. The dean of St. Andrew's Seminary in Winnipeg, Father Tymofii Minenko, traveled to Ukraine, where he visited Patriarch Mstyslav and demonstrated support for the UAOC. UAOC circles criticized him for visiting Metropolitan Filaret. See *Blahovisnyk vidrodzhennia,* no. 15 (1 August 1991), p. 5. The UOC tried to exploit the Canadian situation to its advantage. In a distorted account of the situation, Metropolitan Filaret maintained: "Pay attention to the following fact—in Canada there exists a Ukrainian Greek Orthodox Church, which Metropolitan Vasyl' (Fedak) heads. Metropolitan Vasyl' does not have any spiritual contacts and Eucharistic communion with Mstyslav (Skrypnyk). Why? Because he does not wish to soil his white robe with an uncanonical link." See press

conference of October 28, 1990, *Pravosvoslavnyi visnyk,* no. 1 (1991). p. 11.

53. Before the arrival of Patriarch Mstyslav, Bishop (later Metropolitan) Ioan, whom the ROC defrocked after he declared that he left its jurisdiction, joined with a bishop of a dissident Russian Orthodox church and an anonymous bishop of the Moscow Patriarchate to consecrate bishops. For an account of this issue by Bishop Antonii of Rivne, see his interview, "Rozum peremozhe emotsii."

54. On the Berestechko celebrations, see Kolomayets, "Battle of Berestechko." The Communist press charged that the UAOC was merely an arm of *Rukh.* See "Pochemu miriane prishli k sovminu," *Pravda Ukrainy* (7 November 1990). See also "Patriiarkh Mstyslav zustrivsia z L. Kravchukom," *Ukrains'ki visti,* no. 25 (23 June 1991), p. 4; and "Patriarch Mstyslav Meets with Ukrainian PM Vitold Fokin," *Ukrainian Weekly,* vol. 59, no. 54 (16 June 1991), pp. 1, 4.

55. For an example of the cooperation of Ukrainian groups in Dnipropetrovs'k, see "Rizdvo v Ukraini," *Ukrains'ke slovo* (Paris), 27 January 1991. Members of the UAOC, the Society for Ukrainian Language, and *Rukh* joined to carol and to stage a *vertep* (Christmas pageant), including a version with political figures.

56. See his "The Ukrainian Autocephalous Orthodox Church, 1920–1930: A Study in Religious Modernization," in Dennis Dunn, ed., *Religion and Modernization in the Soviet Union* (Boulder, Colo., 1977), pp. 310–347, repr. in Bohdan R. Bociurkiw, *Ukrainian Churches Under Soviet Rule: Two Case Studies* (Cambridge, Mass., 1984).

57. On concern over the issue of canonicity, see a letter by Father Ihor Shvets' of January 11, 1991, in *Visnyk,* no. 3 (March 1991), p. 6. For expressions of strong desire to be in communion with other Orthodox churches and the mother church of Constantinople, see Metropolitan Ioan's Christmas message in *Blahovisnyk vidrodzhennia,* no. 2 (20 January 1991), pp. 1–2.

58. The ROC in Russia faced a similar problem as national consciousness rose among the Ukrainians, many of whom are settled in Kuban', the Amur Basin, and Kazakhstan. Until now the ROC functioned entirely as a Russian national church, not even preaching in Ukrainian. Parishes of the UAOC were organized as far away from Ukraine as Sakhalin. On Easter 1991 members of the UAOC in Moscow gathered to listen to a recording of a service because they had neither church nor priest. *Blahovisnyk vidrodzhennia,* no. 8 (16 April 1991), p. 6.

59. Statistics from the government materials for a new law on religious freedom provided by a private source.

60. See Frank E. Sysyn, "The Russian Sobor and the Rejection of Ukranian Orthodox Autocephaly," *Ukrainian Weekly,* 60, no. 30 (1992), pp. 8–9.

Reflections on the
Current State of the
Georgian Church and Nation

A close relationship exists between nationality and confessionality in eastern and southeastern Europe, as well as in the Caucasus. This close relationship, or identity, is one of the facts that distinguishes these regions most from western Europe and even more so from the United States, where "nation" means "a community of citizens of a state." Such a nation can include people from many different Christian confessions, or even from religious faiths outside Christianity. Yet, these people consider themselves to be of one nation. Any question regarding their nationality on passport forms, for example, refers to their citizenship within a state. The same forms, however, in the former Soviet Union or in what was formerly Yugoslavia would have asked *two* questions: one regarding "citizenship" and the other "nationality." Nationality, then, in the east European context, means the feeling of national identity based on language, religion, consciousness of a unique historical fate, and a special cultural behavior. When we talk here of nation and nationality, it is this east European notion we have in mind.

Modern east European nationalism has modified the feeling of national identity described above, in which one nation could live together with other nations in a nonnational state or empire,[1] into the desire to have one's own sovereign state with a nationally identical population on its own national soil.[2] However, France, Great Britain, and Germany, unified during the nineteenth century, had a different—Western— notion of the character of their nationality.

The Georgian people nowadays define their identity more or less explicitly by four factors: by their language, by their history, and by two features arising from this history—the imprint of belonging for sixteen hundred years to the Georgian Orthodox church, and the reality of occupying for that long their own historic, and even prehistoric, soil.[3] Thus, they also contribute to modern nationalistic development. Insofar as this feeling is more or less typical of the nations in eastern Europe and the Caucasus (varying only by the specific religion in each case), it is not easy to explain what makes the present-day Georgian feeling of identity unique.

It is even more difficult when we—as Western-educated historians observing this from outside—note that the Georgian struggle for national sovereignty and identity has so much in common with that of the other nations seeking national sovereignty in the former Soviet Union or in the Balkans.[4] This is not only because these people are in the same situation, but also because in these territories there is communication between these nations. In the Georgian case, this communication took place particularly with the Ukrainians, with whom they shared a long-standing relationship of exile and national persecution by the "Muscovites," and also with the people of the Baltic states, with whom they sensed a common fate: that they were part of the Soviet Union not by their own will but by conquest. The Georgians, however, were conquered by the Red Army in 1921 and have suffered from the Soviet Russification violently forced upon them for much longer than have the Balts.[5]

Georgians today share with these nations the fact that they feel ever more suppressed by the Russians. Their feeling of national identity is deeply influenced by this fact. As in the case of other nations of the former Soviet Union, there is also the fact that for them, "Soviet" and "Russian" are identical.[6]

Bolsheviks were a minority in the independent Georgia of 1917–1921; it was the Russian Red Army that forced the Georgians to the bolshevism of the Soviet Union. In addition, their fellow countryman, Joseph Stalin—a totally Russified person, as described by his daughter Svetlana,[7] and a Great Russian chauvinist, as Lenin eventually came to realize[8]—did everything possible to devastate the Georgian nation and its church together with his Russian and Georgian "traitor and renegade" friends, Grigorii Ordzhonikidze and Lavrentii Beria.

Ordzhonikidze, along with other commanders of the Red Army and leaders of socialist Georgia, murdered a large number of Georgian intellectuals, churchmen, and peasants, and drove many others, especially from the intelligentsia, into exile. Beria then managed to reduce the number of Georgian politicians, writers, artists, and scholars; only 5 percent of them survived the slaughter of the 1930s. Georgians are very aware that proportionately far more Georgians than Russians died in these terrible years.

Perestroika finally made it possible to talk of the purges. Not by chance was the first cinematic treatment of this terrible period a Georgian film, *Pokaianie* (Repentance), by Tengiz Abuladze.

Perestroika also made it possible to speak publicly about other facts of Soviet-Russian domination and imperialism. Georgia, for example, had been able to retain only 30 percent of its GNP; 70 percent belonged to Moscow, that is, to Moscow's all-Soviet ministries—"the center," as it was called.

It is especially in this sphere that national autonomy and self-determination are now urged.[9] There has been, the Georgians feel, terrible exploitation of their natural resources and production by the center, with the Georgian Communist party executing commands from Moscow. In addition, there have been unbelievable material privileges of higher-ranking members of the party, the nomenklatura. Above all has loomed the devastating exploitation of Georgian resources without any investment in their maintenance to prevent the terrible pollution of Georgian air and soil.

Until recently, no doctor's or candidate's thesis could be defended at a Georgian university or institute; every piece of scholarly research had to be translated into Russian and submitted to Moscow, the theme of the research having been accepted by the center in advance. This has now changed; an academic degree can be given by Tbilisi State University or Georgian Academy of Sciences, although until 1991 the thesis still had to go to Moscow in Russian translation. Confirmation by the notorious VAK (the Supreme Academic Committee) is now only a formality, no longer a political and national issue. Georgian research institutes, however, still cannot independently use their own scientific or economic innovations, and are hindered in making use of them in joint ventures with Western scholars or firms. The Russians have not been willing even to consider Georgian innovations for Soviet use—on the grounds, Georgians are convinced, of national prejudice and envy.[10]

Georgian anger about Soviet-Russian imperialism and enforced Russification is especially deep for two reasons. First, Georgians see this phenomenon as the continuation of Russian tsarist imperialism from the times of Catherine the Great and Alexander I. Second, Russification profoundly affected the Georgian Orthodox church. The church being such an overriding factor in Georgian national consciousness and identity, Russification tried to destroy not only the language but also the very "soul" of the Georgian nation. Thus, the Communist effort to annihilate the church was, in this light, only a prolongation of tsarist politics.

I must mention this phenomenon, especially, because the very thoroughly researched and documented book of Grigor Suny, *The Making of the Georgian Nation*,[11] almost entirely omits this vital factor in present-day Georgian self-consciousness. Furthermore, it is in this field that there lies a big difference between the Georgian condition and that of the other nations of the Russian empire.

The misfortune of the Georgians was that they were Orthodox, in contradistinction to most of the other non-Slavic nations incorporated into this empire.[12] After breaking the treaty of protection for the east Georgian kingdom of King Heraclius II (Treaty of Georgievsk, 1783), young Tsar Alexander I took over Georgia in 1800. The same Alexander I, who dreamed of a temple in which all existing Christian confessions could be united under one roof, did not hesitate to abolish the office of the autocephalous Georgian catholicos, whose origins lay in ancient times when

Russia did not exist, somewhere in the seventh century or even earlier.[13] The last catholicos patriarch of Georgia, Antoni II (a son of King Heraclius), was "invited" in 1811 to go to St. Petersburg to appear before the Holy Synod of the Russian Orthodox church; he was detained in the capital and eventually was sent into exile at Iaroslavl' in northern Russia, where he died. The Georgian church became merely an exarchate of the Russian church, and the first head of the exarchate, a Georgian metropolitan named Varlam Eristavi, was replaced after six years by a Russian. Russians held the exarchal see until the very end of the tsarist empire, and operated according to the tsar's order.

Even more embittering was the order given by the tsar to replace the Old Georgian language used in worship with the Old Church Slavonic of the Russian church, first in the patriarchal cathedral of Sioni, then in the majority of town churches, and later even in the villages. Nicholas I also issued an edict that all Georgian church paintings were to be covered over by whitewashing them; thus, invaluable Byzantine frescoes by outstanding medieval masters were either destroyed or severely damaged. Old Georgian icons were replaced by icons painted in the Russian Italianate style of the nineteenth century. The singular and, in the view of musicologists, matchless Georgian "heterophonic" church chant was forbidden and had to be replaced with Russian church music composed during the eighteenth and nineteenth centuries in a Western style for a mixed choir of four or more voices. A parallel process of Russification in the administration of domestic politics is described by Suny.

In an age when most European nations identified themselves mainly by their history and culture, this assault upon the Georgian church and the rich heritage of Old Georgian literature and thought was especially cruel. This was done, furthermore, by a nation that had accepted the Christian faith six hundred years later than the Georgians and, in the eyes of the Georgians, had nothing to compare with Georgian cultural riches.

There was no university nor theological academy in Georgia. The lyceum for young noblemen in Tiflis, and later the gymnasiums, taught in the Russian language, and anybody who wanted an academic degree had to go to a Russian university or theological academy. Contact with western Europe, possibly elsewhere in the Russian empire, had become a strong tradition among Georgia's upper classes, even the high-ranking clergy. European romanticism, and with it national pride and the exaltation of the Middle Ages, spread throughout Georgia, together with the glorification of "Caucasian freedom" by Russian poets.

This Georgian national movement brought forth an ever-growing opposition to Russia and Russification. A modern Georgian literature and journalism emerged as part of a broad movement to restore Georgian self-consciousness and national identity. There was, in particular, a struggle to create Georgian popular education and Georgian cultural life, especially in journals and in the theater, and to preserve the country's rich folklore. This struggle included the effort to restore the autocephaly of the Georgian church and the office of the catholicos patriarch.

Parallel with this romantic (let us call it so conditionally) and neoromantic movement seeking to restore a traditional Georgian society and using a medieval model for the role of the estates within it (including the Georgian Orthodox church), there also existed among the Georgian intelligentsia liberal and even socialist and Marxist patterns of thought and action. In enlightened and critical circles there developed the same deep ignorance of their church as that which pervaded the Russian intelligentsia, and the same prejudice toward the clergy: that they were all ignorant, uneducated, and rather primitive. Suny has described this leftist, socially critical movement very well, and also the Georgian secular nationalism within it. This nationalism, absolutely alien to the Georgian Orthodox church, held it in contempt for its being Russified and an instrument of Russian imperialism. The left did not perceive the strong national movement within the church. Such a view of Georgian Orthodoxy was later adopted by Georgian Mensheviks and the government of independent Georgia (1918–1921), although it allowed preparations to restore the Georgian patriarchate and the church's resumption of worship in the Georgian language. In the relatively liberal cultural atmosphere of those days there also flourished a search for new religious ideas, including all sorts of theosophy and, especially, Rudolf Steiner's anthroposophy, along with local ideas of a more esoteric nature. These latter ideas persist today among the Georgian intelligentsia.

The Mensheviks and the other leftist nationalists fell victim to Bolshevik persecution, and so even though contemporary Georgian consciousness of national identity can be linked to a revival of the Christian faith in its Georgian Orthodox form, it must be recognized that the current nation also has its secular martyrs and a nonreligious national identity. This deep rift in the Georgian nation, of which Suny speaks, dates from before World War I and continues today.

Anti-Russian feeling is the dominant note in all forms of Georgian nationalism. There now exists an idea of Georgian identity that says: "The Russians—if not the Soviets—are gloomy religious mystics; we Georgians are bright, rational thinkers with traditions from the Middle Ages. We are of another religiosity than that of the Russians"—or even "Georgians are by nature not religious at all." Still, perhaps the most widespread attitude toward the church today among the more fanatic nationalists is to claim a better knowledge of the true sense of Georgian Orthodoxy than even the leaders of the church. The once popular national leader, Zviad Gamsakhurdia, is a good example of this sort of formerly dissident intellectual.[14]

On the other hand, there was a religious revival among the Georgian intelligentsia during the Brezhnev era, as had occurred in Russia itself. It continues today, and it is now lost upon the Georgians that the church and its Catholicos Ilia II were the first in the Soviet period to allow for national sentiment among its people. For example, soon after Ilia became patriarch (1978), there was introduced a special *paraklis* (the equivalent of the Russian *akafist,* or series of doxological prayers) for the Georgian nation, with text and music by contemporary Georgian authors. The patriarch and his entourage have worked constantly to spread the Gospel both by intensive preaching and by providing a linguistically updated, modern Georgian version of the Bible, which was finally printed in the days of Gorbachev, though it had been ready for publication a few years before his rise to power. In this respect, the situation is not quite comparable with that of the Russian Orthodox church.[15] In addition, Russified icons have been replaced by contemporary Georgian painters' icons and frescoes, if the medieval ones could not be found or had been removed to state museums.

The most significant step taken by the Georgian church occurred in 1987, when it canonized a new saint, Ilia Chavchavadze "the Just"—an outstanding poet, writer, and politician who was murdered/martyred in 1907.[16] The murder, all Georgia is convinced (though it was never proved), was due to machinations of the Bolsheviks and especially Philipp Maharadze. It is important to note that this canonization was the first to take place in the Soviet Union, one year *before* the Russian Orthodox church canonized its first saints under Communist rule.

Like Georgian society in general, the Georgian Orthodox church has deep rifts and splits. They are to a large extent explained by the fact that for the first time in seventy years—or even longer—Georgians can try to conceive their own future, and naturally there are as many opinions and parties as there are thinking individuals. There were more than 135 parties in Georgia in the autumn of 1990, trying to register for the elections. Not all of them could meet the criteria for registration, such as a sufficient membership or membership throughout Georgia. In the end, more than 40 were left, and they were forced by the relative strength of the Communist party to unite into blocs.

There is only one major item that divides Georgian Christians, along with their patriarch, from some of the leading nationalistic movements in Georgia: the question of violence versus nonviolence. Amid the surge of armed and rivalrous nationalistic paramilitary groups that have not hesitated to attack one another, and have even tried to murder the leaders of rival groups, the patriarch published, at the climax of the preelection campaign, an edict that excommunicated anyone who used armed force against his compatriots.

The extent to which minds are divided on this edict was shown in a most impressive way on the night during which Georgians of all political tendencies found their national identity most strongly expressed—the night of April 9, 1989. It was then that the idea of nonviolent protest was predominant. Several hundred thousand Georgians came not only from the city of Tbilisi but also from the countryside to express through peaceful demonstration their wish to be rid of the Communist government. They filled the square in front of the government building and the whole of the adjoining Rustaveli Boulevard. In the side street stood the troops of the Soviet Ministry of Internal Affairs, their tanks ready to attack. The crowd sang Georgian national songs, some of them very old religious hymns. They even danced to show that they meant no violence against the government building.

Then Patriarch Ilia II came to join the people, whom he regards as his flock—an expression of the identity of being Orthodox with being Georgian. He addressed the people, telling them that he foresaw a terrible scene of violence due to the surrounding troops, and proposed that the crowd withdraw to the church for sanctuary. The national leaders—outwardly behaving very reverently—denied this request. Many in the crowd whistled at the patriarch (in Europe you whistle in theaters and concerts, and also in political gatherings, if you disagree). Then the patriarch proposed that they kneel down and recite the Lord's Prayer, which the crowd did. After this there was a joint proposal by the patriarch and the national opposition leaders to stand in silence—and there was deep silence as hundreds of thousands awaited, with candles in hand, the attack by the tanks. When the tanks were heard moving, the crowd resumed singing and dancing and sitting on the ground. At last the crackdown with sharpened spades and poison gas began, leaving twenty-two Georgian citizens dead, mostly women and young people in their teens. Hundreds of others were left sick for weeks and months, in hospitals and at home, from the poison gas.[17]

The conclusion that continues to be drawn from this landmark 1989 event in Georgian society is two-sided: the church, and the patriarch personally, were advocating nonviolence in the struggle to come, while at the same time leaders of the right-wing nationalists were continuing to set up their paramilitary partisan fighting groups. Among the latter were Zviad Gamsakhurdia; his former friend, the dissident Georgi Chanturia; and Djaba Iosseliani with his especially aggressive *mhedrioni* (knights). The patriarch, nevertheless, declared solemnly that whoever shed the blood of his Georgian brothers would be excommunicated. I noticed, when I was in Georgia in 1990, that the voice of the church had no great weight in Georgian society as a whole. A few liberals criticized the patriarch for threatening excommunication only for the killing of Georgians, instead of condemning all bloodshed; the majority, however, supported one or another of the militant groups.

A year later I found it necessary to rewrite the end of this essay. In the original, my conclusion read as follows: "I left Georgia a week before the elections for the Georgian parliament, and I thanked God that I could leave before the beginning of civil war." The war, however, did not break out in the autumn of 1990, but one year later.

As a regular reader of the weekly newspaper *Literaturuli Zak'art'velo* (Literary Georgia) and several Russian papers that report political events and relationships in the states on the territory of the former Soviet Union, I find that, on the whole, only national and nationalistic claims seem to be raised by the various parties. Personal, regional, and family aspirations among peoples of similar convictions continue to be voiced, but religion and Orthodox confession appear to play only a minimal part in such claims. Nevertheless, the recent baptism of Eduard Shevard-nadze into the Georgian Orthodox church reflects how critically linked are Georgian confessional and national identities.

It is quite obvious that the catholicos patriarch continues to try to reconcile the nationalists and to suggest common sense and sympathy for democratic decisions. As far as I know, however, even this venerable and peace-minded hierarch is addicted to the idea of recovering former areas of Georgia, although some of these lands have been for centuries in the hands of other nations. He is heard, in any case, only by some parts of Georgian society.

The position of the catholicos patriarch in interreligious relations and conflicts is not quite clear to me. He has always had very good contacts with Georgian Jews,[18] many of whom emigrated to Israel in the 1970s and 1980s. For example, the Jews tried to help him with certain historical claims of the Georgian church in the Holy Land. Not clear to me, however, is the position of the patriarch on the question of greater Abkhaz[19] autonomy. Also unclear is his position on the Adzhars,[20] who in 1989/1990 were devastated by a combination of heavy snows and floods. The catholicos patriarch visited them the next summer and admonished them to return to Christianity, which their ancestors had given up for Islam under Turkish rule. He told them that the catastrophe that had befallen them was obviously the punishment of God for their unfaithfulness to the Savior.

Another question is what role the patriarch plays in the conflict between the Georgians and the South Ossetians. I have not found any Georgian—no matter his or her political persuasion—who does not express the conviction that the South Ossetians possess no right either to have autonomy or to leave the Georgian Republic in order to join the North Ossetian Autonomous Republic and, through it, the Russian Federation. Here the idea of historical Georgian soil shows its most ugly imperialistic aspect.[21] Religion, however, does not play a role in the feeling of national identity for the South Ossetians, who are Orthodox like the Georgians and yet desire the status of an autonomous republic like their

North Ossetian brethren on the other side of the Caucasus Mountains. They wish to belong to the Russian Federation as the North Ossetians do, or even, perhaps, to be joined independently with them. The North Ossetians, however, are 49 percent Islamic, so religion cannot help in the self-identification and definition of either the Georgians or the Ossetians. The main role here is played by language and cultural behavior, not religious convictions or rituals. We can only conclude that the outcome of this process of Georgian national consciousness, and the part that religion, confession, and the Georgian Orthodox church as social body play in it, is uncertain, now more than ever.

NOTES

1. For example, the Persian, Roman, Ottoman, and Habsburg empires. These were not "national" states in the sense that Spain, France, and Great Britain became during the late Middle Ages and the early modern period. For literature see, e.g., Hans Kohn, *The Idea of Nationalism: A Study of Its Origin and Background* (New York, 1948); Eugen Lemberg, *Geschichte de Nationalismus in Europa* (Stuttgart, 1950); Eugen Lemberg, *Nationalismus*, 2 vols., *Rowohlts Deutsche Enzyklopädie*, vols. 197 and 198 (Hamburg, 1964; 2d ed., 1967/1968); Heinrich Finke, "Weltimperialismus und nationale Regungen im späten Mittelalter," *Rede Gehalten bei der Jahrfeier der Freiburger wissenschaftliche Gessellschaft*, October 28, 1916 (Freiburg im Breisgau, 1916); Karl W. Deutsch and Richard L. Merrit, eds., *Nationalism and National Development: An Interdisciplinary Bibliography* (Cambridge and London, 1970); Heinrich August Winkler and Thomas Schnabel, "Bibliographie des Nationalismus," *Arbeitsbucher zur modernen Geschichte*, vol. 7 (Göttingen, 1979).

2. The most enlightening study on this process in southeast central Europe, and also on the expulsions of other national minorities from this "national" soil, is Gotthold Rhode, "Völker auf dem Wege ... Verschiebungen der Bevölkerung in Ostdeutschland und Osteuropa seit 1917," *Schriften des Schleswig-Holsteinischen Geschichtslehrer-Verbandes* (Kiel), n.s., no. 1, (1952); Gotthold Rhode, "Zwangsumsiedlungen in Osteuropa vor der Oktoberrevolution," in *Festgabe für Hermann Aubin zum 23. Dezember 1950* (Hamburg, 1951). On the theme of *gesamteuropäischer Nationalismus*, see Rex Rexheuser, *Die Deutschen im Osten, von der Ostbewegung im Mittelalter bis zu den Westverschiebungen des 20. Jahrhunderts*, Lüneburger Vorträge zur Geschichte Ostdeutschlands und der Deutschen in Osteuropa, no. 2 (Lüneburg, 1986), pp. 6ff. Rexheuser's work is especially important for its method of investigation and critical questioning of the facts. Much information is also found in Alfred Bohmann, *Menschen und Grenzen*, 4 vols. (Cologne, 1969–1975).

3. This essay is based on my own experiences, frequent travel to

Georgia from 1975 to 1990, and regular reading of Georgian newspapers and other literature.

4. For this development see G. Simon, *Nationalismus und Nationalitätenpolitik in der Sowjetunion* (Baden-Baden, 1986), esp. pp. 453–473; also *Kleine Völker in der Geschichte Osteuropas: Festschrift für Günter Stökl zum 75. Geburtstag*, ed. M. Alexander, F. Kämpfer, and A. Kappeler (Stuttgart, 1991).

5. For the history of Georgia and the Georgians, see Ronald Grigor Suny, *The Making of the Georgian Nation* (Bloomington: Indiana University Press/Stanford, Calif.: Hoover Institution Press, 1988). Older standard surveys of the Georgian history in a Western language are David Marshall Lang, *The Georgians* (London, 1966) and *A Modern History of Soviet Georgia* (New York, 1962). See also N. A. Berdzenishvili, V. D. Dondua, M. K. Dumbadze, G. A. Melichishvili, and S. A. Meskhia, *Istoriia Gruzii: S drevneishikh vremen do 60-kh godov XIX veka*, vol. I (Tbilisi, 1962). The classic Georgian historian is Ivane Javakhishvili, *Kartveli eris istoria* [The History of the Georgian People], 4 vols. (Tbilisi, 1928–1948).

6. This essay was written when the Soviet Union still existed. After the August 1991 coup, "Russia," or the Russian Federated Republic, tried to erase the idea of "Soviet imperialism," but other former republics that wanted to make real their declared autonomy did not see—or want to see—any changes in Russian political behavior in comparison with former times.

7. Svetlana Alleluyeva, *Twenty Letters to a Friend* (New York, 1967).

8. See V. I. Lenin, *Polnoe sobranie sochinenii*, 5th ed. (Gospolizdat, Moscow), vol. 45, pp. 346, 356–362. Lenin does not literally say "chauvinist" but uses the untranslatable Russian expression *derzhimorda* (a person who silences his opponents by using the police billy club or even cruder violence). Lenin calls Stalin, also in this context, "not only a real and true 'social nationalist' but a crude Great Russian *derzhimorda*."

9. Since 1991, Georgia has attained autonomy and self-determination, and now has to cope with the devastating consequences of the Soviet centralized and monopolistic economic dictatorship.

10. During my last stay in Georgia, this was the case with the idea of a Kutaissi (Western Georgia University) professor, who proposed to link Georgian telephone, television, and other communication systems directly with the Western communication satellites in order to have direct access to the international communication network. He had already proposed a concrete building and linkage plan for this purpose. The center, refusing to discuss these plans, forbade him to continue or to enter into international negotiations for them. (Georgia's communications all used to run through Moscow and were controlled and hindered there.)

11. See note 5.

12. The Armenians, for instance, were Monophysite Christians of the Armenian Gregorian Apostolic church, the Azeris (of present-day Azerbaijan) were Shiite Muslims, and other Caucasian mountain tribes and the Tatars on the Volga were Sunni Muslims, as were the Central Asian peoples taken into the Russian Empire in the nineteenth century.

13. The Georgian church has existed since the Georgians were evangelized by the wandering female Christian ascetic and teacher, St. Nino (ca. 324), who advised the Georgian king to send to Constantinople for a bishop and priests (according to the oldest Georgian sources about her). Afterwards the Georgian church belonged to the Patriarchate of Antioch from which it gained autocephaly (according to the majority of Georgian historians) during the fifth-century reign of the great Georgian king Vakhtang Gorgasali. We have written evidence only from the eleventh and twelfth centuries. In the latter, the Byzantine canonist and later patriarch of Antioch, Theodore Balsamon, says that this autocephaly was given according to a decision of the Council of Antioch, but he does not state the exact year. Georgians think it was under Patriarch Peter II Knapheus in the fifth century. In any case, we have documents in which the primate of the Georgian church, Melchisedec I (1010–1030), signs using the title of catholicos patriarch. Before this time the head of the Georgian church was obviously archbishop of an autocephalous church, who in the eastern part of the Eastern Roman Empire (in eastern Syria, Persia, and India) took the title catholicos.

The dearth of historical documentation has contributed to the subsequent quarrel over the canonical legality of Georgian church autocephaly. By an official act recognizing Georgian church autocephaly on January 23, 1990, the Ecumenical Patriarch of Constantinople has settled the major questions of Georgian autocephaly and the patriarch's title. But the historical questions will continue to be the subject of dispute in a debate made more complex because, in interpreting the rare sources, account must be taken of great change in the meaning of "autocephaly" and "patriarchate" over the course of fifteen centuries. (The new facts of canonical recognition of the Georgian church and its patriarch by the Ecumenical Patriarch of Constantinople are taken from an official Georgian Orthodox church publication, *Jvari vazisi* [The Cross of the Vine], March–May 1990, pp. 5–12.)

14. He was elected by a great majority in the spring of 1991 and then overthrown by an armed coup d'état in the winter of 1991/1992, accused of having established an antidemocratic dictatorship.

15. See Stephen K. Batalden's essay on the Russian Bible in this volume.

16. See Fairy von Lilienfeld, "Die Heiligsprechung des Ilia Čavčavadze durch die Georgisch-Orthodoxe Kirche am 20.7.1987," in *Kleine Völker in der Geschichte Osteuropas*, pp. 66–75; see also Peter

Hauptmann, "Ilia Čavčavadze als Heiliger der Georgisch-Orthodoxen Kirche," *Kirche im Osten,* vol. 33 (1990), pp. 103–123.

17. This description is based on interviews with participants in the events of that night and on a videotape that was privately made and circulates freely in Tbilisi.

18. Georgia has never known an anti-Semitic movement, probably because of the peculiar circumstances of its church and cultural history; St. Nino converted the Georgians in collaboration with a Jewish diaspora community in Mtskheta, the old capital of "Iberia." Throughout the Middle Ages and up to the modern period, there has always been a unique Georgian Jewish diaspora. Such a group continues in the "Aliya" in Israel.

19. The Abkhaz Autonomous Republic inside the Georgian Republic seeks full independence. The Abkhaz are mainly Sunni Muslims, but they are a minority in their own republic (17 percent Abkhaz, 43 percent Georgians, the remaining population consisting of other nationalities). Before becoming patriarch, Ilia II was metropolitan of Sukhumi in the Abkhaz part of Georgia, but served only as the religious head of the Georgians there.

20. Adzhars are a southwest Georgian tribe (ethnos) that since 1921 has had its own autonomous republic inside the Georgian Republic.

21. See note 2.

STEPHEN K. BATALDEN

The Contemporary Politics
of the Russian Bible

Religious Publication in a Period of Glasnost

I n 1989, a brief lead article in the *Newsletter of the American Association for the Advancement of Slavic Studies* suggested, with a somewhat tongue-in-cheek lament, that the avalanche of open writing during the era of glasnost was becoming as difficult to interpret as had been the strictly limited and ideologically coded information available in earlier, Stalinist and post-Stalinist periods.[1] Today, just a few years later, that lament rings rather hollow, for the more open publishing marketplace has brought fresh problems that again threaten to limit access to the published word.

The rising price of printed matter has so outstripped the resources of an increasingly impoverished readership that sales have plummeted. The premier glasnost journal *Ogonek,* once boasting a circulation of over four million copies, is currently being printed in an official run well under two million. Furthermore, the ever-present paper deficit continues to haunt publishers, whose print runs are continually being circumscribed by such paper shortages. Finally, problems with international circulation add to the challenges facing distribution and the once powerful book-exporting monopolies. Greatly increased costs of postage have combined with competition from new national and private distribution networks to threaten the existence of the former monopoly vendors of Soviet books and journals. The cutback in 1991 of air mail shipments by *Mezhdunarodnaia kniga,* a one-time monopoly exporter, has forced changes in the operation of trading partners in the West. By mid-1991, the future of the state monopoly of the international book trade seemed most uncertain, with Western access to Russian publications hanging in the balance.[2] The result has been that Western academic libraries and individual subscribers can no longer be sure of the timely receipt of Russian books and journals. The irony, then, of the new openness is that access to the printed word has become, for market reasons, almost as problematic as it was formerly, for political reasons. Even with the introduction of some innovative joint publication ventures employing Western capital, the situation appears unlikely to improve in the immediate future.

Despite these rather grim forebodings, the availability of religious literature—including the Scriptures—in both Russian and non-Russian languages constitutes one of the most significant new developments in publishing. Publication of religious literature has accelerated to a point unimaginable prior to glasnost. A "reconstructed" publishing network turns out in limited *tirazh* (circulation) the works of Berdiaev, Bulgakov, Fedotov, Florovskii, Florenskii, and many contemporary writers whose works were strictly forbidden prior to 1985.[3] Although prices remain steep, texts sanctioned by church authorities, including the Bible, may be purchased at major monasteries and church centers. There continue to be great shortages of devotional literature, service books, and lectionaries, but the principle of open publication of religious literature is unquestioned.

In this dynamic and revitalized world of religious publication, there are some obvious questions that beg to be answered regarding the new publishing environment and the special situation of the religious press. First, does the spate of religious titles reflect a new milieu in which the marketplace, rather than prescribed political, ecclesiastical, or other constraints, limits the output of the religious press? Second, why does Russian religious publishing remain, at least by Western standards, so cautious in its agenda? In addressing these related questions, a focus upon contemporary efforts to translate and publish the Russian Bible is particularly instructive.

Two historical circumstances frame the discussion of the Russian Bible in the period of glasnost. First, the marketplace never determined the course of modern Russian biblical translation and publication in the nineteenth century. Indeed, the original Russian Bible Society in the era of Alexander I issued so many volumes of Scripture—over seven hundred thousand New Testaments and Psalters alone—that it overshot the size of the reading population. John Paterson, the enterprising Scot who administered that operation, sensed that there might be an underdeveloped reading public. Adding his support to Lancastrian schools in the cause of increased popular literacy, he intuitively recognized the need to forge a literate audience—a market—before the pious cause of popular Bible reading could be advanced.[4] Later, after Nicholas I closed the Russian Bible Society and forbade translation of Scripture into modern Russian, the ongoing printing of the Russian Bible became very much a part of the underground press. Even after the resumption of translation of modern Russian texts in the era of the Great Reforms, the press of the Holy Synod maintained monopoly rights on publication of Scripture down to 1917.

A second historical condition also affected the fate of the modern Russian Bible: the Russian biblical text typically had a very circumscribed role in Orthodox spirituality. This limited role of the Russian text resulted from the Russian church's continued use in the nineteenth century of the Church Slavonic, as opposed to the more vernacular Russian text in liturgical worship. Thus, translation and publication of the Bible in modern Russian went hand in hand with the perpetuation of a non-demotic, Slavonic liturgical language. The coexistence of these two languages in modern Russian religious culture (as well as in the religious life of other Eastern Slavs) is what has come to be called "diglossia." Eve Levin has referred to the "use of the vernacular in the Russian Church," but in fact the historic Slavonic text was not vernacular, even though it remained (and remains) the functioning liturgical text within the Russian church.

At the same time, as Levin indicates elsewhere in this volume, the importance of biblical texts for Orthodox spirituality differed from their value in the Protestant West, where after the Reformation faith came to be identified with a formal theology rooted in demotic Scripture. In Russia, Bible reading developed rather late as an element of Orthodox piety. Unlike Protestantism with its early sixteenth-century Luther Bible and its appeal to a Bible-reading "priesthood of believers," Russian Orthodoxy traditionally found the clearest expression of its spirituality in the daily marking of the church calendar with its fasts, its saints' lives, its veneration of icons, and, most important, its liturgical celebration of the Eucharist. Reading simply was not required for the fulfillment of Orthodox religious observances. Only with the growth of literacy and popular education in the late nineteenth century did Bible reading become a significant element of Russian religious life—and then only because of the development of an elaborate colportage network for the dissemination of biblical literature.[5]

These two circumstances—the controls placed upon translation and dissemination of the modern Russian Bible and the more peripheral role assigned to Bible reading in traditional Orthodox piety—offer a historical context for addressing the contemporary printing of religious literature in a period of glasnost. Has the more open publishing environment ushered in an unprecedented era in which the marketplace can be said to determine the output of the religious press? With respect to translation and publication of Russian Scripture, there have clearly been other forces beyond that of market demand that continue to determine the course of religious publishing. For, as in other areas of the emergent religious press, there remain powerful constraints operating in the field of Russian biblical translation and publication.

The first of these major constraints is economic. Russian church presses have typically not enjoyed the kind of capital resources needed to produce large editions of Scripture. Most editions published in the Soviet Union, from the 1956 Moscow Russian Bible to the present, were issued in relatively small circulation runs of twenty-five thousand to fifty

thousand copies. Such small print runs meant that Russian biblical literature printed in the Soviet Union was invariably reserved for the clergy
and for internal church distribution. These economic constraints—especially in the era of glasnost—have increasingly drawn the Russian church
into arrangements with Western, particularly Protestant, disseminators
of biblical literature. The provision by the United Bible Societies (UBS)
of hundreds of thousands of copies of the Russian Bible, printed at modern UBS facilities in Stuttgart, reveals only a small part of that dependency. Such shipments will likely continue. In 1986 the Scandinavian
Bible Societies committed themselves to providing, as a gift for the millennium celebration in the Soviet Union, one hundred fifty thousand
copies of the pre-Revolution Lopukhin-edited *Tolkovaia Bibliia*, an interpreter's Bible with Russian text.[6] The storage and distribution arrangements for so large a multivolume work posed logistical problems for
Russian church authorities, but the more substantive problem—indeed,
the irony—was that the economics of religious publication necessitated cooperation with Western, Protestant religious publishers at a time
when there were signs of retreat from ecumenism in wider Russian
church circles.

The dependency of the Russian church on Western philanthropy has
taken several different forms. There have been conversations between the
UBS and the publications department of the Russian Orthodox church
regarding provision of a large printing press in Moscow for the exclusive
publication of biblical literature.[7] For now, the production of large-*tirazh*
editions of Scripture requires special paper and presses that the Moscow
Patriarchate cannot afford. In 1991, Patriarch Aleksii's aide on biblical
matters, Konstantin Logachev, negotiated an agreement with the UBS
for the publication at Aurora Publishers in Leningrad of an edition of
a children's Bible (*Detskaia Bibliia*), to be patterned after a Dutch
children's Bible in wide circulation throughout the West.[8] Even in this
instance, the dependency upon Western philanthropy was to be seen in
the UBS providing paper for the project from Western stock. Such
cooperation between the UBS and the Russian Orthodox church revealed the tip of an iceberg involving wide-ranging church negotiations
with a variety of Western groups offering assistance to the Russian religious press.[9]

This dependency upon Western philanthropy has yielded a situation in
which sales revenue from Western-published Russian and non-Russian
biblical literature has become a large source of income for churches of
the former Soviet Union. For example, the income derived from the
sale of the Lopukhin *Tolkovaia Bibliia* exceeded fifteen million rubles in
the late 1980s, before the rapid deflation of the ruble. Sale of other
Western-supplied Scripture has yielded comparable revenues. The Russian church's ability to exploit in such a manner the Western purveyors of

biblical literature for church revenue came at a time when the rapid reopening of churches and monasteries throughout the country was creating great financial need.[10]

Although the public demand or market for Scripture was a surface factor in this collaboration between Western Bible organizations and the Russian Orthodox church, the alliance was structured in such a way as to play to the political and financial advantage of the Russian Orthodox church. In practice, this meant that, until 1991, the Russian Orthodox church controlled sales of Scripture in Orthodox communities of the Soviet Union. This pattern of Orthodox church control differs from the nineteenth-century model, when the British and Foreign Bible Society directly addressed the biblical market of the Russian Empire through an elaborate structure of agencies, depots, and colporteurs.[11]

The unprecedented, if still limited, availability of biblical literature in contemporary Russian society—Bibles in numerous languages, Russian children's Bibles, an illustrated Russian edition of the Gustav Doré Bible, the interpreter's Bible, and others—also reflects the priorities and interests of the cooperating Western Bible organizations.[12] This is seen most clearly in the priority assigned to biblical publication and dissemination, as opposed to nonbiblical religious publication. Presumably public demand is as great or greater for liturgical service books (and other nonbiblical religious literature) as it is for Bibles, but the marketing priority of Western Bible organizations has assumed special importance in determining the type of religious literature that becomes accessible.[13] Thus, without minimizing the significance of the local religious press that continues to grow exponentially, larger church publication decisions continue to occur in an environment governed by the politics and economics of international joint ventures in which the mutual interests of the Russian Orthodox church and cooperating Western Bible agencies—and not necessarily the market—take priority.

If, at the external level, ecumenical politics and the economics of biblical publication have influenced the religious press, equally powerful have been the internal, institutional dynamics affecting indigenous translation and publication decisions. Numerous individual and institutional efforts are currently under way to translate and publish editions of Holy Scripture. In this respect, the situation appears analogous to the period of the Great Reforms under Alexander II, when, after the hiatus of the Nicolaevan years, it became possible to issue trial editions, to sponsor competing translations, and to review religious literature in dynamic new theological journals. Then, as now, the religious press was enlivened by contending efforts that reflected deep political and theological divisions within the church. Today, for example, at least four separate and distinct projects are struggling to bring out editions of Russian Scripture. Fueled occasionally by personal rivalries and the desire for control over the dissemination of Scripture, these efforts have built upon translation work already under way in the pre-glasnost years.

Perhaps most important because of the relationship to Patriarch Aleksii are the personal and institutional activities of Konstantin Ivanovich Logachev. A former instructor in modern Greek at the Leningrad Theological Academy, Logachev became the dominant figure in an informal Biblical Commission attached to the academy in the 1970s, during the last years of Metropolitan Nikodim. Logachev's ties with the UBS, including his embrace of the scholarship of Eugene Nida, a UBS linguist and polyglot of international stature, date from that period. In 1978 Logachev published abroad, with UBS support, a trial edition of the Gospel of John (an edition that the UBS unfortunately identified on the title page verso as the "Russian John"). Marking a high point of such experimental work in biblical translation, it came out just prior to the death of Metropolitan Nikodim in 1978.[14]

Following the elevation of Bishop Kirill to the Leningrad Theology Academy rectorate after Metropolitan Nikodim's death, Logachev fell from favor at the academy and took employment in the 1980s as an editor at Aurora Publishing House. He resurfaced in a scholarly position within the Russian church in 1989, when he was appointed by Metropolitan Aleksii of Leningrad to serve as his personal research aide (*sekretar' po issledovaniiam*). In January 1990, before Aleksii was elevated to the Moscow patriarchal throne, Logachev founded the Northwest Biblical Commission (Severno-Zapadnaia Bibleiskaia Komissiia).[15] That commission nominally brought together under the presidency of the metropolitan five separate institutional bodies: the Leningrad Diocese of the Russian Orthodox church, the Archive of the Academy of Sciences, the State University of Leningrad, the Union of Evangelical Christians and Baptists of Leningrad, and the Leningrad Association for Study of Slavonic Cultures and Histories. The commission promised to advance scholarly work on the Slavonic biblical text, to publish needed modern editions of Scripture, and to collaborate with other regional commissions and Western Bible societies. Konstantin Logachev, as executive secretary of the Northwest Bible Commission, remained the major force behind its activities, particularly its ties with Western Bible agencies. The commission immediately began to prepare a modern Russian Bible using the Old Testament text (without the deuterocanonical books of the Septuagint) and employing the popular nineteenth-century illustrations of Gustav Doré. This illustrated work became the first edition of Scripture to sell in regular state bookstores since the 1917 Russian Revolution. It circulated in a run of one hundred thousand copies.[16]

With the election of Metropolitan Aleksii as patriarch in 1990, Logachev continued to serve as the patriarch's adviser on biblical matters and became the secretary to the Russian Orthodox Bible commission—

the Patriarchal and Synodal Bible Commission (Patriarshaia i Sinodal'naia Bibleiskaia Komissiia [hereafter, the PSBK]). The PSBK was established initially as the Synodal Bible Commission in February 1990, during the last months of Patriarch Pimen's life, when administrative matters increasingly devolved into the hands of a ruling Holy Synod of bishops.[17] With the designation of Metropolitan Aleksii as patriarch, the Synodal Bible Commission was renamed the Patriarchal and Synodal Bible Commission. The PSBK soon became the main Russian church negotiator with Western Bible agencies. It has become difficult to imagine any authoritative publication of modern Russian Scripture issued without the imprimatur of the Moscow-based PSBK. Unlike the interconfessional Northwest Bible Commission, the PSBK exists strictly as an Orthodox body tied to the Moscow Patriarchate.

In addition to the Northwest Bible Commission and the PSBK, a third organization took form in January 1990 for the express purpose of providing Russian Scripture in a more readable text. This loosely structured organization, composed of leading Orthodox churchmen as well as prominent Protestants in Moscow and members of the Muscovite religious intelligentsia, came to be called the Bible Society in the Soviet Union. With the demise of the Soviet Union, this group assumed the title the Bible Society in Russia. This translation group included among its members the biblical scholar Father Aleksandr Men' (see the essay by Michael Meerson) and literary scholars Sergei Averintsev and Viktor Zhivov. Before his untimely death in September 1990, Aleksandr Men' had laid the groundwork for a new religious scholarly journal on biblical studies, *Mir Biblii* (The World of the Bible), and had been selected as rector for a new Orthodox institution of higher learning in Moscow.[18] Following the tragic murder of Aleksandr Men', editorship of *Mir Biblii* was assumed by Averintsev, a corresponding member of the Academy of Sciences who also served as an initial participant in the PSBK.

Independent of the aforementioned organizations, although including overlapping membership from the Moscow Bible Society in Russia, is the more recently established Russian Bible Institute (Russkii Bibleiskii Institut), directed in St. Petersburg by Anatolii Alekseev. Alekseev, a senior research scholar at the Institute of Early Russian Literature (Pushkinskii Dom) and an early member of the PSBK, completed his doctoral work on the textology of the Old Testament, particularly the Song of Songs. The Russian Bible Institute announced itself as part of a new Independent Humanities Academy (Nezavisimaia Gumanitarnaia Akademiia) located in the recently renamed St. Petersburg.[19] Projecting an ambitious program of scholarly publication on the Slavonic Bible, as well as a "project for translation of the New Testament into present-day literary Russian," this institute has drawn upon the expertise of such biblical scholars as Archimandrite Ianuarii Ivliev of the St. Petersburg Theological Academy and Averintsev of Moscow. The activities of the Russian Bible Institute conspicuously do not overlap with the work of Konstantin Logachev and his Northwest Bible Commission—despite the fact that both organizations are formally located in St. Petersburg.

Alongside this complex picture of competing biblical organizations must be added the growing number of active national and regional Bible commissions. While those in the Caucasus originated before the onset of perestroika, those in the Baltic emerged in the late 1980s, as did the Belarusian (Belorussian) Bible Commission in Minsk, a pan-Orthodox confessional body under the presidency of Russian Orthodox Metropolitan Filaret of Minsk and Belorussia.[20] These national Bible organizations are at work on modern translations of Scripture into non-Russian languages.

Finally, personal translation projects exist, such as that advanced by the Kievan archpriest L. N. Lutkovskii. The Gospels of the Lutkovskii translation appeared in early 1990 in the journal *Literaturnaia ucheba*, a relatively minor literary periodical.[21] This unusual publication of a Gospels text outside official church direction and in a minor journal stirred a predictable outpouring of response. One million new subscribers joined the rolls of *Literaturnaia ucheba* based upon the advance announcement of the Gospels translation. However, reflecting the conservative and even nativist reaction to such publications in the secular press, the journal received accusations that its Lutkovskii translation constituted a Zionist attempt to destroy Orthodoxy. Although there are other independent translation projects afoot, there has been, to my knowledge, only one significant follow-up to the Lutkovskii publication: a special April 1990 issue of *Dos'e: Prilozhenie k 'Literaturnoi gazete'* that offered a harmony of the synoptic Gospels (Matthew, Mark, and Luke) along with a republication for mass readership of the nineteenth-century synodal edition of the Gospel of John.[22]

This rather considerable private, semiofficial, and official activity in biblical translation and publication may suggest that public demand has begun to assert itself in the spread of religious literature. While the marketplace cannot be entirely discounted, especially in the case of non-Russian national language editions, the fact is that few of these projects have reached the actual stage of publication.[23] In the case of work on the Slavonic and Russian texts, the rush to prepare both revised and new translations of Scripture seems rather to have produced rival organizations and competing translation projects. The personal competition and political rivalry over publication of the Word links religious publishing of the era of glasnost with the much more overt constraints operating in the antecedent Soviet and tsarist periods.

In sorting out the personal and institutional politics of the religious press, it is notable that political differences mirror deeper textological divisions. The latter divisions help to explain the existence of some of the rival translation networks. For instance, in his earlier work, done during the tenure of Metropolitan Nikodim of Leningrad, Konstantin Logachev embraced Western biblical textology as represented in the Nestle-Aland school of scholars. This school developed an extended apparatus of variant textual readings represented by more than two thousand extant texts or fragments of texts known to exist for the Greek New Testament. This critical textual apparatus, drawing together schools of texts, came to dominate Western biblical scholarship from the end of the nineteenth century, the period of the first publication of the critical Greek New Testament of Eberhard Nestle.[24] These textological developments postdated the appearance of the standard Russian synodal text of the nineteenth century—the so-called *sinodal'nyi perevod* (synodal translation).

Nevertheless, for reasons stemming from the politics of nineteenth- and twentieth-century Russian translation, much of Orthodox biblical scholarship in the Soviet Union came to reject the Nestle-Aland tradition, claiming that the Slavonic and Russian translations were grounded upon a separate, Eastern textological tradition. Despite the contention of a separate Eastern textological tradition, the Greek basis for the nineteenth-century Russian synodal translation was Desiderius Erasmus's *textus receptus,* a Greek New Testament compilation based upon the half dozen or so extant texts available in the sixteenth century. The irony here is that, in defending the textology of the synodal translation and the *textus receptus,* conservative Orthodox biblical scholars believe they are defending a peculiarly Eastern tradition, despite the obvious identification of Erasmus with Western, pre-Nestlean textology.

While Logachev had previously been eager to reopen the question of the textology behind the modern Russian Bible, his rise to positions of authority under Patriarch Aleksii has tended to modify his earlier textological critique of the nineteenth-century Russian synodal translation.[25] Responding to the cautious judgment of those in power, Logachev has begun to press for new Russian translations based on more modest revisions of the established synodal text.

The textological position of the Russian Bible Institute (RBI) has not been formally spelled out. Nevertheless, RBI leader Alekseev and some of his collaborating churchmen/scholars have expressed reservations over the much-debated nineteenth-century decision to use the Hebrew Masoretic text in preparing the Russian Old Testament. Alekseev believes this use of the Hebrew Bible conflicts with the traditions of Slavonic biblical scholarship. While some nineteenth-century critics may have rejected use of the Hebrew text out of a general disdain for Jewish traditions, the renewed scholarly interest by Alekseev and others in the Septuagint text accords today with wider, renewed scholarly interest in the Greek Old Testament text.[26] This debate over Old Testament textology also reopens in fresh form the question of the underlying bases for the Slavonic Bible, an open-ended textual debate that was unnaturally closed in the aftermath of the Russian Revolution. Thus, important underlying textological conflicts not only reflect the ongoing politics of modern biblical translation but also bring new life to a once vibrant field of inquiry in Russian religious study—a field that remained largely dormant after 1917.

The cumulative impact of these economic, institutional, and textological issues shows that the publication of biblical texts in the contemporary period remains highly politicized despite the veneer of glasnost. In this atmosphere of continuing debate over modern biblical translation, a second, larger question remains: Why does the publishing agenda of the Russian Orthodox church continue to be so cautious? Why has the church leadership, with considerable resources for publication and translation available from the West, proceeded so slowly in sponsoring the printing of biblical texts, service books, saints' lives, and related religious literature? Surely the public demand for such titles exists in the newly energized religious marketplace.

In addition to general economic constraints, there are two explanations for this caution. First, the popular religious audience in Eastern Slav lands has not always supported textual innovation and modern translations into vernacular languages. Although there is, for the moment, a ready audience for any and all religious literature, there also exists an underlying uneasiness about change in the wider culture and, particularly, in the religious life of contemporary society. The Orthodox Church has sought to preserve tradition amid the drab ugliness of twentieth-century society, and some of the conservatism of Russian and other Eastern Slav believers is grounded in just such a concern for preservation. Further breakdown of economic and political life is likely only to reinforce such a native conservatism.[27]

This conservative instinct in the popular religious culture is also related to the absence of a linguistic standard for modern Russian religious texts. There is no single linguistic norm for common Russian; rather, there are many. The Synodal Bible, first published in the 1860s and 1870s, was written in a hybrid nineteenth-century churchly language, essentially pre-Pushkin, and separate from the development of the modern Russian literary language.[28] Today the language of the synodal translation is appreciated precisely because of its peculiarity, calling nostalgically to mind a period of more secure religious and linguistic norms. Potential opponents of the recently published Lutkovskii translation, for example, could be found not only among those opposed to all innovation but also among elements of an intelligentsia who fear the kind of degradation of religious language that has occasionally accompanied Western churchly accommodation to the modern secular idiom. The problem of an appropriate

Russian religious language, after seventy-five years of Sovietese, probably makes this question more complicated for Russians than for any other nationality of the empire.

The Polish-American Nobel laureate, Czeslaw Milosz, addressed the issue of religious language when he commented upon his own translation of the modern Polish Bible. Asked why he had begun to study Hebrew and to translate the Bible—Milosz's translations include a very popular Polish version of the Psalter—he answered that he had done so not only in memory of the Holocaust but also because of his fear of the perverse impact of mass media and journalese upon the modern Polish language and upon contemporary Polish literature.[29] This instinctive, antimodernist drive to preserve culture and tradition is shared by many in Eastern Slav lands who seek to give renewed expression to modern Russian religious culture. Although Western observers may occasionally find these sentiments elitist, such organic notions of culture carry added appeal in times of dramatic economic and political change by reasserting the special authority and importance of tradition and of history. There is in modern Russian culture, particularly religious culture, a predisposition to find contemporary solutions by revisiting, reinterpreting, and recanonizing the past. Thus, the current political battles over the printing of religious texts, particularly translation and publication of the modern Russian Bible, inevitably bear the imprint of unresolved textological issues from the nineteenth century.

NOTES

1. Harley Balzer, "Can We Survive Glasnost?" *AAASS Newsletter*, 29, no. 1 (January 1989), pp. 1–2. Addressing the problems posed by glasnost, Balzer claimed that "the most serious difficulty is the information glut" (p. 1).

2. On the many problems associated with the inaccessibility of Soviet publications, see Patricia Polansky, "Western Slavic Collections: Temporary Chaos or Permanent Damage?" *AAASS Newsletter*, 31, no. 3 (May 1991), pp. 1–2.

3. Although independent desktop and other private publishing has mushroomed, there has also been publication of religious writers in the more official presses. In the case of the works of N. A. Berdiaev, for example, the following editions were issued in 1990: (a) *Dukhi russkoi revoliutsii* (Riga, Latvia: Obshchestvo Druzei Knigi Latvii), a reprint of the Paris YMCA Press edition of 1947, issued in fifty thousand copies; (b) *Istoki i smysl russkogo kommunizma* (Moscow: Nauka), a reprint of the Paris YMCA Press edition of 1955, issued in one hundred thousand copies; (c) *Krizis iskusstva* (Moscow: Tsentr Nauchno-Inzhenernykh Problem), a reprint of the Moscow 1918 edition of G. A. Leman and S. I.

Sakharov, issued in one hundred thousand copies, that incorporates the pre-Revolution Russian orthography of the earlier Moscow edition; (d) *Samopoznanie: Opyt filosofskoi avtobiografii* (Moscow: Mezhdunarodnye Otnosheniia [DEM Publishers, a French-Soviet joint publishing venture]), issued in five hundred thousand copies; (e) *Smysl istorii* (Moscow: Mysl'), based on the Paris YMCA Press edition of 1969, and issued in two hundred thousand copies; (f) *Sud'ba Rossii* (Moscow: MGU [Moscow State University]), a reprint of the Moscow 1918 edition of G. A. Leman and S. I. Sakharov in pre-Revolution Russian orthography, issued in one hundred forty thousand copies. Reflecting the inflationary book market and the deflated ruble, these 1990 editions were marked at prices ranging from 1.9 rubles for the thirty-page *Dukhi russkoi revoliutsii* to 7.8 rubles for *Samopoznanie*. Their actual sale price in 1990–1991 often was four or more times the list price.

4. On Paterson and the press of the early nineteenth-century Russian Bible Society, see S. K. Batalden, "Printing the Bible in the Reign of Alexander I: Toward a Reinterpretation of the Imperial Russian Bible Society," in Geoffrey A. Hosking, ed., *Church, Nation and State in Russia and Ukraine* (London: Macmillan/University of London School of Slavonic and East European Studies, 1991), pp. 65–78.

5. On the development of literacy, see Jeffrey Brooks, *When Russia Learned to Read: Literacy and Popular Literature, 1861–1917* (Princeton: Princeton University Press, 1985). On the specific question of colportage, see S. K. Batalden, "Colportage and the Distribution of Holy Scripture in Late Imperial Russia," a paper read at the Kennan Institute conference "A Millennium of Christianity in Rus'," 1988 (forthcoming in *California Slavic Studies,* 1993).

6. The title of the original interpreter's edition launched by A. P. Lopukhin (1852–1904) is *Tolkovaia Bibliia ili kommentarii na vsie knigi sv. pisaniia Vetkhago i Novago Zavieta,* 12 pts. in 3 vols. (St. Petersburg: 1904–1913). For a discussion of the distribution of the Lopukhin reprint and the UBS-printed Bibles, see "Bible Distribution in the USSR," *UBS Background Paper,* June 1989, pp. 1–2.

7. The precedent for such a printing establishment is that provided for churches of the People's Republic of China. On this question, see the news release of the American Bible Society, "Could 'Memorandum of Understanding' Mean Organized Bible Work, Printing Press for USSR?," 6 June 1989. To date, no such press has been established, but a regular UBS representative and sales office are now in Moscow.

8. On this three-way agreement involving the UBS, Aurora Publishers, and the Northwest Bible Commission, see "Secular Publishers Keen to Produce Bibles," *UBS World Report,* no. 239 (July 1990), p. 3. Since that agreement, the issue of rights to the text has put a strain upon relations between the UBS and Russian publishers.

9. In addition to Russian Orthodox church ties with the UBS, there have been conversations with other Western Bible agencies, denominational bodies, and such self-proclaimed Bible "smuggling" agencies as that of "Brother Andrew."

10. On this calculation of Bible sales revenue, see S. K. Batalden, "The Politics of Modern Russian Biblical Translation," in Philip C. Stine, ed., *Bible Translation and the Spread of the Church* (Leiden: E. J. Brill, 1990), p. 78.

11. Despite the more direct link to the market in nineteenth-century Russia, the Press of the Holy Synod still held a monopoly on the publication of Scripture. On this, see Batalden, "Colportage and the Distribution of Holy Scripture."

12. Among the agencies providing Scripture in non-Russian languages of the empire, one of the most significant is that of Boris Arapovic's Institute for Bible Translation in Stockholm. In addition to commissioning some of its own new translations, the Institute has republished several of the Asian-language texts formerly circulated in the Russian Empire by the British and Foreign Bible Society. On the illustrated Gustav Doré Bible, see note 16 below.

13. Originating in the earliest years of the nineteenth century, evangelical Bible societies (such as the British and Foreign Bible Society, founded in 1804) typically had as their function the translation, publication, and distribution of Bibles in major spoken languages of the world. Since World War II, most national Bible societies have collaborated under the common umbrella of the UBS, but the focus of their activity remains unchanged.

14. Logachev's translation was entitled *Evangelie po Ioannu v novom russkom aperevode* (Brussels: United Bible Societies, 1978). It was published in two thousand copies as a supplement to the UBS periodical publication, *The Bible Translator.*

15. On the establishment of the Northwest Bible Commission (SZBK), see the news release of the UBS, "Bible Organisations Blossom in the USSR," 29 February 1990. A "memorandum of understanding," signed 14 February 1990, between the UBS and the SZBK, identifies the constituencies of the latter, and indicates that it was established in Leningrad on 11 January 1990.

16. Published in Leningrad in 1990, the Gustave Doré illustrated edition was entitled *Bibliia: Knigi sviashchennogo pisaniia Vetkhogo i Novogo Zaveta (Kanonicheskie) s illiustratsiiami Giustava Dore*. The title page verso identifies the work as actually published in Vyborg, under the sponsorship of the Northwest Bible Commission and with the approval of the Northwest Agency for Authors' Rights. The text of this edition is that of the standard synodal edition of the nineteenth century, but without the deuterocanonical books. The absence of Septuagint readings for

the Old Testament distinguishes this text from earlier biblical printings done since 1956 in the Soviet Union.

17. According to the 8 May 1990 session of the Holy Synod of the Russian Orthodox church (*Sinodal'nyi biulleten'*, no. 78), the Synodal Bible Commission of the Russian Orthodox church was established on 20 February 1990. The same issue of the bulletin identifies the initial membership, and indicates that Konstantin Logachev was appointed secretary of the commission.

18. The Bible Society in Russia is identified in the UBS news release of 29 February 1990 (see note 15). Regarding the role of Father Aleksandr Men' in biblical scholarship, see the obituaries by Andrei Bessmertnyi in *Russkaia mysl'* (Paris), no. 3845 (14 September 1990) and by Aleksandr Borisov, no. 3846 (21 September 1990).

19. See the Russian Bible Institute's flyer/announcement, "Russkii Bibleiskii Institut" [undated], which gives a Leningrad address of 1-ia Liniia 52, Leningrad (199053). The founding director is identified as A. A. Alekseev, with N. L. Gorina as secretary and M. V. Babitskaia, S. A. Davydova, and T. V. Tkacheva as project secretaries.

20. The UBS news release of 29 February 1990 (see note 15) dates the founding of both the Belorussian Bible Commission in Minsk and the Latvian Bible Society in Riga to late 1989. In fact, Bible societies in many national regions were first established in the early nineteenth century, during the era of the Russian Bible Society. For a reliable survey history of Bible societies in Russia and the Soviet Union, see Kathleen Cann, "Bible Societies in Russia and the Soviet Union: 1806–1988," *UBS Background Paper*, March 1991. On the situation in Belarus, see Ihor Zawerucha, "The Situation of Roman Catholicism in Belorussia," *Radio Liberty Report on the USSR*, 2, no. 19 (11 May 1990), pp. 19–29. Zawerucha cites, in addition to the New Testament translation of the Orthodox Belorussian Bible Commission, a New Testament translation by the Catholic priest Uladzislav Tsarnyavsky. Because the Tsarnyavsky translation is from Polish (and not from original sources), it has not been accepted even within Catholic circles in Belarus'.

21. *Literaturnaia ucheba* published the translation of the four Gospels by Father Leonid Lutkovskii in nos. 1–4 (1990), pp. 89–138. The Gospels text was preceded (pp. 89–96) by three prefaces. The first, by A. Ch. Kozarzhevskii, "O novom zavete" (pp. 89–90), addressed in broad terms the form and content of the New Testament. The second, by K. I. Logachev, "Russkaia Bibliia: Vchera, segodnia i zavtra" (pp. 91–94), presented a subtle and succinct history of nineteenth- and twentieth-century translations of the Russian Bible. Placing the problem of the adherence to the original Greek text alongside the problem of the aesthetic and artistic presentation of the text in modern Russian, Logachev noted the problems posed in earlier translation efforts. The final preface (pp.

246 STEPHEN K. BATALDEN

95–96), compiled by the editor of the journal, documented the meeting in late September 1989 of translator Lutkovskii and members of the editorial board, representatives of the publications department of the Moscow Patriarchate, Konstantin Logachev of the Leningrad Metropolitanate, and others. After considering the strengths and limitations of the translation—Logachev, for example, while supporting publication, noted that he considered the work to be an excessively "free translation"—the editorial board of the journal stated its support for publication, declaring it important that translations be made available for "today's reader." At the conclusion of its preface, the journal committed itself to a much larger undertaking, "to publish during 1990–91 the whole New Testament in contemporary translations" (p. 96). At the conclusion of the Lutkovskii Gospels text, the journal announced the intention to begin publication in 1991 of a three-year course on the Church Slavonic language (p. 138).

22. "V nachale bylo Slovo," *Dos'e: Prilozhenie k 'Literaturnoi gazete,'* April 1990. The richly illustrated tabloid publication *Dos'e* includes an opening interview (p. 2) with Father Leonid Lutkovskii, whose Russian translation of the Gospels published in *Literaturnaia ucheba* (see note 21) had become well known to a broad Russian readership. Father Leonid, a graduate of the Leningrad Theological Seminary, is chief priest of St. Nicholas Orthodox Church, in the Kievan oblast town of Rogozovo. A secretary of the Ukrainian League of Christian Democratic Unity, Lutkovskii is also president of the educational and benevolent association Put' k Istine (Path Toward Truth). He also lectures in the philosophical faculty of Kiev University on the Bible as a masterpiece of world literature. Following the interview, *Dos'e* published Lutkovskii's harmony of the three synoptic Gospels, "Soglasovanie sinopticheskikh evangelii" (pp. 4–19). In a second section, *Dos'e* provided a reprint of the nineteenth-century synodal Russian translation of the Gospel of John (pp. 22–26). In a third section, the tabloid added fragments from the Lopukhin-edited *Tolkovaia Bibliia* and religious poems by Boris Pasternak and Anna Akhmatova (pp. 28–32).

23. Although the years of glasnost have not witnessed numerous published editions of the Bible, there have been several scholarly publications pertaining to the history and textology of the Slavonic Bible. See, for example, A. A. Alekseev, ed., *Ostrozhskaia Bibliia: Sbornik statei* (Moscow: TsKTBI Press, 1990). This latest Alekseev anthology, including articles by Ia. D. Isaevich, Igumen Innokentii (Pavlor), A. M. Pentkovskii, and Alekseev, is credited on the title page as coming from the Slavonic Bible Commission of the Academy of Science's Russian Language Institute. A small circulation run of seven hundred copies is identified on the back cover.

24. The critical Greek text of Eberhard Nestle has been issued in numerous editions since the end of the nineteenth century. Its standard

title is *Novum Testamentum graece, cum apparatu critico curavit* (United Bible Societies); see, e.g., the 17th ed., Stuttgart, 1949.

25. For an example of this more conservative Orthodox response in defense of the *textus receptus* during a time of reaction against a new Russian New Testament translation being readied in Paris, see A. I. Ivanov, "K voprosu o vosstanovlenii pervonachal'nogo grecheskogo teksta Novogo Zaveta," *Zhurnal moskovskoi patriarkhii* (1954), no. 3, pp. 38–50. For a description of how the debate over biblical textology resurfaced in the Soviet Union during the translation activity of Bishop Kassian Bezobrazov in Paris, see S. K. Batalden, "Revolution and Emigration: The Russian Files of the British and Foreign Bible Society, 1917–1970," in Janet M. Hartley, ed., *The Study of Russian History from British Archival Sources* (London: Mansell, 1986), pp. 156–171. In contrast with this more conservative strain of biblical textology, K. I. Logachev offered a more critical view of the *textus receptus* and of the lexical problems of the synodal translation in a series of articles published in the late 1960s and 1970s in *Zhurnal moskovskoi patriarkhii* and *Bogoslovskie trudy*. See, for example, his essay "K voprosu ob uluchshenii russkogo perevoda novogo zaveta," *Bogoslovskie trudy* 14 (1975), pp. 160–165.

26. The importance of contemporary Septuagint studies hardly needs to be documented, and is clear from such series as the Supplements to Vetus Testamentus (Leiden: E. J. Brill). In this series are such standard studies as L. C. Allen, *The Greek Chronicles: The Relation of the Septuagint I and II Chronicles to the Massoretic Text*, 2 vols. (Leiden: E. J. Brill, 1974).

27. There are, of course, countervailing elements that welcome textual innovation, occasionally seeing in such changes a potential political or national response to conservative and Russifying elements within the Orthodox church of the Moscow Patriarchate. For example, the platform of Rukh, the Ukrainian popular front, includes a subsection on religion with the provision that "Rukh will support the strivings of parishioners for Ukrainian-language services in parishes of the Russian Orthodox Church." See *Rukh: Program and Charter*, trans. Martha Oliynyk (Ellicott City, Md.: Smoloskyp Publishers, 1990), p. 35. For a similar appeal for use of Belorussian in the Greek Catholic church of Belarus', see *Uniya*, 1, no. 1 (August 1990), pp. 1–3.

28. For treatment of Russian linguistic norms in the eighteenth and nineteenth centuries, see the works of V. M. Zhivov, including his most recent book, *Kul'turnye konflikty v istorii russkogo literaturnogo iazyka XVIII-nachala XIX veka* (Moscow: Institut Russkogo Iazyka AN SSSR, 1990).

29. Milosz's comments are from his lecture "Problems of Biblical Translation," delivered at Arizona State University, 20 January 1984.

Part Three

Sources for Study of
Religious Identity in the Orthodox East

STEPHEN K. BATALDEN

and

MICHAEL D. PALMA

Orthodox Pilgrimage and Russian Landholding in Jerusalem

The British Colonial Record

Pilgrimage to the Holy Places of Jerusalem and the surrounding sites of the life and death of Jesus Christ has long given expression to one of the deepest strains of Christian piety. At the Church of the Holy Sepulchre, the site of Jesus' tomb, the annual miracle of the holy fire on the eve of Orthodox Easter—that is, the angel's lighting of the lamp over the tomb and the Patriarch's sharing of that light—drew countless thousands. Robert Curzon, in his description of the miracle of the holy fire on the disastrous Easter of 1834, noted how, in the presence of the Egyptian Ibrahim Pasha, seventeen thousand pilgrims crowded near or into the Church of the Holy Sepulchre. That Easter, after the miracle had been performed and the Patriarch had been carried aloft from the chapel, pandemonium broke loose. The panic worsened when Muslim guards outside misinterpreted the action of the pilgrims as an attack upon themselves. The guards then rushed into the church, brandishing bayonets. By Curzon's reckoning, hundreds perished and many more were badly wounded.[1]

The events of 1834 and the annual flood of pilgrims to the Holy Places—a flood that reached its high-water mark on the eve of World War I—offer needed perspective in understanding the involvement of the Russian Empire in Palestine landholding from the second half of the nineteenth century. For not only did the Russian Orthodox ecclesiastical missions to Jerusalem and the later Orthodox Palestine Society seek to bring order and control to the rival Greek and Arab Orthodox interests in the Holy Places, but this Russian presence became more complicated with the annual arrival of thousands of Russian pilgrims—as many as twenty thousand a year by the eve of World War I.

Partly in order to work among rival Greek and Arab factions within the Jerusalem Patriarchate, but increasingly also to handle the logistical problem of masses of Russian pilgrims in Jerusalem, the Russian Orthodox

Ecclesiastical Mission to Jerusalem and, later, the Imperial Russian Orthodox Palestine Society bought large parcels of land and erected educational, religious, and charitable institutions, as well as accommodations for pilgrims. The account of Russian land purchases, particularly by the Palestine Society and the most prominent heads of the Jerusalem Ecclesiastical Mission, Archimandrites Antonin (Kapustin) and Leonid (Kavelin), has been well documented elsewhere and need not be detailed here.[2] However, the staggering number of these purchases forms the basis for the question I wish to ask.

In the period between 1857 and 1914, the Russian Ecclesiastical Mission in Jerusalem and the Imperial Russian Orthodox Palestine Society acquired over sixty-five parcels of land involving a total area of approximately 1,500,000 square meters (about 150 hectares). The Ecclesiastical Mission and the Palestine Society thereby came to own approximately six times the area enclosed today by the walls of the Moscow Kremlin. To be sure, some portions of that landholding involved territories outside of Jerusalem—in Bethlehem, Jericho, the Sea of Galilee, and other areas. Most of the holdings, however, were in and around the city of Jerusalem. The Ecclesiastical Mission, which owned most of the large Russian compound in Jerusalem as well as churches and monasteries, held over five times as much property as did the Palestine Society. Still, the Palestine Society holdings of over 23 hectares (235,000 square meters) remained substantial. One of its large buildings, for example, could accommodate up to seven thousand pilgrims.[3]

What happened to these very considerable Russian Orthodox and Palestine Society landholdings in the aftermath of World War I and the October Bolshevik Revolution? One of the consequences of the creation of the British-held Palestine Mandate as successor to Ottoman authority in the region was that many of the important sources for understanding the fate of Russian landholding in Palestine were preserved in the British Public Record Office, particularly within Foreign Office and Colonial Office records.[4] With the possible exception of records remaining in Jerusalem, this British archival documentation affords the clearest picture to date concerning the fate of Russian Orthodox landholding during the Palestine Mandate.

In reconstructing from these records the fate of Russian landholding in Palestine, a complicated pattern of British policy emerges. It is the thesis of this essay that British policy, driven by concerns for the internationally recognized religious and charitable nature of the Russian holdings, sought to avoid by all means handing over the properties to Soviet authorities, whose avowed atheism they regarded as contrary to the intended use of Holy Places. However, in not transferring title to Soviet representatives—indeed, discouraging any visit by Soviet delegations until the outbreak of World War II—the British Mandate authorities played into the hands of the representatives of the Russian Church in Exile, the followers of the Karlovatskii Synod, who sought, albeit with very limited success, to exploit the fears of Soviet atheism to secure their own authority over the prewar Russian holdings.

In the end, the party that gained the most from the issue of Russian landholding was the Palestine Mandate (the British authorities). For by securing lease to the land and the buildings on the land, that government at minimal cost maintained and developed its own offices on Russian lands. The importance of this precedent cannot be overestimated inasmuch as the leased buildings in the former Russian compound and elsewhere continue to house some of the highest legal and bureaucratic offices of the Israeli state, including its supreme court. The ultimate irony, then, is that for the ostensible purpose of protecting the religious and charitable intent of Russian Orthodox landholding in Jerusalem, the Palestine Mandate developed its own system of control that, while permitting limited monastic and religious institutional life on isolated properties, fundamentally contributed to the secularization of lands formerly held by the Imperial Russian Orthodox Palestine Society and the Russian Ecclesiastical Mission in Jerusalem.

The issue of Russian landholding in Jerusalem, while it undoubtedly was a part of Palestine Mandate concerns from the origin of the League of Nations and the mandate system, surfaced as a significant concern for the British in 1923 with the appeal of Leonid B. Krassin, member of the Soviet trade delegation in London, for Soviet rights to the prewar Russian properties. In May 1923, Krassin turned to the British Foreign Office, requesting that the Russian property in Palestine be turned over to the Soviet government.[5] In his memorandum and in subsequent appeals, including those of Konstantin Rakovskii, Soviet chargé d'affaires in England, the argument was put forward that the January 1918 decree of the Council of Peoples' Commissariats concerning separation of church and state specifically included the provision that no religious societies could own property and that all such properties were henceforth to be properties of the people—that is, under state ownership. By extension, properties once held in Jerusalem by the imperial government or by a religious association chartered in the Russian Empire had, according to the claim, become de jure the property of the Soviet government.[6]

The appeals of the Soviet government forced a lengthy British review of the matter, setting in motion a series of responses that effectively undermined Soviet claims upon the Russian properties for the entire period of the Palestine Mandate. In their initial search for a response to Soviet claims, the British turned to the provision of the League of Nations' "Mandate for Palestine," issued by the League's Council in July 1922. Article 13 vested "all responsibility in connection with the Holy Places and religious buildings or sites in Palestine" in the British mandatory, authority that came to be exercised through the high commissioner for Palestine and the various Palestine Mandate administrative agencies and courts. Article 14 of that document, however, called for the creation of a "special commission" by the mandatory "to define and determine the rights and claims in connection with the Holy Places." That special commission was never convened, owing to unresolved disputes in the Council of the League of Nations over its composition.[7]

For the British, the problem with reliance upon Article 13 and the provision of the original "Mandate" was that they could not be absolutely certain that Palestine courts, if appealed to by Soviet authorities, might not recognize some legality in the Soviet claims. As a result of this uncertainty, British authorities determined that a special ordinance was needed to clarify the status of charitable lands in Palestine. Writing for British State Secretary Ramsay MacDonald in June 1924, the British Foreign Office reported to the Colonial Office that "Mr. MacDonald also agrees as to the necessity of the immediate framing of local legislation in Palestine on the subject of charitable trusts."[8] The timeliness of the matter also related to the ongoing Anglo-Russian conference on normalization of diplomatic and trade relations, a conference at which the issue of Russian landholding was likely to arise.

In the end, the Charitable Trusts Ordinance of 1924 granted the Palestine Mandate and its courts broad jurisdictional authority over charitable, particularly *wakf*, lands, properties of a religious or charitable nature or endowed to a family trust.[9] The crucial section pertaining to the Russian properties concerned the sweeping provisions in Article 37 of the ordinance. According to this article, "notwithstanding anything [else] in the Ordinance," the court, in evaluating "any property in Palestine held by the owner under obligation that the use of the property and its proceeds be devoted to charitable purposes . . . may declare such property to be held in trust." Under the ordinance, "to be held in trust" came to mean that the Palestine Mandate high commissioner or his representative could administer the properties for charitable purposes. The result of the 1924 Charitable Trusts Ordinance was that even if Soviet authorities were to appeal to the Palestine courts, those courts were empowered to declare that the Mandate was legally acting as trustee for the properties, thus nullifying other claims to the land that might—or might not, as the case may be—threaten its secularization. This was, in effect, a broad grant of administrative authority to the British-run mandatory government headed by High Commissioner Herbert Samuel.

While the Charitable Trusts Ordinance effectively undermined Soviet claims upon Palestine properties for the remainder of the interwar period, its impact upon other claimants—including émigré organizations and local Russian monks and nuns—was more complicated. The appeal of Russian émigrés for the Jerusalem properties reached the British Foreign Office directly on the heels of the initial Soviet claims of 1923.

In September 1923, Metropolitan Evlogii, declaring himself to be the "highest representative" in the West of canonically elected Patriarch Tikhon of Moscow, appealed from Paris to the Archbishop of Canterbury for the latter's intercession with the British authorities so that properties formerly belonging to the Russian Orthodox Mission and the Orthodox Palestine Society "should not be given even temporarily into the hands of strangers, but should be left as they formerly were in the possession of the Russian Orthodox church in the person of her abovementioned loyal representative [i.e., Evlogii himself]."[10] In claiming authority as head of the diocesan administration for the Russian Orthodox Church in western Europe, Metropolitan Evlogii said that none of the properties owned by the Ecclesiastical Mission in Jerusalem and the Orthodox Palestine Society had belonged to the Russian state, a matter the Soviet claims had sought to deflect by noting the 1918 decree secularizing church property. Evlogii also identified the representatives of the two pre-Revolution organizations as still being in Jerusalem: Archimandrite Ieronim, head of the Ecclesiastical Mission, and N. R. Seleznev, former secretary and current manager of the Orthodox Palestine Society.

In addition to the appeals of Metropolitan Evlogii, representatives of the Russian Church Abroad, the Karlovatskii Synod, also began to press their claims to the Jerusalem properties. Counting among their followers some of the Orthodox Palestine Society's former members, such as Seleznev, the Synod sought to play its hand by cultivating the support of Russian monks and nuns who remained in Jerusalem. Toward that end, Metropolitan Antonii (Khrapovitskii), leader of the Russian Church Abroad, traveled to Jerusalem in June/July 1924. In his correspondence from Jerusalem, he noted the continuing presence of some three hundred Russian nuns in two convents and a dozen Russian officials of clerical rank who still headed the Russian Ecclesiastical Mission.[11] In the years that followed Metropolitan Antonii's visit, especially through the intercession of a Karlovatskii Synod loyalist, former Kishinev Archbishop Anastasii, the Russian Church Abroad sought to lay claim to the loyalties of the remaining Russians in and around Jerusalem, even publishing a journal from there, *Sviataia zemlia*. By the end of the interwar period, it could successfully claim the loyalties of some, but not all, of the monks and nuns remaining in Jerusalem.

More to the point, however, was the fact that the October Bolshevik Revolution and the ensuing collapse of Russian pilgrimage had left the local Russian representatives of the Russian Ecclesiastical Mission and Orthodox Palestine Society without their traditional sources of financial support. Metropolitan Antonii (Khrapovitskii) put the matter succinctly in 1924, during his Jerusalem visit:

> Almost all the huge and numerous buildings of the compound, as well as
> the premises of its former superintendent, are occupied by British govern-

> mental institutions, and the rent for these constitutes the sole revenue-producing item of the Russian mission, consisting now of just ten to twelve persons of parish and monastic clerical rank.[12]

What Khrapovitskii testified to, in effect, was the utter dependency of the remaining Russian clergy and nuns upon the leasing of Russian properties to the Mandate authorities.

This leasing of buildings is confirmed in the British archival record, wherein rental payments for the subsistence of the remaining Russian clergy and nuns—payments made first through the Spanish consulate and later through a special administrator appointed by the Palestine high commissioner—are cataloged for over twenty buildings formerly a part of the Russsian Ecclesiastical Mission and Orthodox Palestine Society. Annual rent for these premises was, as of 1924, calculated to be in excess of forty-eight hundred pounds.[13] By 1930, following promulgation of the special Russian Properties Administration Ordinance (Ordinance no. 31, 1925, promulgated in 1926), the properties had been brought under formal bureaucratic custody of a British administrator, with annual rent of over seventy-seven hundred pounds received by local representatives for the Orthodox Palestine Society and the Russian Ecclesiastical Mission. This income from leases accounted for over 90 percent of the total annual revenue raised by the pre-Revolution organizations.[14] The buildings were leased for a variety of purposes ranging from housing the Spanish consulate and housing of Palestine Mandate law courts, to storage depots, hospitals, prisons, and barracks and warehouses for the British gendarmerie. While most of the leased property was in Jerusalem, the British gendarmerie also leased Russian property in Nazareth, and there were other leased properties in Acre, Haifa, and Jericho. Based upon the 1924 figures, over one-third of the annual revenue from leases came from just three Jerusalem properties:

> 1. The Palestine law courts operating on property of the Ecclesiastical Mission in the former Russian compound (600 pounds).
> 2. A large hospital functioning on property of the Orthodox Palestine Society (630 pounds).
> 3. A storage facility on property of the Orthodox Palestine Society (600 pounds).

Part of the explanation for the subsequent increase in revenue is that by 1930, 20 percent of the rental income was coming from leases to private persons—an indication that the local representatives of the Orthodox Palestine Society and the Russian Ecclesiastical Mission were moving beyond sole dependency upon the Palestine Mandate. Still, within the terms of the Russian Properties Administration Ordinance, the pre-Revolution Russian religious agencies and the local Russian monks and nuns remained largely dependent upon rents from the Palestine Mandate authorities.

In the end, the Palestine Mandate authorities were anxious to keep the legal claims of the Soviets at bay while retaining maximum flexibility in responding to the appeals of pre-Revolution Russian figures, such as Seleznev and Metropolitans Evlogii and Antonii. As a result the Palestine Mandate proceeded, paying minimal rent, to occupy many of the former Russian buildings for the very secular purposes that they believed would result from recognition of the claims by "atheist" Soviet representatives. Meanwhile, fearing the independent leasing of Russian properties already under way by Seleznev and other Russian émigré representatives, the Mandate authorities continued to press Seleznev and others to demonstrate clear title to the holdings before continuing to undertake activity with respect to the properties. Playing both sides against each other, the British recognized the impossibility of documenting such title in the wake of the January 1918 Soviet secularization of church property—an act that the Palestine Mandate recognized only insofar as it helped to undermine the position of Seleznev and the Russian Church Abroad.[15]

The irony, here, of course is that it was the same secularization decree that the British, perhaps with justification, also turned against the Soviets. For under the original title, much of the Russian landholding fell within the Ottoman land classification system as *wakf* land. Such *wakf* properties were recognized by both the Muslim courts and their Mandate successors as usable exclusively for charitable purposes and not subject to secularization.[16]

Thus, in the period following World War I, the Palestine Mandate established a powerful precedent of leasing Russian properties for governmental accommodation. Refusing to recognize the claims of either the atheist Soviet government or the Russian religious émigrés, the British positioned themselves in between as trustee of the properties while paying rent through the Spanish consulate, or later through their own administrator, for distribution to the dwindling numbers of Russian monks and nuns in and around Jerusalem. The British government's reluctance to recognize the legitimacy of the Soviet claims put forward by Krassin, Rakovskii, Litvinov, and others may be attributed in part to the official ideology of atheism embraced by the new Soviet state.

While the post–World War II picture pertaining to these properties has remained clouded amid lawsuits and rival claims, the appeal of the Holy Places for the Moscow Patriarchate and the Russian Orthodox Church Abroad has its origins in the piety of the Russian faithful—a piety given expression through pilgrimage and philanthropy. The recent travel of delegations from Russia to the Holy Places, while reflecting the ongoing official interest in the Russian properties, continues this tradition of Russian ties to the Orthodox East.

APPENDIX: Table 1. Properties Belonging to the Russian Mission

No.	Location	Description	Area (m²)	Acquired	Registration	Land Tenure	Occupancy (1930)
1	Jerusalem	Building, Land & Cathedral	N.A.	1857–60	Russian Govt.	Mulk	Mission & Law Courts
2	Jerusalem	Building	N.A.	1857	Elias N. Haddad	Mulk	Palestine Govt.
3	Jerusalem	House & Building	249,024	1889	Russian Convent on Mt. Olives	Mulk	Private Lease
4	Jerusalem	House	495	1905	Russian Mission	Wakf	Russian Mission
5	Mt. Olives	2 Churches, Bell Tower & Buildings	53,748	1868–89	Russian Mission & Grand Duke Sergei	Miri	Convent
6	Mt. Olives	Stone Shed & Cave "Prophet's Tomb"	1503	1882	Grand Duke Sergei	Miri	Unoccupied
7	Mt. Olives	Land	4137	1881	Russian Govt.	Miri	Unoccupied
8	Silwan	Land	684	1878–82	Grand Duke Sergei	Miri	Unoccupied
9	Silwan	2 Caves	409	1875	Russian Mission	Miri	Unoccupied
10	Bethany	Buildings & Chapel	2000	1905	Russian Mission	Mulk	Private Lease
11	Ein Karem	Church, Bell Tower	226,776	1871–89	Russian Mission	Miri	Convent
12	Ein Karem	Land & Building	6000	1871	Russian Mission	Miri	Private Lease
13	Anata	Land	370	1879	Grand Duke Sergei	Mulk	Private Lease
15	Bair Jala	Land, House & Shed	9519	1873	Grand Duke Sergei	Miri	Govt. Lease
16	Bair Sahur	Land	12,000	1909–14	Helen Rumman	Miri	Unoccupied
17	Bair Sha'an	Land & Houses	151,154	1903	Russian Mission	Miri	Russian Mission
18	Hedron Valley	Land & Caves	2493	1866–72	Grand Duke Sergei	Miri	Unoccupied
19	Jaffa	Orange Grove, Church "St. Tabitha's Tomb"	31,154	1868	Russian Mission	Wakf	Russian Mission

No.	Location	Description	Size	Date	Owner	Tenure	Status
20	Hedron Valley	Land	18,158	1910	Russian Mission	Miri	Unoccupied
21	Hebron	Land, Church & "Abraham's Oak"	72,355	1868–89	Russian Mission	Wakf	Russian Mission
22	Hebron	Land & Olive Trees	1861	1877	Jacob Kapustin	Mulk	Private Lease
23	Jericho	Buildings & Fruit Trees	15,128	1874	Russian Mission	Miri	Russian Mission
24	Jericho Rd.	Land & Cistern	6360	1911	Russian Mission	Miri	Private Lease
25	Haifa	Buildings & Land	6600	1906–09	Russian Mission	Miri	Private Lease
26	Mt. Carmel	Church & Buildings	21,000	1908	Russian Mission	Miri	Russian Mission
27	Nazareth	Olive Trees & House	5000	1909	Russian Mission	Miri	Private Lease
28	Galilee	Garden	1800	1913	Russian Mission	Miri	Private Lease
29	Galilee	Land	3767	1912	Russian Mission	Miri	Unoccupied
30	Tiberias	Building	77,391	1879	Antonin Kapustin	N.A.	Private Lease
31	Magdala	Land & Building	43,512	1909	Russian Mission	Miri	Russian Mission
32	Jericho	Land & Chapel	10,000	1914	Russian Mission	Miri	Russian Mission

Sources: PRO F.O. 371/10491, N 1288/1288/38 (13 February 1924); PRO F.O. 371/10514, N 3501/3501/85 (22 April 1924); PRO F.O. 371/10836, E 2435/236/65 (18 April 1925); PRO F.O. 371/52591, R 646/646/31 (17 January 1946). See also Theofanis George Stavrou, *Russian Interests in Palestine, 1882–1914* (Thessaloniki, 1963); Derek Hopwood, *The Russian Presence in Syria and Palestine, 1843–1914* (Oxford, 1969); Arkhimandrit Kiprian, *Antonin Kapustin, arkhimandrit i nachal'nik Russkoi Dukhovnoi Missii v Ierusalime, 1817–1894* (Belgrade, 1934); V. Iushmanov, "Russkiia uchrezhdeniia v Palestine i Sirii pered nachalom voiny s Turtsiei," *Soobshcheniia Imperatorskago pravoslavnago palestinskago obshchestvo,* 25 (1914), 436–464; and V. Iushmanov, "Russkiia uchrezhdeniia v Palestine i Sirii vo vremia voiny s Turtsiei," *Soobshcheniia,* 26 (1915), 147, 181, 373–406, and (1916), 267–288.

APPENDIX: Table 2. Properties Belonging to Palestine Orthodox Society

No.	Location	Description	Area (m²)	Acquired	Registration	Land Tenure	Occupancy (1930)
1	Jerusalem	Land & Cisterns	47,414	1889	Russian Govt.	Mulk	Palestine Society
2	Jerusalem	Building	763	1907	Palestine Society	Mulk	Palestine Govt.
3	Jerusalem	Nikolaevskii Hospice	1895	1906	Palestine Society	Mulk	Palestine Govt.
4	Jerusalem	Stone Barracks	1170	1906–10	Palestine Society	Mulk	Palestine Govt.
5	Jerusalem	Elizavetskii Hospice	4612	1889	Russian Govt.	Mulk	Palestine Society
6	Jerusalem	Mariianskii Hospice	3706	1889	Russian Govt.	Mulk	Palestine Govt.
7	Jerusalem	Stone Barracks	1423	1907	Palestine Society	Mulk	Palestine Govt.
8	Jerusalem	Building & Hospital	1210	1889	Russian Govt.	Mulk	Palestine Govt.
9	Jerusalem	Building & Hospital	186	1889	Russian Govt.	Mulk	Palestine Govt.
10	Jerusalem	Stone Sheds	12	1889	Russian Govt.	Mulk	Private Lease
11	Jerusalem	Stone Shed	16	1889	Russian Govt.	Mulk	Palestine Govt.
12	Jerusalem	Stone Shed	155	N.A.	Palestine Society	Mulk	Palestine Govt.
13	Jerusalem	Sergievskii Hospice	3405	1890	Grand Duke Sergei	Mulk	Palestine Society
14	Jerusalem	Veniaminskii Hospice	1388	1893	Grand Duke Sergei	Mulk	Palestine Society
15	Jerusalem	Alexandrovskii Hospice	1342	1890	Russian Govt.	Mulk	Palestine Society
16	Jerusalem	Land & Cistern	1933	1891	Russian Govt.	Mulk	Private Lease
17	Jerusalem	Land & Coffee Shop	12,411	1890	Russian Govt.	Mulk	Private Lease
18	Jerusalem	Land	17,465	1890	Russian Govt.	Mulk	Palestine Society
19	Gethsemane	Church St. Mary Magdalene	11,830	1890	Russian Govt.	Mulk	Abbess Mary Robinson

20	Mt. Olives	Land	9727	1890	Russian Govt.	Mulk	Palestine society
21	Bethlehem	Land & Fruit Garden	7955	1897	Grand Duke Sergei	Wakf	Private Lease
22	Bait jalla	Land & Buildings	9725	1886	Russian Govt.	Mulk & Wakf	Private Lease
23	Ein Karem	Land	5748	1890	Russian Govt.	Wakf	Private Lease
24	Jericho	Land, Houses, Garden	11,811	1886	Palestine society	N.A.	Private Lease
25	Haifa	Land Near Seashore	968	1909	Palestine Society	Mulk	Palestine Govt.
26	Haifa	Revenue House	146	1913	Palestine Society	Mulk	Private Lease
27	Haifa	Speranskii Hospice	3596	1899	Grand Duke Sergei	Miri	Private Lease
28	Nazareth	House & Cisterns	2064	1903	Palestine Society	Mulk	Palestine Govt.
29	Nazareth	House & Plantations	1329	1903–6	Palestine Society	Mulk	Private Lease
30	Nazareth	Land & Gardens	3437	1890	Palestine Society	Miri	Palestine Society
31	Nazareth	Land	47,157	1914	Palestine Society	Miri	Private Lease
32	Affula	Land	8266	1914	Palestine Society	Miri	Palestine Society
33	Kafr Kanna	Land	6433	1896	Palestine Society	Miri	Private Lease
34	Er-Rameh	Land & House	689	1893	Palestine Society	Mulk	Private Lease
35	Ramallah	Land	2310	1900	Grand Duke Sergei	Wakf	Palestine Society

Sources: PRO F.O. 371/10491, N 1288/1288/38 (13 February 1924); PRO F.O. 371/10514, N 3501/3501/85 (22 April 1924); PRO F.O. 371/10836, E 2435/236/65 (18 April 1925); PRO F.O. 371/52591, R 646/646/31 (17 January 1946). See also Theofanis George Stavrou, *Russian Interests in Palestine, 1882–1914* (Thessaloniki, 1963); Derek Hopwood, *The Russian Presence in Syria and Palestine, 1843–1914* (Oxford, 1969); Arkhimandrit Kiprian, *Antonin Kapustin, arkhimandrit i nachal'nik Russkoi Dukhovnoi Missii v Ierusalime, 1817–1894* (Belgrade, 1934); V. Iushmanov, "Russkiia uchrezhdeniia v Palestine i Sirii pered nachalom voiny s Turtsiei," *Soobshcheniia Imperatorskago pravoslavnago palestinskago obshchestvo*, 25 (1914); 436–464; and V. Iushmanov, "Russkiia uchrezhdeniia v Palestine i Sirii vo vremia voiny s Turtsiei," *Soobshcheniia*, 26 (1915); 147, 181, 373–406, and (1916), 267–288.

NOTES

SOURCE: An earlier Russian version of this article was presented in Moscow in January 1990, at an international symposium sponsored by the Russian Palestine Society. That Russian text, without accompanying tables, was published by the Palestine Society, which has now assumed the pre-Revolution title, Imperatorskoe Pravoslavnoe Palestinskoe Obshchestvo. See S. K. Batalden, "Sud'ba russkago zemlevladeniia v Ierusalime vo vremia palestinskogo mandata," *Pravoslavnyi palestinskii sbornik* (Moscow, 1992), no. 31(94), pp. 25–31.

1. Robert Curzon, *Visits to Monasteries in the Levant,* quoted in Harry Charles Luke, *Ceremonies at the Holy Places* (London, 1933), pp. 28–29.

2. For the secondary literature on Russian activity and landholding in Palestine, see Theofanis George Stavrou, *Russian Interests in Palestine, 1882–1914* (Thessaloniki, 1963); Derek Hopwood, *The Russian Presence in Syria and Palestine, 1843–1914* (Oxford, 1969); Igor Smolitsch, "Zur Geschichte der Beziehungen zwischen der russischen Kirche und dem orthodoxen Osten," *Ostkirchliche Studien,* 5 (1956); Arkhimandrit Kiprian, *Antonin Kapustin, arkhimandrit i nachal'nik Russkoi Dukhovnoi Missii v Ierusalime, 1817–1894* (Belgrade, 1934); V. Iushmanov, "Russkiia uchrezhdeniia v Palestine i Sirii pered nachalom voiny s Turtsiei," *Soobshcheniia Imperatorskago pravoslavnago palestinskago obshchestva,* 25 (1914), pp. 436–464; and V. Iushmanov, "Russkiia uchrezhdeniia v Palestine i Sirii vo vremia voiny s Turtsiei," *Soobshcheniia,* 26 (1915), pp. 147, 181, 373–408, and (1916), pp. 267–288.

3. The figures for landholding cited here are compiled from records kept by the British Foreign Office during and immediately after the period of the Palestine Mandate. The tables appended to this essay provide a property-by-property description of lands held by the Orthodox Palestine Society and Russian Ecclesiastical Mission. The tables and the summary figures in the essay are compiled from four British Foreign Office files: (a) British Public Record Office, Foreign Office (hereafter PRO F.O.) 371/10491, Northern Department (hereafter N) 1288/1288/38 (13 February 1924); (b) PRO F.O. 371/10514, N 3501/3501/85 (22 April 1924); (c) PRO F.O. 371/10836, Eastern Department (hereafter E) 2435/236/65 (18 April 1925); and (d) PRO F.O. 371/52591, E 646/646/31 (17 January 1946).

4. For a more complete description of the relevant British Foreign Office and Colonial Office records, see the bibliography of Michael Palma, "Russian Landholdings in Palestine, 1917–1948" (M.A. thesis, Arizona State University, 1993).

5. See copy of Krassin's 18 May 1923 memorandum, Annex 1 in PRO F.O. 371/10836, E 2435/236/65.

6. For the Rakovskii claim and its reference to the 1918 secularization decree, see Austen Chamberlain's report of his 1 April 1925 meeting
with Rakovskii, Chamberlain to British Ambassador to Moscow Hodgson, PRO F.O. 371/10836, E 2435/236/65 (1 April 1925).

7. For a copy of the League's "Mandate for Palestine," including
articles 13 and 14, see PRO F.O. 371/10836, E 2435/236/65.

8. PRO F.O. 371/10112, E 4970/4300/65 (D. G. Osborne to Colonial Office, 24 June 1924).

9. For a copy of the Charitable Trusts Ordinance in draft, see PRO
F.O. 371/10111, E 3543/3543/65 (1924).

10. Copy of Metropolitan Evlogii's letter, dated 19 September
1923, is in PRO F.O. 371/9370, N 8612/4560/38.

11. Arkhiepiskop Nikon (Rklitskii), *Zhizneopisanie Blazhenneishago
Antoniia, Mitropolita Kievskago i Galitskago*, vol. 7 (New York, 1961),
p. 43.

12. Ibid.

13. For a list of the properties leased by the Palestine Mandate, in-
cluding the provisions for payment through the Spanish consulate, see
"Annex 5: Russian Properties in Palestine Occupied by Government,"
PRO F.O. 371/10836, E2435/236/65 (1925).

14. For the Russian Properties Administration Ordinance, see PRO
Colonial Office 733/212, 97024/1/32 (1932). That file also contains the
audited income and expenditure figures for the Orthodox Palestine Society and the Russian Ecclesiastical Mission for the year ending 31 December 1930. Total income for the Orthodox Palestine Society was
6,005 pounds, of which 5,732 derived from rent of leased properties. Total income for the Russian Ecclesiastical Mission was 2,799 pounds, of
which 2,034 derived from rent of leased properties. Another 451 pounds
came to the Ecclesiastical Mission as a grant in aid from the Orthodox
Palestine Society.

15. For evidence of the Mandate's opposition to Seleznev, see copy
of High Commissioner Herbert Samuel's report of 26 October 1923 in
PRO F.O. 371/10836, E 2435/236/65.

16. On the history of charitable *wakf* landholding, see Aharon Lay-
ish, "The Muslim Waqf in Israel," *Asian and African Studies*, 2 (1966),
pp. 41–76; and Kenneth W. Stein, *The Land Question in Palestine, 1917–
1939* (Chapel Hill, N.C., 1986). *Wakf* lands were those designated by the
state for some religious or charitable purpose, or to be held by a family
trust. They could not be resold. *Mulk* lands were held in complete free-
hold. The owner of *mulk* land could dispose of the land as he or she saw
fit: through sale, mortgage, or bequeathal. *Miri* landowners did not hold
their land by title. The owner could not mortgage or sell the land without
the consent of the state. Nevertheless, the owner did have legal right to
the property and to the profits from it.

Using Vatican Archives
in the Study of Eastern Christianity

T he need for recordkeeping by Christian church officials was evident as soon as the community at Rome grew to be large enough to become an institution. Along with copies of biblical literature, church collections included correspondence and documents as well as theological treatises and liturgical books.

THE PAPAL LIBRARY IN THE MIDDLE AGES

Early records and documents were at risk until Constantine granted toleration to Christians in the early fourth century. Then it appears that certain churches and buildings were used as depositories. Some Roman documents went to the Church of San Lorenzo in Damaso; others were placed in the Turris Certelaria near the Roman Forum.[1]

A library for the use of the pope and his household was collected at the Lateran Palace, which Constantine placed at the disposal of the bishops of Rome. A large complex developed here, for the Lateran was the papal residence for almost the next thousand years. It included several monasteries, halls, the living quarters of the popes, and a building to hold the papal library. During the early Middle Ages both the manuscript collections and archival material continued to grow, but in a haphazard way. Often the popes' secretaries simply carried around with them or kept in their offices the documents they thought useful.

Until the beginning of the ninth century, the popes considered themselves Romans, and both emperors and churchmen in Constantinople often received letters from Italy. The extensive registers of Pope Gregory the Great, which have been preserved in copies, show the active correspondence between this pope and Eastern churchmen. The archbishop of Thessalonika was the pope's vicar to the Greek-speaking Catholic churches in the East.[2]

Despite an obvious need to provide a permanent location for the papal archives and library of manuscripts that came into the pope's possession, not much seems to have been done to organize a system for gathering and filing correspondence until the papacy of Innocent III early in the thirteenth century. As a result there is only a scattering of documents in the Vatican Archive that antedate Innocent's papacy (1198–1216). Among these, by chance, are 314 letters of Pope John VIII (872–882), whose correspondence dealt with the mission of Cyril and Methodius to the Moravian Slavs. They are the oldest records in the Vatican Archive.[3] Whatever other church documents existed before Innocent, at a time when relations between Rome and the Eastern churches were often of great importance, are almost entirely lost. One reason for this was the insistence of Vatican scribes using highly perishable papyrus rather than the more expensive parchment.

Innocent's archive was placed at St. Peter's Basilica in the Vatican. His registers, which contain his correspondence with Eastern churchmen, are still extant, many of them now published.[4]

The papal collection, one of Europe's largest libraries, must have rivaled the collection of the emperors in Constantinople and perhaps surpassed it. However, libraries are always in danger, and events of the late thirteenth and early fourteenth centuries brought disaster to the pope's manuscripts. In 1303 King Philip IV sent French soldiers to arrest Pope Boniface VIII. They used the occasion to despoil his library as well as to insult his person. Five years later a fire swept through the Lateran, burning much of it to the ground and destroying many of its records.[5]

Soon afterward the papacy moved to Avignon, and a demand was made that the library and archives of the Roman church also be transferred to France. This task, begun in 1329, was both expensive and difficult, extending over several decades. Avignon was the heart of a great bureaucracy. The volumes of paperwork that flowed back and forth between the papacy and its officials outside of Rome reached immense quantities.

The difficult decades of the later fourteenth century and early fifteenth century kept the manuscripts and archives in Avignon although the popes were once more living in the Eternal City. After some delay the laborious task of returning the popes' books and documents to Rome commenced. The first collections arrived sometime before 1431, but the cost of transferring material was so great that the moves were made in stages. It was only in 1783 that the last Avignon documents reached Rome.[6]

THE RECORDS OF THE RENAISSANCE POPES

The honor of creating the present Vatican Library is held by Pope Nicholas V, who began gathering books and documents soon after the Jubilee Year of 1450 provided him with the necessary funds. He set up an endowment for a building and dispatched agents to scour both Eastern and Western libraries for manuscripts that were for sale. By the time of his death the Vatican Library held a collection of approximately eight-hundred Latin and four hundred Greek codices, making it the largest library in western Europe.[7]

In June 1475, Pope Sixtus IV officially founded the library, assigning it rooms and an endowment. He appointed Bartolomeo Sacchi of Cremona, known as Platina, to be his librarian. Platina's catalog of 1481 showed that the library then held thirty-five hundred items.[8]

Renaissance popes who followed Sixtus saw much of their work destroyed early in the sixteenth century. In 1527 the imperial army marched into the city, sparing nothing that could be perceived as valuable—including the papal library. The lead seals of charters were melted down to make ammunition. The golden seals went into officers' pockets (except those that were hidden). Manuscript parchment was used for cleaning stables.[9]

Rome in the Reformation era quickly recovered from its losses, and once more the collection of books and manuscripts belonging to the church was reconstituted. In 1548 Pope Paul III thought the task of overseeing his library so important that he appointed a cardinal as librarian. That tradition extends to the present. The first cardinal librarian was Marcello Cervini (later Pope Marcellus II).

In 1565 Pope Pius IV ordered the cardinal librarian to assemble his papers into an archive. Until then not much had been done to keep abreast of current affairs; interest had been focused on old manuscripts. The purpose of the archive, according to Pius, was to assist the various Vatican departments and congregations in conducting their business. The documents placed there were considered confidential.

As more volumes arrived from Avignon and Roman records increased, it became obvious that a new building was needed to house all the material. In 1587 Pope Sixtus V began the construction of a larger library to house the papal collection. It took over twenty years to accomplish the assembly of his books. The staff was few, their pay was poor, and the work went on very slowly. Employees were considered part of the "family" of the pope, and as members of his household the workers received a bread allowance.[10]

There was always a problem regarding who should have access to the library. Gregory XIV felt the administration much too lax, and ordered that no document should be released without his explicit permission. Only officials in the Curia and historians who were also "official" had access. Among these were Cardinal Caesar Baronio, who worked on the *Annales ecclesiastici,* and Cardinal Pietro Pallavicino, whose history of the Council of Trent was the papal response to unofficial histories.[11]

THE DIVISION BETWEEN LIBRARY AND ARCHIVE

Early in the seventeenth century Pope Clement VIII decided that there should be a physical division between the papal library and the archive. The library was to contain the manuscripts and books belonging to the pope. Into the archive went the working papers of the Curia. As a result Clement had his most important papers located in a hall of Castel Sant'Angelo. In 1612 this division was confirmed on orders of Pope Paul V, who appointed a separate head for the archive. His rank was not so high, since the archival prefect was not a cardinal.[12]

The archive received 279 papal registers, extending from the papacy of John VIII to that of Sixtus IV, as well as the records of most curial offices. The most important documents it obtained for the study of Eastern Christianity were those from the Vatican's secretary of state, who took over the funding of the archive. Most valuable for the researcher are the reports of various sixteenth-century papal nuncios resident in Poland, Hungary, and Dalmatia. The archivists, still few and underpaid, were at the mercy of curial secretaries for the documents they received. The archive was secret, a name it still keeps in its title, and over its door was a sign that anyone not authorized to enter would be excommunicated. Its motto was succinct: "No one goes in, and nothing comes out."[13]

Since access was so limited, nephews of early seventeenth-century popes, who headed various Vatican offices, frequently sent no documents to the archive. Once their uncle-patrons were dead and their continued appointment in jeopardy, the nephews dispatched important records off to family collections, where some still remain.[14]

Fortunately for the researcher, in 1696 Pope Innocent XII ordered that all his records should go into the archive, so that from that date curial secretaries had no choice but to forward complete sets. By this time the archive had moved back to the Vatican Palace, in close proximity to the Vatican Library. The Castel Sant'Angelo depository kept only part of its records. After the mid-seventeenth century, the records of the Vatican secretaries of state are presumed to be complete.

When the scholar Benedict XIV was elected pope in the mid-eighteenth century, he sought to improve the archive's organization. Arrangement of materials had been highly subjective, and it was well known that documents were often lost. As a result Benedict appointed a fellow scholar, Giuseppe Garampi, to order the collection. Garampi complained that it would take a hundred archivists to accomplish the task, but obediently began making lists of material that have been superseded only in modern times.[15]

Meanwhile, the Vatican Library's manuscript collections continued to receive new material and to be better cataloged. The Greek manuscripts were inventoried and placed into a Biblioteca Greca under the direction of Leon Allatios, a Greek from Chios. In 1623 Allatios went to Heidelberg to bring the library of the Palatine to Rome. This collection is still extant, listed under the rubric Biblioteca Palatina.[16]

Over the decades that followed, the Vatican Library continued to receive major additions. These include the Fondo Urbinate (1658); the

Reginese, brought by Queen Christina of Sweden; the Fondo Cap-
poniano (1746); and the Fondo Ottoboniano (1748), purchased by Pope
Benedict XIV. The Ottoboniano included important manuscripts from
Mt. Athos, totaling 473 Greek codices.[17]

THE NAPOLEONIC PERIOD

Just as the figure of Napoleon dominated Europe for a generation, so the
Corsican general who became emperor of the French left his mark on the
history of the Vatican Archive. In December 1809 the emperor, who en-
visaged a universal library in Paris of all European documents, sent orders to his Roman governor to move the archive to the French capital.
Along with the person of the pope, Napoleon would also have his books
and records.

The archival materials were packed, and began their laborious journey
across the Alps in February 1811. Two years later the task was finished.
The cost was six hundred thousand francs. As might be expected, some
damage occurred and several boxes never reached France. Nevertheless,
an inventory showed that Paris obtained 3,239 crates holding 102,435
items. The French did not get everything. The pope's archivist, Gaetano
Marini, managed to hide a few records and buried those of Pius VI in the
Vatican gardens.

Napoleon's archivist had only a short time to try to make sense of his
windfall before Napoleon's empire came crashing down and he found his
work halted. The victorious allies told the French to return the archives
to Rome, but the restored Bourbons claimed poverty—they had only
sixty thousand francs available, a tenth of the sum needed.

The Vatican emissary to Paris, Marino Marini, a nephew of the archivist, supervised the return of the most important documents. He
wrote to the Curia to see if anyone would be willing to forgo the return
of "useless" papers. Of course, none consented to call their records "useless," and all demanded the return of complete sets.

Since Marini had no way to pay for the transfer, he took it upon himself to sort out what he thought could be disposed of in order to meet the
freight charges. Some documents were sold to university libraries, others
went to cardboard makers for recycling. The records of Galileo's trial
were stolen. The move, completed in 1817, brought back twenty-two
hundred crates, a little more than two-thirds of the original collection.
Marini undertook the task of reestablishing the archive, a work completed only in the 1890s, long after his death.[18]

As prefect of the archive, Marini took a proprietary view of his collection. Protecting the contents from prying eyes was his major concern.
Yet in the decade following the restoration, European scholars were anxious to get a look inside, in order to write national histories that could be
complete only if this major untapped source was made available.

OPENING THE ARCHIVES

When G. H. Pertz, a Protestant Prussian, arrived in Rome, seeking permission to use the documents in the archive, it caused no end of anxiety. The Prussian government wanted Pertz to be let into the archive, and the Curia of the 1820s could not afford to make an enemy of Prussia. In November 1822, Pope Pius VII gave permission for Marini to let Pertz have the documents he wanted, the registers of Pope Honorius III.

Soon other scholars, financed by their governments, began to arrive. Anyone interested in writing a national history came to Rome, convinced that in the secret archive a treasure of information might be unearthed. The secrecy attached to the documents made them all the more appealing. Reluctantly, in the view of most curial officials, the archives were opened, even to scholars who had no sympathy for the church. Marini limited the damage. Copies had to be requested from him personally. He brought documents to his apartment for an appropriate fee, where for only a few hours scholars were permitted to scan them and make copies. Marini also checked to be sure the copies matched the original.

Agitation for the release of documents in the secret archive continued to build within the European scholarly community, and at last found a pope in Leo XIII (1878–1903) who was willing to take the chance that if the archive were open the credibility of the church would be enhanced rather than damaged.

Although he was no historian, Leo showed his hand when he named Josef Hergenrother, a German professor of church history, both cardinal and prefect of the secret archive. Another welcome change was to provide a reading room for scholars, opened in January 1881, but it was unheated and rather gloomy. Moreover, the pope did not at once change the staff of the archive, who tended to ignore his directives. This continued to be a problem. Nevertheless, in theory any record before 1815 was to be made available so long as the researcher needed it for a historical purpose. Eventually institutes were set up in Rome to print these sources: German, French, Austrian, and Swiss.[19]

In 1921 Ludwig von Pastor, the great historian of the papacy, was at last allowed inside the archive to see the rooms that housed the documents upon which he had worked for decades. Another milestone had been passed.

CONTENTS OF THE ARCHIVE

The exact number of documents and records in the archive remains unknown. They number in the thousands, and much cataloging and description remain unfinished because even now the staff is quite small and daily demands are great. Some materials are in bound volumes that contain about two thousand documents each. Others are in bundles or envelopes whose contents the researcher must examine piece by piece.

There are eight major collections: (1) the Secret Archives, (2) the Archives of Avignon, (3) the Apostolic Chamber, (4) the Castel Sant'Angelo, (5) the Dataria, (6) the Consistorial Archives, (7) the Archives of the Secretariat of State, and (8) a catchall, Various Collections.[20] As has been mentioned, the student of Eastern Christianity will find the papers of the secretary of state (*segreteria di stato*) from the sixteenth through the eighteenth centuries the most useful. This was a time when nuncios from Rome were engaged in a battle with Islam and the Protestant powers in Europe while trying to convert Eastern Christians to the Roman persuasion. The nuncios' descriptions of events in Eastern Europe and the Mediterranean give a firsthand view of those contests.[21]

The Archives of the Secretariat of State are further divided into three major chronological sections: Fondo Vecchio, Fondo Napoleonica, and Fondo Moderno. The Fondo Vecchio holds materials prior to the eighteenth century. For the student of Eastern Christianity the division Nunziature e Legazioni will be most important, for here the volumes or bundles are organized according to nations and time periods. There are 367 volumes or bundles for Poland covering the years 1567 to 1783; 30 for what is known as Polonia-Russia, extending over the years when there was a papal ambassador at the Tsar's court in St. Petersburg (1793–1806). The largest collection is that of Germania, which includes both German and Austrian documents (818 volumes).[22]

Polish (and therefore Ukrainian and Belorussian) archival material from 1607 to 1770 is found under the rubric Gruppo Avvisi.[23] Letters and notices from nuncios in Dalmatia and the Levant are also located here.

Under the division Lettere is correspondence between the Curia and local churchmen, foreign governments, and private individuals. This numbers twelve hundred volumes or bundles.

Under Varia Miscellanea and Fondo Diverse are extremely varied collections, from concordats with states to personal family correspondence. Other collections that are located here contain papal papers of Paul III, Clement VIII, Urban VIII, Paul V, and Alexander VII, popes of the mid-sixteenth through mid-seventeenth centuries.

Much of the material in the Epoca Napoleonica was lost in Paris or during transit back and forth to Rome. The Fondo Moderno, on the other hand, is rich in letters, dispatches, and reports. This Fondo is important for students of Eastern Christianity, particularly the division known as Esteri. Here, under IX, Affari Esteri: Rubriche, the Eastern Christian researcher can discover material under the following:

247. Nunzii in Vienne
260. Austria Ambasciatore
268. Russia Ministro

292. Consoli Pontificio in Corfu e Isole Ionie
295. Consoli Pontificio in Dalmezi
301. (Provisioni) Delegato di Constantinopoli.[24]

There are also recent papal documents in the archive listed under the heading Congregazione per gli Affari Ecclesiastici Straordinari; they are considered so delicate that they are still off limits to researchers without explicit permission of the pope.

The mass of material in the secret archive is so great that although numerous efforts at indexing and cataloging have been conducted over the years, much remains unfinished. In 1901 an index of indexes was produced. To illustrate the point, there are 681 volumes of indexes in a special room, the Sala degli Indici. For the sixteenth and seventeenth centuries, lists of the archivists Guiseppe Garampi and Petrus Doninus de Pretis are still useful. Printed indexes have appeared in the twentieth century. The most useful work has been done by Karl Fink. His first edition, *Das Vatikanische Archiv*, appeared in 1942, and a revision followed in 1951. This may now be supplemented by the most recent guide of Leonard Boyle, *A Survey of the Vatican Archives and of Its Medieval Holdings*, a book of the Medieval Institute of Toronto published in 1972. Boyle currently is prefect of the Vatican Library.[25]

The numbering of indexes is consecutive, without regard for subject. Older indexes are handwritten in Italian or Latin, usually the former.

THE VATICAN LIBRARY TODAY

The Vatican Library continues to receive material of interest to a scholar in Eastern Christianity. In 1902, Cardinal Stefano Borgia's collection arrived. For the study of Eastern Christianity its wealth can hardly be overestimated: 276 Arabic, 136 Coptic, 88 Aramaic, 37 Ethiopian, 15 Georgian, 178 Syrian, and 27 Greek manuscripts were included. This was supplemented by the Fondo Barberiniano, which added 595 Greek and 160 Oriental manuscripts to the collection.

In addition the Vatican purchased the library of Stavrakis Aristarchis, once the grand logothete of the Phanar, which included a ninth-century Greek manuscript of St. Basil's works. It is now in the Fondo Chigi. In summary, the total of Greek manuscripts held by the Vatican Library is 2,608. In addition to the Greek, there are significant Armenian, Slavic, Coptic, Georgian, Syrian, and Ethiopian works, nearly all now cataloged.[26]

It is important for scholars to be aware that in using either the Vatican Archive or the Vatican Library, they are working in a private collection. The staff expects scholars who come there to realize it is a privilege, not a right, to be admitted. Only about five hundred researchers gain access in a year. It should also be noted that the archival materials are open only to the year 1878.

The directors of the archive and of the library require a researcher to furnish an introduction from a scholarly institution or a church official. After explaining the purpose of the research, the scholar must fill out an admission card that includes a picture of him or her. Since the archive and library are separate, it is necessary to apply to both directors. Today the library and archive are adjacent, separated by a courtyard.

It is best to know exactly what one wants beforehand, since the archive's attendants who bring materials have only a limited knowledge of any language besides Italian. They are courteous and efficient but cannot give much help. The Vatican Library has a card catalog and hence is easier to use. The hours of the reading rooms at the archive and the library extend from 8:00 in the morning until 1:30 in the afternoon every day but Sunday. Unless a researcher can afford a lengthy stay in Rome, these short hours can be a serious problem. At Christmas there is a ten-day holiday, and Easter week also finds both institutions closed. Summers are difficult, because the archive and library are shut from July 15 to September 15. For special reasons the director of the archive may allow a scholar access during the summer. A researcher may use the Italian National Library in the afternoon, since it reopens later in the day.[27]

Another useful shortcut before proceeding to Rome is to examine the printed archival sources, especially those of papal registers, found in university libraries. Some of these are listed in the bibliography of this article. Printed registers now extend from the first century to the fifteenth.[28]

The most valuable printed source for researching Eastern churches is the thirteen volumes published under the title *Fontes,* series III of the Pontifical Commission for the Compilation of the Code of Eastern Canon Law (Pontificia Commissio ad Redigendum Codicem Juris Canonici Orientalis). The first volume extends from Clement I through the pontificate of Celestine III (1198). The second picks up with Innocent III. Volume XIII, which appeared in 1971, reached Gregory XII, pope from 1406 to 1415.

There are other archives and libraries in Rome that deserve special attention. One is the archive of the Inquisition, later called the Holy Office and now the Congregation for Christian Doctrine. This archive has its own separate administration. For the student of Russian history it is important, for it contains the correspondence between False Dmitrii and the Roman Curia.

ST. LOUIS FILM LIBRARY

For the American researcher who would prefer to work closer to home, St. Louis University's Pius XII Memorial Library contains a film collection of most Greek, Latin, and west European manuscripts in the Vatican Library. The photographing was carried out during the 1950s thanks to a grant from the Knights of Columbus, and has continued on a smaller scale ever since. Arabic and Ethiopic manuscripts are now included. The collection contains manuscripts from the fifth through the nineteenth centuries. Archival materials are also included. The Greek manuscript collection is third in size, after Latin and Italian. The color slide collection of illuminated manuscripts numbers fifty-two thousand units.

Since 1957 the film library has published a journal, *Manuscripta,* that deals with manuscripts in the Vatican Library. In the 1985 and 1986 volumes (29 and 30), lists of the Vatican Library collection, giving collection and codex numbers, are found. The Andrew W. Mellon Foundation offers fellowships to researchers for travel and per diem expenses for a two-to-eight-week stay at the St. Louis library.

ADDITIONAL LIBRARIES OF ROME

In addition to the Vatican Library and Vatican Archive there are other depositories that the student of Eastern Christianity will find useful. One is the archive of the Congregation for the Propagation of the Faith. Found here are the reports of bishops who were considered to be living "in partibus infidelium," lands where there were few Catholics. Under categories such as Armenia, Romania, and Archipelago are the reports of the bishops stationed in these locations. The archive reading room has desks for only a few scholars.[29]

The national colleges for training priests have their own libraries, but they are usually not open to the public. The Russicum, or Russian College, has only a small library for its students. The Maronites also have a collection. The Greek College is now several centuries old, and hence holds a larger number of volumes. Although most of the monks are Italian Albanians, the monastery of Grottaferatta, just outside Rome, has a major collection of Greek works.

The religious orders that have worked in Eastern Europe, the Orient, and India hold a variety of documents sent back by missionaries of their congregations over the years. In this regard the Franciscan and Dominican libraries are Rome's oldest. In time the Carmelites, Capuchins, Jesuits, Lazarists (or Vincentians), and Augustinians of the Assumption joined the religious orders working in Eastern Christian lands. The Lazarists, officially the Congregation of the Mission, have their archive in Paris.[30] Generally permission to work in these collections is given for very limited periods.

For Russian Orthodox studies, Rome's most important resource is the Pontifical Oriental Institute, with a library open to all scholars. Founded in October 1917, it was entrusted in 1922 to the Jesuits, and three years later the library assumed the task of creating a major resource for the study of all Eastern Christianity, especially of the Russian and Ukrainian churches.

Today it contains 109,000 items; 17,000 books and periodicals deal with Russian Orthodox liturgy, theology, and history. The pre-Revolution collection of periodicals may well be the most complete in the West. In all, the library holds 523 Russian, 109 Ukrainian, and 15 Belorussian journals.

The collection is especially strong in monastic literature, with over 500 titles. The earliest holding is a Gospel Book of 1560; the collection broadens as a result of donations by Cardinal Andrew Archetti, who in 1783 served as nuncio to the court of Catherine the Great. It also holds in its special collection the archives of Prince Vorontsov, totaling 30 volumes.

The Institute obtained a major addition from the Archeographical Commission of St. Petersburg, totaling nearly 50 volumes. It also has 6 volumes of the *Novgorodskie pistsovye knigi* and 39 volumes of the *Russkaia istoricheskaia biblioteka*. The library has a complete set of Russian chronicles. In addition the collection contains the 264 volumes of the *Chteniia v Imperatorskom obshchestve istorii i drevnostei rossiikikh pri Moskovskom Universitete*.

In more recent times the librarians have assembled many works of the theological academies of Moscow, St. Petersburg, and Kazan, as well as modern antireligious works published by the Soviet government. In this regard there is another depository in Rome: the Gustave Wetter Library, which supplements and complements the Pontifical Institute's collection.[31] For Ukrainian church affairs a major resource is the library of the newly formed Ukrainian Catholic University.

VALUE OF THE ROMAN LIBRARIES AND ARCHIVES

From this brief overview of library and archival materials it is possible to reach the conclusion that Old Rome is of great importance for the study of Eastern Christianity. The Vatican Library is one of the major repositories in the world of Byzantine and Oriental manuscripts. The Vatican Archive, supplemented by Rome's other repositories and libraries, provides ample information on Eastern Christianity since the sixteenth century.

Roman church sources are not always friendly to Eastern Christians. In both medieval and early modern times papal delegations and nuncios were not always welcome. When in the seventeenth and eighteenth centuries Western missionary orders began work in the East, they were viewed with suspicion. Suspicion turned to hostility once independent Eastern Catholic churches were established.

Missionary literature can hardly be expected to be nonpartisan, nor are papal nuncios without their prejudices. However, to neglect the views and reports of these foreigners observing Eastern Christian churches is to produce incomplete histories of the Greek, Slavic, and Oriental churches. If not all roads, at least some very important ones, still lead to Rome.

NOTES

1. The early history of the papal library may best be followed in Owen Chadwick, *Catholicism and History: The Opening of the Vatican Archives* (New York, 1978). See also Natalie Summers and Willard Allen Fletcher, "Vatican City," in *Guide to the Diplomatic Archives of Western Europe,* ed. Daniel H. Thomas and Lynn M. Case (Philadelphia, 1959), pp. 285–288. A new edition of the *Guide* by Raymond Cummings (Philadelphia, 1975) has a more recent bibliography. For a popular description of the archive, see M. C. Ambrosini, *The Secret Archives of the Vatican* (Boston, 1969).

2. See Gregory the Great, *Epistolae,* vols. 140 and 141 of *Corpus Christianorum, series latina, Registrum epistularum libri I–VIII,* ed. Dag Norberg (Turnhout, Belgium, 1982).

3. M. Giusti, "I Registri vaticani e loro provenienze originarie," in *Miscellanea archivistica Angelo Mercati* (Vatican City, 1952), pp. 384ff.; Leonard E. Boyle, *A Survey of the Vatican Archives and of Its Medieval Holdings* (Toronto, 1972), pp. 103ff.

4. For Innocent's correspondence consult *Innocentii III Romani pontificis regestorum sive epistolarum libri,* vols. 214–216, in J. P. Migne, ed., *Patrologiae latinae cursus completus* (Paris, 1844–1864).

5. See P. Laver, *Le palais de Latran* (Paris, 1911), pp. 242–250; H. Leclercq, "Lateran," in *Dictionnaire d'archéologie chrétienne et de liturgie* (Paris, 1953) VIII, 2, 1529–1887.

6. G. Mollat, *The Popes at Avignon, 1305–1378* (New York, 1965), pp. 285–305.

7. Ludwig Pastor, *The History of the Popes,* 7th ed., ed. F. I. Antrobus (St. Louis, 1949), II, pp. 165–168.

8. Pastor, *History,* IV, pp. 432–442. Platina wrote a life of the pope, in L. A. Muratori, *Rerum italicarum scriptores ab anno 500 ad 1500,* 2d ser. (Città di Costello, 1900–1925) III, 1, pp. 1053–1068.

9. Judith Hosh, *The Sack of Rome, 1527* (London, 1972), pp. 156–180; H. M. Vaughn, *The Medici Popes, Leo X and Clement VII* (London, 1908).

10. Chadwick, *Catholicism,* p. 12; J. A. de Hübner, *Der eiserne Papst* (Berlin, 1932).

11. Caesar Baronio, *Annales ecclesiastici,* 12 vols. (Rome, 1578–1607); Pietro Pallavicino, *Istoria del Concilio di Trento,* 5 vols. (Rome, 1656–1657).

12. Karl Fink, *Das Vatikanische Archiv*, 2d ed. (Rome, 1951), pp. 1–13.

13. Boyle, *Survey*, p. 10; Chadwick, *Catholicism*, p. 12.

14. Boyle, *Survey*, p. 69.

15. Chadwick, *Catholicism*, pp. 11, 12; Garampi's lists have been published in vol. 45 of *Studi e Testi* (Vatican City, 1926).

16. Charles Frazee, "Leon Allatios, a Greek Scholar of the Seventeenth Century," *Modern Greek Studies Yearbook*, 1 (1985), pp. 63–76.

17. The library's history is best followed in Jeanne B. Odier, *La Bibliothèque vaticane de Sixte IV à Pie XI: Recherches sur l'histoire des collections de manuscrits*, vol. 272 of *Studi e Testi* (Vatican City, 1973).

18. M. Gachard, *Les Archives du Vatican* (Brussels, 1874), pp. 113–128; Chadwick, *Catholicism*, pp. 14–15; Gaetano Marini, *Memorie istoriche degli archivi della S. Sede* (Rome, 1825); and Marino Marini, "Memorie istoriche dell'occupazione e restituzione degli Archivii della S. Sede . . . ," in *Regestum Clementis Papae V* (Rome, 1885).

19. V. Berlière, "Aux Archives vaticanes," *Revue Bénédictine*, 20 (1903), pp. 132–173; G. H. Pertz, *Autobiography and Letters*, ed. Leonore Pertz (London, 1894), pp. 37–38.

20. Boyle, *Survey*, pp. 70–78.

21. H. Biaudet, *Les nonciatures apostoliques permanentes jusqu'en 1648* (Helsinki, 1910); L. Kattinnen, *Les nonciatures apostoliques permanentes de 1650 à 1800* (Geneva, 1912); G. de Marchi, *Le nunziature apostoliche dal 1800 à 1956* (Rome, 1957).

22. A. Mercati, "Schema della disposizione dei fondi dell'Archivio Vaticano," *Bulletin of the International Committee of Historical Sciences* (Paris), 5 (1933), pp. 909–912.

23. See V. Meysztowicz, "Repertorium bibliographicum pro rebus Polonicis Archivi Secreti Vaticani," *Studia teologiczne*, 11 (Rome, 1943).

24. Summers and Fletcher, "Vatican City," pp. 294–300.

25. See also the guides to the archive printed in vols. 45, 55, and 134 of *Studi e Testi*, entitled *Sussidi per la consultazione dell' Archivio Vaticano* (Vatican City).

26. See bibliography of this article for guides to the fonds. Consult also Marcel Richard, *Répertoire des bibliothèques et des catalogues de manuscrits grecs*, 2d ed. (Paris, 1958), pp. 199ff.

27. See Gary B. Blumenshine, "The Apostolic Vatican Library and *Studi e Testi*," *Southeastern Medieval Association Newsletter*, 4, no. 1 (1978), pp. 4–12.

28. The papal registers have been published under the auspices of the Bibliothèque des Écoles Françaises d'Athènes et de Rome, and are listed in the bibliography of this essay.

29. See the bibliography for guides by G. Metzler and B. Millet.

30. The address for the Congregation of the Mission is 95 Rue de

Sèvres, Paris. Here may be found the papers of Eugene Boré, probably the most active missionary of the nineteenth century.

31. Richard C. Lewanski, *Eastern Europe and Russia/Soviet Union: A Handbook of West European Archival and Library Resources* (New York, 1980), pp. 240–241. The fascinating story of Catholics in the Soviet Union has been documented in Antoine Wenger, *Rome et Moscou, 1900–1950* (Paris, 1987); and in Léon Tretjakewitsch, *Bishop Michel d'Herbigny, S.J. and Russia: A Pre-ecumenical Approach to Christian Unity* (Würzburg, 1990). For the rich correspondence of Pie-Eugène Beveu, Roman Catholic bishop of Moscow during the Stalinist period, see the archives of the Assumptionist Fathers (Assunzionisti, 55 Via San Pio V, Rome).

A SELECT BIBLIOGRAPHY
General Reference Works on Archival Material

Djaparidze, David. *Medieval Slavic Manuscripts.* Medieval Academy Publications, 64. Cambridge, Mass., 1957.

Kristeller, Paul Oskar. *Latin Manuscript Books before 1600.* 3d ed. New York, 1965.

Lewanski, Richard C. *Eastern Europe and Russia/Soviet Union: A Handbook of West European Archival and Library Resources.* New York, 1980.

Powell, J. Enoch. "A List of Printed Catalogues of Greek Manuscripts in Italy." *The Library.* 4th ser. *Transactions of the Bibliographical Society,* 17 (1937), 200–213.

Richard, Marcel. *Répertoire des bibliothèques et des catalogues de manuscrits grecs.* 2d ed. Publications de l'Institut de Recherche et d'Histoire des Textes 1. Paris, 1958.

Seydoux, Marianne. "Les périodiques antireligieux en U.R.S.S.: Bibliographie et état des collections dans les bibliothèques occidentales," *Cahiers du monde russe et soviétique,* 11 (1970), 124–143.

Spatharakis, Iohannis. *Corpus of Dated Illuminated Manuscripts to the Year 1453.* 2 vols. Leiden, 1981.

General Works on Sources for the Study of Rome and the Eastern Churches

Allen, T. W. *Notes on Greek Manuscripts in Italian Libraries.* London, 1890.

De Vries, Wilhelm. *Rom und die Patriarchat des Ostens.* Munich, 1963.

Ehrhard, A. *Überlieferung und Bestand der hagiographischen und homiletischen Literatur der griechischen Kirche von den Anfägen bis zum Ende des 16 Jahrhunderts.* Ed. Carl Schmidt, Walter Eltester, and Erich Klostermann. 4 vols. Leipzig, 1936–1952.

Fedalto, Giorgio. *La chiesa latina in Oriente.* 2 vols. Verona, 1973–1976.

Frazee, Charles. *Catholics and Sultans*. Cambridge, England, 1983.
Gill, Joseph. *Byzantium and the Papacy, 1198–1400*. New Brunswick, N.J., 1979.
Hatch, William H. *An Album of Dated Syriac Manuscripts*. Boston, 1946.
Hussey, Joan M. *The Orthodox Church in the Byzantine Empire*. Oxford, 1986.
Ker, N. R. *Medieval Scribes, Manuscripts and Libraries*. London, 1978.
Neale, John Mason. *Voices from the East: Documents on the Present State and Working of the Oriental Church*. Repr. New York, 1974.
Nicol, Donald. *Byzantium: Its Ecclesiastical History and Relations with the Western World*. London, 1972.
Norden, Walter. *Das Papsttum und Byzanz*. Repr. New York, 1958.
Pierling, Paul. *La Russie et le Saint-Siège*. 5 vols. Paris, 1896–1912.
Senyk, Sophia. *Women's Monasteries in Ukraine and Belorussia to the Period of Suppressions*. Vol. 222 of Orientalia Christiana Analecta. Rome, 1983.
Siegmund, A. *Die Überlieferung der griechischen christlichen Literatur in der lateinischen Kirche bis zum zwölften Jahrhundert*. Munich, 1949.
Stehle, Hansjakob. *Die Ostpolitik des Vatikan, 1917–1975*. Munich, 1975.
Stickler, Alfons M. and Leonard E. Boyle, eds. *The Vatican Library, Its History and Treasures*. Yorktown Heights, N.Y., 1989.
Treadgold, Donald. *The West in Russia and China: Religion and Secular Thought in Modern Times; Russia, 1472–1917*. Cambridge, Mass., 1973.
Tretjakewitsch, Léon. *Bishop Michel d'Herbigny, S.J. and Russia. A Pre-ecumenical Approach to Christian Unity*. Würzburg, 1990.
Turyn, A. *Dated Greek Manuscripts of the Thirteenth and Fourteenth Centuries in Italy*. Urbana, Ill., 1972.
Wenger, Antoine. *Rome et Moscou, 1900–1950*. Paris, 1987.

Works on Vatican Archives (Archivo Segreto Vaticano)

Ambrosini, Maria L. *The Secret Archives of the Vatican*. Boston, 1969.
Boyle, Leonard E. *A Survey of the Vatican Archives and of Its Medieval Holdings*. Toronto, 1972.
Chadwick, Owen. *Catholicism and History: The Opening of the Vatican Archives*. New York, 1978.
Diener, H. *Die grossen Registerserien im Vatikanischen Archiv, 1378–1523*. Tübingen, 1972.
Fink, Karl A. *Das Vatikanische Archiv*. 2d ed. Rome, 1951.
Macfarlane, L. "The Vatican Archive . . . with Special Reference to Sources for British Medieval History." *Archives*, 4 (1959), pp. 29–44, 84–101.
Summers, Natalie and Willard Allen Fletcher, "Vatican City." In *Guide to*

the Diplomatic Archives of Western Europe. Ed. Daniel H. Thomas and Lynn M. Case. Philadelphia, 1959.

———. "Vatican City." In *New Guide to the Diplomatic Archives of Western Europe.* Ed. Raymond Cummings. Philadelphia, 1975.

Printed Archival Material

Acta et decreta Concilii nationalis Armenorum Romae habiti anno Domini 1911. Rome, 1913.

Acta nuntiaturae Polonae. Vol. I: *De fontibus eorumque investigatione et editionibus. Instructio ad editionem. Nuntiorum series chronologica.* By Henricus Damianus Wojtyska, C.P. Rome, 1990.

Acta sanctorum.

Actes et documents du Saint-Siège relatifs à la Seconde Guerre mondiale. 11 vols. Rome, 1965–1981.

Analecta Bollandiana.

Analecta Carmelitarum Discalceatorum. Rome, 1926–.

Annaisi, T. *Bullarium Maronitarium.* Rome, 1911.

Archivum Franciscarum Historicum. Florence, 1908–.

Archivum Fratrum Praedicatorum. Rome, 1931–.

Archivum historicum Societatis Jesu. Rome, 1931–.

Baronius, C. *Annales ecclesiastici.* 12 vols. Rome, 1598–1607.

Beccari, C. *Rerum Aethiopicarum scriptores occidentales.* 15 vols. Rome, 1903–1917.

Boratynski, L. *Iohannis Andreae Caligarii, nuntii apostolici in Polonia, epistolae et acta, 1571–1581.* Krakow, 1915.

Bullarium Romanum. 23 vols. Turin, 1857–1872.

Collectanea S. Congregationis de Propaganda Fide. 2 vols. Rome, 1907.

Collin, Bernadin, ed. *Recueil de documents concernant Jerusalem et les Lieux Saints.* Jerusalem, 1982.

Corpus scriptorum christianorum orientalium.

D'Avril, A. *Documents relatifs aux églises de l'Orient et à leurs rapports avec Rome.* Paris, 1885.

De Martinis, R. *Juris pontificii de propaganda fide.* Pars prima, 7 vols. Rome, 1888–1902.

Diaz, F., N. Carranza, and Francesco Buonvisi. *Nunziatura a Varsavia 1673–1675.* 2 vols. Rome, 1965.

Dujčev, I. *Innocentii P.P. III epistolae ad Bulgariae historiam spectantes.* Sofia, 1942.

Giamil, S. *Genuinae relationes inter Sedem Apostolicam et Assyriorum orientalium seu Chaldaeorum ecclesiam.* Rome, 1902.

Glorieux, P. *Monumenta christiana selecta.* Tournai, 1957.

Golubovich, G. *Bibliotheca bio-bibliografica della Terra Santa e dell'Oriente Francescano.* 21 vols. Quaracchi, 1906–1933.

Halkin, F. *Bibliotheca hagiographica graeca.* 3d ed. Brussels, 1957.

Hofmann, G. *Epistolae pontificiae ad Concilium Florentinum spectantes, Concilium Florentinum documenta et scriptores,* ser. A, vol. I, pt. 3. Rome, 1940.

Ignazio da Seggiano. *Documenti inediti sull'apostolato dei Minori Cappucini nel Vicino Oriente, 1626–1683.* Rome, 1954.

Izvori za bulgarska istoria. Vol. 2. *Fontes latini.* Ed. I. Duichev, M. Voinov, B. Primov, and V. Velkov. Sofia, 1958.

Jaffe, P. *Regesta pontificum Romanorum e condita ecclesia ad annum post Christum n. 1198.* 2 vols. Leipzig, 1881–1888.

Karmiris, I. N. *Ta dogmatika kai symvolika mnēmeia tēs Orthodoxou Katholikēs Ekklēseias.* 2d ed. Athens, 1960.

Kuntze, E., and C. Nanke. *Alberti Bolognetti, nuntii apostolici in Polonia, epistolae et acta, 1581–1585.* 2 vols., Krakow, 1933–1938.

Lefevre, R. "S. Sede e Russia e i colloqui dello Czar Nicola I nei documenti vaticani (1843–1846)." *Gregorio XVI: Miscellanaea commemorativa,* pt. 2, pp. 159–293. Rome, 1948.

Mei, A. *Patrum nova bibliotheca.* 8 vols. Rome, 1870.

Mercati, G. *Scritti d'Isidoro il Cardinale Ruteno.* Studi e Testi, 46. Rome, 1926.

Meysztowicz, V. *De Archivo nuntiature Varsaviensis.* Rome, 1944.

Migne, J. P., ed. *Patrologiae cursus completus.* 167 vols. Paris, 1857–1866.

Monumenta Germaniae historica.

Olszamowska-Skowranska, S. *La correspondence des papes et des empereurs de Russie, 1814–1876, selon les documents authentiques.* Rome, 1970.

Paska, Walter. *Sources of Particular Law for the Ukrainian Catholic Church in the United States.* Catholic University of America, Canon Law Studies. No. 485. Washington, D.C., 1975.

Patrologia orientalis.

Pontificia Commissio ad Redigendum Codicem Juris Canonici Orientalis. *Fontes: Series III.* 13 vols. Rome, 1943–1971.

Rabbath, A., ed. *Documents inédits pour servir à l'histoire du Christianisme en Orient.* 2 vols. Paris, 1905–1926.

Raynaldus, Odoricus. *Annales ecclesiastici ex tomis octo ad unum pluribus auctum.* Rome, 1667.

Registres et lettres des papes du XIIIe siècle. Ed. Bibliothèque des Écoles Françaises d'Athènes et de Rome. 14 vols. Paris, 1883–1960.

Registres et lettres des papes du XIVe siècle. Ed. Bibliothèque des Écoles Françaises d'Athènes et de Rome. 14 vols. Paris, 1899–.

Rouët de Journel, M. J. *Nonciatures de Russie, d'après les documents authentiques.* 5 vols. Rome, 1952–1957. Vols. 166–169 and 1194 of Studi e Testi.

Savio, P. *De actis nunciaturae Poloniae.* Rome, 1947.

Sheptyckyj, A. A. *Monumenta Ucrainae historica.* 8 vols. Rome, 1964–1970.

Silva-Tarovca, C. *Epistularum Romanorum pontificum ad vicarios per Illyricum aliosque episcopos collectio Thessalonicensis, ad fidem codicis Vat. lat. 5751.* Rome, 1937.

Sources chrétiennes.

Studi e Testi.

Synodus provincialis Ruthenorum habita in civitate Zamosciae anno 1720. Rome, 1838.

Theiner, A. *Vetera monumenta Poloniae et Lithuaniae gentiumque finitimarum historiam illustrantia.* 4 vols. Rome, 1860–1864.

———. *Vetera monumenta Slavorum meridionalium historiam illustrantia.* 2 vols. Rome, 1863–1875; repr. Osnabrück, 1968.

Wadding, Luke, ed. *Annales Minorum seu trium ordinum a S. Francisco institutorum.* 32 vols. Florence, 1931.

Welykyj, A. G. *Documenta pontificum Romanorum historiam Ucrainae illustrantia.* 2 vols. Rome, 1953–1954.

———. *Documenta Romana historiam ecclesiae in terris Ucrainae et Bielorussiae spectantia.* 25 vols. Rome, 1953–1960.

Welykyj, A. G., and G. Harastej. *Litterae nuntiorum apostolicarum historiam Ucrainae illustrantes, 1550–1850.* 10 vols. Rome, 1959–1965.

Vatican Library (Biblioteca Apostolica Vaticana): Greek and Latin Catalogs and Guides

Biblioteca Casanatense. *Index codicum graecorum Bibliothecae Casanatensis, 161–207.* Ed. Francesco Bancalari. Estratto de Gli Studi Italiani di Filiogia Classica. Vol. 2. 1894.

Bignami-Odier, J. "Guide au Départment des Manuscripts de la Bibliothèque du Vatican." *Mélanges d'archéologie et d'histoire* 51 (1934), pp. 205–239.

Catalogus codicum hagiographicum graecorum Bibliothecae Vaticanae. Ed. Hagiographi Bollandiana and P. Franchi de Cavalieri. Brussels, 1898. Supplement in *Analecta Bollandiana* 21 (1902), pp. 5–22.

Codices Barberiniani. Ed. Seymour de Ricci as "Liste sommaire des mss. grecs de la Bibliotheca Barberina." *Revue des bibliothèques* 17 (1907), pp. 81–125.

Codices Borgiani i codices Chisiani. Ed. Pius Franchi de Cavalieri. Rome, 1927.

Codices Ottoboniani. Ed. H. E. Feron and F. Battaglini. Rome, 1893.

Codices Palatini. Ed. H. Stevenson. Rome, 1885.

Codices Reginenses et Pii II. Ed. H. Stevenson. Rome, 1888.

Codices Urbinates. Ed. C. Stornajolo. Rome, 1895.

Codices Vaticani graeci. Vol. I, Cod. 1–329. Rome, 1923. Vol. II, Cod. 330–603. Vatican City, 1937. Vol. III, Cod. 604–866. Vatican City, 1950. *Codices* after this date have no index.

Codices Vaticani latini. 5 vols. Vatican City, 1902–1959.

Delehaye, H. "Catalogus codicum hagiographicorum graecorum Bibliothecae Barberianae de Urbe." *Analecta Bollandiana,* 19 (1900), pp. 82–118.

De Rossi, G. B. "La Biblioteca della Sede Apostolica ed i cataloghi dei suoi manoscritti." *Studi e documenti di storia e diritto,* 5 (1884), pp. 317–368.

Ehrle, F. "Zur Geschichte der Katalogisierung der Vatikana," *Historisches Jahrbuch,* 11 (1890), pp. 718–727.

Odier, Jeanne B. *La Bibliothèque Vatican de Sixte IV à Pie XI. Recherches sur l'histoire des collections de manuscrits.* Vol. 272 of Studi e Testi. Vatican City, 1973.

Other Archives and Libraries under Church Auspices in Rome

Archivio del S. Ufficio.

Archivio della S. Congregazione de Propaganda: Scritture non riferite [and] Scritture riferite: (1) Romania, (2) Armenia, (3) Acta, (4) Archipelago. Guides include G. Metzler, "Indici dell'Archivio Storico della S.C. De Propaganda Fide," *Euntes docete,* 11 (1968), pp. 109–130; and B. Millet, "The Archives of the Congregatio de Propaganda Fide," *Proceedings of the Irish Catholic Historical Committee* (Dublin), 2 (1956), pp. 20–27.

Biblioteca Angelica. An index of the Greek codices of the 130 manuscripts located here is in *Studi Italiani di Filologia Classica,* 6 (1898), pp. 167–184.

Biblioteca Grottaferrata.

Biblioteca Vallicelliana. This library holds 221 Greek manuscripts.

Collegio Greco. The catalog was published by Sp. P. Lambros, "To en Rōmē Hellēnikon Gymnasion kai en tō archeiō autou hellēnikoi kōdikes," *Neos Hellēnomnēmōn,* 10 (1913), pp. 3–32.

Institutum Historicum Societatis Jesu. Via Penitenzieri 20.

Pontificio Instituto Orientale, Piazza S. Maria Maggiore. Guides are Johann Gardner, "Russische Neumen—Handschriften der Bibliothek des Papstlichen Orientalischen Instituts in Rom," *Die Welt der Slaven,* 8 (1964), pp. 426–433; and Jan Krajcar, "The East European Holdings in the Library of the Pontifical Oriental Institute, Rome," *Slavonic and East European Review,* 48, no. 111 (April 1970), pp. 265–272.

List of Contributors

STEPHEN K. BATALDEN is Associate Professor of History and Coordinator of the Russian & East European Studies Consortium at Arizona State University. He is the author of *Eugenios Voulgaris in Russia, 1771–1806* (1982) and numerous articles on the history of the Russian Bible, and coauthor (with Sandra Batalden) of *The Newly Independent States of Eurasia: Handbook of Former Soviet Republics* (1993).

ROBERT O. CRUMMEY is Professor of History and Dean of the College of Letters and Science at the University of California, Davis. In addition to his volume on Old Belief, *The Old Believers and the World of Antichrist* (1970), his major publications include *Aristocrats and Servitors: The Boyar Elite in Russia, 1613–1689* (1983) and *The Formation of Muscovy, 1304–1613* (1987).

CHARLES FRAZEE is Professor of History and Director of the Humanities Institute at California State University in Fullerton. His many published works on church history in the Near East include *The Orthodox Church and Independent Greece, 1821–1852* (1969) and *Catholics and Sultans: The Church and the Ottoman Empire* (1983).

GREGORY L. FREEZE is Professor of History and Chair of the History Department at Brandeis University. His published work on the social and institutional history of the Russian church includes *The Russian Levites: Parish Clergy in the Eighteenth Century* (1977), *The Parish Clergy in Nineteenth-Century Russia: Crisis, Reform, Couter-reform* (1983), and *Description of the Clergy in Rural Russia* (1985), a translation of I. S. Belliustin's memoir.

EVE LEVIN is Associate Professor of History and Director of the Center for Medieval and Renaissance Studies at Ohio State University. Her work on popular religion in early modern Russia includes *Sex and Society in the World of the Orthodox Slavs, 900–1700* (1989).

FAIRY VON LILIENFELD is Professor Emeritus at Friedrich-Alexander University in Erlangen, Germany, and Honorary Member of the Faculty of the Moscow Theological Academy. Her voluminous published work addresses issues in the history and theology of the Byzantine and Slavic worlds. Her most recent book is *Der Himmel im Herzen: Altrussische Heiligenlegenden* (1990). She is currently working on a biography of St. Nino of Georgia.

BRENDA MEEHAN is Professor of History and Religion at the University of Rochester. She is the author of *Holy Women of Russia* (1993) and *Autocracy and Aristocracy: The Russian Service Elite of 1730* (1982).

MICHAEL A. MEERSON is Rector of Christ the Savior Orthodox Church in New York and freelance writer and broadcaster for Radio Liberty/Radio Free Europe. He is the author of *Pravoslavie i svoboda: Sbornik statei* (1986) and editor of *Political, Social and Religious Thought of the Russian Samizdat* (1977) and *Georgii Fedotov, Rossiia i svoboda: Sbornik statei* (1981).

MICHAEL D. PALMA is a graduate student in the History Department at Arizona State University.

ROY R. ROBSON is Adjunct Assistant Professor of History at Boston College and Fellow of the Harvard University Russian Research Center. He is the author of several articles, published in the United States and abroad, on the Old Believer experience in Russia, Poland, and America.

FRANK E. SYSYN is Director of the Peter Jacyk Centre for Ukrainian Historical Research at the University of Alberta. His published work on Ukrainian history and Ukrainian Orthodoxy includes *Between Poland and the Ukraine: The Dilemma of Adam Kysil, 1600–1653* (1985) and *The Ukrainian Orthodox Question in the USSR* (1987).

BORIS A. USPENSKY is Professor of Philology at Moscow State University and Visiting Professor in the Department of Slavic Languages and Literatures at Harvard University. Widely published in the field of semiotics and historical linguistics, his most recent books include *Istoriia russkogo literaturnogo iazyka (XI–XVII vv.)* (1987) and an edited collection of essays, *The Semiotics of Russian Cultural History* (1985).

Index

DATE DUE

			Printed in USA